Software Testing and Continuous Quality Improvement

Software Testing and Continuous Quality Improvement

Second Edition

William E. Lewis

Gunasekaran Veerapillai, Technical Contributor

AUERBACH PUBLICATIONS

A CRC Press Company

Boca Raton   London   New York   Washington, D.C.

Library of Congress Cataloging-in-Publication Data

Lewis, William E.
   Software testing and continuous quality improvement / William E. Lewis ; Gunasekaran
Veerapillai, technical contributor.--2nd ed.
       p. cm.
   Includes bibliographical references and index.
   ISBN 0-8493-2524-2 (alk. paper)
       1. Computer software--Testing. 2. Computer software--Quality control. I. Veerapillai,
Gunasekaran. II. Title.

   QA76.76.T48L495 2004
   005.1'4--dc22

                                                                                  2004052492

Visit the Auerbach Web site at www.auerbach-publications.com

© 2005 by CRC Press LLC
Auerbach is an imprint of CRC Press LLC

No claim to original U.S. Government works
International Standard Book Number 0-8493-2524-2
Library of Congress Card Number 2004052492
Printed in the United States of America 1 2 3 4 5 6 7 8 9 0

About the Authors

William E. Lewis holds a B.A. in Mathematics and an M.S. in Operations Research and has 38 years experience in the computer industry. Currently he is the founder, president, and CEO of Smartware Technologies, Inc., a quality assurance consulting firm that specializes in software testing. He is the inventor of Test Smart™, a patented software testing tool that creates optimized test cases/data based upon the requirements (see www.smartwaretechnologies.com for more information about the author).

He is a certified quality analyst (CQA) and certified software test engineer (CSTE) sponsored by the Quality Assurance Institute (QAI) of Orlando, Florida. Over the years, he has presented several papers to conferences. In 2004 he presented a paper to QAI's *Annual International Information Technology Quality Conference*, entitled "Cracking the Requirements/Test Barrier." He also speaks at meetings of the American Society for Quality and the Association of Information Technology Practitioners.

Mr. Lewis was a quality assurance manager for CitiGroup where he managed the testing group, documented all the software testing, quality assurance processes and procedures, actively participated in the CitiGroup CMM effort, and designed numerous WinRunner automation scripts.

Mr. Lewis was a senior technology engineer for Technology Builders, Inc. of Atlanta, Georgia, where he trained and consulted in the requirements-based testing area, focusing on leading-edge testing methods and tools.

Mr. Lewis was an assistant director with Ernst & Young, LLP, located in Las Colinas, Texas. He joined E & Y in 1994, authoring the company's software configuration management, software testing, and application evolutionary handbooks, and helping to develop the navigator/fusion methodology application improvement route maps. He was the quality assurance manager for several application development projects and has extensive experience in test planning, test design, execution, evaluation, reporting, and automated testing. He was also the director of the ISO initiative, which resulted in ISO9000 international certification for Ernst & Young.

Lewis also worked for the Saudi Arabian Oil Company (Aramco) in Jeddah, Saudi Arabia, on an overseas contract assignment as a quality assurance consultant. His duties included full integration and system testing, and he served on the automated tool selection committee and made recommendations to management. He also created software testing standards and procedures.

In 1998 Lewis retired from IBM after 28 years. His jobs included 12 years as a curriculum/course developer and instructor, and numerous years as a system programmer/analyst and performance analyst. An overseas assignment included service in Seoul, Korea, where he was the software engineering curriculum manager for the Korean Advanced Institute of Science and Technology (KAIST), which is considered the MIT of higher education in Korea. Another assignment was in Toronto, Canada, at IBM Canada's headquarters, where he was responsible for upgrading the corporate education program. In addition, he has traveled throughout the United States, Rome, Amsterdam, Southampton, Hong Kong, and Sydney, teaching software development and quality assurance classes with a specialty in software testing.

He has also taught at the university level for five years as an adjunct professor. While so engaged he published a five-book series on computer problem solving.

For further information about the training and consulting services provided by Smartware Technologies, Inc., contact:

Smartware Technologies, Inc.
2713 Millington Drive
Plano, Texas 75093
(972) 985-7546

Gunasekaran Veerapillai, a certified software quality analyst (CSQA), is also a project management professional (PMP) from the PMI USA. After his 15 years of retail banking experience with Canara Bank, India he was manager of the EDP section for 4 years at their IT department in Bangalore. He was in charge of many critical, internal software development, testing, and maintenance projects. He worked as project manager for testing projects with Thinksoft Global Services, a company that specializes in testing in the BFSI sector.

Currently Guna is working as project manager in the Testing Center of Excellence of HCL Technologies (www.hcltechnologies.com), a level-5 CMM Company that has partnered itself with major test automation tool vendors such as Mercury Interactive and IBM Rational. Guna has successfully turned out various testing projects for international bankers such as Citibank, Morgan Stanley, and Discover Financial. He also contributes articles to software testing Web sites such as Sticky Minds.

Contents

Acknowledgments

I would like to express my sincere gratitude to Carol, my wife, who has demonstrated Herculean patience and love in the preparation of this second edition, and my mother and father, Joyce and Bill Lewis, whom I will never forget.

I thank John Wyzalek, Senior Acquisitions Editor at Auerbach Publications, for recognizing the importance of developing a second edition of this book, and Gunasekaran Veerapillai who was a technical contributor and editor. He has demonstrated an in-depth knowledge of software testing concepts and methodology.

Finally, I would like to thank the numerous software testing vendors who provided descriptions of their tools in the section, "Modern Software Testing Tools."

Introduction

Numerous textbooks address software testing in a structured development environment. By "structured" is meant a well-defined development cycle in which discretely defined steps provide measurable outputs at each step. It is assumed that software testing activities are based on clearly defined requirements and software development standards, and that those standards are used to develop and implement a plan for testing. Unfortunately, this is often not the case. Typically, testing is performed against changing, or even wrong, requirements.

This text aims to provide a quality framework for the software testing process in the traditional structured as well as unstructured environments. The goal is to provide a continuous quality improvement approach to promote effective testing methods and provide tips, techniques, and alternatives from which the user can choose.

The basis of the continuous quality framework stems from Edward Deming's quality principles. Deming was the pioneer in quality improvement, which helped turn Japanese manufacturing around. Deming's principles are applied to software testing in the traditional "waterfall" and rapid application "spiral" development (RAD) environments. The waterfall approach is one in which predefined sequential steps are followed with clearly defined requirements. In the spiral approach, these rigid sequential steps may, to varying degrees, be lacking or different.

Section I, Software Quality in Perspective, reviews modern quality assurance principles and best practices. It provides the reader with a detailed overview of basic software testing techniques, and introduces Deming's concept of quality through a continuous improvement process. The Plan, Do, Check, Act (PDCA) quality wheel is applied to the software testing process.

The Plan step of the continuous improvement process starts with a definition of the test objectives, or what is to be accomplished as a result of testing. The elements of a test strategy and test plan are described. A test strategy is a concise statement of how to meet the goals of testing and precedes test plan development. The outline of a good test plan is provided, including an introduction, the overall plan, testing requirements, test procedures, and test plan details.

The Do step addresses how to design or execute the tests included in the test plan. A cookbook approach describes how to perform component, integration, and system acceptance testing in a spiral environment.

The Check step emphasizes the importance of metrics and test reporting. A test team must formally record the results of tests and relate them to the test plan and system objectives. A sample test report format is provided, along with several graphic techniques.

The Act step of the continuous improvement process provides guidelines for updating test cases and test scripts. In preparation for the next spiral, suggestions for improving the people, process, and technology dimensions are provided.

Section II, Life Cycle Testing Review, reviews the waterfall development methodology and describes how continuous quality improvement can be applied to the phased approach through technical reviews and software testing. The requirements, logical design, physical design, program unit design, and coding phases are reviewed. The roles of technical reviews and software testing are applied to each. Finally, the psychology of software testing is discussed.

Section III, Software Testing Methodology, contrasts the waterfall development methodology with the rapid application spiral environment from a technical and psychological point of view. A spiral testing approach is suggested when the requirements are rapidly changing. A spiral methodology is provided, broken down into parts, steps, and tasks, applying Deming's continuous quality improvement process in the context of the PDCA quality wheel.

Section IV, Test Project Management, discusses the fundamental challenges of maintaining and improving existing systems. Software changes are described and contrasted. Strategies for managing the maintenance effort are presented, along with the psychology of the software maintenance activity. A maintenance testing methodology is then broken down into parts, steps, and tasks, applying Deming's continuous quality improvement process in the context of the PDCA quality wheel.

Section V, Modern Software Testing Tools, provides a brief historical perspective from the 1950s to date, and a preview of future testing tools. Next, an overview of tools and guidelines for when to consider a testing tool and when not to is described. It also provides a checklist for selecting testing tools, consisting of a series of questions and responses. Examples are given of some of the most popular products. Finally, a detailed methodology for evaluating testing tools is provided, ranging from the initial test goals through training and implementation.

Section I
Software Quality in Perspective

SOFTWARE QUALITY IN PERSPECTIVE

The new century has started with a major setback to the information technology world, which was booming in the last decade of the twentieth century. When the Year 2000 issues evaporated there was a major breakdown in the growth of the IT industry. Hundreds of new companies vanished with closures and mergers and a state of consolidation began to occur in the industry. Major restructuring started happening in the multinational companies across the globe. The last three years were a period of consolidation and the one good thing that emerged is the importance of software quality.

- The adventure of Web business has necessitated the importance of sound, robust, reliable software else the hackers would vanish with millions of dollars. So all businesses have started giving special importance to their software quality assurance departments that were hitherto a neglected sector.
- The Sarbanes–Oxley Act, the new legislation passed in reaction to Enron, WorldCom, and similar fiascos, has greatly improved the importance of QA and testing in the United States and the corporate heads have started giving equal importance to their QA teams, which were another previously neglected sector.

Software quality is something everyone wants. Managers know that they want high quality, software developers know they want to produce a quality product, and users insist that software work consistently and be reliable.

The American Software Quality (ASQ) Institute and Quality Assurance Institute (QAI) have defined various quality assurance practices that are being adopted by various organizations. Many organizations form software quality assurance groups to improve and evaluate their software applications. However, there is no commonly accepted practice for quality assurance. Thus the quality assurance groups in various organizations may perform different roles and may execute their planning using different procedures. In some organizations, software testing is a responsibility of that group. In others, software testing is the responsibility of the development group or an independent organization.

Many software quality groups develop software quality assurance plans, which are similar to test plans. However, a software quality assurance plan may include a variety of activities beyond those included in a test plan. Although the quality assurance plan encompasses the entire quality gambit, the test plan is a part of the quality assurance plan that is one of the quality control tools.

The objectives of this section are to:

- Define quality and its cost.
- Differentiate quality prevention from quality detection.
- Differentiate verification from validation.

- Outline the components of quality assurance.
- Outline common testing techniques.
- Describe how the continuous improvement process can be instrumental in achieving quality.

Part 1
Quality Assurance Framework

<hr>

What Is Quality?

In Webster's Dictionary, quality is defined as "the essential character of something, an inherent or distinguishing character, degree or grade of excellence." If you look at the computer literature, you will see that there are two generally accepted meanings of quality. The first is that quality means "meeting requirements." With this definition, to have a quality product, the requirements must be measurable, and the product's requirements will either be met or not met. With this meaning, quality is a binary state; that is, it is a quality product or it is not. The requirements may be very complete or they may be simple, but as long as they are measurable, it can be determined whether quality has or has not been met. This is the producer's view of quality as meeting the producer's requirements or specifications. Meeting the specifications becomes an end in itself.

Another definition of quality, the customer's, is the one we use. With this definition, the customer defines quality as to whether the product or service does what the customer needs. Another way of wording it is "fit for use." There should also be a description of the purpose of the product, typically documented in a customer's "requirements specification" (see Appendix C, Requirements Specification, for more details). The requirements are the most important document, and the quality system revolves around it. In addition, quality attributes are described in the customer's requirements specification. Examples include usability, the relative ease with which a user communicates with the application; portability, the capability of the system to be executed across a diverse range of hardware architectures; and reusability, the ability to transfer software components constructed in one software system into another.

Everyone is committed to quality; however, the following show some of the confusing ideas shared by many individuals that inhibit achieving a quality commitment:

- Quality requires a commitment, particularly from top management. Close cooperation of management and staff is required in order to make it happen.

- Many individuals believe that defect-free products and services are impossible, and accept certain levels of defects as normal and acceptable.
- Quality is frequently associated with cost, meaning that high quality equals high cost. This is a confusion between quality of design and quality of conformance.
- Quality demands requirement specifications in enough detail that the products produced can be quantitatively measured against those specifications. Many organizations are not capable or willing to expend the effort to produce specifications at the level of detail required.
- Technical personnel often believe that standards stifle their creativity, and thus do not abide by standards compliance. However, for quality to happen, well-defined standards and procedures must be followed.

Prevention versus Detection

Quality cannot be achieved by assessing an already completed product. The aim, therefore, is to prevent quality defects or deficiencies in the first place, and to make the products assessable by quality assurance measures. Some quality assurance measures include: structuring the development process with a software development standard and supporting the development process with methods, techniques, and tools. The undetected bugs in the software that caused millions of losses to business have necessitated the growth of independent testing, which is performed by a company other than the developers of the system.

In addition to product assessments, process assessments are essential to a quality management program. Examples include documentation of coding standards, prescription and use of standards, methods, and tools, procedures for data backup, test methodology, change management, defect documentation, and reconciliation.

Quality management decreases production costs because the sooner a defect is located and corrected, the less costly it will be in the long run. With the advent of automated testing tools, although the initial investment can be substantial, the long-term result will be higher-quality products and reduced maintenance costs.

The total cost of effective quality management is the sum of four component costs: prevention, inspection, internal failure, and external failure. Prevention costs consist of actions taken to prevent defects from occurring in the first place. Inspection costs consist of measuring, evaluating, and auditing products or services for conformance to standards and specifications. Internal failure costs are those incurred in fixing defective products before they are delivered. External failure costs consist of the costs of defects discovered after the product has been released. The latter can be devastating because they may damage the organization's reputation or result in the loss of future sales.

The greatest payback is with prevention. Increasing the emphasis on prevention costs reduces the number of defects that go to the customer undetected, improves product quality, and reduces the cost of production and maintenance.

Verification versus Validation

Verification is proving that a product meets the requirements specified during previous activities carried out correctly throughout the development life cycle, and validation checks that the system meets the customer's requirements at the end of the life cycle. It is a proof that the product meets the expectations of the users, and it ensures that the executable system performs as specified. The creation of the test product is much more closely related to validation than to verification. Traditionally, software testing has been considered a validation process, that is, a life cycle phase. After programming is completed, the system is validated or tested to determine its functional and operational performance.

When verification is incorporated into testing, testing occurs throughout the development life cycle. For best results, it is good practice to combine verification with validation in the testing process. Verification includes systematic procedures of review, analysis, and testing, employed throughout the software development life cycle, beginning with the software requirements phase and continuing through the coding phase. Verification ensures the quality of software production and maintenance. In addition, verification imposes such an organized, systematic development practice that the resulting program can be easily understood and evaluated by an independent party.

Verification emerged about 20 years ago as a result of the aerospace industry's need for extremely reliable software in systems in which an error in a program could cause mission failure and result in enormous time and financial setbacks, or even life-threatening situations. The concept of verification includes two fundamental criteria: the software must adequately and correctly perform all intended functions, and the software must not perform any function that either by itself or in combination with other functions can degrade the performance of the entire system. The overall goal of verification is to ensure that each software product developed throughout the software life cycle meets the customer's needs and objectives as specified in the software requirements document.

Verification also establishes tractability between the various sections of the software documentation and the associated parts of the requirements specification. A comprehensive verification effort ensures that all software performance and quality requirements in the specification are adequately tested and that the test results can be repeated after changes are installed. Verification is a "continuous improvement process" and has no definite termination. It should be used throughout the system life cycle to maintain configuration and operational integrity.

Verification ensures that the software functions as intended and has the required attributes (e.g., portability), and increases the chances that the software will contain few errors (i.e., an acceptable number in the final product). It provides a method for closely monitoring the software development project and provides management with a detailed status of the project at any point in time. When verification procedures are used, management can be assured that the developers follow a formal, sequential, traceable software development process, with a minimum set of activities to enhance the quality of the system.

One criticism of verification is that it increases software development costs considerably. When the cost of software throughout the total life cycle from inception to the final abandonment of the system is considered, however, verification actually reduces the overall cost of the software. With an effective verification program, there is typically a four-to-one reduction in defects in the installed system. Because error corrections can cost 20 to 100 times more during operations and maintenance than during design, overall savings far outweigh the initial extra expense.

Software Quality Assurance

A formal definition of software quality assurance is that it is the systematic activities providing evidence of the fitness for use of the total software product. Software quality assurance is achieved through the use of established guidelines for quality control to ensure the integrity and prolonged life of software. The relationships between quality assurance, quality control, the auditing function, and software testing are often confused.

Quality assurance is the set of support activities needed to provide adequate confidence that processes are established and continuously improved in order to produce products that meet specifications and are fit for use. Quality control is the process by which product quality is compared with applicable standards and the action taken when nonconformance is detected. Auditing is the inspection/assessment activity that verifies compliance with plans, policies, and procedures.

Software quality assurance is a planned effort to ensure that a software product fulfills these criteria and has additional attributes specific to the project, for example, portability, efficiency, reusability, and flexibility. It is the collection of activities and functions used to monitor and control a software project so that specific objectives are achieved with the desired level of confidence. It is not the sole responsibility of the software quality assurance group but is determined by the consensus of the project manager, project leader, project personnel, and users.

Quality assurance is the function responsible for managing quality. The word "assurance" means that if the processes are followed, management can be assured of product quality. Quality assurance is a catalytic function that should encourage quality attitudes and discipline on the part of management and workers. Successful quality assurance managers know how to make people quality conscious and to make them recognize the benefits of quality to themselves and to the organization.

The objectives of software quality are typically achieved by following a software quality assurance plan that states the methods the project will employ to ensure the documents or products produced and reviewed at each milestone are of high quality. Such an explicit approach ensures that all steps have been taken to achieve software quality and provides management with documentation of those actions. The plan states the criteria by which quality activities can be monitored rather than setting impossible goals, such as no software defects or 100 percent reliable software.

Software quality assurance is a strategy for risk management. It exists because software quality is typically costly and should be incorporated into the formal risk management of a project. Some examples of poor software quality include:

- Delivered software frequently fails.
- Consequences of system failure are unacceptable, from financial to life-threatening scenarios.
- Systems are often not available for their intended purpose.
- System enhancements are often very costly.
- Costs of detecting and removing defects are excessive.

Although most quality risks are related to defects, this only tells part of the story. A defect is a failure to comply with a requirement. If the requirements are inadequate or even incorrect, the risks of defects are more pervasive. The result is too many built-in defects and products that are not verifiable. Some risk management strategies and techniques include software testing, technical reviews, peer reviews, and compliance verification.

Components of Quality Assurance

Most software quality assurance activities can be categorized into software testing, that is, verification and validation, software configuration management, and quality control. But the success of a software quality assurance program also depends on a coherent collection of standards, practices, conventions, and specifications, as shown in Exhibit 1.1.

Exhibit 1.1. Quality Assurance Components

Software Testing

Software testing is a popular risk management strategy. It is used to verify that functional requirements were met. The limitation of this approach, however, is that by the time testing occurs, it is too late to build quality into the product. Tests are only as good as the test cases, but they can be inspected to ensure that all the requirements are tested across all possible combinations of inputs and system states. However, not all defects are discovered during testing. Software testing includes the activities outlined in this text, including verification and validation activities. In many organizations, these activities, or their supervision, are included within the charter for the software quality assurance function. The extent to which personnel independent of design and coding should participate in software quality assurance activities is a matter of institutional, organizational, and project policy.

The major purpose of verification and validation activities is to ensure that software design, code, and documentation meet all the requirements imposed on them. Examples of requirements include user requirements; specifications derived from and designed to meet user requirements; code review and inspection criteria; test requirements at the modular, subsystem, and integrated software levels; and acceptance testing of the code after it has been fully integrated with hardware.

During software design and implementation, verification helps determine whether the products of one phase of the software development life cycle fulfill the requirements established during the previous phase. The verification effort takes less time and is less complex when conducted throughout the development process.

Quality Control

Quality control is defined as the processes and methods used to monitor work and observe whether requirements are met. It focuses on reviews and removal of defects before shipment of products. Quality control should be the responsibility of the organizational unit producing the product. It is possible to have the same group that builds the product perform the quality control function, or to establish a quality control group or department within the organizational unit that develops the product.

Quality control consists of well-defined checks on a product that are specified in the product quality assurance plan. For software products, quality control typically includes specification reviews, inspections of code and documents, and checks for user deliverables. Usually, document and product inspections are conducted at each life cycle milestone to demonstrate that the items produced are within the criteria specified by the software quality assurance plan. These criteria are normally provided in the requirements specifications, conceptual and detailed design documents, and test plans. The documents given to users are the requirement specifications, design documentation, results from the user acceptance test, the software code, user guide, and the operations and maintenance guide. Additional documents are specified in the software quality assurance plan.

Quality control can be provided by various sources. For small projects, the project personnel's peer group or the department's software quality coordinator can inspect the documents. On large projects, a configuration control board may be responsible for quality control. The board may include the users or a user representative, a member of the software quality assurance department, and the project leader.

Inspections are traditional functions of quality control, that is, independent examinations to assess compliance with some stated criteria. Peers and subject matter experts review specifications and engineering work products to identify defects and suggest improvements. They are used to examine the software project for adherence to the written project rules at a project's milestones and at other times during the project's life cycle as deemed necessary by the project leader or the software quality assurance personnel. An inspection may be a detailed checklist for assessing compliance or a brief checklist to determine the existence of such deliverables as documentation. A report stating the purpose of the inspection and the deficiencies found goes to the project supervisor, project leader, and project personnel for action.

Responsibility for inspections is stated in the software quality assurance plan. For small projects, the project leader or the department's quality coordinator can perform the inspections. For large projects, a member of the software quality assurance group may lead an inspection performed by an audit team, which is similar to the configuration control board mentioned previously. Following the inspection, project personnel are assigned to correct the problems on a specific schedule.

Quality control is designed to detect and correct defects, whereas quality assurance is oriented toward preventing them. Detection implies flaws in the processes that are supposed to produce defect-free products and services. Quality assurance is a managerial function that prevents problems by heading them off, and by advising restraint and redirection.

Software Configuration Management

Software configuration management is concerned with labeling, tracking, and controlling changes in the software elements of a system. It controls the evolution of a software system by managing versions of its software components and their relationships.

The purpose of software configuration management is to identify all the interrelated components of software and to control their evolution throughout the various life cycle phases. Software configuration management is a discipline that can be applied to activities including software development, document control, problem tracking, change control, and maintenance. It can provide a high cost savings in software reusability because each software component and its relationship to other software components have been defined.

Software configuration management consists of activities that ensure that design and code are defined and cannot be changed without a review of the effect of the change itself and its documentation. The purpose of configuration management is to control code and its associated documentation so that final code and its description are consistent and represent those items that were actually reviewed and tested. Thus, spurious, last-minute software changes are eliminated.

For concurrent software development projects, software configuration management can have considerable benefits. It can organize the software under development and minimize the probability of inadvertent changes. Software configuration management has a stabilizing effect on all software when there is a great deal of change activity or a considerable risk of selecting the wrong software components.

Elements of Software Configuration Management

Software configuration management identifies a system configuration in order to systematically control changes, maintain integrity, and enforce tractability of the configuration throughout its life cycle. Components to be controlled include planning, analysis, and design documents, source code,

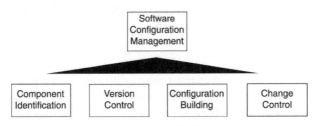

Exhibit 1.2. Software Configuration Management

executable code, utilities, job control language (JCL), test plans, test scripts, test cases, and development reports. The software configuration process typically consists of four elements: software component identification, software version control, configuration building, and software change control, as shown in Exhibit 1.2.

Component Identification

A basic software configuration management activity is the identification of the software components that make up a deliverable at each point of its development. Software configuration management provides guidelines to identify and name software baselines, software components, and software configurations.

Software components go through a series of changes. In order to manage the development process, one must establish methods and name standards for uniquely identifying each revision. A simple way to name component revisions is to use a series of discrete digits. The first integer could refer to a software component's external release number. The second integer could represent the internal software development release number. The transition from version number 2.9 to 3.1 would indicate that a new external release 3 has occurred. The software component version number is automatically incremented when the component is checked into the software library. Further levels of qualifiers could also be used as necessary, such as the date of a new version.

A software configuration is a collection of software elements that comprise a major business function. An example of a configuration is the set of program modules for an order system. Identifying a configuration is quite similar to identifying individual software components. Configurations can have a sequence of versions. Each configuration must be named in a way that distinguishes it from others. Each configuration version must be differentiated from other versions. The identification of a configuration must also include its approval status and a description of how the configuration was built.

13

A simple technique for identifying a configuration is to store all its software components in a single library or repository. The listing of all the components can also be documented.

Version Control

As an application evolves over time, many different versions of its software components are created, and there needs to be an organized process to manage changes in the software components and their relationships. In addition, there is usually the requirement to support parallel component development and maintenance.

Software is frequently changed as it evolves through a succession of temporary states called versions. A software configuration management facility for controlling versions is a software configuration management repository or library. Version control provides the tractability or history of each software change, including who did what, why, and when.

Within the software life cycle, software components evolve, and at a certain point each reaches a relatively stable state. But as defects are corrected and enhancement features are implemented, the changes result in new versions of the components. Maintaining control of these software component versions is called versioning.

A component is identified and labeled to differentiate it from all other software versions of the component. When a software component is modified, both the old and new versions should be separately identifiable. Therefore, each version, except for the initial one, has a predecessor. The succession of component versions is the component's history and tractability. Different versions also act as backups so that one can return to previous versions of the software.

Configuration Building

To build a software configuration one needs to identify the correct component versions and execute the component build procedures. This is often called configuration building.

A software configuration consists of a set of derived software components. An example is executable object programs derived from source programs. Derived software components are correctly associated with each source component to obtain an accurate derivation. The configuration build model defines how to control the way derived software components are put together.

The inputs and outputs required for a configuration build model include the primary inputs such as the source components, the version selection procedures, and the system model, which describes how the software components are related. The outputs are the target configuration and respectively derived software components.

Software configuration management environments use different approaches for selecting versions. The simplest approach to version selection is to maintain a list of component versions. Other approaches entail selecting the most recently tested component versions, or those modified on a particular date.

Change Control

Change control is the process by which a modification to a software component is proposed, evaluated, approved or rejected, scheduled, and tracked. Its basic foundation is a change control process, a component status reporting process, and an auditing process.

Software change control is a decision process used in controlling the changes made to software. Some proposed changes are accepted and implemented during this process. Others are rejected or postponed, and are not implemented. Change control also provides for impact analysis to determine the dependencies.

Modification of a configuration has at least four elements: a change request, an impact analysis of the change, a set of modifications and additions of new components, and a method for reliably installing the modifications as a new baseline (see Appendix D, Change Request Form, for more details).

A change often involves modifications to multiple software components. Therefore, a storage system that provides for multiple versions of a single file is usually not sufficient. A technique is required to identify the set of modifications as a single change. This is often called delta storage.

Every software component has a development life cycle. A life cycle consists of states and allowable transitions between those states. When a software component is changed, it should always be reviewed and frozen from further modifications until a new version is created. The reviewing authority must approve or reject the modified software component. A software library holds all software components as soon as they are frozen and also acts as a repository for approved components.

A derived component is linked to its source and has the same status as its source. In addition, a configuration cannot have a more complete status than any of its components, because it is meaningless to review a configuration when some of the associated components are not frozen.

All components controlled by software configuration management are stored in a software configuration library, including work products such as business data and process models, architecture groups, design units, tested application software, reusable software, and special test software. When a software component is to be modified, it is checked out of the repository into a private workspace. It evolves through many states, which are temporarily beyond the scope of configuration management control.

When a change is completed, the component is checked into the library and becomes a new software component version. The previous component version is also retained.

Software Quality Assurance Plan

The software quality assurance (SQA) plan is an outline of quality measures to ensure quality levels within a software development effort. The plan is used as a baseline to compare the actual levels of quality during development with the planned levels of quality. If the levels of quality are not within the planned quality levels, management will respond appropriately as documented within the plan.

The plan provides the framework and guidelines for development of understandable and maintainable code. These ingredients help ensure the quality sought in a software project. An SQA plan also provides the procedures for ensuring that quality software will be produced or maintained inhouse or under contract. These procedures affect planning, designing, writing, testing, documenting, storing, and maintaining computer software. It should be organized in this way because the plan ensures the quality of the software rather than describing specific procedures for developing and maintaining the software.

Steps to Develop and Implement a Software Quality Assurance Plan

Step 1. Document the Plan

The software quality assurance plan should include the sections below (see Appendix B, Software Quality Assurance Plan, which contains a template for the plan):

- *Purpose Section* — This section delineates the specific purpose and scope of the particular SQA plan. It should list the name(s) of the software items covered by the SQA plan and the intended use of the software. It states the portion of the software life cycle covered by the SQA plan for each software item specified.
- *Reference Document Section* — This section provides a complete list of documents referenced elsewhere in the text of the SQA plan.
- *Management Section* — This section describes the project's organizational structure, tasks, and responsibilities.
- *Documentation Section* — This section identifies the documentation governing the development, verification and validation, use, and maintenance of the software. It also states how the documents are

to be checked for adequacy. This includes the criteria and the identification of the review or audit by which the adequacy of each document will be confirmed.

- *Standards, Practices, Conventions, and Metrics Section* — This section identifies the standards, practices, conventions, and metrics to be applied, and also states how compliance with these items is to be monitored and assured.
- *Reviews and Inspections Section* — This section defines the technical and managerial reviews, walkthroughs, and inspections to be conducted. It also states how the reviews, walkthroughs, and inspections are to be accomplished including follow-up activities and approvals.
- *Software Configuration Management Section* — This section is addressed in detail in the project's software configuration management plan.
- *Problem Reporting and Corrective Action Section* — This section is addressed in detail in the project's software configuration management plan.
- *Tools, Techniques, and Methodologies Section* — This section identifies the special software tools, techniques, and methodologies that support SQA, states their purposes, and describes their use.
- *Code Control Section* — This section defines the methods and facilities used to maintain, store, secure, and document the controlled versions of the identified software during all phases of development. This may be implemented in conjunction with a computer program library and/or may be provided as a part of the software configuration management plan.
- *Media Control Section* — This section states the methods and facilities to be used to identify the media for each computer product and the documentation required to store the media, including the copy and restore process, and protects the computer program physical media from unauthorized access or inadvertent damage or degradation during all phases of development. This may be provided by the software configuration management plan.
- *Supplier Control Section* — This section states the provisions for assuring that software provided by suppliers meets established requirements. In addition, it should state the methods that will be used to assure that the software supplier receives adequate and complete requirements. For previously developed software, this section states the methods to be used to assure the suitability of the product for use with the software items covered by the SQA plan. For software to be developed, the supplier will be required to prepare and implement an SQA plan in accordance with this standard. This section will also state the methods to be employed to assure that the developers comply with the requirements of this standard.

- *Records Collection, Maintenance, and Retention Section* — This section identifies the SQA documentation to be retained. It states the methods and facilities to assemble, safeguard, and maintain this documentation, and will designate the retention period. The implementation of the SQA plan involves the necessary approvals for the plan as well as development of a plan for execution. The subsequent evaluation of the SQA plan will be performed as a result of its execution.
- *Testing Methodology* — This section defines the testing approach, techniques, and automated tools that will be used.

Step 2. Obtain Management Acceptance

Management participation is necessary for the successful implementation of an SQA plan. Management is responsible both for ensuring the quality of a software project and for providing the resources needed for software development.

The level of management commitment required for implementing an SQA plan depends on the scope of the project. If a project spans organizational boundaries, approval should be obtained from all affected areas. Once approval has been obtained, the SQA plan is placed under configuration control.

In the management approval process, management relinquishes tight control over software quality to the SQA plan administrator in exchange for improved software quality. Software quality is often left to software developers. Quality is desirable, but management may express concern as to the cost of a formal SQA plan. Staff should be aware that management views the program as a means of ensuring software quality, and not as an end in itself.

To address management concerns, software life cycle costs should be formally estimated for projects implemented both with and without a formal SQA plan. In general, implementing a formal SQA plan makes economic and management sense.

Step 3. Obtain Development Acceptance

Because the software development and maintenance personnel are the primary users of an SQA plan, their approval and cooperation in implementing the plan are essential. The software project team members must adhere to the project SQA plan; everyone must accept it and follow it.

No SQA plan is successfully implemented without the involvement of the software team members and their managers in the development of the plan. Because project teams generally have only a few members, all team members should actively participate in writing the SQA plan. When projects become much larger (i.e., encompassing entire divisions or departments), representatives of project subgroups should provide input. Constant feedback from representatives to team members helps gain acceptance of the plan.

Step 4. Plan for Implementation of the SQA Plan

The process of planning, formulating, and drafting an SQA plan requires staff and word-processing resources. The individual responsible for implementing an SQA plan must have access to these resources. In addition, the commitment of resources requires management approval and, consequently, management support. To facilitate resource allocation, management should be made aware of any project risks that may impede the implementation process (e.g., limited availability of staff or equipment). A schedule for drafting, reviewing, and approving the SQA plan should be developed.

Step 5. Execute the SQA Plan

The actual process of executing an SQA plan by the software development and maintenance team involves determining necessary audit points for monitoring it. The auditing function must be scheduled during the implementation phase of the software product so that improper monitoring of the software project will not hurt the SQA plan. Audit points should occur either periodically during development or at specific project milestones (e.g., at major reviews or when part of the project is delivered).

Quality Standards

The following section describes the leading quality standards for IT.

ISO9000

ISO9000 is a quality series and comprises a set of five documents developed in 1987 by the International Standards Organization (ISO). ISO9000 standards and certification are usually associated with non-IS manufacturing processes. However, application development organizations can benefit from these standards and position themselves for certification, if necessary. All the ISO9000 standards are guidelines and interpretive because of their lack of stringency and rules. ISO certification is becoming more and more important throughout Europe and the United States for the manufacture of hardware. Software suppliers will increasingly be required to have certification. ISO9000 is a definitive set of quality standards, but it represents quality standards as part of a total quality management (TQM) program. It consists of ISO9001, ISO9002, or ISO9003, and it provides the guidelines for selecting and implementing a quality assurance standard.

ISO9001 is a very comprehensive standard and defines all the quality elements required to demonstrate the supplier's ability to design and deliver

19

Exhibit 1.3. Companion ISO Standards

International	U.S.	Europe	U.K.
ISO9000	ANSI/ASQA	EN29000	BS5750 (Part 0.1)
ISO9001	ANSI/ASQC	EN29001	BS5750 (Part 1)
ISO9002	ANSI/ASQC	EN29002	BS5750 (Part 2)
ISO9003	ANSI/ASQC	EN29003	BS5750 (Part 3)
ISO9004	ANSI/ASQC	EN29004	BS5750 (Part 4)

a quality product. ISO9002 covers quality considerations for the supplier to control the design and development activities. ISO9003 demonstrates the supplier's ability to detect and control product nonconformity during inspection and testing. ISO9004 describes the quality standards associated with ISO9001, ISO9002, and ISO9003 and provides a comprehensive quality checklist.

Exhibit 1.3 shows the ISO9000 and companion international standards.

Capability Maturity Model (CMM)

The Software Engineering Institute–Capability Maturity Model (SEI–CMM) is a model for judging the maturity of the software processes of an organization and for identifying the key practices that are required to increase the maturity of these processes. As organizations enhance their software process capabilities, they progress through the various levels of maturity. The achievement of each level of maturity signifies a different component in the software process, resulting in an overall increase in the process capability of the organization. The Capability Maturity Model for Software describes the principles and practices underlying software process maturity and is intended to help software organizations improve the maturity of their software processes in terms of an evolutionary path from ad hoc chaotic processes to mature, disciplined software processes.

The CMM is organized into five maturity levels (see Exhibit 1.4):

1. *Initial.* The software process is characterized as ad hoc, and occasionally even chaotic. Few processes are defined, and success depends on individual effort and heroics.
2. *Repeatable.* Basic project management processes are established to track cost, schedule, and functionality. The necessary process discipline is in place to repeat earlier successes on projects with similar applications.
3. *Defined.* The software process for both management and engineering activities is documented, standardized, and integrated into a standard software process for the organization. All projects use an

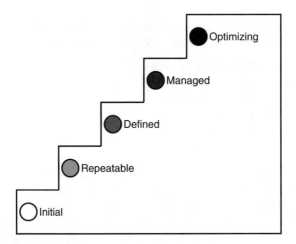

Exhibit 1.4. Maturity Levels

approved, tailored version of the organization's standard software process for developing and maintaining software.

4. *Managed.* Detailed measures of the software process and product quality are collected. Both the software process and products are quantitatively understood and controlled.

5. *Optimizing.* Continuous process improvement is enabled by quantitative feedback from the process and from piloting innovative ideas and technologies

Level 1 — Initial. The organization typically does not provide a stable environment for developing and maintaining software. This period is chaotic without any procedure and process established for software development and testing. When an organization lacks sound management practices, ineffective planning and reaction-driven commitment systems undermine the benefits of good software engineering practices.

In this phase, projects typically abandon planned procedures and revert to coding and testing. Success depends entirely on having an exceptional manager and effective software team. The project performance depends upon capable and forceful project managers. But when they leave the project, their stabilizing influence leaves with them. Even a strong engineering process cannot overcome the instability created by the absence of sound management practices.

Level 2 — Repeatable. During this phase measures and metrics will be reviewed to include percent compliance to various processes, percent of allocated requirements delivered, number of changes to requirements, number of changes to project plans, variance between estimated and actual size of deliverables, and variance between actual PQA audits performed and planned and number of change requests processed over a period of time. The following are the key process activities during level 2:

- Software configuration management
- Software quality assurance
- Software subcontract management
- Software project tracking and oversight
- Software project planning
- Requirements management

Level 3 — Defined. During this phase measures and metrics will be reviewed to include percentage of total project time spent on test activities, testing efficiency, inspection rate for deliverables, inspection efficiency, variance between actual attendance and planned attendance for training programs, and variance between actual and planned management effort. Level 3 compliance means an organization's processes for management and engineering activities have been formally defined, documented, and integrated into a standard process that is understood and followed by the organization's staff when developing and maintaining software. Once an organization has reached this level, it has a foundation for continuing progress. New processes and tools can be added with minimal disruption and new staff members can be easily trained to adapt to the organization's practices. The following are the key process areas for Level 3:

- Peer reviews
- Intergroup coordination
- Software product engineering
- Integrated software management
- Training program
- Organization process definition
- Organization process focus

The software process capability of Level 3 organizations can be summarized as standard and consistent because both software engineering and management activities are stable and repeatable. Within established product lines, cost, schedule, and functionality are under control, and software quality is tracked. This process capability is based on a common organizationwide understanding of the activities, roles, and responsibilities in a defined software process.

Level 4 — Managed. This phase denotes that the processes are well defined and professionally managed. The quality standards are on an upswing. With sound quality processes in place, the organization is better equipped to meet customer expectations of high-quality/high-performance software at reasonable cost and committed deliveries. Delivering consistency in software work products and consistency throughout the software development life cycle including plans, process, requirements, design, code, and testing helps create satisfied customers. Projects achieve control over their products and processes by narrowing the variation in their process performance to fall within acceptable quantitative boundaries. Meaningful variations in process performance can be distinguished from random variations (noise), particularly within established product lines. The risks involved in moving up the learning curve of a new application domain are known and carefully managed:

- Software quality management
- Quantitative process management

The software process capability of Level 4 organizations can be summarized as predictable because the process is measured and operates within measurable limits. The level of process capability allows an organization to predict trends in process and product quality within the quantitative bounds of these limits. When these limits are exceeded, action is taken to correct the situation. Software products are of predictably high quality.

Level 5 — Optimized. A continuous emphasis on process improvement and defect reduction avoids process stagnancy or degeneration and ensures continual improvement, translating into improved productivity, reduced defect leakage, and greater timeliness. Tracing requirements across each development phase improves the completeness of software, reduces rework, and simplifies maintenance. Verification and validation activities are planned and executed to reduce defect leakage. Customers have access to the project plan, receive regular status reports, and their feedback is sought and used for process tuning. The KPA at Level 5 are:

- Process change management
- Technology change management
- Defect prevention

Software project teams in Level 5 organizations analyze defects to determine their causes. Software processes are evaluated to prevent known types of defects from recurring, and lessons learned are disseminated to other projects. The software process capability of Level 5 organizations can be characterized as continuously improving because Level 5 organizations are continuously striving to improve the range of their process capability, thereby improving the process performance of their projects. Improvement occurs both by incremental advancements in the existing process and by innovations using new technologies and methods.

PCMM

The People Capability Maturity Model (People CMM) is a framework that helps organizations successfully address their critical people issues. Based on the best current practices in fields such as human resources, knowledge management, and organizational development, the People

CMM guides organizations in improving their processes for managing and developing their workforces. The People CMM helps organizations characterize the maturity of their workforce practices, establish a program of continuous workforce development, set priorities for improvement actions, integrate workforce development with process improvement, and establish a culture of excellence. Since its release in 1995, thousands of copies of the People CMM have been distributed, and it is used worldwide by organizations small and large.

The People CMM consists of five maturity levels that establish successive foundations for continuously improving individual competencies, developing effective teams, motivating improved performance, and shaping the workforce the organization needs to accomplish its future business plans. Each maturity level is a well-defined evolutionary plateau that institutionalizes new capabilities for developing the organization's workforce. By following the maturity framework, an organization can avoid introducing workforce practices that its employees are unprepared to implement effectively.

CMMI

The CMMI Product Suite provides the latest best practices for product and service development and maintenance.[1] The CMMI models as the best process improvement models available for product and service development and maintenance. These models extend the best practices of the Capability Maturity Model for Software (SW-CMM®), the Systems Engineering Capability Model (SECM), and the Integrated Product Development Capability Maturity Model (IPD-CMM).

Organizations reported that CMMI is adequate for guiding their process improvement activities and that CMMI training courses and appraisal methods are suitable for their needs, although there are specific opportunities for improvement. The cost of CMMI is an issue that affected adoption decisions for some but not for others. Finally, return-on-investment information is usually helpful to organizations when making the business case to adopt CMMI.

Malcom Baldrige National Quality Award

As the National Institute of Standards and Technology (NIST) says,

> In the early and mid-1980s, many industry and government leaders saw that a renewed emphasis on quality was no longer an option for American companies but a necessity for doing business in an ever expanding, and more demanding, competitive world market. But many American businesses either did not believe quality mattered for them or did not know where to begin.[2]

Public Law 100-107, signed into law on August 20, 1987, created the Malcolm Baldrige National Quality Award. The Award Program led to the creation of a new public–private partnership. Principal support for the program comes from the Foundation for the Malcolm Baldrige National Quality Award, established in 1988. The Award is named for Malcolm Baldrige, who served as Secretary of Commerce from 1981 until his tragic death in a rodeo accident in 1987.

> The Baldrige Award is given by the President of the United States to businesses — manufacturing and service, small and large — and to education and health care organizations that apply and are judged to be outstanding in seven areas: leadership, strategic planning, customer and market focus, information and analysis, human resource focus, process management, and business results. . . . While the Baldrige Award and the Baldrige recipients are the very visible centerpiece of the U.S. quality movement, a broader national quality program has evolved around the award and its criteria. A report, Building on Baldrige: American Quality for the 21st Century, by the private Council on Competitiveness, said, 'More than any other program, the Baldrige Quality Award is responsible for making quality a national priority and disseminating best practices across the United States.'

> Each year, more than 300 experts from industry, educational institutions, governments at all levels, and non-profit organizations volunteer many hours reviewing applications for the award, conducting site visits, and providing each applicant with an extensive feedback report citing strengths and opportunities to improve. In addition, board members have given thousands of presentations on quality management, performance improvement, and the Baldrige Award.[2]

The Baldrige performance excellence criteria are a framework (see Exhibit 1.5) that any organization can use to improve overall performance. Seven categories make up the award criteria:

1. *Leadership* — Examines how senior executives guide the organization and how the organization addresses its responsibilities to the public and practices good citizenship. Evaluations are based upon the appropriateness, effectiveness, and extent of the leader's and the company's involvement in relation to the size and type of business.
2. *Measurement, analysis, and knowledge management* — Examines the management, effective use, analysis, and improvement of data and information to support key organization processes and the organization's performance management system. The scope, management, and analysis of data depend upon the type of business, its resources, and the geographical distribution.
3. *Strategic planning* — Examines how the organization sets strategic directions and how it determines key action plans. Evaluations are based upon the thoroughness and effectiveness of the processes.

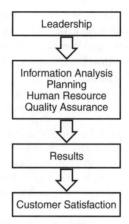

Exhibit 1.5. Baldrige Performance Framework

4. *Human resource focus* — Examines how the organization enables its workforce to develop its full potential and how the workforce is aligned with the organization's objectives. Evaluation depends upon the human resource approach of the company.

5. *Process management* — Examines aspects of how key production/delivery and support processes are designed, managed, and improved. The types of products and services, customer and government requirements, regulatory requirements, and number of business locations are the factors influencing this.

6. *Business results* — Examines the organization's performance and improvement in its key business areas: customer satisfaction, financial and marketplace performance, human resources, supplier and partner performance, operational performance, and governance and social responsibility. The category also examines how the organization performs relative to competitors.

7. *Customer and market focus* — Examines how the organization determines requirements and expectations of customers and markets; builds relationships with customers; and acquires, satisfies, and retains customers.

The system for scoring examination items is based upon these evaluation dimensions:

1. *Approach:* Approach indicates the method that the company uses to achieve the purposes. The degree to which the approach is prevention-based, the appropriateness of the tools, techniques, and methods, the effectiveness of their use, whether the approach is systematic, integrated, and consistently applied, effective self-evaluation and feedback, quantitative information gathered, and the

uniqueness and innovativeness of the approach are the factors to decide on the correct approach.

2. *Deployment:* This concerns the areas where the approach is deployed. It evaluates whether the approach is implemented in all the products and services and all internal processes, activities, facilities, and employees.

3. *Results:* This refers to the outcome of the approach. The quality levels demonstrated, rate of quality improvement, breadth, significance, and comparison of the quality improvement and the extent to which quality improvement is demonstrated are the key factors to this.

As compared to other programs like ISO, Japan's Deming award and America's Baldrige Award:

- Focus more on results and service
- Rely upon the involvement of many different professional and trade groups
- Provide special credits for innovative approaches to quality
- Include a strong customer and human resource focus
- Stress the importance of sharing information

Notes

1. http://www.sei.cmu.edu/cmmi/adoption/cmmi-start.html.
2. http://www.nist.gov/public_affairs/factsheet/baldfaqs.htm.

Part 2
Overview of Testing Techniques

As software testing, as a separate process, witnessed vertical growth and received the attention of project stakeholders and business sponsors in the last decade, various new techniques have been continuously introduced in the arena of software testing. Apart from the traditional testing techniques, various new techniques necessitated by the complicated business and development logic were realized to make software testing more meaningful and purposeful. This part discusses some of the popular testing techniques that have been adopted by the testing community.

Black-Box Testing (Functional)

Black-box or functional testing is one in which test conditions are developed based on the program or system's functionality; that is, the tester requires information about the input data and observed output, but does not know how the program or system works. Just as one does not have to know how a car works internally to drive it, it is not necessary to know the internal structure of a program to execute it. The tester focuses on testing the program's functionality against the specification. With black-box testing, the tester views the program as a black-box and is completely unconcerned with the internal structure of the program or system. Some examples in this category include: decision tables, equivalence partitioning, range testing, boundary value testing, database integrity testing, cause-effect graphing, orthogonal array testing, array and table testing, exception testing, limit testing, and random testing.

A major advantage of black-box testing is that the tests are geared to what the program or system is supposed to do, and it is natural and understood by everyone. This should be verified with techniques such as structured walkthroughs, inspections, and joint application designs (JADs). A limitation is that exhaustive input testing is not achievable, because this requires that every possible input condition or combination be tested. In addition, because there is no knowledge of the internal structure or logic, there could be errors or deliberate mischief on the part of a programmer that may not be detectable with black-box testing. For example, suppose a payroll programmer wants to insert some job security into a payroll application he is developing. By inserting the following extra code into the application, if the employee were to be terminated, that is, his employee ID no longer existed in the system, justice would sooner or later prevail.

```
if my employee ID exists
deposit regular pay check into my bank account
else
deposit an enormous amount of money into my bank account
erase any possible financial audit trails
erase this code
```

White-Box Testing (Structural)

In white-box or structural testing test conditions are designed by examining paths of logic. The tester examines the internal structure of the program or system. Test data is driven by examining the logic of the program or system, without concern for the program or system requirements. The tester knows the internal program structure and logic, just as a car mechanic knows the inner workings of an automobile. Specific examples in this category include basis path analysis, statement coverage, branch coverage, condition coverage, and branch/condition coverage.

An advantage of white-box testing is that it is thorough and focuses on the produced code. Because there is knowledge of the internal structure or logic, errors or deliberate mischief on the part of a programmer have a higher probability of being detected.

One disadvantage of white-box testing is that it does not verify that the specifications are correct; that is, it focuses only on the internal logic and does not verify the logic to the specification. Another disadvantage is that there is no way to detect missing paths and data-sensitive errors. For example, if the statement in a program should be coded "if $|a-b| < 10$" but is coded "if $(a-b) < 1$," this would not be detectable without specification details. A final disadvantage is that white-box testing cannot execute all possible logic paths through a program because this would entail an astronomically large number of tests.

Gray-Box Testing (Functional and Structural)

Black-box testing focuses on the program's functionality against the specification. White-box testing focuses on the paths of logic. Gray-box testing is a combination of black- and white-box testing. The tester studies the requirements specifications and communicates with the developer to understand the internal structure of the system. The motivation is to clear up ambiguous specifications and "read between the lines" to design implied tests. One example of the use of gray-box testing is when it appears to the tester that a certain functionality seems to be reused throughout an application. If the tester communicates with the developer and understands the internal design and architecture, many tests will be eliminated, because it may be possible to test the functionality only once. Another example is when the syntax of a command consists of seven possible parameters that can be entered in any order, as follows:

```
Command parm1, parm2, parm3, parm4, parm5, parm6, parm7
```

In theory, a tester would have to create 7! or 5040 tests. The problem is compounded further if some of the parameters are optional. If the tester uses gray-box testing, by talking with the developer and understanding the parser algorithm, if each parameter is independent, only seven tests may be required.

Manual versus Automated Testing

The basis of the manual testing categorization is that it is not typically carried out by people and it is not implemented on the computer. Examples include structured walkthroughs, inspections, JADs, and desk checking.

The basis of the automated testing categorization is that it is implemented on the computer. Examples include boundary value testing, branch coverage testing, prototyping, and syntax testing. Syntax testing is performed by a language compiler, and the compiler is a program that executes on a computer

Static versus Dynamic Testing

Static testing approaches are time independent and are classified in this way because they do not necessarily involve either manual or automated execution of the product being tested. Examples include syntax checking, structured walkthroughs, and inspections. An inspection of a program occurs against a source code listing in which each code line is read line by line and discussed. An example of static testing using the computer is a static flow analysis tool, which investigates another program for errors without executing the program. It analyzes the other program's control and data flow to discover problems such as references to a variable that has not been initialized and unreachable code.

Dynamic testing techniques are time dependent and involve executing a specific sequence of instructions on paper or by the computer. Examples include structured walkthroughs, in which the program logic is simulated by walking through the code and verbally describing it. Boundary testing is a dynamic testing technique that requires the execution of test cases on the computer with a specific focus on the boundary values associated with the inputs or outputs of the program.

Taxonomy of Software Testing Techniques

A testing technique is a set of interrelated procedures that, together, produce a test deliverable. There are many possible classification schemes for software testing and Exhibit 2.1 describes one way. The exhibit reviews formal popular testing techniques and also classifies each per the above discussion as manual, automated, static, dynamic, functional (black-box), or structural (white-box).

Exhibit 2.2 describes each of the software testing methods.

Exhibit 2.1. Testing Technique Categories

Technique	Manual	Automated	Static	Dynamic	Functional	Structural
Acceptance testing	x	x		x	x	
Ad hoc testing	x				x	
Alpha testing	x			x	x	
Basis path testing		x		x		x
Beta testing	x			x	x	
Black-box testing		x		x	x	
Bottom-up testing		x		x		x
Boundary value testing		x		x	x	
Branch coverage testing		x		x		x
Branch/condition coverage		x		x		x
Cause-effect graphing		x		x	x	
Comparison testing	x	x		x	x	x
Compatibility testing	x	x				x
Condition coverage testing		x		x		x
CRUD testing		x		x	x	
Database testing		x		x		x
Decision tables		x		x	x	
Desk checking	x			x		x
End-to-end testing	x	x		x	x	

Exhibit 2.1. Testing Technique Categories (Continued)

Technique	Manual	Automated	Static	Dynamic	Functional	Structural
Equivalence partitioning		x		x		
Exception testing		x		x	x	
Exploratory testing	x			x	x	
Free form testing		x		x	x	
Gray-box testing		x		x	x	x
Histograms	x				x	
Incremental integration testing	x	x		x	x	
Inspections	x		x		x	x
Integration testing	x	x		x	x	
JADs	x				x	x
Load testing	x	x		x		x
Mutation testing	x	x		x	x	
Orthogonal array testing	x		x		x	
Pareto analysis	x				x	
Performance testing	x	x		x	x	x
Positive and negative testing		x		x	x	
Prior defect history testing	x		x	x	x	
Prototyping		x		x	x	
Random testing		x		x	x	

Technique							
Range testing		X				X	
Recovery testing	X	X	X		X		X
Regression testing		X			X	X	
Risk-based testing	X		X	X	X		
Run charts	X		X		X		
Sandwich testing		X			X		X
Sanity testing	X	X			X	X	
Security testing	X	X					X
State transition testing		X			X	X	
Statement coverage testing		X			X		X
Statistical profile testing	X		X			X	
Stress testing	X	X			X	X	
Structured walkthroughs	X				X	X	
Syntax testing		X	X		X	X	
System testing	X	X			X	X	
Table testing		X			X		X
Thread testing		X			X		X
Top-down testing	X	X			X	X	
Unit testing	X	X		X	X		X
Usability testing	X	X			X	X	
User acceptance testing	X	X			X	X	
White-box testing		X			X		X

35

Exhibit 2.2. Testing Technique Descriptions

Technique	Brief Description
Acceptance testing	Final testing based on the end-user/customer specifications, or based on use by end-users/customers over a defined period of time
Ad hoc testing	Similar to exploratory testing, but often taken to mean that the testers have significant understanding of the software before testing it
Alpha testing	Testing of an application when development is nearing completion; minor design changes may still be made as a result of such testing. Typically done by end-users or others, not by programmers or testers
Basis path testing	Identifying tests based on flow and paths of a program or system
Beta testing	Testing when development and testing are essentially completed and final bugs and problems need to be found before final release. Typically done by end-users or others, not by programmers or testers
Black-box testing	Testing cases generated based on the system's functionality
Bottom-up testing	Integrating modules or programs starting from the bottom
Boundary value testing	Testing cases generated from boundary values of equivalence classes
Branch coverage testing	Verifying that each branch has true and false outcomes at least once
Branch/condition coverage testing	Verifying that each condition in a decision takes on all possible outcomes at least once
Cause–effect graphing	Mapping multiple simultaneous inputs that may affect others to identify their conditions to test
Comparison testing	Comparing software weaknesses and strengths to competing products
Compatibility testing	Testing how well software performs in a particular hardware/software/operating system/network environment
Condition coverage testing	Verifying that each condition in a decision takes on all possible outcomes at least once
CRUD testing	Building a CRUD matrix and testing all object creations, reads, updates, and deletions
Database testing	Checking the integrity of database field values
Decision tables	Table showing the decision criteria and the respective actions
Desk checking	Developer reviews code for accuracy

Exhibit 2.2. Testing Technique Descriptions (Continued)

Technique	Brief Description
End-to-end testing	Similar to system testing; the "macro" end of the test scale; involves testing of a complete application environment in a situation that mimics real-world use, such as interacting with a database, using network communications, or interacting with other hardware, applications, or systems if appropriate
Equivalence partitioning	Each input condition is partitioned into two or more groups. Test cases are generated from representative valid and invalid classes
Exception testing	Identifying error messages and exception handling processes and conditions that trigger them
Exploratory testing	Often taken to mean a creative, informal software test that is not based on formal test plans or test cases; testers may be learning the software as they test it
Free form testing	Ad hoc or brainstorming using intuition to define test cases
Gray-box testing	A combination of black-box and white-box testing to take advantage of both
Histograms	A graphical representation of measured values organized according to the frequency of occurrence used to pinpoint hot spots
Incremental integration testing	Continuous testing of an application as new functionality is added; requires that various aspects of an application's functionality be independent enough to work separately before all parts of the program are completed, or that test drivers be developed as needed; done by programmers or by testers
Inspections	Formal peer review that uses checklists, entry criteria, and exit criteria
Integration testing	Testing of combined parts of an application to determine if they function together correctly. The "parts" can be code modules, individual applications, or client and server applications on a network. This type of testing is especially relevant to client/server and distributed systems.
JADs	Technique that brings users and developers together to jointly design systems in facilitated sessions
Load testing	Testing an application under heavy loads, such as testing of a Web site under a range of loads to determine at what point the system's response time degrades or fails
Mutation testing	A method for determining if a set of test data or test cases is useful, by deliberately introducing various code changes ("bugs") and retesting with the original test data/cases to determine if the "bugs" are detected. Proper implementation requires large computational resources.

Exhibit 2.2. Testing Technique Descriptions (Continued)

Technique	Brief Description
Orthogonal array testing	Mathematical technique to determine which variations of parameters need to be tested
Pareto analysis	Analyze defect patterns to identify causes and sources
Performance testing	Term often used interchangeably with "stress" and "load" testing. Ideally "performance" testing (and any other "type" of testing) is defined in requirements documentation or QA or Test Plans
Positive and negative testing	Testing the positive and negative values for all inputs
Prior defect history testing	Test cases are created or rerun for every defect found in prior tests of the system
Prototyping	General approach to gather data from users by building and demonstrating to them some part of a potential application
Random testing	Technique involving random selection from a specific set of input values where any value is as likely as any other
Range testing	For each input identifies the range over which the system behavior should be the same
Recovery testing	Testing how well a system recovers from crashes, hardware failures, or other catastrophic problems
Regression testing	Testing a system in light of changes made during a development spiral, debugging, maintenance, or the development of a new release
Risk-based testing	Measures the degree of business risk in a system to improve testing
Run charts	A graphical representation of how a quality characteristic varies with time
Sandwich testing	Integrating modules or programs from the top and bottom simultaneously
Sanity testing	Typically an initial testing effort to determine if a new software version is performing well enough to accept it for a major testing effort. For example, if the new software is crashing systems every five minutes, bogging down systems to a crawl, or destroying databases, the software may not be in a "sane" enough condition to warrant further testing in its current state
Security testing	Testing how well the system protects against unauthorized internal or external access, willful damage, etc.; may require sophisticated testing techniques

Exhibit 2.2. Testing Technique Descriptions (Continued)

Technique	Brief Description
State transition testing	Technique in which the states of a system are first identified and then test cases are written to test the triggers to cause a transition from one condition to another state
Statement coverage testing	Every statement in a program is executed at least once
Statistical profile testing	Statistical techniques are used to develop a usage profile of the system that helps define transaction paths, conditions, functions, and data tables
Stress testing	Term often used interchangeably with "load" and "performance" testing. Also used to describe such tests as system functional testing while under unusually heavy loads, heavy repetition of certain actions or inputs, input of large numerical values, or large complex queries to a database system
Structured walkthroughs	A technique for conducting a meeting at which project participants examine a work product for errors
Syntax testing	Data-driven technique to test combinations of input syntax
System testing	Black-box type testing that is based on overall requirements specifications; covers all combined parts of a system
Table testing	Testing access, security, and data integrity of table entries
Thread testing	Combining individual units into threads of functionality which together accomplish a function or set of functions
Top-down testing	Integrating modules or programs starting from the top
Unit testing	The most "micro" scale of testing; to test particular functions or code modules. Typically done by the programmer and not by testers, as it requires detailed knowledge of the internal program design and code. Not always easily done unless the application has a well-designed architecture with tight code; may require developing test driver modules or test harnesses
Usability testing	Testing for "user-friendliness." Clearly this is subjective, and will depend on the targeted end-user or customer. User interviews, surveys, video recording of user sessions, and other techniques can be used. Programmers and testers are usually not appropriate as usability testers
User acceptance testing	Determining if software is satisfactory to an end-user or customer
White-box testing	Test cases are defined by examining the logic paths of a system

Part 3
Quality through Continuous Improvement Process

Contribution of Edward Deming

Although Henry Ford and Fredrick Winslow Taylor made enormous contributions to factory production, Dr. Edward Deming has gone beyond them. He has influenced every facet of work in every industry, including government, schools, and hospitals. Deming has had a profound effect on how people think, how they see themselves, and how they relate to their customers, to one another, and to society.

In 1928 he earned his Ph.D. in physics and in the next four years published papers about the effect of electrons on the structure of materials. He started his career at the frontiers of physics. In 1934 he began to move away from physics and physical chemistry and published his first paper in the field of statistics. In 1937 he wrote a paper on the statistical theory of errors.

By law the federal government is required to take a population census every ten years, and in 1940 Deming became involved with the Census Bureau of the Department of Commerce. The proper tool for this task was statistics, and so we find in his list of publications a series of 26 papers dealing almost solely with problems of sampling. One paper published in 1944, during World War II, introduced Shewhart's methods of quality control to engineers. He took the lead in getting this subject into the wartime training of engineers, giving the first course himself at Stanford University. From around 1945 onward, people did not think of Deming as a physicist but as a statistician. It is not surprising, therefore, that when General MacArthur needed to make a population survey in Japan in 1948, he called upon Deming. In 1953 — three years after he started to work with Japanese managers — he started his crusade to bring quality management principles to American managers. In 1953 he published *Management's Responsibility for the Use of Statistical Techniques in Industry*, thus marking the start of a theme he would pursue for the next 40 years. He had begun to see the transformation in Japan.

Role of Statistical Methods

Deming's quality method includes the use of statistical methods that he believed were essential to minimize confusion when there is variation in a process. Statistics also help us to understand the processes themselves, gain control, and improve them. This is brought home by the quote, "In God we trust. All others must use data." Particular attention is paid to locating a problem's major causes which, when removed, improve quality significantly. Deming points out that many statistical techniques are not difficult and require a strong background in mathematics. Education, however, is a very powerful tool and is required on all levels of an organization to make it work.

The following is an outline of some of the statistical methods that are further described and applied to software testing. More details are provided in Section III.

Cause-and-Effect Diagram

Often called the "fishbone" diagram, this method can be used in brainstorming sessions to locate factors that may influence a situation. This is a tool used to identify possible causes of a problem by representing the relationship between some effect and its possible cause.

Flow Chart

This is a graphical method of documenting a process. It is a diagram that shows the sequential steps of a process or of a workflow that go into creating a product or service. The justification of flow charts is that in order to improve a process, one needs first to understand it.

Pareto Chart

This is a commonly used graphical technique in which events to be analyzed are named. The incidents are counted by name; the events are ranked by frequency in a bar chart in ascending sequence. Pareto analysis applies the 80/20 rules. An example of this is when 20 percent of an organization's customer's account for 80 percent of the revenue, for example, focuses on the 20 percent.

Run Chart

A run chart is a graphical technique that graphs data points in chronological order to illustrate trends of a characteristic being measured in order to assign a potential cause rather than random variation.

Histogram

A histogram is a graphical description of measured values organized according to the frequency or relative frequency of occurrence. It also provides the average and variation.

Scatter Diagram

A scatter diagram is a graph designed to show where there is a relationship between two variables or changing factors.

Control Chart

A control chart is a statistical method for distinguishing between special and common variations exhibited by processes. It is a run chart with statistically determined upper and lower limits drawn on either side of the process averages.

Deming's 14 Quality Principles

Deming outlined 14 quality principles, which must be used concurrently in order to achieve quality. Although these principles were applied to industry, influencing government, schools, and hospitals, many are also applicable to achieving software quality from an information technology perspective. The following is a brief discussion of each point, followed by a description of how a quality assurance organization might apply each.

Point 1: Create Constancy of Purpose

Most companies tend to dwell on their immediate problems without adequate attention to the future. According to Deming, "It is easy to stay bound up in the tangled knots of the problems of today, becoming ever more and more efficient in the future, but no company without a plan for the future will stay in business." A constancy of purpose requires innovation (e.g., long-term planning for it), investment in research and education, and continuous improvement of products and service.

To apply this point, an information technology quality assurance organization can:

- Develop a quality assurance plan that provides a long-range quality direction.
- Require software testers to develop and maintain comprehensive test plans for each project.
- Encourage quality analysts and testers to come up with new and innovative ideas to maximize quality.
- Strive to continuously improve quality processes.

43

Point 2: Adopt the New Philosophy

Quality must become the new religion. According to Deming, "The cost of living depends inversely on the goods and services that a given amount of money will buy, for example, reliable service reduces costs. Delays and mistakes raise costs." Consumers of goods and services end up paying for delays and mistakes, which reduces their standard of living. Tolerance of acceptability levels and defects in systems is the roadblock between quality and productivity.

To apply this point, an information technology quality assurance organization can:

- Educate the information technology organization on the need and value of quality.
- Promote the quality assurance department to the same level as any other department.
- Defuse the notion that quality assurance is negative and the "watch dogs."
- Develop a risk management plan and not accept any anomalies outside the range of acceptable risk tolerance.

Point 3: Cease Dependence on Mass Inspection

The old way of thinking is to inspect bad quality out. A better approach is that inspection should be used to see how we are doing, and not be left to the final product, when it is difficult to determine where in the process a defect took place. Quality should be built in without the dependence on mass inspections.

To apply this point, an information technology quality assurance organization can:

- Promote and interject technical reviews, walkthroughs, and inspections as nondefensive techniques for achieving quality throughout the entire development cycle.
- Instill the need for the whole organization to be quality conscious and treat it as a tangible, measurable work product deliverable.
- Require statistical evidence of information technology quality.

Point 4: End the Practice of Awarding Business on Price Tag Alone

"Two or more suppliers for the same item will multiply the evils that are necessarily inherent and bad enough with any one supplier." A buyer will serve her company best by developing a long-term relationship of loyalty and trust with a single vendor. Rather than using standards manuals by which vendors must qualify for business, a better approach is active involvement by the supplier's management with Deming's 14 points.

To apply this point, an information technology quality assurance organization can:

- Require software quality and test vendors to provide statistical evidence of their quality.
- Pick the best vendor for each quality assurance tool, testing tool, or service, and develop a working relationship consistent with the quality plan.

Point 5: Improve Constantly and Forever the System of Production and Service

Improvement is not a one-time effort: management is obligated to improve quality continuously. "Putting out fires is not improvement. Finding a point out of control, finding the special cause and removing it, is only putting the process back to where it was in the first place. The obligation for improvement is a ceaseless process."

To apply this point, an information technology quality assurance organization can:

- Constantly improve quality assurance and testing processes.
- Not rely on judgment.
- Use statistical techniques such as root cause and effect analysis to uncover the sources of problems and test analysis.

Point 6: Institute Training and Retraining

Often there is little or no training and workers do not know when they have done their jobs correctly. It is very difficult to erase improper training. Deming stresses that training should not end as long as performance is not in statistical control and there is something to be gained.

To apply this point, an information technology quality assurance organization can:

- Institute modern training aids and practices.
- Encourage quality staff to constantly increase their knowledge of quality and testing techniques by attending seminars and classes.
- Reward staff for creating new seminars and special interest groups.
- Use statistical techniques to determine when training is needed and completed.

Point 7: Institute Leadership

"There is no excuse to offer for putting people on a job that they know not how to do. Most so-called 'goofing off' — somebody seems to be lazy, doesn't seem to care — that person is almost always in the wrong job, or has very poor management." It is the responsibility of management to discover the inhibitors that prevent workers from taking pride in their jobs. From an information technology point of view, development often views the job of quality to be the QA department's responsibility. QA should be very aggressive as quality leaders and point out that quality is everyone's responsibility.

To apply this point, an information technology quality assurance organization can:

- Take the time to train a developer on how to unit test code effectively if he or she has an excessive number of defects discovered by QA testing.
- Improve supervision, which is the responsibility of management.
- Allow the project leader to have more time to help people on the job.
- Use statistical methods to indicate where there are faults.

Point 8: Drive Out Fear

There is often no incentive for problem solving. Suggesting new ideas is too risky. People are afraid of losing their raises, promotions, or jobs. "Fear takes a horrible toll. Fear is all around, robbing people of their pride, hurting them, robbing them of a chance to contribute to the company. It is unbelievable what happens when you unloose fear." A common problem is the fear of inspections.

To apply this point, an information technology quality assurance organization can:

- Promote the idea that quality is goodness and should be rewarded, and promote any new ideas to improve quality.
- Prior to a structured walkthrough, inspection, or JAD session, make sure everyone understands the ground rules and promote an "egoless" environment.
- Periodically schedule a "Quality Day" in which quality improvement ideas are openly shared.

Point 9: Break Down Barriers between Staff Areas

There are numerous problems when departments have different goals and do not work as a team to solve problems, set policies, or define new directions. "People can work superbly in their respective departments, but if their goals are in conflict, they can ruin the company. It is better to have teamwork, working for the company."

To apply this point, an information technology quality assurance organization can:

- Promote the need for the quality assurance and other departments (particularly development) to work closely together; QA should be viewed as the "good guys" trying to make the software products the best in the world.
- Point out that a defect discovered before production is one that won't be discovered by the users.

Point 10: Eliminate Slogans, Exhortations, and Targets for the Workforce

"Slogans never helped anybody do a good job. They generate frustration and resentment." Slogans such as "Zero Defects" or "Do It Right the First Time" are fine on the surface. The problem is that they are viewed as signals that management does not understand employees' problems, or care. There is a common practice of setting goals without describing how they are going to be accomplished.

To apply this point, an information technology quality assurance organization can:

- Encourage management to avoid the use of slogans.
- Rather than generate slogans, develop and document quality standards, procedures, and processes that the rest of the organization can use to help maximize quality.

Point 11: Eliminate Numerical Goals

"Quotas or other work standards, such as measured day work or rates, impede quality perhaps more than any other single working condition. As work standards are generally used, they guarantee inefficiency and high costs." A proper work standard would define what is and is not acceptable in terms of quality.

To apply this point, an information technology quality assurance organization can:

- Look not just at the numbers but look carefully at the quality standards.
- Avoid formally publicizing defect rates by individual or department.
- Work with the development organization to define quality standards and procedures to improve quality.
- When there are specific quality issues, have the department manager address them informally.

Point 12: Remove Barriers to Pride of Workmanship

People are regarded as a commodity, to be used as needed. If not needed, they are returned to the market. Managers cope with many problems but tend to shy away from people problems. They often form "Quality Control Circles," but this is often a way for a manager to pretend to be doing something about a problem. Management seldom invests employees with any authority, nor does it act upon their recommendations.

To apply this point, an information technology quality assurance organization can:

- Instill an image that quality is their deliverable and is a very valuable commodity.
- Delegate responsibility to the staff to seek out quality and do whatever it takes to accomplish it.

Point 13: Institute a Vigorous Program of Education and Retraining

People must acquire new knowledge and skills. Education and retraining is an investment in people, which is required for long-term planning. Education and training must fit people into new jobs and responsibilities.

To apply this point, an information technology quality assurance organization can:

- Encourage quality staff to constantly increase their knowledge of quality and testing techniques by attending seminars and classes.
- Reward staff for creating new seminars and special interest groups.
- Retrain individuals in new quality skills.

Point 14: Take Action to Accomplish the Transformation

Top management needs to push these 13 points. Every employee, including managers, should acquire a precise idea of how to improve quality continually, but the initiative must come from top management. The following discusses a process that can be used to apply Deming's Point 14. It is also the process that is constantly reinforced in this text to improve software-testing processes.

Continuous Improvement through the Plan, Do, Check, Act Process

The term control has various meanings, including supervising, governing, regulating, or restraining. The control in quality control means defining the objective of the job, developing and carrying out a plan to meet that objective, and checking to determine if the anticipated results are achieved. If the anticipated results are not achieved, modifications are made in the work procedure to fulfill the plan.

One way to describe the above is with the "Deming Cycle" (or PDCA circle; see Exhibit 3.1), named after Deming in Japan because he introduced it there, although it was originated by Shewhart. It was the basis of the turnaround of the Japanese manufacturing industry, in addition to other

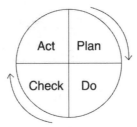

Exhibit 3.1. The Deming Quality Circle

Deming management principles. The word management describes many different functions, encompassing policy management, human resources management, and safety control, as well as component control and management of materials, equipment, and daily schedules. In this text, the Deming model is applied to software quality.

In the Plan quadrant of the circle, one defines her objectives and determines the conditions and methods required to achieve them. It is crucial to clearly describe the goals and policies needed to achieve the objectives at this stage. A specific objective should be documented numerically, if possible. The procedures and conditions for the means and methods to achieve the objectives are described.

In the Do quadrant of the circle, the conditions are created and the necessary training to execute the plan is performed. It is paramount that everyone thoroughly understands the objectives and the plan. Workers need to be taught the procedures and skills they need to fulfill the plan and thoroughly understand the job. The work is then performed according to these procedures.

In the Check quadrant of the circle, one must check to determine whether work is progressing according to the plan and whether the expected results are obtained. The performance of the set procedures must be checked against changes in conditions, or abnormalities that may appear. As often as possible, the results of the work should be compared with the objectives. If a check detects an abnormality — that is, if the actual value differs from the target value — then a search for the cause of the abnormality must be initiated to prevent its recurrence. Sometimes it is necessary to retrain workers and revise procedures. It is important to make sure these changes are reflected and more fully developed in the next plan.

In the Action quadrant of the circle, if the checkup reveals that the work is not being performed according to plan or results are not what was anticipated, measures must be devised for appropriate action.

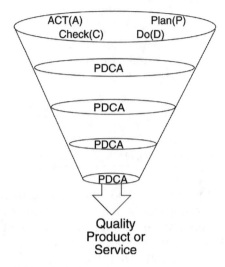

Exhibit 3.2. The Ascending Spiral

Going around the PDCA Circle

The above procedures not only ensure that the quality of the products meets expectations, but they also ensure that the anticipated price and delivery date are fulfilled. Sometimes our preoccupation with current concerns makes us unable to achieve optimal results. By going around the PDCA circle, we can improve our working methods and obtain the desired results. Repeated use of PDCA makes it possible to improve the quality of the work, the work methods, and the results. Sometimes this concept is depicted as an ascending spiral as illustrated in Exhibit 3.2.

Section II
Life Cycle Testing Review

The life cycle development methodology consists of distinct phases from requirements to coding. Life cycle testing means that testing occurs in parallel with the development life cycle and is a continuous process. Deming's continuous improvement process is applied to software testing using the quality circle, principles, and statistical techniques.

The psychology of life cycle testing encourages testing to be performed outside the development organization. The motivation for this is that there are clearly defined requirements, and it is more efficient for a third party to verify these requirements.

The test plan is the bible of software testing and is a document prescribing the test objectives, scope, strategy approach, and test details. There are specific guidelines for building a good test plan.

The two major quality assurance verification approaches for each life cycle phase are technical reviews and software testing. Technical reviews are more preventive; that is, they aim to remove defects as soon as possible. Software testing verifies the actual code that has been produced.

The objectives of this section are to:

- Discuss how life cycle testing is a parallel activity.
- Describe how Deming's process improvement is applied.
- Discuss the psychology of life cycle development and testing.
- Discuss the components of a good test.
- List and describe how technical review and testing are verification techniques.

Part 4
Overview

The following provides an overview of the "waterfall" life cycle development methodology and the associated testing activities. Deming's continuous quality improvement is applied with technical review and testing techniques.

Waterfall Development Methodology

The life cycle development or waterfall approach breaks the development cycle down into discrete phases, each with a rigid sequential beginning and end (see Exhibit 4.1). Each phase is fully completed before the next is started. Once a phase is completed, in theory during development, one never goes back to change it.

In Exhibit 4.1 you can see that the first phase in the waterfall is user requirements. In this phase, the users are interviewed, their requirements are analyzed, and a document is produced detailing what the users' requirements are. Any reengineering or process redesign is incorporated into this phase.

In the next phase, entity relation diagrams, process decomposition diagrams, and data flow diagrams are created to allow the system to be broken into manageable components from a data and functional point of view. The outputs from the logical design phase are used to develop the physical design of the system. During the physical and program unit design phases, various structured design techniques, such as database schemas, Yourdon structure charts, and Warnier/Orr diagrams, are used to produce a design specification that will be used in the next phase.

In the program unit design phase, programmers develop the system according to the physical design produced in the previous phase. Once complete, the system enters the coding phase, where it will be written in a programming language, unit or component tested, integration tested, system tested, and finally user tested, often called acceptance testing.

Now the application is delivered to the users for the operation and maintenance phase, not shown in Exhibit 4.1. Defects introduced during the life cycle phases are detected, corrected, and new enhancements are incorporated into the application.

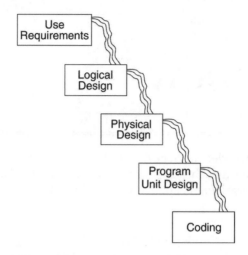

Exhibit 4.1. Waterfall Development Methodology

Continuous Improvement "Phased" Approach

Deming's continuous improvement process, which was discussed in the previous section, is effectively applied to the waterfall development cycle using the Deming quality cycle, or PDCA; that is, Plan, Do, Check, and Act. It is applied from two points of view: software testing, and quality control or technical reviews.

As defined in Section I, Software Quality in Perspective, the three major components of quality assurance include software testing, quality control, and software configuration management. The purpose of software testing is to verify and validate the activities to ensure that the software design, code, and documentation meet all the requirements imposed on them. Software testing focuses on test planning, test design, test development, and test execution. Quality control is the process and methods used to monitor work and observe whether requirements are met. It focuses on structured walkthroughs and inspections to remove defects introduced during the software development life cycle.

Psychology of Life Cycle Testing

In the waterfall development life cycle there is typically a concerted effort to keep the testing and development departments separate. This testing organization is typically separate from the development organization with a different reporting structure. The basis of this is that because require-ments and design documents have been created at specific phases in the development life cycle, a separate quality assurance organization should be able to translate these documents into test plans, test cases, and test specifi-cations. Underlying assumptions include the belief that (1) programmers should not test their own programs and (2) programming organizations should not test their own programs.

It is thought that software testing is a destructive process and that it would be very difficult for a programmer to suddenly change his perspective from developing a software product to trying to find defects, or breaking the software. It was believed that programmers cannot effectively test their own programs because they cannot bring themselves to attempt to expose errors.

Part of this argument was that there will be errors due to the programmer's misunderstanding of the requirements of the programs. Thus, a programmer testing his own code would have the same bias and would not be as effective testing it as someone else.

It is not impossible for a programmer to test her own programs, but testing is more effective when performed by someone who does not have a stake in it, as a programmer does. Because the development deliverables have been documented, why not let another individual verify them?

It is thought that a programming organization is measured by its ability to produce a program or system on time and economically. It is difficult for the programming organization to be objective, just as it is for an individual programmer. If a concerted effort were made to find as many defects as possible, it was believed that the project would probably be late and not cost effective. Less quality is the result.

From a practical point of view, an independent organization should be responsible for the quality of the software products. Such organizations as product test or quality assurance were created to serve as independent parties.

Software Testing as a Continuous Improvement Process

Software life cycle testing means that testing occurs in parallel with the development cycle and is a continuous process (see Exhibit 4.2). The software testing process should start early in the application life cycle, not just in the traditional validation testing phase after the coding phase has been completed. Testing should be integrated into application development. In order to do so, there needs to be a commitment on the part of the development organization and close communication with the quality assurance function.

A test plan is started during the requirements phase. It is an organization of testing work. It is a document describing the approach to be taken for the intended testing activities and includes the items to be tested, the types of tests to be performed, test schedules, human resources, reporting procedures, evaluation criteria, and so on.

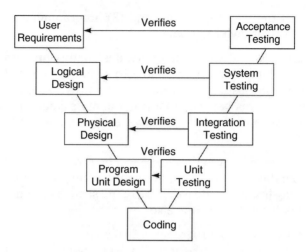

Exhibit 4.2. Development Phases versus Testing Types

During logical, physical, and program unit design, the test plan is refined with more details. Test cases are also created. A test case is a specific set of test data and test scripts. A test script guides the tester through a test and ensures consistency among separate executions of the test. A test also includes the expected results to verify whether the test met the objective correctly. During the coding phase, test scripts and test data are generated. During application testing, the test scripts are executed and the results are analyzed.

Exhibit 4.2 shows a correspondence between application development and the testing activities. The application development cycle proceeds from user requirements and design until the code is completed. During test design and development, the acceptance test criteria were established in a test plan. As more details are refined, the system, integration, and unit testing requirements are established. There may be a separate test plan for each test type, or one plan may be used.

During test execution, the process is reversed and starts with unit testing. Integration tests are performed that combine individual, unit-tested pieces of code. Once this is completed, the system is tested from a total system point of view. This is known as system testing. System testing is a multifaceted test to evaluate the functionality, performance, and usability of the system. The final test is the acceptance test, which is a user-run test that verifies the ability of the system to meet the original user objectives and requirements. In some cases the system test serves as the acceptance test.

If you will recall, the PDCA approach (i.e., Plan, Do, Check, and Act) is a control mechanism used to control, supervise, govern, regulate, or restrain a system. The approach first defines the objectives of a process, develops and carries out the plan to meet those objectives, and checks to determine if the anticipated results are achieved. If they are not achieved, the plan is modified to fulfill the objectives. The PDCA quality cycle can be applied to software testing.

The Plan step of the continuous improvement process, when applied to software testing, starts with a definition of the test objectives; for example, what is to be accomplished as a result of testing. Testing criteria do more than simply ensure that the software performs according to specifications. Objectives ensure that all responsible individuals contribute to the definition of the test criteria to maximize quality.

A major deliverable of this step is a software test plan. A test plan is the basis for accomplishing testing. The test plan should be considered an ongoing document. As the system changes, so does the plan. The test plan also becomes part of the system maintenance documentation after the application is delivered to the user. The outline of a good test plan includes an introduction, the overall plan, and testing requirements. As more detail is available, the business functions, test logs, problem and summary reports, test software, hardware, data, personnel requirements, test schedule, test entry criteria, and exit criteria are added.

The Do step of the continuous improvement process when applied to software testing describes how to design and execute the tests included in the test plan. The test design includes test cases, test procedures and scripts, expected results, function/test case matrix, test logs, and so on. The more definitive a test plan is, the easier the test design will be. If the system changes between development of the test plan and when the tests are to be executed, the test plan should be updated accordingly; that is, whenever the system changes, the test plan should change.

The test team is responsible for the execution of the tests and must ensure that the test is executed according to the plan. Elements of the Do step include selecting test tools, defining the resource requirements, defining the test setup conditions and environment, test requirements, and the actual testing of the application.

The Check step of the continuous improvement process when applied to software testing includes the evaluation of how the testing process is progressing. Again, the credo for statisticians, "In God we trust. All others must use data," is crucial to the Deming method. It is important to base decisions as much as possible on accurate and timely data. Testing metrics such as the number and types of defects, the workload effort, and the schedule status are key.

It is also important to create test reports. Testing began with setting objectives, identifying functions, selecting tests to validate the test functions, creating test conditions, and executing the tests. To construct test reports, the test team must formally record the results and relate them to the test plan and system objectives. In this sense, the test report reverses all the previous testing tasks.

Summary and interim test reports should be written at the end of testing and at key testing checkpoints. The process used for report writing is the same whether it is an interim or a summary report, and, like other tasks in testing, report writing is also subject to quality control; that is, it should be reviewed. A test report should at least include a record of defects discovered, data reduction techniques, root cause analysis, the development of findings, and recommendations to management to improve the testing process.

The Act step of the continuous improvement process when applied to software testing includes devising measures for appropriate actions relating to work that was not performed according to the plan or results that were not anticipated in the plan. This analysis is fed back to the plan. Examples include updating the test suites, test cases, and test scripts, and reevaluating the people, process, and technology dimensions of testing.

The Testing Bible: Software Test Plan

A test plan is a document describing the approach to be taken for intended testing activities and serves as a service-level agreement between the quality assurance testing function and other interested parties, such as development. A test plan should be developed early in the development cycle and help improve the interactions of the analysis, design, and coding activities. A test plan defines the test objectives, scope, strategy and approach, test procedures, test environment, test completion criteria, test cases, items to be tested, the tests to be performed, the test schedules, personnel requirements, reporting procedures, assumptions, risks, and contingency planning.

While developing a test plan, one should be sure that it is simple, complete, current, and accessible by the appropriate individuals for feedback and approval. A good test plan flows logically and minimizes redundant testing, demonstrates full functional coverage, provides workable procedures for monitoring, tracking, and reporting test status, contains a clear definition of the roles and responsibilities of the parties involved, has target delivery dates, and clearly documents the test results.

There are two ways of building a test plan. The first approach is a master test plan that provides an overview of each detailed test plan, that is, a test plan of a test plan. A detailed test plan verifies a particular phase in the waterfall development life cycle. Test plan examples include unit, integration, system, and acceptance. Other detailed test plans include application enhancements, regression testing, and package installation. Unit test plans are code oriented and very detailed but short because of their limited

Exhibit 4.3. Test Case Form

Date: _____	Tested by: _____
System: _____	Environment: _____
Objective: _____	Test ID _____ Req. ID _____
Function: _____	Screen: _____
Version: _____	Test Type: _____
	(Unit, Integ., System, Accept.)

Condition to test:

_____

_____

Data/steps to perform

_____

_____

Expected results:

_____

_____

_____

Actual results: Passed ____Failed ____

_____

_____

_____

scope. System or acceptance test plans focus on the functional test or black-box view of the entire system, not just a software unit. See Appendix E1, Unit Test Plan, and Appendix E2, System/Acceptance Test Plan, for more details.

The second approach is one test plan. This approach includes all the test types in one test plan, often called the acceptance/system test plan, but covers unit, integration, system, and acceptance testing and all the planning considerations to complete the tests.

A major component of a test plan, often in the Test Procedure section, is a test case, as shown in Exhibit 4.3. (Also see Appendix E8, Test Case.) A test case defines the step-by-step process whereby a test is executed. It includes the objectives and conditions of the test, the steps needed to set up the test, the data inputs, the expected results, and the actual results.

Other information such as the software, environment, version, test ID, screen, and test type are also provided.

Major Steps to Develop a Test Plan

A test plan is the basis for accomplishing testing and should be considered a living document; that is, as the application changes, the test plan should change.

A good test plan encourages the attitude of "quality before design and coding." It is able to demonstrate that it contains full functional coverage, and the test cases trace back to the functions being tested. It also contains workable mechanisms for monitoring and tracking discovered defects and report status. Appendix E2 is a System/Acceptance Test Plan template that combines unit, integration, and system test plans into one. It is also used in this section to describe how a test plan is built during the waterfall life cycle development methodology.

The following are the major steps that need to be completed to build a good test plan.

1. Define the Test Objectives

The first step for planning any test is to establish what is to be accomplished as a result of the testing. This step ensures that all responsible individuals contribute to the definition of the test criteria that will be used. The developer of a test plan determines what is going to be accomplished with the test, the specific tests to be performed, the test expectations, the critical success factors of the test, constraints, scope of the tests to be performed, the expected end products of the test, a final system summary report (see Appendix E11, System Summary Report), and the final signatures and approvals. The test objectives are reviewed and approval for the objectives is obtained.

2. Develop the Test Approach

The test plan developer outlines the overall approach or how each test will be performed. This includes the testing techniques that will be used, test entry criteria, test exit criteria, procedures to coordinate testing activities with development, the test management approach, such as defect reporting and tracking, test progress tracking, status reporting, test resources and skills, risks, and a definition of the test basis (functional requirement specifications, etc.).

3. Define the Test Environment

The test plan developer examines the physical test facilities, defines the hardware, software, and networks, determines which automated test tools and support tools are required, defines the help desk support required, builds special software required for the test effort, and develops a plan to support the above.

4. Develop the Test Specifications

The developer of the test plan forms the test team to write the test specifications, develops test specification format standards, divides up the work tasks and work breakdown, assigns team members to tasks, and identifies features to be tested. The test team documents the test specifications for each feature and cross-references them to the functional specifications. It also identifies the interdependencies and work flow of the test specifications and reviews the test specifications.

5. Schedule the Test

The test plan developer develops a test schedule based on the resource availability and development schedule, compares the schedule with deadlines, balances resources and workload demands, defines major checkpoints, and develops contingency plans.

6. Review and Approve the Test Plan

The test plan developer or manager schedules a review meeting with the major players, reviews the plan in detail to ensure it is complete and workable, and obtains approval to proceed.

Components of a Test Plan

A system or acceptance test plan is based on the requirement specifications and is required in a very structured development and test environment. System testing evaluates the functionality and performance of the whole application and consists of a variety of tests including performance, usability, stress, documentation, security, volume, recovery, and so on. Acceptance testing is a user-run test that demonstrates the application's ability to meet the original business objectives and system requirements and usually consists of a subset of system tests.

Exhibit 4.4 cross-references the sections of Appendix E2, System/Acceptance Test Plan, against the waterfall life cycle development phases. "Start" in the intersection indicates the recommended start time, or first-cut of a test activity. "Refine" indicates a refinement of the test activity started in a previous life cycle phase. "Complete" indicates the life cycle phase in which the test activity is completed.

Technical Reviews as a Continuous Improvement Process

Quality control is a key preventive component of quality assurance. Defect removal via technical reviews during the development life cycle is an example of a quality control technique. The purpose of technical reviews is to

Exhibit 4.4. System/Acceptance Test Plan versus Phase

Test Section	Requirements Phase	Logical Design Phase	Physical Design Phase	Program Unit Design Phase	Coding Phase
1. Introduction					
a. System description	Start	Refine	Refine	Complete	
b. Objective	Start	Refine	Refine	Complete	
c. Assumptions	Start	Refine	Refine	Complete	
d. Risks	Start	Refine	Refine	Complete	
e. Contingencies	Start	Refine	Refine	Complete	
f. Constraints	Start	Refine	Refine	Complete	
g. Approval signatures	Start	Refine	Refine	Complete	
2. Test approach and strategy					
a. Scope of testing	Start	Refine	Refine	Complete	
b. Test approach	Start	Refine	Refine	Complete	
c. Types of tests	Start	Refine	Refine	Complete	
d. Logistics	Start	Refine	Refine	Complete	
e. Regression policy	Start	Refine	Refine	Complete	
f. Test facility		Start	Refine	Complete	
g. Test procedures		Start	Refine	Complete	
h. Test organization		Start	Refine	Complete	
i. Test libraries		Start	Refine	Complete	
j. Test tools		Start	Refine	Complete	

k. Version control	Start	Refine	Complete	
l. Configuration building	Start	Refine	Complete	
m. Change control	Start	Refine	Complete	
3. Test execution setup				
a. System test process	Start	Refine	Complete	
b. Facility	Start	Refine	Complete	
c. Resources	Start	Refine	Complete	
d. Tool plan	Start	Refine	Complete	
e. Test organization	Start	Refine	Complete	
4. Test specifications				
a. Functional decomposition	Start	Refine	Refine	Complete
b. Functions not to be tested	Start	Refine	Refine	Complete
c. Unit test cases			Start	Complete
d. Integration test cases		Start	Complete	
e. System test cases	Start	Refine	Complete	
f. Acceptance test cases	Start	Refine	Complete	
5. Test procedures				
a. Test case, script, data development	Start	Refine	Refine	Complete
b. Test execution	Start	Refine	Refine	Complete
c. Correction	Start	Refine	Refine	Complete
d. Version control	Start	Refine	Refine	Complete
e. Maintaining test libraries	Start	Refine	Refine	Complete
f. Automated test tool usage	Start	Refine	Refine	Complete

Exhibit 4.4. System/Acceptance Test Plan versus Phase (Continued)

Test Section	Requirements Phase	Logical Design Phase	Physical Design Phase	Program Unit Design Phase	Coding Phase
g. Project management	Start	Refine	Refine	Refine	Complete
h. Monitoring and status reporting	Start	Refine	Refine	Refine	Complete
6. Test tools					
a. Tools to use		Start	Refine	Complete	
b. Installation and setup		Start	Refine	Complete	
c. Support and help		Start	Refine	Complete	
7. Personnel resources					
a. Required skills	Start	Refine	Refine	Complete	
b. Roles and responsibilities	Start	Refine	Refine	Complete	
c. Numbers and time required	Start	Refine	Refine	Complete	
d. Training needs	Start	Refine	Refine	Complete	
8. Test schedule					
a. Development of test plan		Start	Refine	Refine	Complete
b. Design of test cases		Start	Refine	Refine	Complete
c. Development of test cases		Start	Refine	Refine	Complete
d. Execution of test cases		Start	Refine	Refine	Complete
e. Reporting of problems		Start	Refine	Refine	Complete
f. Developing test summary report		Start	Refine	Refine	Complete
g. Documenting test summary report		Start	Refine	Refine	Complete

increase the efficiency of the development life cycle and provide a method to measure the quality of the products. Technical reviews reduce the amount of rework, testing, and "quality escapes," that is, undetected defects. They are the missing links to removing defects and can also be viewed as a testing technique, even though we have categorized testing as a separate quality assurance component.

Originally developed by Michael Fagan of IBM in the 1970s, inspections have several aliases. They are often referred to interchangeably as "peer reviews," "inspections," or "structured walkthroughs." Inspections are performed at each phase of the development life cycle from user requirements through coding. In the latter, code walkthroughs are performed in which the developer walks through the code for the reviewer.

Research demonstrates that technical reviews can be a lot more productive than automated testing techniques in which the application is executed and tested. A technical review is a form of testing, or manual testing, not involving program execution on the computer. Structured walkthroughs and inspections are a more efficient means of removing defects than software testing alone. They also remove defects earlier in the life cycle, thereby reducing defect-removal costs significantly. They represent a highly efficient, low-cost technique of defect removal and can potentially result in a reduction of defect-removal costs of greater than two thirds when compared to dynamic software testing. A side benefit of inspections includes the ability to periodically analyze the defects recorded and remove the root causes early in the software development life cycle.

The purpose of the following section is to provide a framework for implementing software reviews. Discussed is the rationale for reviews, the roles of the participants, planning steps for effective reviews, scheduling, allocation, agenda definition, and review reports.

Motivation for Technical Reviews

The motivation for a review is that it is impossible to test all software. Clearly, exhaustive testing of code is impractical. Technology also does not exist for testing a specification or high-level design. The idea of testing a software test plan is also bewildering. Testing also does not address quality issues or adherence to standards, which are possible with review processes.

There is a variety of software technical reviews available for a project, depending on the type of software product and the standards that affect the review processes. The types of reviews depend on the deliverables to be produced. For example, for a Department of Defense contract, there are certain stringent standards for reviews that must be followed. These requirements may not be required for in-house application development.

A review increases the quality of the software product, reduces rework and ambiguous efforts, reduces testing and defines test parameters, and is a repeatable and predictable process. It is an effective method for finding defects and discrepancies; it increases the reliability of the delivered product, has a positive impact on the schedule, and reduces development costs.

Early detection of errors reduces rework at later development stages, clarifies requirements and design, and identifies interfaces. It reduces the number of failures during testing, reduces the number of retests, identifies requirements testability, and helps identify missing or ambiguous requirements.

Types of Reviews

There are formal and informal reviews. Informal reviews occur spontaneously among peers, and the reviewers do not necessarily have any responsibility and do not have to produce a review report. Formal reviews are carefully planned meetings in which reviewers are held responsible for their participation and a review report is generated that contains action items.

The spectrum of review ranges from very informal peer reviews to extremely formal and structured inspections. The complexity of a review is usually correlated to the complexity of the project. As the complexity of a project increases, the need for more formal reviews increases.

Structured Walkthroughs

A structured walkthrough is a presentation review in which a review participant, usually the developer of the software being reviewed, narrates a description of the software, and the remainder of the group provides feedback throughout the presentation. Testing deliverables such as test plans, test cases, and test scripts can also be reviewed using the walkthrough technique. These are referred to as presentation reviews because the bulk of the feedback usually occurs only for the material actually presented.

Advanced preparation of the reviewers is not necessarily required. One potential disadvantage of a structured walkthrough is that, because of its informal structure, it may lead to disorganized and uncontrolled reviews. Walkthroughs may also be stressful if the developer is conducting the walkthrough.

Inspections

The inspection technique is a formally defined process for verification of the software product throughout its development. All software deliverables are examined at defined phases to assess the current status and quality effectiveness from the requirements to coding phase. One of the major decisions within an inspection is whether a software deliverable is eligible to proceed to the next development phase.

Software quality is achieved in a product during the early stages when the cost to remedy defects is 10 to 100 times less than it would be during testing or maintenance. It is, therefore, advantageous to find and correct defects as near to their point of origin as possible. Exit criteria are the standard against which inspections measure completion of the product at the end of a phase.

The advantages of inspections are that they are very systematic, controlled, and less stressful. The inspection process promotes the concept of egoless programming. If managed properly, it is a forum in which developers need not become emotionally protective of the work produced. An inspection requires an agenda to guide the review preparation and the meeting itself. Inspections have rigorous entry and exit requirements for the project work deliverables.

A major difference between structured walkthroughs and inspections is that inspections collect information to improve the development and review processes themselves. In this sense, an inspection is more of a quality assurance technique than walkthroughs.

Phased inspections apply the PDCA (Plan, Do, Check, and Act) quality model. Each development phase has entrance requirements, for example, how to qualify to enter an inspection and exit criteria, and how to know when to exit the inspection. In between the entry and exit are the project deliverables that are inspected. In Exhibit 4.5, the steps of a phased inspection and the corresponding PDCA steps are shown.

Exhibit 4.5. PDCA Process and Inspections

Inspection Step	Description	Plan	Do	Check	Act
1. Planning	Identify participants, get materials together, schedule the overview	√			
2. Overview	Educate for the inspections	√			
3. Preparation	Individual preparation for the inspections		√		
4. Inspection	Actual inspection to identify defects		√	√	
5. Rework	Rework to correct any defects				√
6. Follow-up	Follow up to ensure all defects are corrected				√

The Plan step of the continuous improvement process consists of inspection planning and preparing an education overview. The strategy of an inspection is to design and implement a review process that is timely, efficient, and effective. Specific products are designated, as are acceptable criteria, and meaningful metrics are defined to measure and maximize the efficiency of the process. Inspection materials must meet inspection entry criteria. The right participants are identified and scheduled. In addition, a suitable meeting place and time is arranged. The group of participants is educated on what is to be inspected and their roles.

The Do step includes individual preparation for the inspections and the inspection itself. Participants learn the material, prepare for their assigned roles, and the inspection proceeds. Each review is assigned one or more specific aspects of the product to be reviewed in terms of technical accuracy, standards and conventions, quality assurance, and readability.

The Check step includes the identification and documentation of the defects uncovered. Defects are discovered during the inspection, but solution hunting and the discussion of design alternatives are discouraged. Inspections are a review process, not a solution session.

The Act step includes the rework and follow-up required to correct any defects. The author reworks all discovered defects. The team ensures that all the potential corrective actions are effective and no secondary defects are inadvertently introduced.

By going around the PDCA cycle for each development phase using inspections we verify and improve each phase deliverable at its origin and stop it dead in its tracks when defects are discovered (see Exhibit 4.6). The

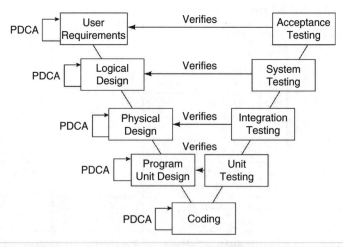

Exhibit 4.6. Phased Inspections as an Ascending Spiral

next phase cannot start until the discovered defects are corrected. The reason is that it is advantageous to find and correct defects as near to their point of origin as possible. Repeated application of the PDCA results in an ascending spiral to facilitate quality improvement at each phase. The end product is dramatically improved, and the bewildering task of the software testing process will be minimized; for example, a lot of the defects will have been identified and corrected by the time the testing team receives the code.

Participant Roles

Roles will depend on the specific review methodology being followed, that is, structured walkthroughs or inspections. These roles are functional, which implies that it is possible in some reviews for a participant to execute more than one role. The role of the review participants after the review is especially important because many errors identified during a review may not be fixed correctly by the developer. This raises the issue of who should follow up on a review and whether another review is necessary.

The review leader is responsible for the review. This role requires scheduling the review, conducting an orderly review meeting, and preparing the review report. The review leader may also be responsible for ensuring that action items are properly handled after the review process. Review leaders must possess both technical and interpersonal management characteristics. The interpersonal management qualities include leadership ability, mediator skills, and organizational talents. The review leader must keep the review group focused at all times and prevent the meeting from becoming a problem-solving session. Material presented for review should not require the review leader to spend more than two hours for preparation.

The recorder role in the review process guarantees that all information necessary for an accurate review report is preserved. The recorder must digest complicated discussions and capture their essence in action items. The role of the recorder is clearly a technical function and one that cannot be performed by a nontechnical individual.

The reviewer role is to objectively analyze the software and be accountable for the review. An important guideline is that the reviewer must keep in mind that the software is being reviewed and not the producer of the software. This cannot be overstated. Also, the number of reviewers should be limited to six. If too many reviewers are involved, productivity will decrease.

In a technical review, the producer may actually lead the meeting in an organized discussion of the software. A degree of preparation and planning is needed in a technical review to present material at the proper level and pace. The attitude of the producer is also important, and it is essential that he does not take a defensive approach. This can be facilitated by the group leader's emphasizing that the purpose of the inspection is to uncover defects and produce the best product possible.

Steps for an Effective Review

1. Plan for the Review Process

Planning can be described at both the organizational level and the specific review level. Considerations at the organizational level include the number and types of reviews that are to be performed for the project. Project resources must be allocated for accomplishing these reviews.

At the specific review level, planning considerations include selecting participants and defining their respective roles, scheduling the review, and developing a review agenda. There are many issues involved in selecting the review participants. It is a complex task normally performed by management, with technical input. When selecting review participants, care must be exercised to ensure that each aspect of the software under review can be addressed by at least some subset of the review team.

In order to minimize the stress and possible conflicts in the review processes, it is important to discuss the role that a reviewer plays in the organization and the objectives of the review. Focus on the review objectives will lessen personality conflicts.

2. Schedule the Review

A review should ideally take place soon after a producer has completed the software but before additional effort is expended on work dependent on the software. The review leader must state the agenda based on a well thought-out schedule. If all the inspection items have not been completed, another inspection should be scheduled.

The problem of allocating sufficient time to a review stems from the difficulty in estimating the time needed to perform the review. The approach that must be taken is the same as that for estimating the time to be allocated for any meeting; that is, an agenda must be formulated and time estimated for each agenda item. An effective technique is to estimate the time for each inspection item on a time line.

Another scheduling problem is the duration of the review when the review is too long. This requires that review processes be focused in terms of their objectives. Review participants must understand these review objectives and their implications in terms of actual review time, as well as preparation time, before committing to the review. The deliverable to be reviewed should meet a certain set of entry requirements before the review is scheduled. Exit requirements must also be defined.

3. Develop the Review Agenda

A review agenda must be developed by the review leader and the producer prior to the review. Although review agendas are specific to any particular product and the objective of its review, generic agendas should be produced for related types of products. These agendas may take the form of checklists (see Appendix F, Checklists, for more details).

4. Create a Review Report

The output of a review is a report. The format of the report is not important. The contents should address the management perspective, user perspective, developer perspective, and quality assurance perspective.

From a management perspective, the review report serves as a summary of the review that highlights what was reviewed, who did the reviewing, and their assessment. Management needs an estimate of when all action items will be resolved to successfully track the project.

The user may be interested in analyzing review reports for some of the same reasons as the manager. The user may also want to examine the quality of intermediate work products in an effort to monitor the development organization's progress.

From a developer's perspective, the critical information is contained in the action items. These may correspond to actual errors, possible problems, inconsistencies, or other considerations that the developer must address.

The quality assurance perspective of the review report is twofold: quality assurance must ensure that all action items in the review report are addressed, and it should also be concerned with analyzing the data on the review forms and classifying defects to improve the software development and review process. For example, a high number of specification errors might suggest a lack of rigor or time in the requirements specifications phase of the project. Another example is a high number of defects reported, suggesting that the software has not been adequately unit tested.

Part 5
Verifying the Requirements Phase

The testing process should begin early in the application development life cycle, not just at the traditional testing phase at the end of coding. Testing should be integrated with the application development phases.

During the requirements phase of the software development life cycle, the business requirements are defined on a high level and are the basis of the subsequent phases and the final implementation. Testing in its broadest sense commences during the requirements phase (see Exhibit 5.1), which increases the probability of a quality system based on the user's expectations. The result is the requirements are verified as correct and complete. Unfortunately, more often than not, poor requirements are produced at the expense of the application. Poor requirements ripple down the waterfall and result in a product that does not meet the user's expectations. Some examples of poor requirements include:

- Partial set of functions defined
- Performance not considered
- Ambiguous requirements
- Security not defined
- Interfaces not documented
- Erroneous and redundant requirements
- Requirements too restrictive
- Contradictory requirements

The functionality is the most important part of the specification and should include a hierarchic decomposition of the functions. The reason for this is that it provides a description that is described in levels to enable all the reviewers to read as much detail as needed. Specifically, this will make the task of translating the specification to test requirements much easier.

Another important element of the requirements specification is the data description (see Appendix C, Requirements Specification, for more details). It should contain details such as whether the database is relational or hierarchical. If it is hierarchical, a good representation is with a data model or entity relationship diagram in terms of entities, attributes, and relationships.

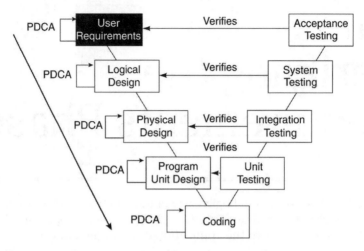

Exhibit 5.1. Requirements Phase and Acceptance Testing

Another section in the requirements should be a description of the interfaces between the system and external entities that interface with the system, such as users, external software, or external hardware. The human interaction should include a description of how the users will interact with the system. This would include the form of the interface and the technical capabilities of the users.

During the requirements phase, the testing organization needs to perform two functions simultaneously. It needs to build the system/acceptance test plan and also verify the requirements. The requirements verification entails ensuring the correctness and completeness of the documentation prepared by the development team.

Testing the Requirements with Technical Reviews

The requirements definition is the result of creative thinking and is the basis for design. The requirements phase is verified with static techniques, that is, nonexecution of the application because it does not yet exist. These techniques check adherence to specification conventions, completeness, and language syntax, and include the following (see Appendix G, Software Testing Techniques, for more details).

Inspections and Walkthroughs

These are formal techniques to evaluate the documentation form, interface requirements, and solution constraints as described in the previous section.

Checklists

These are oriented toward quality control and include questions to ensure the completeness of the requirements.

Exhibit 5.2. Requirements Phase Defect Recording

Defect Category	Missing	Wrong	Extra	Total
1. Operating rules (or information) are inadequate or partially missing				
2. Performance criteria (or information) are inadequate or partially missing				
3. Environment information is inadequate or partially missing				
4. System mission information is inadequate or partially missing				
5. Requirements are incompatible				
6. Requirements are incomplete				
7. Requirements are missing				
8. Requirements are incorrect				
9. The accuracy specified does not conform to the actual need				
10. The data environment is inadequately described				

Methodology Checklist

This provides the methodology steps and tasks to ensure that the methodology is followed.

If the review is totally successful with no outstanding issues or defects discovered, the requirements specification is frozen, and any further refinements are monitored rigorously. If the review is not totally successful and there are minor issues during the review, the author corrects them and it is reviewed by the moderator and signed off. On the other hand, if major issues and defects are discovered during the requirements review process, the defects are corrected and a new review occurs with the same review members at a later time.

Each defect uncovered during the requirements phase review should be documented. Requirement defect trouble reports are designed to assist in the proper recording of these defects. It includes the defect category and defect type. The description of each defect is recorded under the missing, wrong, or extra columns. At the conclusion of the requirements review, the defects are summarized and totaled. Exhibit 5.2 shows a partial requirements phase defect recording form (see Appendix F1, Requirements Phase Defect Checklist, for more details).

Requirements Traceability Matrix

A requirements traceability matrix is a document that traces user requirements from analysis through implementation. It can be used as a completeness check to verify that all requirements are present or that there are no unnecessary/extra features, and as a maintenance guide for new personnel. At each step in the development cycle, the requirements, code, and associated test cases are recorded to ensure that the user requirement is addressed in the final system. Both the user and developer have the ability to easily cross-reference the requirements to the design specifications, programming, and test cases. See Appendix E3, Requirements Traceability Matrix, for more details.

Building the System/Acceptance Test Plan

Acceptance testing verifies that a system satisfies the user's acceptance criteria. The acceptance test plan is based on the requirement specifications and is required in a formal test environment. This test uses black-box techniques to test the system against its specifications and is generally tested by the end user. During acceptance testing, it is important for the project team to coordinate the testing process and update the acceptance criteria, as needed. Acceptance testing is often combined with the system-level test plan, which is the case in this discussion.

The requirements phase is the first development phase that is completed before proceeding to the logical design, physical design, program unit design, and coding phases. During the requirements phase, it is not expected that all sections in the test plan will be completed, for not enough information is available.

In the Introduction section of the test plan (see Appendix E2, System/Acceptance Test Plan), the documentation of "first-cut" test activities starts. Included are the system description, the overall system description, acceptance test objectives, assumptions, risks, contingencies, and constraints. At this point some thought about the appropriate authorities for the approval signatures begins.

The key parts in the Test Approach and Strategy section include: (1) the scope of testing, (2) test approach, (3) types of tests, (4) logistics, and (5) the regression policy. The scope of testing defines the magnitude of the testing effort; for example, whether to test the whole system or part. The testing approach documents the basis of the test design approach, for example, black-box, white-box, gray-box testing, incremental integration, and so on. The types of tests identify the test types, such as unit, integration, system, or acceptance, that will be performed within the testing scope. Details of the types of system-level tests may not be available at this point because of the lack of details but will be available during the next

Test / Requirement	Test Case									Comment
	1	2	3	4	5	6	7	8	9	
Functional										
1										
2		Q						T		
3										
4	Q						Q			
Performance										
1										
2			T							
3	Q					Q		Q		
4										
Security										
1				U						
2										
3					Q					
4				U				T		

U – Users reviewed
Q – QA reviewed
T – Ready for testing

Exhibit 5.3. Requirements/Test Matrix

phase. Logistics documents the working relationship between the development and testing organizations and other interested parties. It defines such issues as how and when the testing group will receive the software, and how defects will be recorded, corrected, and verified. The regression policy determines whether previously tested system functions perform properly after changes are introduced.

A major difficulty in testing the requirements document is that testers have to determine whether the problem definition has been translated properly to the requirements document. This requires envisioning the final product and coming up with what should be tested to determine that the requirement solves the problem.

A useful technique to help analyze, review, and document the initial cut at the functional decomposition of the system in the Test Specifications section is the requirement/test matrix (see Exhibit 5.3). This matrix defines the scope of the testing for the project and ensures that tests are specified for each requirement as documented in the requirements specification. It also helps identify the functions to be tested as well as those not to be tested.

Some benefits of the requirements/test matrix are that it:

1. Correlates the tests and scripts with the requirements
2. Facilitates status of reviews
3. Acts as a traceability mechanism throughout the development cycle, including test design and execution

The requirement/test matrix in Exhibit 5.3 documents each requirement and correlates it with the test cases and scripts to verify it. The requirements listed on the left side of the matrix can also aid in defining the types of system tests in the Test Approach and Strategy section.

It is unusual to come up with a unique test case for each requirement and, therefore, it takes several test cases to test a requirement thoroughly. This enables reusability of some test cases to other requirements. Once the requirement/test matrix has been built, it can be reviewed, and test case design and script building can commence.

The status column is used to track the status of each test case as it relates to a requirement. For example, "Q" in the status column can indicate that the requirement has been reviewed by QA, "U" can indicate that the users had reviewed the requirement, and "T" can indicate that the test case specification has been reviewed and is ready.

In the Test Specifications section of the test plan, information about the acceptance tests is available and can be documented. These tests must be passed in order for the user to accept the system. A procedure is a series of related actions carried out using an operational mode, that is, one which tells how to accomplish something. The following information can be documented in the Test Procedures section: test case, script, data development, test execution, correction, version control, maintaining test libraries, automated test tool usage, project management, monitoring, and status reporting.

It is not too early to start thinking about the testing personnel resources that will be needed. This includes the required testing skills, roles and responsibilities, the numbers and time required, and the personnel training needs.

Part 6
Verifying the Logical Design Phase

The business requirements are defined during the requirements phase. The logical design phase refines the business requirements in preparation for system specification that can be used during physical design and coding. The logical design phase further refines the business requirements that were defined in the requirement phase from a functional and information model point of view.

Data Model, Process Model, and the Linkage

The logical design phase establishes a detailed system framework for building the application. Three major deliverables from this phase are the data model, also known as an entity relationship diagram, a process model, and the linkage between the two.

A data model is a representation of the information needed or data object types required by the application. It establishes the associations between people, places, and things of importance to the application and is used later in physical database design, which is part of the physical design phase. A data model is a graphical technique used to define the entities and the relationships. An entity is something about which we want to store data. It is a uniquely identifiable person, place, thing, or event of interest to the user, about which the application is to maintain and report data. Examples of entities are customers, orders, offices, and purchase orders.

Each entity is a table divided horizontally into rows and columns. Each row is a specific occurrence of each entity, much like records in a file. Each column is an attribute that helps describe the entity. Examples of attributes include size, date, value, and address. Each entity in a data model does not exist by itself and is linked to other entities by relationships. A relationship is an association between two or more entities of interest to the user, about which the application is to maintain and report data. There are three types of relationships: a one-to-one relationship links a single occurrence of an entity to zero or one occurrence of another entity; a one-to-many relationship links one occurrence of an entity to zero or more occurrences of an entity; and a many-to-many relationship links many occurrences of an entity to many occurrences of an entity. The type of relationship defines the cardinality of the entity relationships. See Appendix G10, Database Testing, for more details about data modeling.

A process is a business activity and the associated inputs and outputs. Examples of processes are: accept order, update inventory, ship orders, and schedule class. A process model is a graphical representation and should describe what the process does but not refer to why, how, or when the process is carried out. These are physical attributes of a process that are defined in the physical design phase.

A process model is a decomposition of the business. Process decomposition is the breakdown of the activities into successively more detail. It starts at the top until elementary processes, the smallest unit of activity that has meaning to the user, are defined.

A process decomposition diagram is used to illustrate processes in a hierarchical structure showing successive levels of detail. The diagram is built iteratively as processes and nonelementary processes are decomposed. The root of a process is the starting point of the decomposition. A parent is the process at a higher level than lower levels. A child is the lower level that is joined to a higher level, or parent. A data flow diagram is often used to verify the process decomposition. It shows all the processes, data store accesses, and the incoming and outgoing data flows. It also shows the flows of data to and from entities external to the processes.

An association diagram, often called a CRUD matrix or process/data matrix, links data and process models (see Exhibit 6.1). It helps ensure that the data and processes are discovered and assessed. It identifies and resolves matrix omissions and conflicts and helps refine the data and process models, as necessary. It maps processes against entities showing which processes create, read, update, or delete the instances in an entity.

This is often called "entity life cycle analysis" and analyzes the birth and death of an entity and is performed by process against the entity. The analyst first verifies that there is an associated process to create instances in the entity. If there is an entity that has no associated process that creates it, a process is missing and must be defined. It is then verified that there are associated processes to update, read, or delete instances in an entity. If there is an entity that is never updated, read, or deleted, perhaps the entity may be eliminated. See Appendix G9, CRUD Testing, for more details of how this can be applied to software testing.

Testing the Logical Design with Technical Reviews

The logical design phase is verified with static techniques, that is, non-execution of the application. As utilized in the requirements phase, these techniques check the adherence to specification conventions and

Entity \ Process	Entity Type									Comment
	1	2	3	4	5	6	7	8	9	
Planning	crud				cu			cu		
Selling		ud	c				c			
Scheduling	c				d	crud			d	
Compensation			cu	c	d		cu			
Shipping		crud	ud	u	c	crud				
Operations					crud		crud			
Maintenance		c			cu				cu	
Cost Planning	crud					crud				
Purchasing			ud					d		
Forecasting							c			
Receiving		c	c		c					
Ordering	d					d			cu	
Research			crud		c		crud			
⋮										

Exhibit 6.1. CRUD Matrix

completeness of the models. The same static testing techniques used to verify the requirements are used in the logical design phase. The work products to be reviewed include the data model, the process model, and CRUD matrix.

Each defect discovered during the logical design review should be documented. A defect trouble report is designed to assist in the proper recording of these defects. It includes the defect category and defect type. The description of each defect is recorded under the missing, wrong, or extra columns. At the conclusion of the logical design review, the defects are summarized and totaled. Exhibit 6.2 shows a sample logical design phase defect recording form (see Appendix F2, Logical Design Phase Defect Checklist, for more details).

Refining the System/Acceptance Test Plan

System testing is a multifaceted test that evaluates the functionality, performance, and fit of the whole application. It demonstrates whether the system satisfies the original objectives. During the requirements phase, enough detail was not available to define these types of tests. The logical

Exhibit 6.2. Logical Design Phase Defect Recording

Defect Category	Missing	Wrong	Extra	Total
1. The data has not been adequately defined				
2. Entity definition is incomplete				
3. Entity cardinality is incorrect				
4. Entity attribute is incomplete				
5. Normalization is violated				
6. Incorrect primary key				
7. Incorrect foreign key				
8. Incorrect compound key				
9. Incorrect entity subtype				
10. The process has not been adequately defined				

design provides a great deal more information with data and process models. The scope of testing and types of tests in the Test Approach and Strategy section (see Appendix E2, System/Acceptance Test Plan) can now be refined to include details concerning the types of system-level tests to be performed. Examples of system-level tests to measure the fitness of use include functional, performance, security, usability, and compatibility. The testing approach, logistics, and regression policy are refined in this section. The rest of the items in this section, such as the test facility, test procedures, test organization, test libraries, and test tools, are started. Preliminary planning for the software configuration management elements, such as version and change control and configuration building, can begin. This includes acquiring a software configuration management tool if it does not already exist in the organization.

The Test Execution Setup section deals with those considerations for preparing for testing and includes the system test process, test facility, required testing resources, the testing tool plan, and test organization.

In the Test Specifications section more functional details are available from the data and process models and added in the requirements/test matrix. At this point, system-level test case design is started. However, it is too early to complete detailed test development, for example, test procedures, scripts, and the test case input/output data values associated with each test case. Acceptance test cases should be completed during this phase.

In the Test Procedures section, the items started in the previous phase are refined. Test items in the Test Tools and Test Schedule sections are started.

Part 7
Verifying the Physical Design Phase

The logical design phase translates the business requirements into system specifications that can be used by programmers during physical design and coding. The physical design phase determines how the requirements can be automated. During this phase a high-level design is created in which the basic procedural components and their interrelationships and major data representations are defined.

The physical design phase develops the architecture, or structural aspects, of the system. Logical design testing is functional; however, physical design testing is structural. This phase verifies that the design is structurally sound and accomplishes the intent of the documented requirements. It assumes that the requirements and logical design are correct and concentrates on the integrity of the design itself.

Testing the Physical Design with Technical Reviews

The logical design phase is verified with static techniques, that is, nonexecution of the application. As with the requirements and logical design phases, the static techniques check the adherence to specification conventions and completeness, with a focus on the architectural design. The basis for physical design verification is design representation schemes used to specify the design. Example design representation schemes include structure charts, Warnier–Orr diagrams, Jackson diagrams, data navigation diagrams, and relational database diagrams, which have been mapped from the logical design phase.

Design representation schemes provide mechanisms for specifying algorithms and their inputs and outputs to software modules. Various inconsistencies are possible in specifying the control flow of data objects through the modules. For example, a module may need a particular data item that another module creates but is not provided correctly. Static analysis can be applied to detect these types of control flow errors.

Other errors made during the physical design can also be detected. Design specifications are created by iteratively supplying detail. Although a hierarchical specification structure is an excellent vehicle for expressing the design, it does not allow for inconsistencies between levels of detail. For example, coupling measures the degree of independence between modules. When there is little interaction between two modules, the modules are described as loosely coupled. When there is a great deal of interaction, they are tightly coupled. Loose coupling is considered a good design practice.

Examples of coupling include content, common, control, stamp, and data coupling. Content coupling occurs when one module refers to or changes the internals of another module. Data coupling occurs when two modules communicate via a variable or array (table) that is passed directly as a parameter between the two modules. Static analysis techniques can determine the presence or absence of coupling.

Static analysis of the design representations detects static errors and semantic errors. Semantic errors involve information or data decomposition, functional decomposition, and control flow. Each defect uncovered during the physical design review should be documented, categorized, recorded, presented to the design team for correction, and referenced to the specific document in which the defect was noted. Exhibit 7.1 shows a sample physical design phase defect recording form (see Appendix F3, Physical Design Phase Defect Checklist, for more details).

Exhibit 7.1. Physical Design Phase Defect Recording

Defect Category	Missing	Wrong	Extra	Total
1. Logic or sequencing is erroneous				
2. Processing is inaccurate				
3. Routine does not input or output required parameters				
4. Routine does not accept all data within the allowable range				
5. Limit and validity checks are made on input data				
6. Recovery procedures are not implemented or are not adequate				
7. Required processing is missing or inadequate				
8. Values are erroneous or ambiguous				
9. Data storage is erroneous or inadequate				
10. Variables are missing				

Creating Integration Test Cases

Integration testing is designed to test the structure and the architecture of the software and determine whether all software components interface properly. It does not verify that the system is functionally correct, only that it performs as designed.

Integration testing is the process of identifying errors introduced by combining individual program unit tested modules. It should not begin until all units are known to perform according to the unit specifications. Integration testing can start with testing several logical units or can incorporate all units in a single integration test.

Because the primary concern in integration testing is that the units interface properly, the objective of this test is to ensure that they integrate, that parameters are passed, and the file processing is correct. Integration testing techniques include top-down, bottom-up, sandwich testing, and thread testing (see Appendix G, Software Testing Techniques, for more details).

Methodology for Integration Testing

The following describes a methodology for creating integration test cases.

Step 1: Identify Unit Interfaces

The developer of each program unit identifies and documents the unit's interfaces for the following unit operations:

- External inquiry (responding to queries from terminals for information)
- External input (managing transaction data entered for processing)
- External filing (obtaining, updating, or creating transactions on computer files)
- Internal filing (passing or receiving information from other logical processing units)
- External display (sending messages to terminals)
- External output (providing the results of processing to some output device or unit)

Step 2: Reconcile Interfaces for Completeness

The information needed for the integration test template is collected for all program units in the software being tested. Whenever one unit interfaces with another, those interfaces are reconciled. For example, if program unit A transmits data to program unit B, program unit B should indicate that it has received that input from program unit A. Interfaces not reconciled are examined before integration tests are executed.

Step 3: Create Integration Test Conditions

One or more test conditions are prepared for integrating each program unit. After the condition is created, the number of the test condition is documented in the test template.

Step 4: Evaluate the Completeness of Integration Test Conditions

The following list of questions will help guide evaluation of the completeness of integration test conditions recorded on the integration testing template. This list can also help determine whether test conditions created for the integration process are complete.

- Is an integration test developed for each of the following external inquiries?
  - Record test
  - File test
  - Search test
  - Match/merge test
  - Attributes test
  - Stress test
  - Control test
- Are all interfaces between modules validated so that the output of one is recorded as input to another?
- If file test transactions are developed, do the modules interface with all those indicated files?
- Is the processing of each unit validated before integration testing?
- Do all unit developers agree that integration test conditions are adequate to test each unit's interfaces?
- Are all software units included in integration testing?
- Are all files used by the software being tested included in integration testing?
- Are all business transactions associated with the software being tested included in integration testing?
- Are all terminal functions incorporated in the software being tested included in integration testing?

The documentation of integration tests is started in the Test Specifications section (see Appendix E2, System/Acceptance Test Plan). Also in this section, the functional decomposition continues to be refined, but the system-level test cases should be completed during this phase.

Test items in the Introduction section are completed during this phase. Items in the Test Approach and Strategy, Test Execution Setup, Test Procedures, Test Tool, Personnel Requirements, and Test Schedule continue to be refined.

Part 8
Verifying the Program Unit Design Phase

The design phase develops the physical architecture, or structural aspects, of the system. The program unit design phase is refined to enable detailed design. The program unit design is the detailed design in which specific algorithmic and data structure choices are made. It is the specifying of the detailed flow of control that will make it easily translatable to program code with a programming language.

Testing the Program Unit Design with Technical Reviews

A good detailed program unit design is one that can easily be translated to many programming languages. It uses structured techniques such as while, for, repeat, if, and case constructs. These are examples of the constructs used in structured programming. The objective of structured programming is to produce programs with high quality at low cost. A structured program is one in which only three basic control constructs are used.

Sequence

Statements are executed one after another in the same order as they appear in the source listing. An example of a sequence is an assignment statement.

Selection

A condition is tested and, depending on whether the test is true or false, one or more alternative execution paths are executed. An example of a selection is an if-then-else. With this structure the condition is tested and, if the condition is true, one set of instructions is executed. If the condition is false, another set of instructions is executed. Both sets join at a common point.

Iteration

Iteration is used to execute a set of instructions a number of times with a loop. Examples of iteration are dountil and dowhile. A dountil loop executes a set of instructions and then tests the loop termination condition. If

Exhibit 8.1. Program Unit Design Phase Defect Recording

Defect Category	Missing	Wrong	Extra	Total
1. Is the if-then-else construct used incorrectly?				
2. Is the dowhile construct used incorrectly?				
3. Is the dountil construct used incorrectly?				
4. Is the case construct used incorrectly?				
5. Are there infinite loops?				
6. Is it a proper program?				
7. Are there goto statements?				
8. Is the program readable?				
9. Is the program efficient?				
10. Does the case construct contain all the conditions?				

it is true, the loop terminates and continues to the next construct. If it is false, the set of instructions is executed again until reaching the termination logic. A dowhile loop tests the termination condition. If it is true, control passes to the next construct. If it is false, a set of instructions is executed until control is unconditionally passed back to the condition logic.

Static analysis of the detailed design detects semantic errors involving information and logic control flow. Each defect uncovered during the program unit design review should be documented, categorized, recorded, presented to the design team for correction, and referenced to the specific document in which the defect was noted. Exhibit 8.1 shows a sample program unit design phase defect recording form (see Appendix F4, Program Unit Design Phase Defect Checklist, for more details).

Creating Unit Test Cases

Unit testing is the process of executing a functional subset of the software system to determine whether it performs its assigned function. It is oriented toward the checking of a function or a module. White-box test cases are created and documented to validate the unit logic and black-box test cases to test the unit against the specifications (see Appendix E8, Test Case, for a sample test case form). Unit testing, along with the version control necessary during correction and retesting, is typically performed by the developer. During unit test case development it is important to know which portions of the code have been subjected to test cases and which have not. By knowing this coverage, the developer can discover lines of code that are never executed or program functions that do not perform according to the specifications. When coverage is inadequate, implementing the system is risky because defects may be present in the untested portions of the code (see Appendix G, Software Testing Techniques, for more unit test case development techniques). Unit test case specifications are started and documented in the Test Specification section (see Appendix E2, System/Acceptance Test Plan), but all other items in this section should have been completed.

All items in the Introduction, Test Approach and Strategy, Test Execution Setup, Test Tools, and Personnel Resources should have been completed prior to this phase. Items in the Test Procedures section, however, continue to be refined. The functional decomposition, integration, system, and acceptance test cases should be completed during this section. Refinement continues for all items in the Test Procedures and Test Schedule sections.

Part 9
Verifying the Coding Phase

The program unit design is the detailed design in which specific algorithmic and data structure choices are made. Specifying the detailed flow of control will make it easily translatable to program code with a programming language. The coding phase is the translation of the detailed design to executable code using a programming language.

Testing Coding with Technical Reviews

The coding phase produces executable source modules. The basis of good programming is programming standards that have been defined. Some good standards should include commenting, unsafe programming constructs, program layout, defensive programming, and so on. Commenting refers to how a program should be commented and to what level or degree. Unsafe programming constructions are practices that can make the program hard to maintain. An example is goto statements. Program layout refers to how a standard program should be laid out on a page, indentation of control constructs, and initialization. A defensive programming practice describes the mandatory element of the programming defensive strategy. An example is error condition handling and control to a common error routine.

Static analysis techniques, such as structured walkthroughs and inspections, are used to ensure the proper form of the program code and documentation. This is accomplished by checking adherence to coding and documentation conventions and type checking.

Each defect uncovered during the coding phase review should be documented, categorized, recorded, presented to the design team for correction, and referenced to the specific document in which the defect was noted. Exhibit 9.1 shows a sample coding phase defect recording form (see Appendix F5, Coding Phase Defect Checklist, for more details).

Executing the Test Plan

By the end of this phase, all the items in each section of the test plan should have been completed. The actual testing of software is accomplished through the test data in the test plan developed during the requirements, logical

Exhibit 9.1. Coding Phase Defect Recording

Defect Category	Missing	Wrong	Extra	Total
1. Decision logic or sequencing is erroneous or inadequate				
2. Arithmetic computations are erroneous or inadequate				
3. Branching is erroneous				
4. Branching or other testing is performed incorrectly				
5. There are undefined loop terminations				
6. Programming language rules are violated				
7. Programming standards are violated				
8. The programmer misinterprets language constructs				
9. Typographical errors exist				
10. Main storage allocation errors exist				

design, physical design, and program unit design phases. Because results have been specified in the test cases and test procedures, the correctness of the executions is assured from a static test point of view; that is, the tests have been reviewed manually.

Dynamic testing, or time-dependent techniques, involves executing a specific sequence of instructions with the computer. These techniques are used to study the functional and computational correctness of the code.

Dynamic testing proceeds in the opposite order of the development life cycle. It starts with unit testing to verify each program unit independently and then proceeds to integration, system, and acceptance testing. After acceptance testing has been completed, the system is ready for operation and maintenance. Exhibit 9.2 briefly describes each testing type.

Unit Testing

Unit testing is the basic level of testing. Unit testing focuses separately on the smaller building blocks of a program or system. It is the process of executing each module to confirm that each performs its assigned function. The advantage of unit testing is that it permits the testing and debugging of small units, thereby providing a better way to manage the integration of the units into larger units. In addition, testing a smaller unit of code makes it mathematically possible to fully test the code's logic with fewer tests. Unit testing also facilitates automated testing because the behavior of

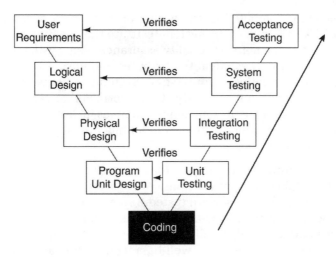

Exhibit 9.2. Executing the Tests

smaller units can be captured and played back with maximized reusability. A unit can be one of several types of application software. Examples include the module itself as a unit, GUI components such as windows, menus, and functions, batch programs, online programs, and stored procedures.

Integration Testing

After unit testing is completed, all modules must be integration tested. During integration testing, the system is slowly built up by adding one or more modules at a time to the core of already integrated modules. Groups of units are fully tested before system testing occurs. Because modules have been unit tested prior to integration testing, they can be treated as blackboxes, allowing integration testing to concentrate on module interfaces. The goals of integration testing are to verify that each module performs correctly within the control structure and that the module interfaces are correct.

Incremental testing is performed by combining modules in steps. At each step one module is added to the program structure, and testing concentrates on exercising this newly added module. When it has been demonstrated that a module performs properly with the program structure, another module is added, and testing continues. This process is repeated until all modules have been integrated and tested.

System Testing

After integration testing, the system is tested as a whole for functionality and fitness of use based on the system/acceptance test plan. Systems are fully tested in the computer operating environment before acceptance testing occurs. The sources of the system tests are the quality attributes that were specified in the software quality assurance plan. System testing is a set of tests to verify these quality attributes and ensure that the acceptance test occurs relatively trouble-free. System testing verifies that the functions are carried out correctly. It also verifies that certain nonfunctional characteristics are present. Some examples include usability testing, performance testing, stress testing, compatibility testing, conversion testing, and document testing.

Black-box testing is a technique that focuses on testing a program's functionality against its specifications. White-box testing is a testing technique in which paths of logic are tested to determine how well they produce predictable results. Gray-box testing is a combination of these two approaches and is usually applied during system testing. It is a compromise between the two and is a well-balanced testing approach that is widely used during system testing.

Acceptance Testing

After systems testing, acceptance testing certifies that the software system satisfies the original requirements. This test should not be performed until the software has successfully completed systems testing. Acceptance testing is a user-run test that uses black-box techniques to test the system against its specifications. The end users are responsible for assuring that all relevant functionality has been tested.

The acceptance test plan defines the procedures for executing the acceptance tests and should be followed as closely as possible. Acceptance testing continues even when errors are found, unless an error itself prevents continuation. Some projects do not require formal acceptance testing. This is true when the customer or user is satisfied with the other system tests, when timing requirements demand it, or when end users have been involved continuously throughout the development cycle and have been implicitly applying acceptance testing as the system is developed.

Acceptance tests are often a subset of one or more system tests. Two other ways to measure acceptance testing are as follows:

1. *Parallel Testing* — A business transaction level comparison with the existing system to ensure that adequate results are produced by the new system.
2. *Benchmarks* — A static set of results produced either manually or from an existing system is used as expected results for the new system.

Defect Recording

Each defect discovered during the above tests is documented to assist in the proper recording of these defects. A problem report is generated when a test procedure gives rise to an event that cannot be explained by the tester. The problem report documents the details of the event and includes at least these items (see Appendix E12, Defect Report, for more details):

- Problem Identification
- Author
- Release/Build Number
- Open Date
- Close Date
- Problem Area
- Defect or Enhancement
- Test Environment
- Defect Type
- Who Detected
- How Detected
- Assigned to
- Priority
- Severity
- Status

Other test reports to communicate the testing progress and results include a test case log, test log summary report, and system summary report.

A test case log documents the test cases for a test type to be executed. It also records the results of the tests, which provides the detailed evidence for the test log summary report and enables reconstructing testing, if necessary. See Appendix E9, Test Case Log, for more information.

A test log summary report documents the test cases from the tester's logs in progress or completed for the status reporting and metric collection. See Appendix E10, Test Log Summary Report.

A system summary report should be prepared for every major testing event. Sometimes it summarizes all the tests. It typically includes the following major sections: general information (describing the test objectives, test environment, references), test results and findings (describing each test), software functions and findings, and analysis and test summary. See Appendix E11, System Summary Report, for more details.

Section III
Software Testing Methodology

Spiral development methodologies are a reaction to the traditional waterfall systems development in which the product evolves in sequential phases. A common problem with the life cycle development model is that the elapsed time to deliver the product can be excessive with user involvement only at the very beginning and very end. As a result, the system that they are given is often not what they originally requested.

By contrast, spiral development expedites product delivery. A small but functioning initial system is built and quickly delivered, and then enhanced in a series of iterations. One advantage is that the users receive at least some functionality quickly. Another advantage is that the product can be shaped by iterative feedback, for example, users do not have to define every feature correctly and in full detail at the beginning of the development cycle, but can react to each iteration.

Spiral testing is dynamic and may never be completed in the traditional sense of a delivered system's completeness. The term "spiral" refers to the fact that the traditional sequence of analysis-design-code-test phases are performed on a microscale within each spiral or cycle in a short period of time, and then the phases are repeated within each subsequent cycle.

The objectives of this section are to:

- Discuss the limitations of waterfall development.
- Describe the complications of client/server.
- Discuss the psychology of spiral testing.
- Describe the iterative/spiral development environment.
- Apply Deming's continuous improvement quality to a spiral development environment in terms of:
  - Information gathering
  - Test planning
  - Test case design
  - Test development
  - Test execution/evaluation
  - Traceability/coverage matrix
  - Preparing for the next spiral
  - System testing
  - Acceptance testing
  - Summarizing/reporting spiral test results

Part 10
Development Methodology Overview

Limitations of Life Cycle Development

In Section II, Life Cycle Testing Review, the waterfall development methodology was reviewed along with the associated testing activities. The life cycle development methodology consists of distinct phases from requirements to coding. Life cycle testing means that testing occurs in parallel with the development life cycle and is a continuous process. Although the life cycle or waterfall development is very effective for many large applications requiring a lot of computer horsepower, for example, DOD, financial, security-based, and so on, it has a number of shortcomings.

- The end users of the system are only involved in the very beginning and the very end of the process. As a result, the system that they were given at the end of the development cycle is often not what they originally visualized or thought they requested.
- The long development cycle and the shortening of business cycles leads to a gap between what is really needed and what is delivered.
- End users are expected to describe in detail what they want in a system, before the coding phase. This may seem logical to developers, however, there are end users who haven't used a computer system before and aren't really certain of its capabilities.
- When the end of a development phase is reached, it is often not quite complete, but the methodology and project plans require that development press on regardless. In fact, a phase is rarely complete and there is always more work than can be done. This results in the "rippling effect," where sooner or later, one must return to a phase to complete the work.
- Often the waterfall development methodology is not strictly followed. In the haste to produce something quickly, critical parts of the methodology are not followed. The worst case is ad hoc development in which the analysis and design phases are bypassed and

99

the coding phase is the first major activity. This is an example of an unstructured development environment.

- Software testing is often treated as a separate phase starting in the coding phase as a validation technique and is not integrated into the whole development life cycle.
- The waterfall development approach can be woefully inadequate for many development projects, even if it were followed. An implemented software system is not worth very much if it is not the system the user wanted. If the requirements are incompletely documented, the system will not survive user validation procedures; that is, it is the wrong system. Another variation is when the requirements are correct, but the design is inconsistent with the requirements. Once again, the completed product will probably fail the system validation procedures.
- Due to the above, experts began to publish methodologies based on other approaches, such as prototyping.

The Client/Server Challenge

The client/server architecture for application development allocates functionality between a client and server so that each performs its task independently. The client cooperates with the server to produce the required results.

The client is an intelligent workstation used as a single user, and because it has its own operating system it can run other applications such as spreadsheets, word processors, and file processors. The user and the server process client/server application functions cooperatively. The server can be a PC, mini-computer, local area network, or even a mainframe. The server receives requests from the clients and processes them. The hardware configuration is determined by the application's functional requirements.

Some advantages of client/server applications include reduced costs, improved accessibility of data, and flexibility. However, justifying a client/server approach and assuring quality is difficult and presents additional difficulties not necessarily found in mainframe applications. Some of these problems include the following:

- The typical graphical user interface has more possible logic paths, and thus the large number of test cases in the mainframe environment is compounded.
- Client/server technology is complicated and often new to the organization. Furthermore, this technology often comes from multiple vendors and is used in multiple configurations and in multiple versions.
- The fact that client/server applications are highly distributed results in a large number of failure sources and hardware/software configuration control problems.

- A short- and long-term cost/benefit analysis must be performed to include the overall organizational costs and benefits to justify a client/server.
- Successful migration to a client/server depends on matching migration plans to the organization's readiness for a client/server.
- The effect of client/server technology on the user's business may be substantial.
- Choosing which applications will be the best candidates for a client/server implementation is not straightforward.
- An analysis needs to be performed of which development technologies and tools enable a client/server.
- Availability of client/server skills and resources, which are expensive, needs to be considered.
- Although the cost of client/server is more expensive than mainframe computing, cost is not the only issue. The function, business benefit, and the pressure from end users have to be balanced.

Integration testing in a client/server environment can be challenging. Client and server applications are built separately. When they are brought together, conflicts can arise no matter how clearly defined the interfaces are. When integrating applications, defect resolutions may have single or multiple solutions, and there must be open communication between quality assurance and development.

In some circles there exists a belief that the mainframe is dead and the client/server prevails. The truth of the matter is that applications using mainframe architecture are not dead, and client/server is not necessarily the panacea for all applications. The two will continue to coexist and complement each other in the future. Mainframes will not prosper as they have in the past but should certainly be part of any client/server strategy.

Psychology of Client/Server Spiral Testing

The New School of Thought

The psychology of life cycle testing encourages testing by individuals outside the development organization. The motivation for this is that with the life cycle approach there typically exist clearly defined requirements, and it is more efficient for a third party to verify the requirements. Testing is often viewed as a destructive process designed to break development's work.

The psychology of spiral testing, on the other hand, encourages cooperation between quality assurance and the development organization. The basis of this argument is that, in a rapid application development environment, requirements may or may not be available, to varying degrees. Without this cooperation, the testing function would have a difficult task defining the test criteria. The only possible alternative is for testing and development to work together.

Testers can be powerful allies to development and, with a little effort, they can be transformed from adversaries into partners. This is possible because most testers want to be helpful; they just need a little consideration and support. In order to achieve this, however, an environment needs to be created to bring out the best of a tester's abilities. The tester and development manager must set the stage for cooperation early in the development cycle and communicate throughout the development life cycle.

Tester/Developer Perceptions

To understand some of the inhibitors to a good relationship between the testing function and development, it is helpful to understand how each views his role and responsibilities.

Testing is a difficult effort. It is the task that's both infinite and indefinite. No matter what testers do, they can't be sure they will find all the problems, or even all the important ones.

Many testers are not really interested in testing and do not have the proper training in basic testing principles and techniques. Testing books or conferences typically treat the testing subject too rigorously and employ deep mathematical analysis. The insistence on formal requirement specifications as a prerequisite to effective testing is not realistic in the real world of a software development project.

It is hard to find individuals who are good at testing. It takes someone who is a critical thinker motivated to produce a quality software product, likes to evaluate software deliverables, and is not caught up in the assumption held by many developers that testing has a lesser job status than development. A good tester is a quick learner and eager to learn, is a good team player, and can effectively communicate both verbally and in written form.

The output from development is something that is real and tangible. A programmer can write code and display it to admiring customers who assume it is correct. From a developer's point of view, testing results in nothing more tangible than an accurate, useful, and all-too-fleeting perspective on quality. Given these perspectives, many developers and testers often work together in an uncooperative, if not hostile, manner.

In many ways the tester and developer roles are in conflict. A developer is committed to building something to be successful. A tester tries to minimize the risk of failure and tries to improve the software by detecting defects. Developers focus on technology, which takes a lot of time and energy when producing software. A good tester, on the other hand, is motivated to provide the user with the best software to solve a problem.

Testers are typically ignored until the end of the development cycle when the application is "completed." Testers are always interested in the progress of development and realize that quality is only achievable when they take a broad point of view and consider software quality from multiple dimensions.

Project Goal: Integrate QA and Development

The key to integrating the testing and developing activities is for testers to avoid giving the impression that they are out to "break the code" or destroy development's work. Ideally, testers are human meters of product quality and should examine a software product, evaluate it, and discover if the product satisfies the customer's requirements. They should not be out to embarrass or complain, but inform development how to make their product even better. The impression they should foster is that they are the "developer's eyes to improved quality."

Development needs to be truly motivated to quality and view the test team as an integral player on the development team. They need to realize that no matter how much work and effort has been expended by development, if the software does not have the correct level of quality, it is destined to fail. The testing manager needs to remind the project manager of this throughout the development cycle. The project manager needs to instill this perception in the development team.

Testers must coordinate with the project schedule and work in parallel with development. They need to be informed about what's going on in development and included in all planning and status meetings. This lessens the risk of introducing new bugs, known as "side-effects," near the end of the development cycle and also reduces the need for time-consuming regression testing.

Testers must be encouraged to communicate effectively with everyone on the development team. They should establish a good communication relationship with the software users, who can help them better understand acceptable standards of quality. In this way, testers can provide valuable feedback directly to development.

Testers should intensively review online help and printed manuals whenever they are available. It will relieve some of the communication burden to get writers and testers to share notes rather than saddle development with the same information.

Testers need to know the objectives of the software product, how it is intended to work, how it actually works, the development schedule, any proposed changes, and the status of reported problems.

Developers need to know what problems were discovered, what part of the software is or is not working, how users perceive the software, what will be tested, the testing schedule, the testing resources available, what the testers need to know to test the system, and the current status of the testing effort.

When quality assurance starts working with a development team, the testing manager needs to interview the project manager and show an interest in working in a cooperative manner to produce the best software product possible. The next section describes how to accomplish this.

Iterative/Spiral Development Methodology

Spiral methodologies are a reaction to the traditional waterfall methodology of systems development, a sequential solution development approach. A common problem with the waterfall model is that the elapsed time for delivering the product can be excessive.

By contrast, spiral development expedites product delivery. A small but functioning initial system is built and quickly delivered, and then enhanced in a series of iterations. One advantage is that the clients receive at least some functionality quickly. Another is that the product can be shaped by iterative feedback; for example, users do not have to define every feature correctly and in full detail at the beginning of the development cycle, but can react to each iteration.

With the spiral approach, the product evolves continually over time; it is not static and may never be completed in the traditional sense. The term "spiral" refers to the fact that the traditional sequence of analysis-design-code-test phases are performed on a microscale within each spiral or cycle, in a short period of time, and then the phases are repeated within each subsequent cycle. The spiral approach is often associated with prototyping and rapid application development.

Traditional requirements-based testing expects that the product definition will be finalized and even frozen prior to detailed test planning. With spiral development, the product definition and specifications continue to evolve indefinitely; that is, there is no such thing as a frozen specification. A comprehensive requirements definition and system design probably never will be documented.

The only practical way to test in the spiral environment, therefore, is to "get inside the spiral." Quality assurance must have a good working relationship with development. The testers must be very close to the development effort, and test each new version as it becomes available. Each iteration of testing must be brief, in order not to disrupt the frequent delivery of the product iterations. The focus of each iterative test must be first to test only the enhanced and changed features. If time within the spiral allows, an automated regression test also should be performed; this requires sufficient time and resources to update the automated regression tests within each spiral.

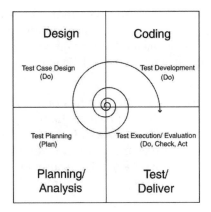

Exhibit 10.1. Spiral Testing Process

Clients typically demand very fast turnarounds on change requests; there may be neither formal release nor a willingness to wait for the next release to obtain a new system feature. Ideally, there should be an efficient, automated regression test facility for the product, which can be used for at least a brief test prior to the release of the new product version (see Section V, Modern Software Testing Tools, for more details).

Spiral testing is a process of working from a base and building a system incrementally. Upon reaching the end of each phase, developers reexamine the entire structure and revise it. Drawing the four major phases of system development — planning/analysis, design, coding, and test/deliver — into quadrants, as shown in Exhibit 10.1, represents the spiral approach. The respective testing phases are test planning, test case design, test development, and test execution/evaluation.

The spiral process begins with planning and requirements analysis to determine the functionality. Then a design is made for the base components of the system and the functionality determined in the first step. Next, the functionality is constructed and tested. This represents a complete iteration of the spiral.

Having completed this first spiral, the users are given the opportunity to examine the system and enhance its functionality. This begins the second iteration of the spiral. The process continues, looping around and around the spiral until the users and developers agree the system is complete; the process then proceeds to implementation.

The spiral approach, if followed systematically, can be effective for ensuring that the users' requirements are being adequately addressed and that the users are closely involved with the project. It can allow for the system to adapt to any changes in business requirements that occurred after the system development began. However, there is one major flaw with this methodology: there may never be any firm commitment to implement a working system. One can go around and around the quadrants, never actually bringing a system into production. This is often referred to as "spiral death."

Although the waterfall development has often proved itself to be too inflexible, the spiral approach can produce the opposite problem. Unfortunately, the flexibility of the spiral methodology often results in the development team ignoring what the user really wants, and thus the product fails the user verification. This is where quality assurance is a key component of a spiral approach. It will make sure that user requirements are being satisfied.

A variation to the spiral methodology is the iterative methodology where the development team is forced to reach a point where the system will be implemented. The iterative methodology recognizes that the system is never truly complete, but is evolutionary. However, it also realizes that there is a point at which the system is close enough to completion to be of value to the end user.

The point of implementation is decided upon prior to the start of the system and a certain number of iterations will be specified with goals identified for each iteration. Upon completion of the final iteration, the system will be implemented in whatever state it may be.

Role of JADs

During the first spiral the major deliverables are the objectives, an initial functional decomposition diagram, and a functional specification. The functional specification also includes an external (user) design of the system. It has been shown that errors defining the requirements and external design are the most expensive to fix later in development. It is, therefore, imperative to get the design as correct as possible the first time.

A technique that helps accomplish this is joint application design sessions (see Appendix G19, JADs, for more details). Studies show that JADs increase productivity over traditional design techniques. In JADs, users and IT professionals jointly design systems in facilitated group sessions. JADs go beyond the one-on-one interviews to collect information. They promote communication, cooperation, and teamwork among the participants by placing the users in the driver's seat.

JADs are logically divided into phases: customization, session, and wrap-up. Regardless of what activity one is pursuing in development, these components will always exist. Each phase has its own objectives.

Role of Prototyping

Prototyping is an iterative approach often used to build systems that users initially are unable to describe precisely (see Appendix G24, Prototyping, for more details). The concept is made possible largely through the power of fourth-generation languages (4GLs) and application generators.

Prototyping is, however, as prone to defects as any other development effort, maybe more so if not performed in a systematic manner. Prototypes need to be tested as thoroughly as any other system. Testing can be difficult unless a systematic process has been established for developing prototypes.

There are various types of software prototypes, ranging from simple printed descriptions of input, processes, and output to completely automated versions. An exact definition of a software prototype is impossible to find; the concept is made up of various components. Among the many characteristics identified by MIS professionals are the following:

- Comparatively inexpensive to build (i.e., less than 10 percent of the full system's development cost).
- Relatively quick development so that it can be evaluated early in the life cycle.
- Provides users with a physical representation of key parts of the system before implementation.
- Prototypes:
  - Do not eliminate or reduce the need for comprehensive analysis and specification of user requirements.
  - Do not necessarily represent the complete system.
  - Perform only a subset of the functions of the final product.
  - Lack the speed, geographical placement, or other physical characteristics of the final system.

Basically, prototyping is the building of trial versions of a system. These early versions can be used as the basis for assessing ideas and making decisions about the complete and final system. Prototyping is based on the premise that, in certain problem domains (particularly in online interactive systems), users of the proposed application do not have a clear and comprehensive idea of what the application should do or how it should operate.

Often, errors or shortcomings overlooked during development appear after a system is operational. Applications prototyping seeks to overcome these problems by providing users and developers with an effective means of communicating ideas and requirements before a significant amount of development effort has been expended. The prototyping process results in a functional set of specifications that can be fully analyzed, understood, and used by users, developers, and management to decide whether an application is feasible and how it should be developed.

Fourth-generation languages have enabled many organizations to undertake projects based on prototyping techniques. They provide many of the capabilities necessary for prototype development, including user functions for defining and managing the user–system interface, data management functions for organizing and controlling access, and system functions for defining execution control and interfaces between the application and its physical environment.

In recent years, the benefits of prototyping have become increasingly recognized. Some include the following:

- Prototyping emphasizes active physical models. The prototype looks, feels, and acts like a real system.
- Prototyping is highly visible and accountable.
- The burden of attaining performance, optimum access strategies, and complete functioning is eliminated in prototyping.
- Issues of data, functions, and user–system interfaces can be readily addressed.
- Users are usually satisfied, because they get what they see.
- Many design considerations are highlighted and a high degree of design flexibility becomes apparent.
- Information requirements are easily validated.
- Changes and error corrections can be anticipated and in many cases made on the spur of the moment.
- Ambiguities and inconsistencies in requirements become visible and correctable.
- Useless functions and requirements can be quickly eliminated.

Methodology for Developing Prototypes

The following describes a methodology to reduce development time through reuse of the prototype and knowledge gained in developing and using the prototype. It does not include how to test the prototype within spiral development. This is included in the next part.

1. Develop the Prototype

In the construction phase of spiral development, the external design and screen design are translated into real-world windows using a 4GL tool such as Visual Basic or Power Builder. The detailed business functionality is not built into the screen prototypes, but a "look and feel" of the user interface is produced so the user can imagine how the application will look.

Using a 4GL, the team constructs a prototype system consisting of data entry screens, printed reports, external file routines, specialized procedures, and procedure selection menus. These are based on the logical database structure developed in the JAD data modeling sessions. The sequence of events for performing the task of developing the prototype in a 4GL is iterative and is described as follows.

Define the basic database structures derived from logical data modeling. The data structures will be populated periodically with test data as required for specific tests.

Define printed report formats. These may initially consist of query commands saved in an executable procedure file on disk. The benefit of a query language is that most of the report formatting can be done automatically by the 4GL. The prototyping team needs only to define what data elements to print and what selection and ordering criteria to use for individual reports.

Define interactive data entry screens. Whether each screen is well designed is immaterial at this point. Obtaining the right information in the form of prompts, labels, help messages, and validation of input is more important. Initially, defaults should be used as often as possible.

Define external file routines to process data that is to be submitted in batches to the prototype or created by the prototype for processing by other systems. This can be done in parallel with other tasks.

Define algorithms and procedures to be implemented by the prototype and the finished system. These may include support routines solely for the use of the prototype.

Define procedure selection menus. The developers should concentrate on the functions as the user would see them. This may entail combining seemingly disparate procedures into single functions that can be executed with one command from the user.

Define test cases to ascertain that:

- Data entry validation is correct.
- Procedures and algorithms produce expected results.
- System execution is clearly defined throughout a complete cycle of operation.

Reiterate this process by adding report and screen formatting options, corrections for errors discovered in testing, and instructions for the intended users. This process should end after the second or third iteration or when changes become predominantly cosmetic rather than functional.

At this point, the prototyping team should have a good understanding of the overall operation of the proposed system. If time permits, the team must now describe the operation and underlying structure of the prototype. This is most easily accomplished through the development of a draft user manual. A printed copy of each screen, report, query, database structure, selection menu, and catalogued procedure or algorithm must be included. Instructions for executing each procedure should include an illustration of the actual dialogue.

2. Demonstrate Prototypes to Management

The purpose of this demonstration is to give management the option of making strategic decisions about the application on the basis of the prototype's appearance and objectives. The demonstration consists primarily of a short description of each prototype component and its effects and a walkthrough of the typical use of each component. Every person in attendance at the demonstration should receive a copy of the draft user manual if one is available.

The team should emphasize the results of the prototype and its impact on development tasks still to be performed. At this stage, the prototype is not necessarily a functioning system, and management must be made aware of its limitations.

3. Demonstrate Prototype to Users

There are arguments for and against letting the prospective users actually use the prototype system. There is a risk that users' expectations will be raised to an unrealistic level with regard to delivery of the production system and that the prototype will be placed in production before it is ready. Some users have actually refused to give up the prototype when the production system was ready for delivery. This may not be a problem if the prototype meets the users' expectations and the environment can absorb the load of processing without affecting others. On the other hand, when users exercise the prototype, they can discover the problems in procedures and unacceptable system behavior very quickly.

The prototype should be demonstrated before a representative group of users. This demonstration should consist of a detailed description of the system operation, structure, data entry, report generation, and procedure execution. Above all, users must be made to understand that the prototype is not the final product, that it is flexible, and that it is being demonstrated to find errors from the users' perspective.

The results of the demonstration include requests for changes, correction of errors, and overall suggestions for enhancing the system. Once the demonstration has been held, the prototyping team reiterates the steps in the prototype process to make the changes, corrections, and enhancements deemed necessary through consensus of the prototyping team, the end users, and management.

For each iteration through prototype development, demonstrations should be held to show how the system has changed as a result of feedback from users and management. The demonstrations increase the users' sense of ownership, especially when they can see the results of their suggestions. The changes should therefore be developed and demonstrated quickly.

Requirements uncovered in the demonstration and use of the prototype may cause profound changes in the system scope and purpose, the conceptual model of the system, or the logical data model. Because these modifications occur in the requirements specification phase rather than in the design, code, or operational phases, they are much less expensive to implement.

4. Revise and Finalize Specifications

At this point, the prototype consists of data entry formats, report formats, file formats, a logical database structure, algorithms and procedures, selection menus, system operational flow, and possibly a draft user manual.

The deliverables from this phase consist of formal descriptions of the system requirements, listings of the 4GL command files for each object programmed (i.e., screens, reports, database structures), sample reports, sample data entry screens, the logical database structure, data dictionary listings, and a risk analysis. The risk analysis should include the problems and changes that could not be incorporated into the prototype and the probable impact that they would have on development of the full system and subsequent operation.

The prototyping team reviews each component for inconsistencies, ambiguities, and omissions. Corrections are made and the specifications are formally documented.

5. Develop the Production System

At this point, development can proceed in one of three directions:

1. The project is suspended or canceled because the prototype has uncovered insurmountable problems or the environment is not ready to mesh with the proposed system.
2. The prototype is discarded because it is no longer needed or because it is too inefficient for production or maintenance.
3. Iterations of prototype development are continued, with each iteration adding more system functions and optimizing performance until the prototype evolves into the production system.

The decision on how to proceed is generally based on such factors as:

- The actual cost of the prototype
- Problems uncovered during prototype development

- The availability of maintenance resources
- The availability of software technology in the organization
- Political and organizational pressures
- The amount of satisfaction with the prototype
- The difficulty in changing the prototype into a production system
- Hardware requirements

Continuous Improvement "Spiral" Testing Approach

The purpose of software testing is to identify the differences between existing and expected conditions, that is, to detect software defects. Testing identifies the requirements that have not been satisfied and the functions that have been impaired. The most commonly recognized test objective is to identify bugs, but this is a limited definition of the aim of testing. Not only must bugs be identified, but they must be put into a framework that enables testers to predict how the software will perform.

In the spiral and rapid application development testing environment there may be no final functional requirements for the system. They are probably informal and evolutionary. Also, the test plan may not be completed until the system is released for production. The relatively long lead-time to create test plans based on a good set of requirement specifications may not be available. Testing is an ongoing improvement process that occurs frequently as the system changes. The product evolves over time and is not static.

The testing organization needs to get inside the development effort and work closely with development. Each new version needs to be tested as it becomes available. The approach is to first test the new enhancements or modified software to resolve defects reported in the previous spiral. If time permits, regression testing is then performed to ensure that the rest of the system has not regressed.

In the spiral development environment, software testing is again described as a continuous improvement process that must be integrated into a rapid application development methodology. Testing as an integrated function prevents development from proceeding without testing. Deming's continuous improvement process using the PDCA model (see Exhibit 10.2) will again be applied to the software testing process.

Before the continuous improvement process begins, the testing function needs to perform a series of information-gathering planning steps to understand the development project objectives, current status, project plans, function specification, and risks.

Once this is completed, the formal Plan step of the continuous improvement process commences. A major step is to develop a software test plan. The test plan is the basis for accomplishing testing and should be considered

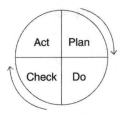

Exhibit 10.2. Spiral Testing and Continuous Improvement

an ongoing document; that is, as the system changes, so does the plan. The outline of a good test plan includes an introduction, the overall plan, testing requirements, test procedures, and test plan details. These are further broken down into business functions, test scenarios and scripts, function/test matrix, expected results, test case checklists, discrepancy reports, required software, hardware, data, personnel, test schedule, test entry criteria, exit criteria, and summary reports.

The more definitive a test plan is, the easier the Plan step will be. If the system changes between development of the test plan and when the tests are to be executed, the test plan should be updated accordingly.

The Do step of the continuous improvement process consists of test case design, test development, and test execution. This step describes how to design test cases and execute the tests included in the test plan. Design includes the functional tests, GUI tests, and fragment system and acceptance tests. Once an overall test design is completed, test development starts. This includes building test scripts and procedures to provide test case details.

The test team is responsible for executing the tests and must ensure that they are executed according to the test design. The Do step also includes test setup, regression testing of old and new tests, and recording any defects discovered.

The Check step of the continuous improvement process includes metric measurements and analysis. As discussed in Section I, Part 3, Quality through Continuous Improvement Process, crucial to the Deming method is the need to base decisions as much as possible on accurate and timely data. Metrics are key to verifying if the work effort and test schedule are on schedule, and to identify any new resource requirements.

During the Check step it is important to publish intermediate test reports. This includes recording of the test results and relating them to the test plan and test objectives.

The Act step of the continuous improvement process involves preparation for the next spiral iteration. It entails refining the function/GUI tests,

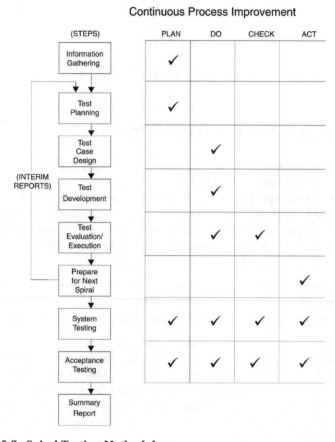

Exhibit 10.3. Spiral Testing Methodology

test suites, test cases, test scripts, and fragment system and acceptance tests, and modifying the defect tracking system and the version and control system, if necessary. It also includes devising measures for appropriate actions relating to work that was not performed according to the plan or results that were not what was anticipated. Examples include a reevaluation of the test team, test procedures, and technology dimensions of testing. All the above are fed back to the test plan, which is updated.

Once several testing spirals have been completed and the application has been verified as functionally stable, full system and acceptance testing starts. These tests are often optional. Respective system and acceptance test plans are developed defining the test objects and the specific tests to be completed.

The final activity in the continuous improvement process is summarizing and reporting the spiral test results. A major test report should be written at the end of all testing. The process used for report writing is the same whether it is an interim or a final report, and, like other tasks in testing, report writing is also subject to quality control. However, the final test report should be much more comprehensive than interim test reports. For each type of test it should describe a record of defects discovered, data reduction techniques, root cause analysis, the development of findings, and follow-on recommendations for current and/or future projects.

Exhibit 10.3 provides an overview of the spiral testing methodology by relating each step to the PDCA quality model. Appendix A, Spiral Testing Methodology, provides a detailed representation of each part of the methodology. The methodology provides a framework for testing in this environment. The major steps include information gathering, test planning, test design, test development, test execution/evaluation, and preparing for the next spiral. It includes a set of tasks associated with each step or a checklist from which the testing organization can choose based on its needs. The spiral approach flushes out the system functionality. When this has been completed, it also provides for classical system testing, acceptance testing, and summary reports.

Part 11
Information Gathering (Plan)

If you will recall, in the spiral development environment, software testing is described as a continuous improvement process that must be integrated into a rapid application development methodology. Deming's continuous improvement process using the PDCA model (see Exhibit 11.1) is applied to the software testing process. We are now in the Plan part of the spiral model.

Exhibit 11.2 outlines the steps and tasks associated with information gathering within the Plan part of spiral testing. Each step and task is described along with valuable tips and techniques.

The purpose of gathering information is to obtain information relevant to the software development project and organize it in order to understand the scope of the development project and start building a test plan. Other interviews may occur during the development project, as necessary.

Proper preparation is critical to the success of the interview. Before the interview, it is important to clearly identify the objectives of the interview to all parties, identify the quality assurance representative who will lead the interview and the scribe, schedule a time and place, prepare any required handouts, and communicate what is required from development.

Although many interviews are unstructured, the interviewing steps and tasks shown in Exhibit 11.2 will be very helpful.

Step 1: Prepare for the Interview

Task 1: Identify the Participants

It is recommended that there be no more than two interviewers representing quality assurance. It is helpful for one of these to assume the role of questioner while the other takes detailed notes. This will allow the interviewer to focus on soliciting information. Ideally the interviewer should be the manager responsible for the project testing activities. The scribe, or note taker, should be a test engineer or lead tester assigned to the project, who supports the interviewer and records each pertinent piece of information and lists the issues, the assumptions, and questions.

Exhibit 11.1. Spiral Testing and Continuous Improvement

The recommended development participants attending include the project sponsor, development manager, or a senior development team member. Although members of the development team can take notes, this is the responsibility of the scribe. Having more than one scribe can result in confusion, because multiple sets of notes will eventually have to be consolidated. The most efficient approach is for the scribe to take notes and summarize at the end of the interview. (See Appendix F20, Project Information Gathering Checklist, which can be used to verify the information available and required at the beginning of the project.)

Task 2: Define the Agenda

The key factor for a successful interview is a well thought-out agenda. It should be prepared by the interviewer ahead of time and agreed upon by the development leader. The agenda should include an introduction, specific points to cover, and a summary section. The main purpose of an agenda is to enable the testing manager to gather enough information to scope out the quality assurance activities and start a test plan. Exhibit 11.3 depicts a sample agenda (details are described in Step 2, Conduct the Interview).

Step 2: Conduct the Interview

A good interview contains certain elements. The first is defining what will be discussed, or "talking about what we are going to talk about." The second is discussing the details, or "talking about it." The third is summarizing, or "talking about what we talked about." The final element is timeliness. The interviewer should state up front the estimated duration of the interview and set the ground rule that if time expires before completing all items on the agenda, a follow-on interview will be scheduled. This is difficult, particularly when the interview is into the details, but nonetheless it should be followed.

Task 1: Understand the Project

Before getting into the project details the interviewer should state the objectives of the interview and present the agenda. As with any type of

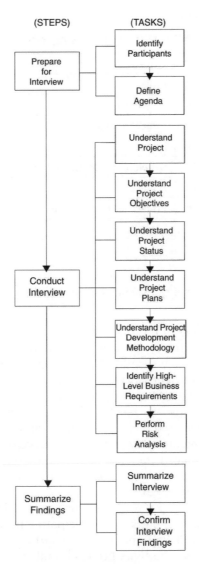

(STEPS)   (TASKS)

Exhibit 11.2. Information Gathering (Steps/Tasks)

interview, he should indicate that only one individual should speak, no interruptions should occur until the speaker acknowledges a request, and focus should be on the material being presented.

He should then introduce himself and the scribe and ask the members of the development team to introduce themselves. Each should indicate name, title, specific roles and job responsibilities, as well as expectations of the interview. The interviewer should point out that the purpose of this task is to obtain general project background information.

Exhibit 11.3. Interview Agenda

I.	Introductions
II.	Project Overview
III.	Project Objectives
IV.	Project Status
V.	Project Plans
VI.	Development Methodology
VII.	High-Level Requirements
VIII.	Project Risks and Issues
IX.	Summary

The following general questions should be asked to solicit basic information:

- What is the name of the project?
- What are the high-level project objectives?
- Who is the audience (users) of the system to be developed?
- When was the project started?
- When is it anticipated to be complete?
- Where is the project in developing the system?
- What is the projected effort in person-months?
- Is this a new, maintenance, or package development project?
- What are the major problems, issues, and concerns?
- Are there plans to address problems and issues?
- Is the budget on schedule?
- Is the budget too tight, too loose, or about right?
- What organizational units are participating in the project?
- Is there an established organization chart?
- What resources are assigned to each unit?
- What is the decision-making structure; that is, who makes the decisions?
- What are the project roles and the responsibilities associated with each role?
- Who is the resource with whom the test team will communicate on a daily basis?
- Has a quality management plan been developed?
- Has a periodic review process been set up?
- Has there been a representative from the user community appointed to represent quality?

Task 2: Understand the Project Objectives

To develop a test plan for a development project it is important to understand the objectives of the project. The purpose of this task is to understand the scope, needs, and high-level requirements of this project.

The following questions should be asked to solicit basic information.

- Purpose:
    - What type of system is being developed, for example, payroll, order entry, inventory, or accounts receivable/payable?
    - Why is the system being developed?
    - What subsystems are involved?
    - What are the subjective requirements, for example, ease of use, efficiency, morale, flexibility?
- Scope:
    - Who are the users of the system?
    - What are the users' job titles and roles?
    - What are the major and subfunctions of the system?
    - What functions will not be implemented?
    - What business procedures are within the scope of the system?
    - Are there analysis diagrams, such as business flow diagrams, data flow diagrams, or data models, to describe the system?
    - Have project deliverables been defined along with completeness criteria?
- Benefits:
    - What are the anticipated benefits that will be provided to the user with this system?
        - Increased productivity
        - Improved quality
        - Cost savings
        - Increased revenue
        - More competitive advantage
- Strategic:
    - What are the strategic or competitive advantages?
    - What impact will the system have on the organization, customers, legal, government, and so on?
- Constraints:
    - What are the financial, organizational, personnel, technological constraints, or limitations for the system?
    - What business functions and procedures are out of scope of the system?

Task 3: Understand the Project Status

The purpose of this task is to understand where the project is at this point, which will help define how to plan the testing effort. For example, if this is the first interview and the project is coding the application, the testing effort is already behind schedule. The following questions should be asked to solicit basic information:

- Has a detailed project work plan, including activities, tasks, dependencies, resource assignments, work effort estimates, and milestones, been developed?
- Is the project on schedule?
- Is the completion time too tight?
- Is the completion time too loose?
- Is the completion time about right?
- Have there been any major slips in the schedule that will have an impact on the critical path?
- How far is the project from meeting its objectives?
- Are the user functionality and quality expectations realistic and being met?
- Are the project work effort hours trends on schedule?
- Are the project costs trends within the budget?
- What development deliverables have been delivered?

Task 4: Understand the Project Plans

Because the testing effort needs to track development, it is important to understand the project work plans. The following questions should be asked to solicit basic information:

- Work breakdown:
  - Has a Microsoft Project (or other tool) plan been developed?
  - How detailed is the plan; for example, how many major and bottom-level tasks have been identified?
  - What are the major project milestones (internal and external)?
- Assignments:
  - Have appropriate resources been assigned to each work plan?
  - Is the work plan well balanced?
  - What is the plan to stage resources?
- Schedule:
  - Is the project plan on schedule?
  - Is the project plan behind schedule?
  - Is the plan updated periodically?

Task 5: Understand the Project Development Methodology

The testing effort must integrate with the development methodology. If considered a separate function, it may not receive the appropriate resources and commitment. Testing as an integrated function should prevent development from proceeding without testing. Testing steps and tasks need to be integrated into the systems development methodology through addition or modification of tasks. Specifically, the testing function needs to know when in the development methodology test design can start. It also needs to know when the system will be available for execution and the recording and correction of defects.

The following questions should be asked to solicit basic information:

- What is the methodology?
- What development and project management methodology does the development organization use?
- How well does the development organization follow the development methodology?
- Is there room for interpretation or flexibility?
- Standards:
    - Are standards and practices documented?
    - Are the standards useful or do they hinder productivity?
    - How well does the development organization enforce standards?

Task 6: Identify the High-Level Business Requirements

A software requirements specification defines the functions of a particular software product in a specific environment. Depending on the development organization, it may vary from a loosely defined document with a generalized definition of what the application will do to a very detailed specification, as shown in Appendix C, Requirements Specification. In either case, the testing manager must assess the scope of the development project in order to start a test plan.

The following questions should be asked to solicit basic information:

- *What are the high-level functions?* The functions at a high level should be enumerated. Examples include order processing, financial processing, reporting capability, financial planning, purchasing, inventory control, sales administration, shipping, cash flow analysis, payroll, cost accounting, and recruiting. This list defines what the application is supposed to do and provides the testing manager an idea of the level of test design and implementation required. The interviewer should solicit as much detail as possible, including a detailed breakdown of each function. If this detail is not available during the interview, a request for a detailed functional decomposition should be made, and it should be pointed out that this information is essential for preparing a test plan.
- *What are the system (minimum) requirements?* A description of the operating system version (Windows, etc.) and minimum microprocessor, disk space, RAM, and communications hardware should be provided.

- *What are the Windows or external interfaces?* The specification should define how the application should behave from an external viewpoint, usually by defining the inputs and outputs. It also includes a description of any interfaces to other applications or subsystems.
- *What are the performance requirements?* This includes a description of the speed, availability, data volume throughput rate, response time, and recovery time of various functions, stress, and so on. This serves as a basis for understanding the level of performance and stress testing that may be required.
- *What other testing attributes are required?* This includes such attributes as portability, maintainability, security, and usability. This serves as a basis for understanding the level of other system-level testing that may be required.
- *Are there any design constraints?* This includes a description of any limitation on the operating environment(s), database integrity, resource limits, implementation language standards, and so on.

Task 7: Perform Risk Analysis

The purpose of this task is to measure the degree of business risk in an application system to improve testing. This is accomplished in two ways: high-risk applications can be identified and subjected to more extensive testing, and risk analysis can help identify the error prone components of an individual application so that testing can be directed at those components. This task describes how to use risk assessment techniques to measure the risk of an application under testing.

Computer Risk Analysis. Risk analysis is a formal method for identifying vulnerabilities (i.e., areas of potential loss). Any area that could be misused, intentionally or accidentally, and result in a loss to the organization is a vulnerability. Identification of risks allows the testing process to measure the potential effect of those vulnerabilities (e.g., the maximum loss that could occur if the risk or vulnerability were exploited).

Risk has always been a testing consideration. Individuals naturally try to anticipate problems and then test to determine whether additional resources and attention need to be directed at those problems. Often, however, risk analysis methods are both informal and ineffective.

Through proper analysis, the test manager should be able to predict the probability of such unfavorable consequences as:

- Failure to obtain all, or even any, of the expected benefits
- Cost and schedule overruns
- An inadequate system of internal control

- Technical performance of the resulting system that is significantly below the estimate
- Incompatibility of the system with the selected hardware and software

The following reviews the various methods used for risk analysis and the dimensions of computer risk and then describes the various approaches for assigning risk priorities. There are three methods of performing risk analysis.

Method 1 — Judgment and Instinct. This method of determining how much testing to perform enables the tester to compare the project with past projects to estimate the magnitude of the risk. Although this method can be effective, the knowledge and experience it relies on are not transferable but must be learned over time.

Method 2 — Dollar Estimation. Risk is the probability for loss. That probability is expressed through this formula:

$$(\text{Frequency of occurrence}) \times (\text{loss per occurrence}) = (\text{annual loss expectation}).$$

Business risk based on this formula can be quantified in dollars. Often, however, the concept, not the formula, is used to estimate how many dollars might be involved if problems were to occur. The disadvantages of projecting risks in dollars are that such numbers (i.e., frequency of occurrence and loss per occurrence) are difficult to estimate and the method implies a greater degree of precision than may be realistic.

Method 3 — Identifying and Weighting Risk Attributes. Experience has demonstrated that the major attributes causing potential risks are the project size, experience with the technology, and project structure. The larger the project is in dollar expense, staffing levels, elapsed time, and number of departments affected, the greater the risk.

Because of the greater likelihood of unexpected technical problems, project risk increases as the project team's familiarity with the hardware, operating systems, database, and application languages decreases. A project that has a slight risk for a leading-edge, large systems development department may have a very high risk for a smaller, less technically advanced group. The latter group, however, can reduce its risk by purchasing outside skills for an undertaking that involves a technology in general commercial use.

In highly structured projects, the nature of the task defines the output completely, from the beginning. Such output is fixed during the life of the project. These projects carry much less risk than those whose output is more subject to the manager's judgment and changes.

Exhibit 11.4. Identifying and Weighting Risk Attributes

Weighting Factor	Project A (Score × Weight)	Project B (Score × Weight)	Project C (Score × Weight)
Project size (2)	$5 \times 2 = 10$	$3 \times 2 = 6$	$2 \times 2 = 4$
Experience with technology (3)	$7 \times 3 = 21$	$1 \times 3 = 3$	$5 \times 3 = 15$
Project structure (1)	$4 \times 1 = 4$	$6 \times 1 = 6$	$3 \times 1 = 3$
Total score	35	15	22

The relationship among these attributes can be determined through weighting, and the testing manger can use weighted scores to rank application systems according to their risk. For example, this method can show application A is a higher risk than application B.

Risk assessment is applied by first weighting the individual risk attributes. For example, if an attribute is twice as important as another it can be multiplied by the weight of two. The resulting score is compared with other scores developed for the same development organization and is used to determine a relative risk measurement among applications, but it is not used to determine an absolute measure.

Exhibit 11.4 compares three projects using the weighted risk attribute method. Project size has a 2 weight factor, experience with technology has a 3 weight factor, and project structure has a 1 weight factor. When the project scores are each multiplied by each of the three weight factors, it is clear that project A has the highest risk.

Information gathered during risk analysis can be used to allocate test resources to test application systems. For example, high-risk applications should receive extensive testing; medium-risk systems, less testing; and low-risk systems, minimal testing. The area of testing can be selected on the basis of high-risk characteristics. For example, if computer technology is a high-risk characteristic, the testing manager may want to spend more time testing how effectively the development team is using that technology.

Step 3: Summarize the Findings

Task 1: Summarize the Interview

After the interview is completed, the interviewer should review the agenda and outline the main conclusions. If there is the need for a follow-up session, one should be scheduled at this point while the members are present.

Typically, during the interview, the notes are unstructured and hard to follow by anyone except the note taker. However, the notes should have at least followed the agenda. After the interview concludes, the notes should be formalized into a summary report. This should be performed by the scribe note taker. The goal is to make the results of the session as clear as possible for quality assurance and the development organization. However, the interview leader may have to embellish the material or expand in certain areas. (See Appendix E16, Minutes of the Meeting, which can be used to document the results and follow-up actions for the project information gathering session).

Task 2: Confirm the Interview Findings

The purpose of this task is to bring about agreement between the interviewer and the development organization to ensure an understanding of the project. After the interview notes are formalized, it is important to distribute the summary report to the other members who attended the interview. A sincere invitation for their comments or suggestions should be communicated. The interviewer should then actively follow up interview agreements and disagreements. Any changes should then be implemented. Once there is full agreement, the interviewer should provide a copy of the summary report.

Part 12
Test Planning (Plan)

The purpose of the test project plan is to provide the basis for accomplishing testing in an organized manner. From a managerial point of view it is the most important document, because it helps manage the test project. If a test plan is comprehensive and carefully thought out, test execution and analysis should proceed smoothly. (See Appendix E1 for a sample unit test plan, Appendix E4 for a sample system test plan, and Appendix F24, which can be used to verify that unit testing has been thorough and comprehensive.)

The test project plan is an ongoing document, particularly in the spiral environment because the system is constantly changing. As the system changes, so does it. A good test plan is one that:

- Has a good chance of detecting a majority of the defects
- Provides test coverage for most of the code
- Is flexible
- Is executed easily and automatically and is repeatable
- Defines the types of tests to be performed
- Clearly documents the expected results
- Provides for defect reconciliation when a defect is discovered
- Clearly defines the test objectives
- Clarifies the test strategy
- Clearly defines the test exit criteria
- Is not redundant
- Identifies the risks
- Documents the test requirements
- Defines the test deliverables

Although there are many ways a test plan can be created, Exhibit 12.1 provides a framework that includes most of the essential planning considerations. It can be treated as a checklist of test items to consider. Some of the items, such as defining the test requirements and test team, are obviously required, however, others may not be. It depends on the nature of the project and the time constraints.

The planning test methodology includes three steps: building the test project plan, defining the metrics, and reviewing/approving the test project plan. Each of these is then broken down into its respective tasks, as shown in Exhibit 12.1.

129

(STEPS) (TASKS)

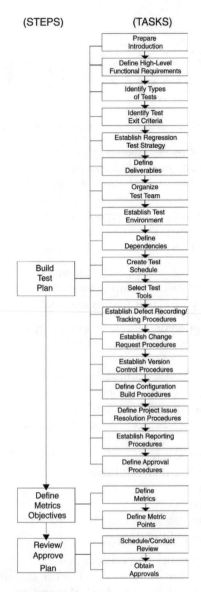

Exhibit 12.1. Test Planning (Steps/Tasks)

Step 1: Build a Test Plan

Task 1: Prepare an Introduction

The first bit of test plan detail is a description of the problem(s) to be solved by the application of the associated opportunities. This defines the summary background describing the events or current status leading up to the decision to develop the application. Also, the application's

130

risks, purpose, objectives, and benefits, and the organization's critical success factors should be documented in the introduction. A critical success factor is a measurable item that will have a major influence on whether a key function meets its objectives. An objective is a measurable end state that the organization strives to achieve. Examples of objectives include:

- New product opportunity
- Improved efficiency (internal and external)
- Organizational image
- Growth (internal and external)
- Financial (revenue, cost profitability)
- Competitive position
- Market leadership

The introduction should also include an executive summary description. The executive sponsor (often called the project sponsor) is the individual who has ultimate authority over the project. This individual has a vested interest in the project in terms of funding, project results, resolving project conflicts, and is responsible for the success of the project. An executive summary describes the proposed application from an executive's point of view. It should describe the problems to be solved, the application goals, and the business opportunities. The objectives should indicate whether the application is a replacement of an old system and document the impact the application will have, if any, on the organization in terms of management, technology, and so on.

Any available documentation should be listed and its status described. Examples include requirements specifications, functional specifications, project plan, design specification, prototypes, user manual, business model/flow diagrams, data models, and project risk assessments. In addition to project risks, which are the potential adverse effects on the development project, the risks relating to the testing effort should be documented. Examples include the lack of testing skills, scope of the testing effort, lack of automated testing tools, and the like. See Appendix E4, Test Plan (Client/Server and Internet Spiral Testing), for more details.

Task 2: Define the High-Level Functional Requirements (in Scope)

A functional specification consists of the hierarchical functional decomposition, the functional window structure, the window standards, and the minimum system requirements of the system to be developed. An example of window standards is the Windows 95 GUI Standards. An example of a minimum system requirement could be Windows 95, a Pentium II microprocessor, 24-MB RAM, 3-gig disk space, and a modem. At this point in development, a full functional specification may not have been defined. However, a list of at least the major business functions of the basic window structure should be available.

Exhibit 12.2. High-Level Business Functions

Order processing (ex. create new order, edit order, etc.)
Customer processing (create new customer, edit customer, etc.)
Financial processing (receive payment, deposit payment, etc.)
Inventory processing (acquire products, adjust product price, etc.)
Reports (create order report, create account receivable report, etc.)

Exhibit 12.3. Functional Window Structure

The Main-Window (menu bar, customer order window, etc.)
The Customer-Order-Window (order summary list, etc.)
The Edit-Order-Window (create order, edit order, etc.)
The Menu Bar (File, Order, View, etc.)
The Tool Bar with icons (FileNew, OrderCreate)

A basic functional list contains the main functions of the system with each function named and described with a verb–object paradigm. This list serves as the basis for structuring functional testing (see Exhibit 12.2).

A functional window structure describes how the functions will be implemented in the windows environment. At this point, a full functional window structure may not be available but a list of the major windows should be (see Exhibit 12.3).

Task 3: Identify Manual/Automated Test Types

The types of tests that need to be designed and executed depend totally on the objectives of the application, that is, the measurable end state the organization strives to achieve. For example, if the application is a financial application used by a large number of individuals, special security and usability tests need to be performed. However, three types of tests that are nearly always required are function, user interface, and regression testing. Function testing comprises the majority of the testing effort and is concerned with verifying that the functions work properly. It is a black-box-oriented activity in which the tester is completely unconcerned with the internal behavior and structure of the application. User interface testing, or GUI testing, checks the user's interaction or functional window structure. It ensures that object state dependencies function properly and provide useful navigation through the functions. Regression testing tests the application in light of changes made during debugging, maintenance, or the development of a new release.

Other types of tests that need to be considered include system and acceptance testing. System testing is the highest level of testing and evaluates the functionality as a total system, its performance, and overall fitness of use. Acceptance testing is an optional user-run test that demonstrates the ability of the application to meet the user's requirements. This test may or may not be performed based on the formality of the project. Sometimes the system test suffices.

Finally, the tests that can be automated with a testing tool need to be identified. Automated tests provide three benefits: repeatability, leverage, and increased functionality. Repeatability enables automated tests to be executed more than once, consistently. Leverage comes from repeatability from tests previously captured and tests that can be programmed with the tool, which may not have been possible without automation. As applications evolve, more and more functionality is added. With automation, the functional coverage is maintained with the test library.

Task 4: Identify the Test Exit Criteria

One of the most difficult and political problems is deciding when to stop testing, because it is impossible to know when all the defects have been detected. There are at least four criteria for exiting testing.

1. *Scheduled testing time has expired* — This criterion is very weak, inasmuch as it has nothing to do with verifying the quality of the application. This does not take into account that there may be an inadequate number of test cases or the fact that there may not be any more defects that are easily detectable.
2. *Some predefined number of defects discovered* — The problems with this are knowing the number of errors to detect and also overestimating the number of defects. If the number of defects is underestimated, testing will be incomplete. Potential solutions include experience with similar applications developed by the same development team, predictive models, and industrywide averages. If the number of defects is overestimated, the test may never be completed within a reasonable time frame. A possible solution is to estimate completion time, plotting defects detected per unit of time. If the rate of defect detection is decreasing dramatically, there may be "burnout," an indication that a majority of the defects have been discovered.
3. *All the formal tests execute without detecting any defects* — A major problem with this is that the tester is not motivated to design destructive test cases that force the tested program to its design limits; for example, the tester's job is completed when the test program fields no more errors. The tester is motivated not to find errors and may subconsciously write test cases that show the program is error free. This criterion is only valid if there is a rigorous and totally comprehensive test case suite created that approaches 100 percent coverage. The problem with this is determining when

there is a comprehensive suite of test cases. If it is felt that this is the case, a good strategy at this point is to continue with ad hoc testing. Ad hoc testing is a black-box testing technique in which the tester lets her mind run freely to enumerate as many test conditions as possible. Experience has shown that this technique can be a very powerful supplemental or add-on technique.

4. *Combination of the above* — Most testing projects utilize a combination of the above exit criteria. It is recommended that all the tests be executed, but any further ad hoc testing will be constrained by time.

Task 5: Establish Regression Test Strategy

Regression testing tests the application in light of changes made during a development spiral, debugging, maintenance, or the development of a new release. This test must be performed after functional improvements or repairs have been made to a system to confirm that the changes have no unintended side effects. Correction of errors relating to logic and control flow, computational errors, and interface errors are examples of conditions that necessitate regression testing. Cosmetic errors generally do not affect other capabilities and do not require regression testing.

It would be ideal if all the tests in the test suite were rerun for each new spiral but, due to time constraints, this is probably not realistic. A good regression strategy during spiral development is for some regression testing to be performed during each spiral to ensure that previously demonstrated capabilities are not adversely affected by later development spirals or error corrections. During system testing after the system is stable and the functionality has been verified, regression testing should consist of a subset of the system tests. Policies need to be created to decide which tests to include. (See Appendix E21.)

A retest matrix is an excellent tool that relates test cases to functions (or program units) as shown in Exhibit 12.4. A check entry in the matrix indicates that the test case is to be retested when the function (or program unit) has been modified due to an enhancement(s) or correction(s). No entry means that the test does not need to be retested. The retest matrix can be built before the first testing spiral but needs to be maintained during subsequent spirals. As functions (or program units) are modified during a development spiral, existing or new test cases need to be created and checked in the retest matrix in preparation for the next test spiral. Over time with subsequent spirals, some functions (or program units) may be stable with no recent modifications. Consideration to selectively remove their check entries should be undertaken between testing spirals. Also see Appendix E14, Retest Matrix.

Other considerations of regression testing are as follows:

Exhibit 12.4. Retest Matrix

	Test Case				
	1	**2**	**3**	**4**	**5**
Business function					
Order processing					
Create new order	√	√	√	√	
Fulfill order					
Edit order	√			√	
Delete order					
Customer processing					
Create new customer					
Edit customer					
Delete customer		√			
Financial processing					
Receive customer payment		√	√		√
Deposit payment					
Pay vendor					
Write a check	√	√	√	√	√
Display register					
Inventory processing					
Acquire vendor products					
Maintain stock					
Handle back orders	√	√	√	√	√
Audit inventory					
Adjust product price					
Reports					
Create order report					
Create account receivables report	√	√	√	√	√
Create account payables report					
Create inventory report					

- Regression tests are potential candidates for test automation when they are repeated over and over in every testing spiral.
- Regression testing needs to occur between releases after the initial release of the system.

- The test that uncovered an original defect should be rerun after it has been corrected.
- An in-depth effort should be made to ensure that the original defect was corrected and not just the symptoms.
- Regression tests that repeat other tests should be removed.
- Other test cases in the functional (or program unit) area where a defect is uncovered should be included in the regression test suite.
- Client-reported defects should have high priority and should be regression tested thoroughly.

Task 6: Define the Test Deliverables

Test deliverables result from test planning, test design, test development, and test defect documentation. Some spiral test deliverables from which you can choose include the following:

- Test plan: Defines the objectives, scope, strategy, types of tests, test environment, test procedures, exit criteria, and so on (see Appendix E4, sample template).
- Test design: The tests for the application's functionality, performance, and appropriateness for use. The tests demonstrate that the original test objectives are satisfied.
- Change request: A documented request to modify the current software system, usually supplied by the user (see Appendix D, Change Request Form, for more details). It is typically different from a defect report, which reports an anomaly in the system.
- Metrics: The measurable indication of some quantitative aspect of a system. Examples include the number of severe defects, and the number of defects discovered as a function of the number of testers.
- Test case: A specific set of test data and associated procedures developed for a particular objective. It provides a detailed blueprint for conducting individual tests and includes specific input data values and the corresponding expected result(s) (see Appendix E8, Test Case, for more details).
- Test log summary report: Specifies the test cases from the tester's individual test logs that are in progress or completed for status reporting and metric collection (see Appendix E10, Test Log Summary Report).
- Test case log: Specifies the test cases for a particular testing event to be executed during testing. It is also used to record the results of the test performed, to provide the detailed evidence for the summary of test results, and to provide a basis for reconstructing the testing event if necessary (see Appendix E9, Test Case Log).
- Interim test report: A report published between testing spirals indicating the status of the testing effort (see Part 16, Step 3, Publish Interim Report).

- System summary report: A comprehensive test report after all spiral testing that has been completed (see Appendix E11, System Summary Report).
- Defect report: Documents defect(s) discovered during spiral testing (see Appendix E12, Defect Report).

Task 7: Organize the Test Team

The people component includes human resource allocations and the required skill sets. The test team should comprise the highest-caliber personnel possible. They are usually extremely busy because their talents put them in great demand, and it therefore becomes vital to build the best case possible for using these individuals for test purposes. A test team leader and test team need to have the right skills and experience, and be motivated to work on the project. Ideally, they should be professional quality assurance specialists but can represent the executive sponsor, users, technical operations, database administration, computer center, independent parties, and so on. In any event, they should not represent the development team, for they may not be as unbiased as an outside party. This is not to say that developers shouldn't test. For they should unit and function test their code extensively before handing it over to the test team.

There are two areas of responsibility in testing: testing the application, which is the responsibility of the test team, and the overall testing processes, which is handled by the test manager. The test manager directs one or more testers, is the interface between quality assurance and the development organization, and manages the overall testing effort. Responsibilities include:

- Setting up the test objectives
- Defining test resources
- Creating test procedures
- Developing and maintaining the test plan
- Designing test cases
- Designing and executing automated testing tool scripts
- Test case development
- Providing test status
- Writing reports
- Defining the roles of the team members
- Managing the test resources
- Defining standards and procedures
- Ensuring quality of the test process
- Training the team members
- Maintaining test statistics and metrics

The test team must be a set of team players and have these responsibilities:

- Executing test cases according to the plan
- Evaluating the test results
- Reporting errors
- Designing and executing automated testing tool scripts
- Recommending application improvements
- Recording defects

The main function of a team member is to test the application and report defects to the development team by documenting them in a defect tracking system. Once the development team corrects the defects, the test team reexecutes the tests that discovered the original defects.

It should be pointed out that the roles of the test manager and team members are not mutually exclusive. Some of the team leader's responsibilities are shared with the team members and vice versa.

The basis for allocating dedicated testing resources is the scope of the functionality and the development time frame; for example, a medium development project will require more testing resources than a small one. If project A of medium complexity requires a testing team of five, project B with twice the scope would require ten testers (given the same resources).

Another rule of thumb is that the testing costs approach 25 percent of the total budget. Because the total project cost is known, the testing effort can be calculated and translated to tester headcount.

The best estimate is a combination of the project scope, test team skill levels, and project history. A good measure of required testing resources for a particular project is the histories of multiple projects, that is, testing resource levels and performance compared to similar projects.

Task 8: Establish a Test Environment

The purpose of the test environment is to provide a physical framework for testing necessary for the testing activity. For this task, the test environment needs are established and reviewed before implementation.

The main components of the test environment include the physical test facility, technologies, and tools. The test facility component includes the physical setup. The technologies component includes the hardware platforms, physical network and all its components, operating system software, and other software such as utility software. The tools component includes any specialized testing software such as automated test tools, testing libraries, and support software.

The testing facility and workplace need to be established. This may range from an individual workplace configuration to a formal testing lab. In any event, it is important that the testers be together and in close proximity to the development team. This facilitates communication and the sense of a common goal. The testing tools that were acquired need to be installed.

The hardware and software technologies need to be set up. This includes the installation of test hardware and software, and coordination with vendors, users, and information technology personnel. It may be necessary to test the hardware and coordinate with hardware vendors. Communication networks need to be installed and tested.

Task 9: Define the Dependencies

A good source of information is previously produced test plans on other projects. If available, the sequence of tasks in the project work plans can be analyzed for activity and task dependencies that apply to this project.

Examples of test dependencies include:

- Code availability
- Tester availability (in a timely fashion)
- Test requirements (reasonably defined)
- Test tools availability
- Test group training
- Technical support
- Defects fixed in a timely manner
- Adequate testing time
- Computers and other hardware
- Software and associated documentation
- System documentation (if available)
- Defined development methodology
- Test lab space availability
- Agreement with development (procedures and processes)

The support personnel need to be defined and committed to the project. This includes members of the development group, technical support staff, network support staff, and database administrator support staff.

Task 10: Create a Test Schedule

A test schedule should be produced that includes the testing steps (and perhaps tasks), target start and end dates, and responsibilities. It should also describe how it will be reviewed, tracked, and approved. A simple test schedule format, as shown in Exhibit 12.5, follows the spiral methodology.

Also, a project management tool such as Microsoft Project can format a Gantt chart to emphasize the tests and group them into test steps. A Gantt chart consists of a table of task information and a bar chart that graphically displays the test schedule. It also includes task time duration and links the task dependency relationships graphically. People resources can

Exhibit 12.5. Test Schedule

Test Step	Begin Date	End Date	Responsible
First Spiral			
Information gathering			
Prepare for interview	6/1/04	6/2/04	Smith, Test Manager
Conduct interview	6/3/04	6/3/04	Smith, Test Manager
Summarize findings	6/4/04	6/5/04	Smith, Test Manager
Test planning			
Build test plan	6/8/04	6/12/04	Smith, Test Manager
Define the metric objectives	6/15/04	6/17/04	Smith, Test Manager
Review/approve plan	6/18/04	6/18/04	Smith, Test Manager
Test case design			
Design function tests	6/19/04	6/23/04	Smith, Test Manager
Design GUI tests	6/24/04	6/26/04	Smith, Test Manager
Define the system/acceptance			
Tests	6/29/04	6/30/04	Smith, Test Manager
Review/approve design	7/3/04	7/3/04	Smith, Test Manager
Test development			
Develop test scripts	7/6/04	7/16/04	Jones, Baker, Brown, Testers
Review/approve test development	7/17/04	7/17/04	Jones, Baker, Brown, Testers
Test execution/evaluation			
Setup and testing	7/20/04	7/24/04	Smith, Jones, Baker, Brown, Testers
Evaluation	7/27/04	7/29/04	Smith, Jones, Baker, Brown, Testers
Prepare for the next spiral			
Refine the tests	8/3/04	8/5/04	Smith, Test Manager
Reassess team, procedures, and test environment	8/6/04	8/7/04	Smith, Test Manager
Publish interim report	8/10/04	8/11/04	Smith, Test Manager
	•		
	•		
	•		

Exhibit 12.5. Test Schedule (Continued)

Test Step	Begin Date	End Date	Responsible
Last spiral...			
Test execution/evaluation			
Setup and testing	10/5/04	10/9/04	Jones, Baker, Brown, Testers
Evaluation	10/12/04	10/14/04	Smith, Test Manager
	•		
	•		
	•		
Conduct system testing			
Complete system test plan	10/19/04	10/21/04	Smith, Test Manager
Complete system test cases	10/22/04	10/23/04	Smith, Test Manager
Review/approve system tests	10/26/04	10/30/04	Jones, Baker, Brown, Testers
Execute the system tests	11/2/04	11/6/04	Jones, Baker, Brown, Testers
Conduct acceptance testing			
Complete acceptance test plan	11/9/04	11/10/04	Smith, Test Manager
Complete acceptance test cases	11/11/04	11/12/04	Smith, Test Manager
Review/approve acceptance			
Test plan	11/13/04	11/16/04	Jones, Baker, Brown, Testers
Execute the acceptance tests	11/17/04	11/20/04	
Summarize/report spiral test results			
Perform data reduction	11/23/04	11/26/04	Smith, Test Manager
Prepare final test report	11/27/04	11/27/04	Smith, Test Manager
Review/approve the final			
Test report	11/28/04	11/29/04	Smith, Test Manager Baylor, Sponsor

also be assigned to tasks for workload balancing. See Appendix E13, Test Schedule, and template file Gantt spiral testing methodology template.

Another way to schedule testing activities is with "relative scheduling" in which testing steps or tasks are defined by their sequence or precedence. It

Exhibit 12.6. Project Milestones

Project Milestone	Due Date
Sponsorship approval	7/1/04
First prototype available	7/20/04
Project test plan	6/18/04
Test development complete	7/1704
Test execution begins	7/20/04
Final spiral test summary report published	11/27/04
System ship date	12/1/04

does not state a specific start or end date but does have a duration, such as days. (Also see Appendix E18, Test Execution Plan, which can be used to plan the activities for the Execution phase, and Appendix E20, PDCA Test Schedule, which can be used to plan and track the Plan-Do-Check-Act test phases.)

It is also important to define major external and internal milestones. External milestones are events that are external to the project but may have a direct impact on the project. Examples include project sponsorship approval, corporate funding, and legal authorization. Internal milestones are derived for the schedule work plan and typically correspond to key deliverables that need to be reviewed and approved. Examples include test plan, design, and development completion approval by the project sponsor and the final spiral test summary report. Milestones can be documented in the test plan in table format as shown in Exhibit 12.6. (Also see Appendix E19, Test Project Milestones, which can be used to identify and track the key test milestones.)

Task 11: Select the Test Tools

Test tools range from relatively simple to sophisticated software. New tools are being developed to help provide the high-quality software needed for today's applications.

Because test tools are critical to effective testing, those responsible for testing should be proficient in using them. The tools selected should be most effective for the environment in which the tester operates and the specific types of software being tested. The test plan needs to name specific test tools and their vendors. The individual who selects the test tool should also conduct the test and be familiar enough with the tool to use it effectively. The test team should review and approve the use of each test tool, because the tool selected must be consistent with the objectives of the test plan.

The selection of testing tools may be based on intuition or judgment. However, a more systematic approach should be taken. Section V, Modern Software Testing Tools, provides a comprehensive methodology for acquiring testing tools. It also provides an overview of the types of modern testing tools available.

Task 12: Establish Defect Recording/Tracking Procedures

During the testing process a defect is discovered. It needs to be recorded. A defect is related to individual tests that have been conducted, and the objective is to produce a complete record of those defects. The overall motivation for recording defects is to correct defects and record metric information about the application. Development should have access to the defects reports, which they can use to evaluate whether there is a defect and how to reconcile it. The defect form can either be manual or electronic, with the latter being preferred. Metric information such as the number of defects by type or open time for defects can be very useful in understanding the status of the system.

Defect control procedures need to be established to control this process from initial identification to reconciliation. Exhibit 12.7 shows some possible defects states from open to closed with intermediate states. The testing department initially opens a defect report and also closes it. A "Yes" in a cell indicates a possible transition from one state to another. For example, an "Open" state can change to "Under Review," "Returned by Development," or "Deferred by Development." The transitions are initiated by either the testing department or development.

A defect report form also needs to be designed. The major fields of a defect form include (see Appendices E12 and E27, Defect Report, for more details):

- Identification of the problem, for example, functional area, problem type, and so on
- Nature of the problem, for example, behavior
- Circumstances that led to the problem, for example, inputs and steps
- Environment in which the problem occurred, for example, platform, and so on
- Diagnostic information, for example, error code and so on
- Effect of the problem, for example, consequence

It is quite possible that a defect report and a change request form are the same. The advantage of this approach is that it is not always clear whether a change request is a defect or an enhancement request. The differentiation can be made with a form field that indicates whether it is a defect or enhancement request. On the other hand, a separate defect report can be very useful during the maintenance phase when the expected behavior of

Exhibit 12.7. Defect States

	Open	Under Review	Returned by Development	Ready for Testing	Returned by QA	Deferred by Development	Closed
Open	—	Yes	Yes	—	—	Yes	—
Under review	—	—	Yes	Yes	—	Yes	Yes
Returned by development	—	—	—	—	Yes	—	Yes
Ready for testing	—	—	—	—	Yes	—	Yes
Returned by QA	—	—	Yes	—	—	Yes	Yes
Deferred by development	—	Yes	Yes	Yes	—	—	Yes
Closed	Yes	—	—	—	—	—	—

the software is well known and it is easier to distinguish between a defect and an enhancement.

Task 13: Establish Change Request Procedures

If it were a perfect world, a system would be built and there would be no future changes. Unfortunately, it is not a perfect world and after a system is deployed, there are change requests.

Some of the reasons for change are:

- The requirements change.
- The design changes.
- The specification is incomplete or ambiguous.
- A defect is discovered that was not discovered during reviews.
- The software environment changes, for example, platform, hardware, and so on.

Change control is the process by which a modification to a software component is proposed, evaluated, approved or rejected, scheduled, and tracked. It is a decision process used in controlling the changes made to software. Some proposed changes are accepted and implemented during this process. Others are rejected or postponed, and are not implemented. Change control also provides for impact analysis to determine the dependencies (see Appendix D, Change Request Form, for more details).

Each software component has a life cycle. A life cycle consists of states and allowable transitions between those states. Any time a software component is changed, it should always be reviewed. While being reviewed, it is frozen from further modifications and the only way to change it is to create a new version. The reviewing authority must approve the modified software component or reject it. A software library should hold all components as soon as they are frozen and also act as a repository for approved components.

The formal title of the organization to manage changes is a configuration control board, or CCB. The CCB is responsible for the approval of changes and for judging whether a proposed change is desirable. For a small project, the CCB can consist of a single person, such as a project manager. For a more formal development environment, it can consist of several members from development, users, quality assurance, management, and the like.

All components controlled by software configuration management are stored in a software configuration library, including work products such as business data and process models, architecture groups, design units, tested application software, reusable software, and special test software. When a component is to be modified, it is checked out of the repository into a private workspace. It evolves through many states that are temporarily outside the scope of configuration management control.

When a change is completed, the component is checked in to the library and becomes a new component version. The previous component version is also retained.

Change control is based on the following major functions of a development process: requirements analysis, system design, program design, testing, and implementation. At least six control procedures are associated with these functions and need to be established for a change control system (see Appendix B, Software Quality Assurance Plan, for more details).

1. *Initiation Procedures* — This includes procedures for initiating a change request through a change request form, which serves as a communication vehicle. The objective is to gain consistency in documenting the change request document and routing it for approval.
2. *Technical Assessment Procedures* — This includes procedures for assessing the technical feasibility and technical risks, and scheduling a technical evaluation of a proposed change. The objectives are to ensure integration of the proposed change, the testing requirements, and the ability to install the change request.
3. *Business Assessment Procedures* — This includes procedures for assessing the business risk, effect, and installation requirements of the proposed change. The objectives are to ensure that the timing of the proposed change is not disruptive to the business goals.
4. *Management Review Procedures* — This includes procedures for evaluating the technical and business assessments through management review meetings. The objectives are to ensure that changes meet technical and business requirements and that adequate resources are allocated for testing and installation.
5. *Test Tracking Procedures* — This includes procedures for tracking and documenting test progress and communication, including steps for scheduling tests, documenting the test results, deferring change requests based on test results, and updating test logs. The objectives are to ensure that testing standards are utilized to verify the change, including test plans and test design, and that test results are communicated to all parties.
6. *Installation Tracking Procedure* — This includes procedures for tracking and documenting the installation progress of changes. It ensures that proper approvals have been completed, adequate time and skills have been allocated, installation and backup instructions have been defined, and proper communication has occurred. The objectives are to ensure that all approved changes have been made, including scheduled dates, test durations, and reports.

Task 14: Establish Version Control Procedures

A method for uniquely identifying each software component needs to be established via a labeling scheme. Every software component must have a unique name. Software components evolve through successive revisions, and each needs to be distinguished. A simple way to distinguish component revisions is with a pair of integers, 1.1, 1.2, . . . , that define the release number and level number. When a software component is first identified, it is revision 1 and subsequent major revisions are 2, 3, and so on.

In a client/server environment it is highly recommended that the development environment be different from the test environment. This requires the application software components to be transferred from the development environment to the test environment. Procedures need to be set up.

Software needs to be placed under configuration control so that no changes are being made to the software while testing is being conducted. This includes source and executable components. Application software can be periodically migrated into the test environment. This process must be controlled to ensure that the latest version of software is tested. Versions will also help control the repetition of tests to ensure that previously discovered defects have been resolved.

For each release or interim change between versions of a system configuration, a version description document should be prepared to identify the software components.

Task 15: Define Configuration Build Procedures

Assembling a software system involves tools to transform the source components, or source code, into executable programs. Examples of tools are compilers and linkage editors.

Configuration build procedures need to be defined to identify the correct component versions and execute the component build procedures. The configuration build model addresses the crucial question of how to control the way components are built.

A configuration typically consists of a set of derived software components. An example of derived software components is executable object programs derived from source programs. Derived components must be correctly associated with each source component to obtain an accurate derivation. The configuration build model addresses the crucial question of how to control the way derived components are built.

The inputs and outputs required for a configuration build model include primary inputs and primary outputs. The primary inputs are the source components, which are the raw materials from which the configuration is built; the version selection procedures; and the system model, which describes the relationship between the components. The primary outputs are the target configuration and derived software components.

Different software configuration management environments use different approaches for selecting versions. The simplest approach to version selection is to maintain a list of component versions. Other automated approaches allow for the most recently tested component versions to be selected, or those updated on a specific date. Operating system facilities can be used to define and build configurations including the directories and command files.

Task 16: Define Project Issue Resolution Procedures

Testing issues can arise at any point in the development process and must be resolved successfully. The primary responsibility of issue resolution is with the project manager who should work with the project sponsor to resolve those issues. Typically, the testing manager will document test issues that arise during the testing process. The project manager or project sponsor should screen every issue that arises. An issue can be rejected or deferred for further investigation but should be considered relative to its impact on the project. In any case, a form should be created that contains the essential information. Examples of testing issues include lack of testing tools, lack of adequate time to test, inadequate knowledge of the requirements, and so on.

Issue management procedures need to be defined before the project starts. The procedures should address how to:

- Submit an issue
- Report an issue
- Screen an issue (rejected, deferred, merged, or accepted)
- Investigate an issue
- Approve an issue
- Postpone an issue
- Reject an issue
- Close an issue

Task 17: Establish Reporting Procedures

Test reporting procedures are critical to manage the testing progress and manage the expectations of the project team members. This will keep the project manager and sponsor informed of the testing project progress and minimize the chance of unexpected surprises. The testing manager needs to define who needs the test information, what information they need, and how often the information is to be provided. The objectives of test status reporting are to report the progress of the testing toward its objectives and report test issues, problems, and concerns.

Exhibit 12.8. Deliverable Approvals

Test Deliverable	Approval Status	Suggested Approver
Test plan	Required	Project Manager, Development Manager, Sponsor
Test design	Required	Development Manager
Change request	Required	Development Manager
Metrics	Recommended	Development Manager
Test case	Required	Development Manager
Test log summary report	Recommended	Development Manager
Interim test report	Required	Project Manager, Development Manager
System summary report	Required	Project Manager, Development Manager, Sponsor
Defect report	Required	Development Manager

Two key reports that need to be published are:

1. *Interim Test Report* — An interim test report is a report published between testing spirals indicating the status of the testing effort.
2. *System Summary Report* — A test summary report is a comprehensive test report after all spiral testing has been completed.

Task 18: Define Approval Procedures

Approval procedures are critical in a testing project. They help provide the necessary agreement between members of the project team. The testing manager needs to define who needs to approve a test deliverable, when it will be approved, and what the backup plan is if an approval cannot be obtained. The approval procedure can vary from a formal sign-off of a test document to an informal review with comments. Exhibit 12.8 shows test deliverables for which approvals are required or recommended, and by whom. (Also see Appendix E17, Test Approvals, for a matrix that can be used to formally document management approvals for test deliverables.)

Step 2: Define the Metric Objectives

"You can't control what you can't measure." This is a quote from Tom DeMarco's book, *Controlling Software Projects,*[20] in which he describes how to organize and control a software project so it is measurable in the context of time and cost projections. Control is the extent to which a manager can ensure minimum surprises. Deviations from the plan should be signaled as early as possible in order to react. Another quote from DeMarco's book, "The only unforgivable failure is the failure to learn from past failure," stresses the importance of estimating and measurement. Measurement is a recording of past effects to quantitatively predict future effects.

Task 1: Define the Metrics

Software testing as a test development project has deliverables such as test plans, test design, test development, and test execution. The objective of this task is to apply the principles of metrics to control the testing process. A metric is a measurable indication of some quantitative aspect of a system and has the following characteristics:

- *Measurable* — A metric point must be measurable for it to be a metric, by definition. If the phenomenon can't be measured, there is no way to apply management methods to control it.
- *Independent* — Metrics need to be independent of human influence. There should be no way of changing the measurement other than changing the phenomenon that produced the metric.
- *Accountable* — Any analytical interpretation of the raw metric data rests on the data itself and it is, therefore, necessary to save the raw data and the methodical audit trail of the analytical process.
- *Precise* — Precision is a function of accuracy. The key to precision is, therefore, that a metric is explicitly documented as part of the data collection process. If a metric varies, it can be measured as a range or tolerance.

A metric can be a "result" or a "predictor." A result metric measures a completed event or process. Examples include actual total elapsed time to process a business transaction or total test costs of a project. A predictor metric is an early warning metric that has a strong correlation to some later result. An example is the predicted response time through statistical regression analysis when more terminals are added to a system when the amount of terminals has not yet been measured. A result or predictor metric can also be a derived metric. A derived metric is one that is derived from a calculation or graphical technique involving one or more metrics.

The motivation for collecting test metrics is to make the testing process more effective. This is achieved by carefully analyzing the metric data and taking the appropriate action to correct problems. The starting point is to define the metric objectives of interest. Some examples include the following:

- *Defect analysis* — Every defect must be analyzed to answer such questions as the root causes, how detected, when detected, who detected, and so on.
- *Test effectiveness* — How well is testing doing, for example, return on investment?
- *Development effectiveness* — How well is development fixing defects?

- *Test automation* — How much effort is expended on test automation?
- *Test cost* — What are the resources and time spent on testing?
- *Test status* — Another important metric is status tracking, or where are we in the testing process?
- *User involvement* — How much is the user involved in testing?

Task 2: Define the Metric Points

Exhibit 12.9 lists some metric points associated with the general metrics selected in the previous task and the corresponding actions to improve the testing process. Also shown is the source, or derivation, of the metric point.

Exhibit 12.9. Metric Points

Metric	Metric Point	Derivation
Defect analysis:	Distribution of defect causes	Histogram, Pareto
	Number of defects by cause over time	Multi-line graph
	Number of defects by how found over time	Multi-line graph
	Distribution of defects by module	Histogram, Pareto
	Distribution of defects by priority (critical, high, medium, low)	Histogram
	Distribution of defects by functional area	Histogram
	Distribution of defects by environment (platform)	Histogram, Pareto
	Distribution of defects by type (architecture, connectivity, consistency, database integrity, documentation, GUI, installation, memory, performance, security, standards and conventions, stress, usability, bad fixes)	Histogram, Pareto
	Distribution of defects by who detected (external customer, internal customer, development, QA, other)	Histogram, Pareto
	Distribution by how detected (technical review, walkthroughs, JAD, prototyping, inspection, test execution)	Histogram, Pareto

Exhibit 12.9. Metric Points (Continued)

Metric	Metric Point	Derivation
	Distribution of defects by severity (high, medium, low defects)	Histogram
Development effectiveness:	Average time for development to repair defect	Total repair time ÷ number of repaired defects
Test automation:	Percent of manual vs. automated testing	Cost of manual test effort ÷ total test cost
Test cost:	Distribution of cost by cause	Histogram, Pareto
	Distribution of cost by application	Histogram, Pareto
	Percent of costs for testing	Test testing cost ÷ total system cost
	Total costs of testing over time	Line graph
	Average cost of locating a defect	Total cost of testing ÷ number of defects detected
	Anticipated costs of testing vs. actual cost	Comparison
	Average cost of locating a requirements defect with requirements reviews	Requirements review costs ÷ number of defects uncovered during requirement reviews
	Average cost of locating a design defect with design reviews	Design review costs ÷ number of defects uncovered during design reviews
	Average cost of locating a code defect with reviews	Code review costs ÷ number of defects uncovered during code reviews
	Average cost of locating a defect with test execution	Test execution costs ÷ number of defects uncovered during test execution
	Number of testing resources over time	Line plot
Test effectiveness:	Percentage of defects discovered during maintenance	Number of defects discovered during maintenance ÷ total number of defects uncovered

Exhibit 12.9. Metric Points (Continued)

Metric	Metric Point	Derivation
	Percentage of defects uncovered due to testing	Number of detected errors through testing ÷ total system defects
	Average effectiveness of a test	Number of tests ÷ total system defects
	Value returned while reviewing requirements	Number of defects uncovered during requirements review ÷ requirements test costs
	Value returned while reviewing design	Number of defects uncovered during design review ÷ design test costs
	Value returned while reviewing programs	Number of defects uncovered during program review ÷ program test costs
	Value returned during test execution	Number of defects uncovered during testing ÷ test costs
	Effect of testing changes	Number of tested changes ÷ problems attributable to the changes
	People's assessment of effectiveness of testing	Subjective scaling (1–10)
	Average time for QA to verify fix	Total QA verification time ÷ total number of defects to verify
	Number of defects over time	Line graph
	Cumulative number of defects over time	Line graph
	Number of application defects over time	Multi-line graph
Test extent:	Percentage of statements executed	Number of statements executed ÷ total statements
	Percentage of logical paths executed	Number of logical paths ÷ total number of paths
	Percentage of acceptance criteria tested	Acceptance criteria tested ÷ total acceptance criteria

Exhibit 12.9. Metric Points (Continued)

Metric	Metric Point	Derivation
	Number of requirements tested over time	Line plot
	Number of statements executed over time	Line plot
	Number of data elements exercised over time	Line plot
	Number of decision statements executed over time	Line plot
Test status:	Number of tests ready to run over time	Line plot
	Number of tests run over time	Line plot
	Number of tests run without defects uncovered	Line plot
	Number of defects corrected over time	Line plot
User involvement:	Percentage of user testing	User testing time ÷ total test time

Step 3: Review/Approve the Plan

Task 1: Schedule/Conduct the Review

The test plan review should be scheduled well in advance of the actual review and the participants should have the latest copy of the test plan.

As with any interview or review, it should contain certain elements. The first is defining what will be discussed, or "talking about what we are going to talk about." The second is discussing the details, or "talking about it." The third is summarization, or "talking about what we talked about." The final element is timeliness. The reviewer should state up front the esti- mated duration of the review and set the ground rule that if time expires before completing all items on the agenda, a follow-on review will be sched- uled.

The purpose of this task is for development and the project sponsor to agree and accept the test plan. If there are any suggested changes to the test plan during the review, they should be incorporated into the test plan.

Task 2: Obtain Approvals

Approval is critical in a testing effort, for it helps provide the necessary agreements between testing, development, and the sponsor. The best approach is with a formal sign-off procedure of a test plan. If this is the case, use the management approval sign-off forms. However, if a formal agreement procedure is not in place, send a memo to each key participant, including at least the project manager, development manager, and sponsor. In the document attach the latest test plan and point out that all their feedback comments have been incorporated and that if you do not hear from them, it is assumed that they agree with the plan. Finally, indicate that in a spiral development environment, the test plan will evolve with each iteration but that you will include them in any modification.

Part 13
Test Case Design (Do)

If you will recall, in the spiral development environment, software testing is described as a continuous improvement process that must be integrated into a rapid application development methodology. Deming's continuous improvement process using the PDCA model is applied to the software testing process. We are now in the Do part of the spiral model (see Exhibit 13.1).

Exhibit 13.2 outlines the steps and tasks associated with the Do part of spiral testing. Each step and task is described along with valuable tips and techniques.

Step 1: Design Function Tests

Task 1: Refine the Functional Test Requirements

At this point, the functional specification should have been completed. It consists of the hierarchical functional decomposition, the functional window structure, the window standards, and the minimum system requirements of the system to be developed. An example of windows standards is the Windows 2000 GUI Standards. A minimum system requirement could consist of Windows 2000, a Pentium IV microprocessor, 1-GB RAM, 40-gigdisk space, and a 56-KB modem.

A functional breakdown consists of a list of business functions, hierarchical listing, group of activities, or set of user profiles defining the basic functions of the system and how the user will use it. A business function is a discrete controllable aspect of the business and the smallest component of a system. Each should be named and described with a verb–object paradigm. The criteria used to determine the successful execution of each function should be stated. The functional hierarchy serves as the basis for function testing in which there will be at least one test case for each lowest-level function. Examples of functions include: approve customer credit, handle order, create invoice, order components, receive revenue, pay bill, purchase items, and so on. Taken together, the business functions constitute the total application including any interfaces. A good source of these functions (in addition to the interview itself) is a process decomposition and/or data flow diagram, or CRUD matrix, which should be requested during the information-gathering interview.

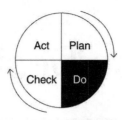

Exhibit 13.1. Spiral Testing and Continuous Improvement

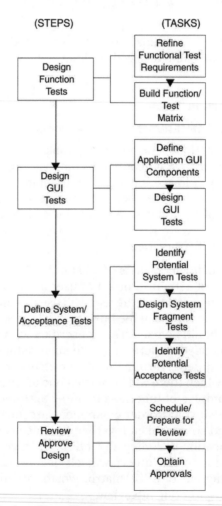

Exhibit 13.2. Test Design (Steps/Tasks)

The requirements serve as the basis for creating test cases. The following quality assurance test checklists can be used to assure that the requirements are clear and comprehensive:

- Appendix E22: Clarification Request that can be used to document questions that may arise while the tester analyzes the requirements.
- Appendix F25: Ambiguity Review Checklist that can be used to assist in the review of a Functional Specification of structural ambiguity (not to be confused with content reviews).
- Appendix F26: Architecture Review Checklist that can be used to review the architecture for completeness and clarity.
- Appendix F27: Data Design Review Checklist that can be used to review the logical and physical design for clarity and completeness.
- Appendix F28: Functional Specification Review Checklist that can be used in Functional Specification for content completeness and clarity (not to be confused with ambiguity reviews).
- Appendix F29: Prototype Review Checklist that can be used to review a prototype for content completeness and clarity.
- Appendix F30: Requirements Review Checklist that can be used to verify that the testing project requirements are comprehensive and complete.
- Appendix F31: Technical Design Review Checklist that can be used to review the technical design for clarity and completeness.

A functional breakdown is used to illustrate the processes in a hierarchical structure showing successive levels of detail. It is built iteratively as processes and nonelementary processes are decomposed (see Exhibit 13.3).

A data flow diagram shows processes and the flow of data among these processes. It is used to define the overall data flow through a system and consists of external agents that interface with the system, processes, data flow, and stores depicting where the data is stored or retrieved. A data flow diagram should be reviewed, and each major and leveled function should be listed and organized into a hierarchical list.

A CRUD matrix, or association matrix, links data and process models. It identifies and resolves matrix omissions and conflicts and helps refine the data and process models, as necessary.

A functional window structure describes how the functions will be implemented in the windows environment. Exhibit 13.4 shows a sample functional window structure for order processing.

Task 2: Build a Function/Test Matrix

The function/test matrix cross-references the tests to the functions. This matrix provides proof of the completeness of the test strategies, illustrating

Exhibit 13.3. Functional Breakdown

Functional Test Requirements (Breakdown)
Order Processing Create new order Fulfill order Edit order Delete order ***Customer Processing*** Create new customer Edit customer Delete customer ***Financial Processing*** Receive customer payment Deposit payment Pay vendor Write a check Display register ***Inventory Processing*** Acquire vendor products Maintain stock Handle back orders Audit inventory Adjust product price ***Reports*** Create order report Create account receivable report Create account payable report Create inventory report

in graphic format which tests exercise which functions. See Exhibit 13.5 and Appendix E5, Function/Test Matrix for more details.

The matrix is used as a control sheet during testing and can also be used during maintenance. For example, if a function is to be changed, the maintenance team can refer to the function/test matrix to determine which tests need to be run or changed. The business functions are listed vertically and the test cases are listed horizontally. The test case name is recorded on the matrix along with the number. (Also see Appendix E24, Test Condition Versus Test Case, Matrix I, which can be used to associate a requirement with each condition that is mapped to one or more test cases.)

Exhibit 13.4. Functional Window Structure

The Main Window
a. The top line of the main window has the standard title bar with Min/Max controls.
b. The next line contains the standard Windows menu bar.
c. The next line contains the standard Windows tool bar.
d. The rest of the Main-Application Window is filled with the Customer-Order Window.

The Customer-Order Window
a. This window shows a summary of each previously entered order.
b. Several orders will be shown at one time (sorted by order number and customer name). For each customer order, this window will show:
   1. Order Number
   2. Customer Name
   3. Customer Number
   4. Date
   5. Invoice Number
   6. Model Number
   7. Product Number
   8. Quantity Shipped
   9. Price
c. The scroll bar will be used to select which orders are to be viewed.
d. This window is read-only for viewing.
e. Double-clicking an order will display the Edit-Order Dialog where the order can be modified.

The Edit-Order Window
a. This dialog is used to create new orders or for making changes to previously created orders.
b. This dialog will be centered over the Customer-Order Window. The layout of this dialog will show the following:
   1. Order Number (automatically filled in)
   2. Edit field for: Customer Name
   3. Edit field for: Customer Number
   4. Date (initialized)
   5. Edit field for: Invoice Number
   6. Edit field for: Model Number
   7. Edit field for: Product Number
   8. Edit field for: Quantity Shipped
   9. Price (automatically filled in)
   10. Push buttons for: OK and Cancel

The Menu Bar Will Include the Following Menus:
File:
  New:
    Used to create a new order file
  Open:
    Used to open the order file

Exhibit 13.4. Functional Window Structure (Continued)

Save:
  Used to save the order file
Save As...:
  Used to save the current order file under a new name
Exit:
  Used to exit Windows
Order:
  Create New Order:
  Display Edit-Order Window with blank fields (except date)
  Fulfill Order:
    This dialog will be used to verify that the order quantity is available in inventory stock and validate customer credit.
    The dialog will include:
      1. Edit field for: Order Number
      2. Edit field for: Customer Name
      3. Edit field for: Customer Number
      4. Date (initialized)
      5. Invoice Number (initialized)
      6. Model Number (initialized)
      7. Product Number (initialized)
      8. Quantity Shipped (initialized)
      9. Price (initialized)
      10. Push buttons for: OK and Cancel
          a. The quantity order is checked against the inventory stock level. If the order cannot be filled, a back order note is sent to purchasing.
          b. The customer history will be displayed (the scroll bar will be used to view the history information).
          c. An Accept button will fulfill the order and create an invoice for shipping.
          d. A Reject button deletes the order and creates a customer order rejection letter.

Edit an Order:
  This dialog will be used to edit an existing order. The dialog will include:
    1. Edit field for: Order Number
    2. Edit field for: Customer Name
    3. Edit field for: Customer Number
    4. Push buttons for: OK and Cancel

Delete an Order:
  This dialog will be used to delete an existing order. The dialog will include:
    1. Edit field for: Order Number
    2. Edit field for: Customer Name
    3. Edit field for: Customer Number
    4. Push buttons for: OK and Cancel
      a. A confirmation message will be displayed with Yes, No, or Cancel options.

Order Report:
  This dialog will display one or more orders based upon order number or date ranges.

Exhibit 13.4. Functional Window Structure (Continued)

The layout of the dialog will include:
1. Radio buttons for: Order, Date
2. First Order Number (if report by Order)
3. Optional last Order Number (if report by Order)
4. First Date (if report by Date)
5. Optional last Date (if report by Date)

The user is prompted with the message "Would you like a hard copy printout?"
The user is prompted with the message "Would you like another report (Y/N)?"
after each report.

View:
Toolbar:
   Used to toggle the display of the toolbar on and off.
Status bar:
   Used to toggle the display of the status bar on or off.

The Tool Bar with Icons to Execute the Following Menu Commands:

File	→	New
File	→	Open
Order	→	Create
Order	→	Validate
Order	→	Edit
Order	→	Delete
File	→	Exit

It is also important to differentiate those test cases that are manual and those that are automated. One way to accomplish this is to come up with a naming standard that will highlight an automated test case; for example, the first character of the name is "A."

Exhibit 13.5 shows an example of a function/test matrix.

Step 2: Design GUI Tests

The goal of a good graphical user interface (GUI) design should be consistent in "look and feel" for the users of the application. Good GUI design has two key components: interaction and appearance. Interaction relates to how the user interacts with the application. Appearance relates to how the interface looks to the user.

GUI testing involves the confirmation that the navigation is correct; for example, when an ICON, menu choice, or ratio button is clicked, the desired response occurs. The following are some good GUI design principles the tester should look for while testing the application.

Exhibit 13.5. Functional/Test Matrix

Business Function	Test Case				
	1	2	3	4	5
Order processing					
Create new order	CNO01	CNO02			
Fulfill order	AO01				
Edit order	EO01	EO02	EO03	EO04	
Delete order	DO01	DO02	DO03	DO04	DO05
Customer processing					
Create new customer	ANC01	ANC02	ANC03		
Edit customer	EC01	EC02	EC03	EC04	EC05
Delete customer	DC01	DC02			
Financial processing					
Receive customer payment	RCP01	RCP02	RCP03	RCP04	
Deposit payment	AP01	AP02			
Pay vendor	PV01	PV02	PV03	PV04	PV05
Write a check	WC01	WC02			
Display register	DR01	DR02			
Inventory processing					
Acquire vendor products	AP01	AP02	AP03		
Maintain stock	MS01	MS02	MS03	MS04	MS05
Handle back orders	HB01	HB02	HB03		
Audit inventory	AI01	AI02	AI03	AI04	
Adjust product price	AC01	AC02	AC03		
Reports					
Create order report	CO01	CO02	CO03	CO04	CO05
Create account receivables report	CA01	CA02	CA03		
Create account payables	AY01	AY02	AY03		
Create inventory report	CI01	CI02	CI03	CI04	

Ten Guidelines for Good GUI Design

1. Involve users.
2. Understand the user's culture and experience.
3. Prototype continuously to validate the requirements.
4. Let the user's business workflow drive the design.

5. Do not overuse or underuse GUI features.
6. Create the GUI, help, and training concurrently.
7. Do not expect users to remember secret commands or functions.
8. Anticipate mistakes and don't penalize the user.
9. Continually remind the user of the application status.
10. Keep it simple.

Task 1: Identify the Application GUI Components

The graphical user interface provides multiple channels of communication using words, pictures, animation, sound, and video. Five key foundation components of the user interface are windows, menus, forms, icons, and controls.

1. *Windows* — In a windowed environment, all user interaction with the application occurs through the windows. These include a primary window, along with any number of secondary windows generated from the primary one.
2. *Menus* — Menus come in a variety of styles and forms. Examples include action menus (push button, radio button), pull-down menus, pop-up menus, option menus, and cascading menus.
3. *Forms* — Forms are windows or screens into which the user can add information.
4. *Icons* — Icons, or "visual push buttons," are valuable for instant recognition, ease of learning, and ease of navigation through the application.
5. *Controls* — A control component appears on a screen that allows the user to interact with the application and is indicated by its corresponding action. Controls include menu bars, pull-down menus, cascading menus, pop-up menus, push buttons, check boxes, radio buttons, list boxes, and drop-down list boxes.

A design approach to GUI test design is to first define and name each GUI component by name within the application as shown in Exhibit 13.6. In the next step, a GUI component checklist is developed that can be used to verify each component in the table above. (Also see Appendix E6, GUI Component Test Matrix.)

Task 2: Define the GUI Tests

In the previous task the application GUI components were defined, named, and categorized in the GUI component test matrix. In the present task, a checklist is developed against which each GUI component is verified. The list should cover all possible interactions and may or may not apply to a particular component. Exhibit 13.7 is a partial list of the items to check. (See Appendix E23, Screen Data Mapping, which can be used to document the properties of the screen data and Appendix F32, Test Case Preparation

Exhibit 13.6. GUI Component Test Matrix

Name	Window	Menu	Form	ICON	Control	P/F	Date	Tester
			GUI Type					
Main window	√							
Customer-order window	√							
Edit-order window	√							
Menu bar		√						
Tool bar					√			
•								
•								
•								

Exhibit 13.7. GUI Component Checklist

Access via Double-Click	Multiple Windows Open	Tabbing Sequence
Access via menu	Ctrl menu (move)	Push buttons
Access via toolbar	Ctrl + function keys	Pull-down menu and submenus options
Right-mouse options	Color	Dialog controls
Help links	Accelerators and hot keys	Labels
Context-sensitive help	Cancel	Chevrons
Button bars	Close	Ellipses
Open by double-click	Apply	Gray-out unavailability
Screen images and graphics	Exit	Check boxes
Open by menu	OK	Filters
Open by toolbar	Tile horizontal/vertical	Spin boxes
ICON access	Arrange icons	Sliders
Access to DOS	Toggling	Fonts
Access via single-click	Expand/contract tree	Drag/drop
Resize window panels	Function keys	Horizontal/vertical scrolling
Fields accept allowable values	Minimize the window Maximize the window	Cascade Window open
Fields handle invalid values	Tabbing sequence	

Review Checklist, which can be used to ensure that test cases have been prepared as per specifications.)

In addition to the GUI component checks above, if there is a GUI design standard, it should be verified as well. GUI standards are essential to ensure that the internal rules of construction are followed to achieve the desired level of consistency. Some of the typical GUI standards that should be verified include the following:

- Forms "enterable" and display-only formats
- Wording of prompts, error messages, and help features
- Use of color, highlight, and cursors
- Screen layouts
- Function and shortcut keys, or "hot keys"
- Consistently locating screen elements on the screen
- Logical sequence of objects
- Consistent font usage
- Consistent color usage

It is also important to differentiate manual from automated GUI test cases. One way to accomplish this is to use an additional column in the GUI component matrix that indicates if the GUI test is manual or automated.

Step 3: Define the System/Acceptance Tests

Task 1: Identify Potential System Tests

System testing is the highest level of testing and evaluates the functionality as a total system, its performance, and overall fitness of use. This test is usually performed by the internal organization and is oriented to systems' technical issues rather than acceptance, which is a more user-oriented test.

Systems testing consists of one or more tests that are based on the original objectives of the system that were defined during the project interview. The purpose of this task is to select the system tests that will be performed, not how to implement the tests. Some common system test types include the following:

- *Performance Testing* — Verifies and validates that the performance requirements have been achieved; measures response times, transaction rates, and other time-sensitive requirements.
- *Security Testing* — Evaluates the presence and appropriate functioning of the security of the application to ensure the integrity and confidentiality of the data.
- *Volume Testing* — Subjects the application to heavy volumes of data to determine if it can handle the volume of data.
- *Stress Testing* — Investigates the behavior of the system under conditions that overload its resources. Of particular interest is the impact that this has on system processing time.

- *Compatibility Testing* — Tests the compatibility of the application with other applications or systems.
- *Conversion Testing* — Verifies the conversion of existing data and loads a new database.
- *Usability Testing* — Determines how well the user will be able to use and understand the application.
- *Documentation Testing* — Verifies that the user documentation is accurate and ensures that the manual procedures work correctly.
- *Backup Testing* — Verifies the ability of the system to back up its data in the event of a software or hardware failure.
- *Recovery Testing* — Verifies the system's ability to recover from a software or hardware failure.
- *Installation Testing* — Verifies the ability to install the system successfully.

Task 2: Design System Fragment Tests

System fragment tests are sample subsets of full system tests that can be performed during each spiral loop. The objective of doing a fragment test is to provide early warning of pending problems that would arise in the full system test. Candidate fragment system tests include function, performance, security, usability, documentation, and procedure. Some of these fragment tests should have formal tests performed during each spiral, whereas others should be part of the overall testing strategy. Nonfragment system tests include installation, recovery, conversion, and the like, which are probably going to be performed until the formal system test.

Function testing on a system level occurs during each spiral as the system is integrated. As new functionality is added, test cases need to be designed, implemented, and tested during each spiral.

Typically, security mechanisms are introduced fairly early in the development. Therefore, a set of security tests should be designed, implemented, and tested during each spiral as more features are added.

Usability is an ongoing informal test during each spiral and should always be part of the test strategy. When a usability issue arises, the tester should document it in the defect tracking system. A formal type of usability test is the end user's review of the prototype, which should occur during each spiral.

Documentation (such as online help) and procedures are also ongoing informal tests. These should be developed in parallel with formal system development during each spiral and not be put off until a formal system test. This will avoid last-minute surprises. As new features are added, documentation and procedure tests should be designed, implemented, and tested during each spiral.

Some performance testing should occur during each spiral at a noncontended unit level, that is, one user. Baseline measurements should be performed on all key functions as they are added to the system. A baseline measurement is a measurement taken for the specific purpose of determining the initial value of the state or performance measurement. During subsequent spirals, the performance measurements can be repeated and compared to the baseline. Exhibit 13.8 provides an example of baseline performance measurements.

Task 3: Identify Potential Acceptance Tests

Acceptance testing is an optional user-run test that demonstrates the ability of the application to meet the user's requirements. The motivation for this test is to demonstrate rather than be destructive, that is, to show that the system works. Less emphasis is placed on technical issues and more is placed on the question of whether the system is a good business fit for the end user. The test is usually performed by users, if performed at all. Typically, 20 percent of the time this test is rolled into the system test. If performed, acceptance tests typically are a subset of the system tests. However, the users sometimes define "special tests," such as intensive stress or volume tests, to stretch the limits of the system even beyond what was tested during the system test.

Step 4: Review/Approve Design

Task 1: Schedule/Prepare for Review

The test design review should be scheduled well in advance of the actual review, and the participants should have the latest copy of the test design.

As with any interview or review, it should contain certain elements. The first is defining what will be discussed, or "talking about what we are going to talk about." The second is discussing the details, or "talking about it." The third is summarization, or "talking about what we talked about." The final element is timeliness. The reviewer should state up front the estimated duration of the review and set the ground rule that if time expires before completing all items on the agenda, a follow-on review will be scheduled.

The purpose of this task is for development and the project sponsor to agree and accept the test design. If there are any suggested changes to the test design during the review, they should be incorporated into the test design.

Task 2: Obtain Approvals

Approval is critical in a testing effort, because it helps provide the necessary agreements among testing, development, and the sponsor. The best approach is with a formal sign-off procedure of a test design. If this is the

Exhibit 13.8. Baseline Performance Measurements

Business Function	Baseline Seconds – Rel 1.0 (1/1/04)	Measure and Delta Seconds – Rel 1.1 (2/1/04)	Measure and Delta Seconds – Rel 1.2 (2/15/04)	Measure and Delta Seconds – Rel 1.3 (3/1/04)	Measure and Delta Seconds – Rel 1.4 (3/15/04)	Measure and Delta Seconds – Rel 1.5 (4/1/04)
Order processing						
Create new order	1.0	1.5 (+50%)	1.3 (−13%)	1.0 (−23%)	.9 (−10%)	.75 (−17%)
Fulfill order	2.5	2.0 (−20%)	1.5 (−25%)	1.0 (−33%)	1.0 (0%)	1.0 (0%)
Edit order	1.76	2.0 (+14%)	2.5 (+25%)	1.7 (−32%)	1.5 (−12%)	1.2 (−20%)
Delete order	1.1	1.1 (0%)	1.4 (+27%)	1.0 (−29%)	.8 (−20%)	.75 (−6%)
•	•	•	•	•	•	•
•	•	•	•	•	•	•
•	•	•	•	•	•	•
•	•	•	•	•	•	•
•	•	•	•	•	•	•

Reports						
Create order report	60	55 (-8%)	35 (-36%)	28 (-20%)	20 (-29%)	15 (-25%)
Create account receivables report	55	65 (+18%)	55 (-15%)	35 (-36%)	25 (-29%)	20 (-20%)
Create account payables	120	90 (-25%)	65 (-28%)	45 (-31%)	65 (+44%)	25 (-62%)
Create inventory report	85	70 (-18%)	50 (-29%)	39 (-22%)	28 (-28%)	25 (-11%)

case, use the management approval sign-off forms. However, if a formal agreement procedure is not in place, send a memo to each key participant, including at least the project manager, development manager, and sponsor. In the document attach the latest test design and point out that all their feedback comments have been incorporated and that if you do not hear from them, it is assumed that they agree with the design. Finally, indicate that in a spiral development environment, the test design will evolve with each iteration but that you will include them in any modification.

Part 14
Test Development (Do)

Exhibit 14.1 outlines the steps and tasks associated with the Do part of spiral testing. Each step and task is described along with valuable tips and techniques.

Step 1: Develop Test Scripts

Task 1: Script the Manual/Automated GUI/Function Tests

In a previous step, a GUI/Function Test Matrix was built that cross-references the tests to the functions. The business functions are listed vertically, and the test cases are listed horizontally. The test case name is recorded on the matrix along with the number.

In the current task, the functional test cases are documented and transformed into reusable test scripts with test data created. To aid in the development of the script of the test cases, the GUI-based Function Test Matrix template in Exhibit 14.2 can be used to document function test cases that are GUI-based (see Appendix E7, GUI-Based Functional Test Matrix, for more details).

Consider the script in Exhibit 14.2, which uses the template to create a new customer order. The use of this template shows the function, the case number within the test case (a variation of a specific test), the requirement identification cross-reference, the test objective, the case steps, the expected results, the pass/fail status, the tester name, and the date the test was performed. Within a function, the current GUI component is also documented. In Exhibit 14.2, a new customer order is created by first invoking the menu bar to select the function, followed by the Edit-Order Window to enter the order number, customer number, model number, product number, and quantity.

Task 2: Script the Manual/Automated System Fragment Tests

In a previous task, the system fragment tests were designed. They are sample subsets of full system tests, which can be performed during each spiral loop.

In this task, the system fragment tests can be scripted using the GUI-based Function Test Matrix discussed in the previous task. The test objective description is probably more broad than the Function/GUI tests, as

173

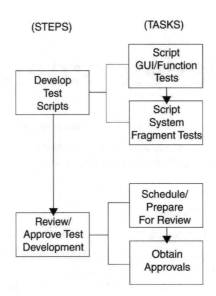

(STEPS)   (TASKS)

Exhibit 14.1. Test Development (Steps/Tasks)

they involve more global testing issues such as performance, security, usability, documentation, procedure, and so on.

Step 2: Review/Approve Test Development

Task 1: Schedule/Prepare for Review

The test development review should be scheduled well in advance of the actual review and the participants should have the latest copy of the test design.

As with any interview or review, it should contain certain elements. The first is defining what will be discussed, or "talking about what we are going to talk about." The second is discussing the details, or "talking about it." The third is summarization, or "talking about what we talked about." The final element is timeliness. The reviewer should state up front the estimated duration of the review and set the ground rule that if time expires before completing all items on the agenda, a follow-on review will be scheduled.

The purpose of this task is for development and the project sponsor to agree and accept the test development. If there are any suggested changes to the test development during the review, they should be incorporated into the test development.

Task 2: Obtain Approvals

Approval is critical in a testing effort, because it helps provide the necessary agreements among the testing, development, and the sponsor. The

Exhibit 14.2. Function/GUI Test Script

Function (Create a New Customer Order)								
Case No.	Req. No.	Test Objective	Case Steps	Expected Results	(P/F)	Tester	Date	
Menu Bar								
15	67	Create a valid new customer order	Select File/Create Order from the menu bar	Edit-Order Window appears	Passed	Jones	7/21/04	
Edit-Order Window								
			1. Enter order number	Order validated	Passed	Jones	7/21/04	
			2. Enter customer number	Customer validated	Passed	Jones	7/21/04	
			3. Enter model number	Model validated	Passed	Jones	7/21/04	
			4. Enter product number	Product validated	Passed	Jones	7/21/04	
			5. Enter quantity	Quantity validated date, invoice number, and total price generated	Passed	Jones	7/21/04	
			6. Select OK	Customer is created successfully	Passed	Jones	7/21/04	

best approach is with a formal sign-off procedure of a test development. If this is the case, use the management approval sign-off forms. However, if a formal agreement procedure is not in place, send a memo to each key participant, including at least the project manager, development manager, and sponsor. In the document, attach the latest test development and point out that all their feedback comments have been incorporated and that if you do not hear from them, it is assumed that they agree with the development. Finally, indicate that in a spiral development environment, the test development will evolve with each iteration but that you will include them in any modification.

Part 15
Test Coverage through Traceability

As already pointed out previously, most businesses have reconciled to the fact that a percent error-free software cannot be produced and only over a period of time the soft base gets stabilized. But the system cannot go live with critical defects unresolved. Many of the companies have started stating their acceptance criteria in the test strategy document. It may range from nonexistence of critical and medium defects to business flow acceptance by the end users. The ultimate aim of final testing is to prove that the software delivers what the client requires. A trace between the different test deliverables should ensure that the test covers the requirements comprehensively so that all requirements are tested without any omission.

The business requirement document (BRD), functional specification documents (FS), test conditions/cases, test data, and defects identified during testing are some key components of the traceability matrix. The following discussion illustrates how these components are integrated through the traceability matrix as shown in Exhibit 15.1.

The requirements specified by the users in the business requirement document may not be exactly translated into a functional specification document. Therefore, a trace on specifications between functional specification and business requirements is done on a one-to-one basis. This helps in finding the gap between the documents. These gaps are then closed by the author of the functional specifications, or deferred to the next release after discussion. The final FS may vary from the original, as deferring or taking in a gap may have a ripple effect on the application. Sometimes, these ripple effects may not be properly documented. This is the first-level traceability.

The functional specification documents are divided into smaller modules, functions, and test conditions to percolate down to the test case where various data values are imputted to the test conditions for validating them. A test condition is an abstract extraction of the testable requirements from the functional specification documents. The test conditions may be explicitly or implicitly in the requirement documents. A test condition has one or more associated test cases. Each of the test conditions is

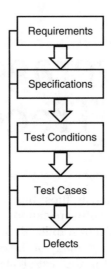

Exhibit 15.1. Traceability Tree Diagram

traced back to its originating requirements. The second level of trace is thus between the functional specification documents and the test condition documents.

A test case is a set of test inputs, execution conditions, and expected results developed for a particular objective to validate a specific functionality in the application under test. The number of test cases for each test condition may vary from multiple to one. Each of these test cases can be traced back to its test conditions and through test conditions to their originating requirements. The third level of traceability is between the test cases and test conditions and ultimately to the baseline requirements.

The final phase of traceability is with the defects identified in the test execution phase. Tracing the defect to the test condition and the specification will lead us to retrospection on the reason why the requirements or the test condition has failed. Whether the requirements have not been stated clearly or the test conditions have not been extracted properly from the requirements will help us to correct ourselves in future assignments. Exhibit 15.2 illustrates how the above deliverables are traced using a traceability matrix.

Use Cases and Traceability

A use case is a scenario that describes the use of a system by an actor to accomplish a specific goal. An actor is a user playing a role with respect to the system. Actors are generally people, although other computer systems may be actors. A scenario is a sequence of steps that describe the interactions

Exhibit 15.2. Traceability Matrix

Item No.	Ref. No. BRD Ref. No.	FS Ref. No.	Application/ Module Name	Test Condition	Test Cases	Test Script ID	Defect ID

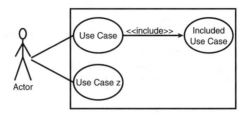

Exhibit 15.3. Use Case Diagram

between an actor and the system. Exhibit 15.3 shows a use case diagram that consists of the collection of all actors and all use cases. Use cases:

- Capture the system's functional requirements from the users' perspective
- Actively involve users in the requirements-gathering process
- Provide the basis for identifying major classes and their relationships
- Serve as the foundation for developing system test cases

The use cases should be traced back to the functional specification document and traced forward to the test conditions and test cases documents. The following have to be considered while deriving traceability:

- Whether the use cases unfold from highest to lowest levels
- If all the system's functional requirements are reflected in the use cases
- If we can trace each use case back to its requirement(s)

Summary

During the progress of the project new requirements are brought in due to the client's additional requirements or as a result of the review process. These additional requirements should be appropriately traced to the test conditions and cases.

Similarly, a change request raised during the course of testing the application should be handled in the traceability matrix. Requirements present in the traceability matrix document should not be deleted at any time even when the requirement is moved for the next release. All the requirements present in the traceability matrix should be covered with at least one test case.

Thus, traceability serves as an effective tool to ensure that the testware is comprehensive. This instills confidence in the client that the test team has tested all the requirements. Various modern testing tools such as Test Director from Mercury Interactive have the facility of creating the traceability documents.

Part 16
Test Execution/ Evaluation (Do/Check)

If you will recall, in the spiral development environment, software testing is described as a continuous improvement process that must be integrated into a rapid application development methodology. Deming's continuous improvement process using the PDCA model is applied to the software testing process. We are now in the Do/Check part of the spiral model (see Exhibit 16.1).

Exhibit 16.2 outlines the steps and tasks associated with the Do/Check part of spiral testing. Each step and task is described along with valuable tips and techniques.

Step 1: Setup and Testing

Task 1: Regression Test the Manual/Automated Spiral Fixes

The purpose of this task is to retest the tests that discovered defects in the previous spiral. The technique used is regression testing. Regression testing is a technique that detects spurious errors caused by software modifications or corrections. See Appendix G27, Regression Testing, for more details.

A set of test cases must be maintained and available throughout the entire life of the software. The test cases should be complete enough so that all the software's functional capabilities are thoroughly tested. The question arises as to how to locate those test cases to test defects discovered during the previous test spiral. An excellent mechanism is the retest matrix.

As described earlier, a retest matrix relates test cases to functions (or program units). A check entry in the matrix indicates that the test case is to be retested when the function (or program unit) has been modified due to an enhancement(s) or correction(s). No entry means that the test case does not need to be retested. The retest matrix can be built before the first

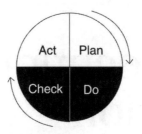

Exhibit 16.1. Spiral Testing and Continuous Improvement

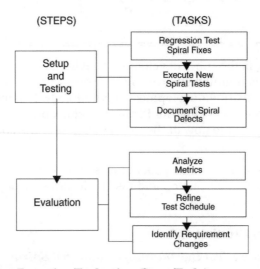

Exhibit 16.2. Test Execution/Evaluation (Steps/Tasks)

testing spiral, but needs to be maintained during subsequent spirals. As functions (or program units) are modified during a development spiral, existing or new test cases need to be created and checked in the retest matrix in preparation for the next test spiral. Over time with subsequent spirals, some functions (or program units) may be stable with no recent modifications. Consideration to selectively remove their check entries should be undertaken between testing spirals.

If a regression test passes, the status of the defect report should be changed to "closed."

Task 2: Execute the Manual/Automated New Spiral Tests
The purpose of this task is to execute new tests that were created at the end of the previous testing spiral. In the previous spiral, the testing team updated the test plan, GUI-based function test matrix, scripts, the GUI, the

system fragment tests, and acceptance tests in preparation for the current testing spiral. During this task those tests are executed.

Task 3: Document the Spiral Test Defects

During spiral test execution, the results of the testing must be reported in the defect tracking database. These defects are typically related to individual tests that have been conducted. However, variations to the formal test cases often uncover other defects. The objective of this task is to produce a complete record of the defects. If the execution step has been recorded properly, the defects have already been recorded on the defect tracking database. If the defects are already recorded, the objective of this step becomes to collect and consolidate the defect information.

Tools can be used to consolidate and record defects depending on the test execution methods. If the defects are recorded on paper, the consolidation involves collecting and organizing the papers. If the defects are recorded electronically, search features can easily locate duplicate defects. A sample defect report is given in Appendix E27, which can be used to report the details of a specific defect.

Step 2: Evaluation

Task 1: Analyze the Metrics

Metrics are used so that we can help make decisions more effectively and support the development process. The objective of this task is to apply the principles of metrics to control the testing process.

In a previous task, the metrics and metric points were defined for each spiral to be measured. During the present task the metrics that were measured are analyzed. This involves quantifying the metrics and putting them into a graphical format.

The following is the key information a test manager needs to know at the end of a spiral:

- *Test Case Execution Status* — How many test cases have been executed, how many not executed, and how many discovered defects? This provides an indication of the tester's productivity. If the test cases are not being executed in a timely manner, this raises a flag that more personnel may need to be assigned to the project.
- *Defect Gap Analysis* — What is the gap between the number of defects that have been uncovered and the number that have been corrected? This provides an indication of development's ability to correct defects in a timely manner. If there is a relatively large gap, this raises the flag that perhaps more developers need to be assigned to the project.

- *Defect Severity Status* — The distribution of the defect severity (e.g., critical, major, and minor) provides an indication of the quality of the system. If there is a large percentage of defects in the critical category, there probably exist a considerable number of design and architecture issues, which also raises a flag.
- *Test Burnout Tracking* — Shows the cumulative and periodic number of defects being discovered. The cumulative number, for example, the running total number of defects, and defects by time period help predict when fewer and fewer defects are being discovered. This is indicated when the cumulative curve "bends" and the defects by time period approach zero. If the cumulative curve shows no indication of bending, it implies that defect discovery is still very robust and that many more still exist to be discovered in other spirals.

Graphical examples of the above metrics can be seen in Part 17, Prepare for the Next Spiral.

Step 3: Publish Interim Report

See Appendix E25, Project Status Report, which can be used to report the status of the testing project for all key process areas; Appendix E26, Test Defect Details Report, which can be used to report the detailed defect status of the testing project for all key process areas; and Appendix E28, Test Execution Tracking Manager, which is an Excel spreadsheet that provides a comprehensive and test cycle view of the number of test cases which passed/failed, the number of defects discovered by application area, the status of the defects, percentage completed, and the defect severities by defect type. The template is located on the CD in the back of the book.

Task 1: Refine the Test Schedule

In a previous task, a test schedule was produced that includes the testing steps (and perhaps tasks), target start dates and end dates, and responsibilities. During the course of development, the testing schedule needs to be continually monitored. The objective of the current task is to update the test schedule to reflect the latest status. It is the responsibility of the test manager to:

- Compare the actual progress to the planned progress.
- Evaluate the results to determine the testing status.
- Take appropriate action based on the evaluation.

If the testing progress is behind schedule, the test manager needs to determine the factors causing the slip. A typical cause is an underestimation of the test effort. Other factors could be that an inordinate number of defects are being discovered, causing a lot of the testing effort to be devoted to retesting old corrected defects. In either case, more testers may be needed and/or overtime may be required to compensate for the slip-page.

Task 2: Identify Requirement Changes

In a previous task, the functional requirements were initially analyzed by the testing function, which consisted of the hierarchical functional decomposition, the functional window structure, the window standards, and the minimum system requirements of the system.

Between spirals new requirements may be introduced into the development process. They can consist of:

- New GUI interfaces or components
- New functions
- Modified functions
- Eliminated functions
- New system requirements, for example, hardware
- Additional system requirements
- Additional acceptance requirements

Each new requirement needs to be identified, recorded, analyzed, and updated in the test plan, test design, and test scripts.

Part 17
Prepare for the Next Spiral (Act)

If you will recall, in the spiral development environment, software testing is described as a continuous improvement process that must be integrated into a rapid application development methodology. Deming's continuous improvement process using the PDCA model is applied to the software testing process. We are now in the Act part of the spiral model (see Exhibit 17.1), which prepares for the next spiral.

Exhibit 17.2 outlines the steps and tasks associated with the Act part of spiral testing. Each step and task is described along with valuable tips and techniques.

Step 1: Refine the Tests

See Appendix F21, Impact Analysis Checklist, which can be used to help analyze the impacts of changes to the system.

Task 1: Update the Function/GUI Tests

The objective of this task is to update the test design to reflect the new functional requirements. The Test Change Function Test Matrix, which cross-references the tests to the functions, needs to be updated. The new functions are added in the vertical list and the respective test cases are added to the horizontal list. The test case name is recorded on the matrix along with the number. (See Appendix E5, Function/Test Matrix.)

Next, any new GUI/function test cases in the matrix need to be documented or scripted. The conceptual test cases are then transformed into reusable test scripts with test data created. Also, any new GUI requirements are added to the GUI tests. (See Appendix E7, GUI-Based Functional Test Matrix.)

Finally, the tests that can be automated with a testing tool need to be updated. Automated tests provide three benefits: repeatability, leverage, and increased functionality. Repeatability enables automated tests to be executed more than once, consistently. Leverage comes from repeatability from tests previously captured and tests that can be programmed with the

Exhibit 17.1. Spiral Testing and Continuous Improvement

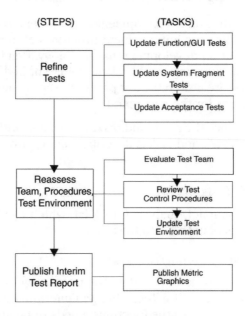

Exhibit 17.2. Prepare for the Next Spiral (Steps/Tasks)

tool, which might not have been possible without automation. As applications evolve, more and more functionality is added. With automation, the functional coverage is maintained with the test library.

Task 2: Update the System Fragment Tests

In a prior task, the system fragment tests were defined. System fragment tests are sample subsets of full system tests that can be performed during each spiral loop. The objective of doing a fragment test is to provide early warning of pending problems that would arise in the full system test.

Candidate fragment system tests include function, performance, security, usability, documentation, and procedure. Some of these fragment tests should have formal tests performed during each spiral, whereas others should be part of the overall testing strategy. The objective of the present task is to update the system fragment tests defined earlier based on new requirements. New baseline measurements are defined.

Finally, the fragment system tests that can be automated with a testing tool need to be updated.

Task 3: Update the Acceptance Tests

In a prior task, the initial list of acceptance tests was defined. Acceptance testing is an optional user-run test that demonstrates the ability of the application to meet the user's requirements. The motivation for this test is to demonstrate rather than be destructive, that is, to show that the system works. If performed, acceptance tests typically are a subset of the system tests. However, the users sometimes define "special tests," such as intensive stress or volume tests, to stretch the limits of the system even beyond what was tested during the system test. The objective of the present task is to update the acceptance tests defined earlier based on new requirements.

Finally, the acceptance tests that can be automated with a testing tool need to be updated.

Step 2: Reassess the Team, Procedures, and Test Environment

Task 1: Evaluate the Test Team

Between each spiral, the performance of the test team needs to be evaluated in terms of its quality and productivity. The test team leader directs one or more testers to ensure that the right skill level is on the project. She makes sure that the test cases are being executed according to the plan, the defects are being reported and retested, and the test automation is successful. The basis for allocating dedicated testing resources is the scope of the functionality and the development timeframe. If the testing is not being completed satisfactorily, the team leader needs to counsel one or more team members and/or request additional testers. On the other hand, if the test is coming to a conclusion, the testing manager needs to start thinking about reassigning testers to other projects.

Task 2: Review the Test Control Procedures

In a prior task, the test control procedures were set up before the first spiral. The objective of this task is to review those procedures and make appropriate modifications. The predefined procedures include the following:

- Defect recording/tracking procedures
- Change request procedures
- Version control procedures
- Configuration build procedures

- Project issue resolution procedures
- Reporting procedures

The purpose of defect recording/tracking procedures is to record and correct defects and record metric information about the application. As the project progresses, these procedures may need tuning. Examples include new status codes or new fields in the defect tracking form, an expanded defect distribution list, and the addition of more verification checks.

The purpose of change request procedures is to allow new change requests to be communicated to the development and testing team. Examples include a new change control review board process, a new sponsor who has ideas of how the change request process should be implemented, a new change request database, and a new software configuration management tool.

The purpose of version control procedures is to uniquely identify each software component via a labeling scheme and allow for successive revisions. Examples include a new software configuration management tool with a new versioning scheme or new labeling standards.

The purpose of configuration build procedures is to provide an effective means to assemble a software system from the software source components into executable components. Examples include the addition of a new 4GL language, a new software configuration management tool, or a new delta build approach.

The purpose of project issue resolution procedures is to record and process testing issues that arise during the testing process. Examples include a new project manager who requests a Lotus Notes approach, a newly formed issue review committee, an updated issue priority categorization scheme, and a new issue submission process.

The purpose of reporting procedures is to facilitate the communication process and reporting. Examples include a new project manager who requires weekly testing status reports, a new interim test report structure, or an expanded reporting distribution.

Task 3: Update the Test Environment

In a prior task, the test environment was defined. A test environment provides a physical framework for testing necessary for the testing activity. During the present task, the test environment needs are reviewed and updated. (See Appendix F22, Environment Readiness Checklist, which can be used to verify the readiness of the environment for testing before starting test execution.)

The main components of the test environment include the physical test facility, technologies, and tools. The test facility component includes the physical setup. The technologies component includes hardware platforms, the physical network and all its components, operating system software, and other software, such as utility software. The tools component includes any specialized testing software, such as automated test tools, testing libraries, and support software. Examples of changes to the test environment include:

- Expanded test lab
- New testing tools required
- Additional test hardware required
- Additional network facilities
- Additional test database space required
- New Lotus Notes log-ons
- Additional software to support testing

Step 3: Publish Interim Test Report

Task 1: Publish the Metric Graphics

Each spiral should produce an interim report to describe the status of the testing. These tests are geared to the testing team, the test manager, and the development manager, and will help them make adjustments for the next spiral. The following minimal graphical reports are recommended between each spiral test.

Test Case Execution Status. The objective of Exhibit 17.3 is to show the status of testing and predict when the testing and development group will be ready for production. Test cases run with errors have not yet been corrected.

If there are a relatively large number of test cases that have not been run, the testing group needs to increase its productivity and/or resources. If there are a large number of test cases run with errors that have not been corrected, the development team also needs to be more productive.

Defect Gap Analysis. The objective of Exhibit 17.4 is to show the gap between the number of defects that has been uncovered compared to the number that has been corrected. A large gap indicates that development needs to increase effort and resources to correct defects more quickly.

Defect Severity Status. The objective of Exhibit 17.5 is to show the distribution of the three severity categories: critical, major, and minor. A large percentage of defects in the critical category indicates that a problem with the design or architecture of the application may exist.

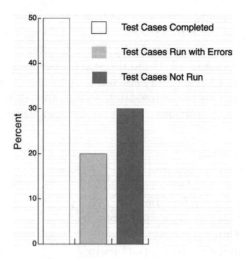

Exhibit 17.3. Test Execution Status

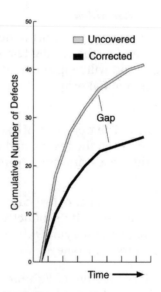

Exhibit 17.4. Defect Gap Analysis

Test Burnout Tracking. The objective of Exhibit 17.6 is to indicate the rate of uncovering defects. The cumulative, for example, running total number of defects and defects by time period help predict when fewer defects are being discovered. This is indicated when the cumulative curve "bends," and the defects by time period approach zero.

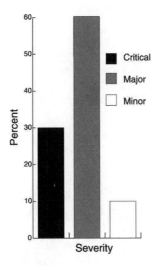

Exhibit 17.5. Defect Severity Status

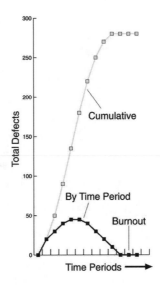

Exhibit 17.6. Test Burnout Tracking

Part 18
Conduct the System Test

System testing evaluates the functionality and performance of the whole application and consists of a variety of tests including: performance, usability, stress, documentation, security, volume, recovery, and so on. Exhibit 18.1 describes how to extend fragment system testing. It includes discussions of how to prepare for the system tests, design and script them, execute them, and report anomalies discovered during the test.

Step 1: Complete System Test Plan

Task 1: Finalize the System Test Types

In a previous task, a set of system fragment tests was selected and executed during each spiral. The purpose of the current task is to finalize the system test types that will be performed during system testing.

If you will recall, systems testing consists of one or more tests that are based on the original objectives of the system, which were defined during the project interview. The purpose of this task is to select the system tests to be performed, not to implement the tests. Our initial list consisted of the following system test types:

- Performance
- Security
- Volume
- Stress
- Compatibility
- Conversion
- Usability
- Documentation
- Backup
- Recovery
- Installation

The sequence of system test type execution should also be defined in this task. For example, related tests such as performance, stress, and volume, might be clustered together and performed early during system testing. Security, backup, and recovery are also logical groupings, and so on.

195

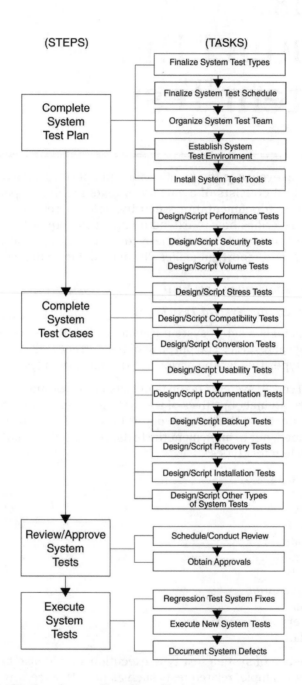

Exhibit 18.1. Conduct System Test (Steps/Tasks)

Finally, the system tests that can be automated with a testing tool need to be finalized. Automated tests provide three benefits: repeatability, leverage, and increased functionality. Repeatability enables automated tests to be executed more than once, consistently. Leverage comes from repeatability from tests previously captured and tests that can be programmed with the tool, which might not have been possible without automation. As applications evolve, more and more functionality is added. With automation the functional coverage is maintained with the test library.

Task 2: Finalize System Test Schedule

In this task, the system test schedule should be finalized and includes the testing steps (and perhaps tasks), target start and target end dates, and responsibilities. It should also describe how it will be reviewed, tracked, and approved. A sample system test schedule is shown in Exhibit 18.2. (Also see the Gantt chart template, Gantt Spiral Testing Methodology template.)

Task 3: Organize the System Test Team

With all testing types, the system test team needs to be organized. The system test team is responsible for designing and executing the tests, evaluating the results, and reporting any defects to development, and using the defect tracking system. When development corrects defects, the test team retests the defects to ensure the correction.

The system test team is led by a test manager whose responsibilities include:

- Organizing the test team
- Establishing the test environment
- Organizing the testing policies, procedures, and standards
- Assurance test readiness
- Working the test plan and controlling the project
- Tracking test costs
- Assuring test documentation is accurate and timely
- Managing the team members

Task 4: Establish the System Test Environment

During this task, the system test environment is also finalized. The purpose of the test environment is to provide a physical framework for the testing activity. The test environment needs are established and reviewed before implementation.

The main components of the test environment include the physical test facility, technologies, and tools. The test facility component includes the physical setup. The technologies component includes the hardware

Exhibit 18.2. Final System Test Schedule

Test Step	Begin Date	End Date	Responsible
General Setup			
Organize the system test team	12/1/04	12/7/04	Smith, Test Manager
Establish the system test environment	12/1/04	12/7/04	Smith, Test Manager
Establish the system test tools	12/1/04	12/10/04	Jones, Tester
Performance Testing			
Design/script the tests	12/11/04	12/15/04	Jones, Tester
Test review	12/16/04	12/16/04	Smith, Test Manager
Execute the tests	12/17/04	12/22/04	Jones, Tester
Retest system defects	12/23/04	12/25/04	Jones, Tester
Stress Testing			
Design/script the tests	12/26/04	12/30/04	Jones, Tester
Test review	12/31/04	12/31/04	Smith, Test Manager
Execute the tests	1/1/04	1/6/04	Jones, Tester
Retest system defects	1/7/04	1/9/04	Jones, Tester
Volume Testing			
Design/script the tests	1/10/04	1/14/04	Jones, Tester
Test review	1/15/04	1/15/04	Smith, Test Manager
Execute the tests	1/16/04	1/21/04	Jones, Tester
Retest system defects	1/22/04	1/24/04	Jones, Tester
Security Testing			
Design/script the tests	1/25/04	1/29/04	Jones, Tester
Test review	1/30/04	1/31/04	Smith, Test Manager
Execute the tests	2/1/04	2/6/04	Jones, Tester
Retest system defects	2/7/04	2/9/04	Jones, Tester
Backup Testing			
Design/script the tests	2/10/04	2/14/04	Jones, Tester
Test review	2/15/04	2/15/04	Smith, Test Manager
Execute the tests	2/16/04	1/21/04	Jones, Tester
Retest system defects	2/22/04	2/24/04	Jones, Tester
Recovery Testing			
Design/script the tests	2/25/04	2/29/04	Jones, Tester

Exhibit 18.2. Final System Test Schedule (Continued)

Test Step	Begin Date	End Date	Responsible
Test review	2/30/04	2/31/04	Smith, Test Manager
Execute the tests	3/1/04	3/6/04	Jones, Tester
Retest system defects	3/7/04	3/9/04	Jones, Tester
Compatibility Testing			
Design/script the tests	3/10/04	3/14/04	Jones, Tester
Test review	3/15/04	3/15/04	Smith, Test Manager
Execute the tests	3/16/04	3/21/04	Jones, Tester
Retest system defects	3/22/04	3/24/04	Jones, Tester
Conversion Testing			
Design/script the tests	4/10/04	4/14/04	Jones, Tester
Test review	4/15/04	4/15/04	Smith, Test Manager
Execute the tests	4/16/04	4/21/04	Jones, Tester
Retest system defects	4/22/04	4/24/04	Jones, Tester
Usability Testing			
Design/script the tests	5/10/04	5/14/04	Jones, Tester
Test review	5/15/04	5/15/04	Smith, Test Manager
Execute the tests	5/16/04	5/21/04	Jones, Tester
Retest system defects	5/22/04	5/24/04	Jones, Tester
Documentation Testing			
Design/script the tests	6/10/04	6/14/04	Jones, Tester
Test review	6/15/04	6/15/04	Smith, Test Manager
Execute the tests	6/16/04	6/21/04	Jones, Tester
Retest system defects	6/22/04	6/24/04	Jones, Tester
Installation Testing			
Design/script the tests	7/10/04	7/14/04	Jones, Tester
Test review	7/15/04	7/15/04	Smith, Test Manager
Execute the tests	7/16/04	7/21/04	Jones, Tester
Retest system defects	7/22/04	7/24/04	Jones, Tester

platforms, physical network and all its components, operating system software, and other software. The tools component includes any specialized testing software, such as automated test tools, testing libraries, and support software.

The testing facility and workplace need to be established. These may range from an individual workplace configuration to a formal testing lab. In any event, it is important that the testers be together and near the development team. This facilitates communication and the sense of a common goal. The system testing tools need to be installed.

The hardware and software technologies need to be set up. This includes the installation of test hardware and software and coordination with vendors, users, and information technology personnel. It may be necessary to test the hardware and coordinate with hardware vendors. Communication networks need to be installed and tested.

Task 5: Install the System Test Tools

During this task, the system test tools are installed and verified for readiness. A trial run of tool test cases and scripts should be performed to verify that the test tools are ready for the actual acceptance test. Some other tool readiness considerations include:

- Test team tool training
- Tool compatibility with operating environment
- Ample disk space for the tools
- Maximizing the tool potentials
- Vendor tool help hotline
- Test procedures modified to accommodate tools
- Installing the latest tool changes
- Assuring the vendor contractual provisions

Step 2: Complete System Test Cases

During this step, the system test cases are designed and scripted. The conceptual system test cases are transformed into reusable test scripts with test data created.

To aid in developing the script test cases, the GUI-based Function Test Matrix template in the Appendix can be used to document system-level test cases with the "function" heading replaced with the system test name.

Task 1: Design/Script the Performance Tests

The objective of performance testing is to measure the system against predefined objectives. The required performance levels are compared against the actual performance levels and discrepancies are documented.

Performance testing is a combination of black-box and white-box testing. From a black-box point of view, the performance analyst does not have to know the internal workings of the system. Real workloads or benchmarks are used to compare one system version with another for performance improvements or degradation. From a white-box point of view, the performance analyst needs to know the internal workings of the system and define specific system resources to investigate, such as instructions, modules, and tasks.

Some of the performance information of interest includes the following:

- CPU utilization
- IO utilization
- Number of IOs per instruction
- Channel utilization
- Main storage memory utilization
- Secondary storage memory utilization
- Percentage of execution time per module
- Percentage of time a module is waiting for IO completion
- Percentage of time module spent in main storage
- Instruction trace paths over time
- Number of times control is passed from one module to another
- Number of waits encountered for each group of instructions
- Number of pages-in and pages-out for each group of instructions
- System response time, for example, last key until first key time
- System throughput, that is, number of transactions per time unit
- Unit performance timings for all major functions

Baseline performance measurements should first be performed on all major functions in a noncontention mode, for example, unit measurements of functions when a single task is in operation. This can be easily done with a simple stopwatch, as was done earlier for each spiral. The next set of measurements should be made in a system contended mode in which multiple tasks are operating and queueing results for demands on common resources such as CPU, memory, storage, channel, network, and so on. Contended system execution time and resource utilization performance measurements are performed by monitoring the system to identify potential areas of inefficiency.

There are two approaches to gathering system execution time and resource utilization. With the first approach, samples are taken while the system is executing in its typical environment with the use of external probes, performance monitors, or a stopwatch. With the other approach, probes are inserted into the system code, for example, calls to a performance monitor program that gathers the performance information. The following is a discussion of each approach, followed by a discussion of test drivers, which are support techniques used to generate data for the performance study.

Monitoring Approach. This approach involves monitoring a system by determining its status at periodic time intervals and is controlled by an elapsed time facility in the testing tool or operating system. Samples taken during each time interval indicate the status of the performance criteria during the interval. The smaller the time interval, the more precise the sampling accuracy is.

Statistics gathered by the monitoring are collected and summarized in performance.

Probe Approach. This approach involves inserting probes or program instructions into the system programs at various locations. To determine, for example, the CPU time necessary to execute a sequence of statements, a problem execution results in a call to the data collection routine that records the CPU clock at that instant. A second probe execution results in a second call to the data collection routine. Subtracting the first CPU time from the second yields the net CPU time used. Reports can be produced showing execution time breakdowns by statement, module, and statement type.

The value of these approaches is their use as performance requirements validation tools. However, formally defined performance requirements must be stated and the system should be designed so that the performance requirements can be traced to specific system modules.

Test Drivers. In many cases test drivers and test harnesses are required to make system performance measurements. A test driver provides the facilities needed to execute a system, for example, inputs. The input data files for the system are loaded with data values representing the test situation to yield recorded data to evaluate against the expected results. Data are generated in an external form and presented to the system.

Performance test cases need to be defined, using one or more of the test templates located in the appendices, and test scripts need to be built. Before any performance test is conducted, however, the performance analyst must make sure that the target system is relatively bug-free. Otherwise, a lot of time will be spent documenting and fixing defects rather than analyzing the performance.

The following are the five recommended steps for any performance study:

1. Document the performance objectives; for example, exactly what the measurable performance criteria are must be verified.
2. Define the test driver or source of inputs to drive the system.
3. Define the performance methods or tools that will be used.
4. Define how the performance study will be conducted; for example, what is the baseline, what are the variations, how can it be verified as repeatable, and how does one know when the study is complete?
5. Define the reporting process, for example, techniques and tools.

Task 2: Design/Script the Security Tests

The objective of security testing is to evaluate the presence and appropriate functioning of the security of the application to ensure the integrity and confidentiality of the data. Security tests should be designed to demonstrate how resources are protected.

A Security Design Strategy. A security strategy for designing security test cases is to focus on the following four security components: the assets, threats, exposures, and controls. In this manner, matrices and checklists will suggest ideas for security test cases.

Assets are the tangible and intangible resources of an entity. The evaluation approach is to list what should be protected. It is also useful to examine the attributes of assets, such as amount, value, use, and characteristics. Two useful analysis techniques are asset value and exploitation analysis. Asset value analysis determines how the value differs among users and potential attackers. Asset exploitation analysis examines different ways to use an asset for illicit gain.

Threats are events with the potential to cause loss or harm. The evaluation approach is to list the sources of potential threats. It is important to distinguish among accidental, intentional, and natural threats, and threat frequencies.

Exposures are forms of possible loss or harm. The evaluation approach is to list what might happen to assets if a threat is realized. Exposures include disclosure violations, erroneous decision, and fraud. Exposure analysis focuses on identifying areas in which exposure is the greatest.

Security functions or controls are measures that protect against loss or harm. The evaluation approach is to list the security functions and tasks and focus on controls embodied in specific system functions or procedures. Security functions assess the protection against human errors and casual attempts to misuse the system. Some functional security questions include the following:

- Do the control features work properly?
- Are invalid and improbable parameters detected and properly handled?
- Are invalid or out-of-sequence commands detected and properly handled?
- Are errors and file accesses properly recorded?
- Do procedures for changing security tables work?
- Is it possible to log in without a password?
- Are valid passwords accepted and invalid passwords rejected?
- Does the system respond properly to multiple invalid passwords?

- Does the system-initialed authentication function properly?
- Are there security features for remote accessing?

It is important to assess the performance of the security mechanisms as well as the functions themselves. Some questions and issues concerning security performance include the following:

- *Availability* — What portion of time is the application or control available to perform critical security functions? Security controls usually require higher availability than other portions of the system.
- *Survivability* — How well does the system withstand major failures or natural disasters? This includes the support of emergency operations during failure, backup operations afterward, and recovery actions to return to regular operation.
- *Accuracy* — How accurate is the security control? Accuracy encompasses the number, frequency, and significance of errors.
- *Response time* — Are response times acceptable? Slow response times can tempt users to bypass security controls. Response time can also be critical for control management, as the dynamic modification of security tables.
- *Throughput* — Does the security control support required use capacities? Capacity includes the peak and average loading of users and service requests.

A useful performance test is stress testing, which involves large numbers of users and requests to attain operational stress conditions. Stress testing is used to attempt to exhaust limits for such resources as buffers, queues, tables, and ports. This form of testing is useful in evaluating protection against service denial threats.

Task 3: Design/Script the Volume Tests

The objective of volume testing is to subject the system to heavy volumes of data to find out if it can handle the volume of data. This test is often confused with stress testing. Stress testing subjects the system to heavy loads or stresses in terms of rates, such as throughputs over a short time period. Volume testing is data oriented, and its purpose is to show that the system can handle the volume of data specified in its objectives.

Some examples of volume testing are:

- Relative data comparison is made when processing date-sensitive transactions.
- A compiler is fed an extremely large source program to compile.
- A linkage editor is fed a program containing thousands of modules.
- An electronic-circuit simulator is given a circuit containing thousands of components.
- An operation system's job queue is filled to maximum capacity.

- Enough data is created to cause a system to span file.
- A test-formatting system is fed a massive document format.
- The Internet is flooded with huge e-mail messages and files.

Task 4: Design/Script the Stress Tests

The objective of stress testing is to investigate the behavior of the system under conditions that overload its resources. Of particular interest is the impact that this has on the system processing time. Stress testing is boundary testing. For example, test with the maximum number of terminals active and then add more terminals than specified in the requirements under different limit combinations. Some of the resources that stress testing subjects to heavy loads include:

- Buffers
- Controllers
- Display terminals
- Interrupt handlers
- Memory
- Networks
- Printers
- Spoolers
- Storage devices
- Transaction queues
- Transaction schedulers
- User of the system

Stress testing studies the system's response to peak bursts of activity in short periods of time and attempts to find defects in a system. It is often confused with volume testing, in which the system's capability of handling large amounts of data is the objective.

Stress testing should be performed early in development because it often uncovers major design flaws that can have an impact on many areas. If stress testing is not performed early, subtle defects, which might have been more apparent earlier in development, may be difficult to uncover.

The following are the suggested steps for stress testing:

1. Perform simple multitask tests.
2. After the simple stress defects are corrected, stress the system to the breaking point.
3. Perform the stress tests repeatedly for every spiral.

Some stress testing examples include the following:

- Word-processing response time for a fixed entry rate, such as 120 words per minute
- Introduce a heavy volume of data in a very short period of time

- Varying loads for interactive, real-time, and process control
- Simultaneous introduction of a large number of transactions
- Thousands of users signing on to the Internet within the same minute

Task 5: Design/Script the Compatibility Tests

The objective of compatibility testing (sometimes called cohabitation testing) is to test the compatibility of the application with other applications or systems. This is a test that is often overlooked until the system is put into production and in which defects are often subtle and difficult to uncover. An example is when the system works perfectly in the testing lab in a controlled environment but does not work when it coexists with other applications. An example of compatibility is when two systems share the same data or data files or reside in the same memory at the same time. The system may satisfy the system requirements but not work in a shared environment and may interfere with other systems.

The following is a compatibility (cohabitation) testing strategy:

1. Update the compatibility objectives to note how the application has actually been developed and the actual environments in which it is to perform. Modify the objectives for any changes in the cohabiting systems or the configuration resources.
2. Update the compatibility test cases to make sure they are comprehensive. Make sure that the test cases in the other systems that can affect the target system are comprehensive. And ensure maximum coverage of instances in which one system could affect another.
3. Perform the compatibility tests and carefully monitor the results to ensure the expected results. Use a baseline approach, which is the system's operating characteristics before the addition of the target system into the shared environment. The baseline needs to be accurate and incorporate not only the functioning but the operational performance to ensure that it is not degraded in a cohabitation setting.
4. Document the results of the compatibility tests and note any deviations in the target system or the other cohabitation systems.
5. Regression test the compatibility tests after the defects have been resolved and record the tests in the retest matrix.

Task 6: Design/Script the Conversion Tests

The objective of conversion testing is to verify the conversion of existing data and load a new database. The most common conversion problem is between two versions of the same system. A new version may have a different data format but must include the data from the old system. Ample time needs to be set aside to carefully think of all the conversion issues that may arise.

Some key factors that need to be considered when designing conversion tests include the following:

- *Auditability* — There needs to be a plan to perform before-and-after comparisons and analysis of the converted data to ensure it was converted successfully. Techniques to ensure auditability include file reports, comparison programs, and regression testing. Regression testing checks to verify that the converted data does not change the business requirements or cause the system to behave differently.
- *Database Verification* — Prior to conversion, the new database needs to be reviewed to verify that it is designed properly, satisfies the business needs, and that the support center and database administrators are trained to support it.
- *Data Cleanup* — Before the data is converted to the new system, the old data needs to be examined to verify that inaccuracies or discrepancies in the data are removed.
- *Recovery Plan* — Roll-back procedures need to be in place before any conversion is attempted to restore the system to its previous state and undo the conversions.
- *Synchronization* — It must be verified that the conversion process does not interfere with normal operations. Sensitive data, such as customer data, may be changing dynamically during conversions. One way to achieve this is to perform conversions during nonoperational hours.

Task 7: Design/Script the Usability Tests

The objective of usability testing is to determine how well the user will be able to use and understand the application. This includes the system functions, publications, help text, and procedures to ensure that the user comfortably interacts with the system. Usability testing should be performed as early as possible during development and should be designed into the system. Late usability testing might be impossible, because it is locked in and often requires a major redesign of the system to correct serious usability problems. This may make it economically infeasible.

Some of the usability problems the tester should look for include:

- Overly complex functions or instructions
- Difficult installation procedures
- Poor error messages, for example, "syntax error"
- Syntax difficult to understand and use
- Nonstandardized GUI interfaces
- User forced to remember too much information
- Difficult log-in procedures
- Help text not context sensitive or not detailed enough
- Poor linkage to other systems

- Unclear defaults
- Interface too simple or too complex
- Inconsistency of syntax, format, and definitions
- User not provided with clear acknowledgment of all inputs

Task 8: Design/Script the Documentation Tests

The objective of documentation testing is to verify that the user documentation is accurate and ensure that the manual procedures work correctly. Documentation testing has several advantages, including improving the usability of the system, reliability, maintainability, and installability. In these cases, testing the document will help uncover deficiencies in the system and/or make the system more usable.

Documentation testing also reduces customer support costs, such as when customers can figure out their questions with the documentation, they are not forced to call the support desk.

The tester verifies the technical accuracy of the documentation to assure that it agrees with and describes the system accurately. She needs to assume the user's point of view and act out the actual behavior as described in the documentation.

Some tips and suggestions for the documentation tester include:

- Use documentation as a source of many test cases.
- Use the system exactly as the documentation describes it.
- Test every hint or suggestion.
- Incorporate defects into the defect tracking database.
- Test every online help hypertext link.
- Test every statement of fact and don't take anything for granted.
- Act like a technical editor rather than a passive reviewer.
- Perform a general review of the whole document first and then a detailed review.
- Check all the error messages.
- Test every example provided in the document.
- Make sure all index entries have documentation text.
- Make sure documentation covers all key user functions.
- Make sure the reading style is not too technical.
- Look for areas that are weaker than others and need more explanation.

Task 9: Design/Script the Backup Tests

The objective of backup testing is to verify the ability of the system to back up its data in the event of a software or hardware failure. This test is complementary to recovery testing and should be part of recovery test planning.

Some backup testing considerations include the following:
- Backing up files and comparing the backup with the original
- Archiving files and data
- Complete system backup procedures
- Checkpoint backups
- Backup performance system degradation
- Effect of backup on manual processes
- Detection of "triggers" to backup system
- Security procedures during backup
- Maintaining transaction logs during backup procedures

Task 10: Design/Script the Recovery Tests

The objective of recovery testing is to verify the system's ability to recover from a software or hardware failure. This test verifies the contingency features of the system for handling interruptions and returning to specific points in the application's processing cycle. The key questions for designing recovery tests are as follows:
- Have the potentials for disasters and system failures, and their respective damages, been identified? Fire-drill brainstorming sessions can be an effective method of defining disaster scenarios.
- Do the prevention and recovery procedures provide for adequate responses to failures? The plan procedures should be tested with technical reviews by subject matter experts and the system users.
- Will the recovery procedures work properly when really needed? Simulated disasters need to be created with the actual system verifying the recovery procedures. This should involve the system users, the support organization, vendors, and so on.

Some recovery testing examples include the following:
- Complete restoration of files that were backed up either during routine maintenance or error recovery
- Partial restoration of file backup to the last checkpoint
- Execution of recovery programs
- Archive retrieval of selected files and data
- Restoration when power supply is the problem
- Verification of manual recovery procedures
- Recovery by switching to parallel systems
- Restoration performance system degradation
- Security procedures during recovery
- Ability to recover transaction logs

Task 11: Design/Script the Installation Tests

The objective of installation testing is to verify the ability to install the system successfully. Customers have to install the product on their systems.

Installation is often the developers' last activity and often receives the least amount of focus during development. Yet, it is the first activity that the customer performs when using the new system. Therefore, clear and concise installation procedures are among the most important parts of the system documentation.

Reinstallation procedures need to be included to be able to reverse the installation process and validate the previous environmental condition. Also, the installation procedures need to document how the user can tune the system options and upgrade from a previous version.

Some key installation questions the tester needs to consider include the following:

- Who is the user installer; for example, what technical capabilities are assumed?
- Is the installation process documented thoroughly with specific and concise installation steps?
- For which environments are the installation procedures supposed to work, for example, platforms, software, hardware, networks, or versions?
- Will the installation change the user's current environmental setup, for example, config.sys and so on?
- How does the installer know the system has been installed correctly; for example, is there an installation test procedure in place?

Task 12: Design/Script Other System Test Types

In addition to the above system tests, the following system tests may also be required.

- *API Testing* — Verify the system uses APIs correctly, for example, operating system calls.
- *Communication Testing* — Verify the system's communications and networks.
- *Configuration Testing* — Verify the system works correctly in different system configurations, for example, software, hardware, and networks.
- *Database Testing* — Verify the database integrity, business rules, access, and refresh capabilities.
- *Degraded System Testing* — Verify the system performs properly with less than full capabilities, for example, line connections down, and the like.
- *Disaster Recovery Testing* — Verify the system recovery processes work correctly.
- *Embedded System Test* — Verify systems that operate on low-level devices, such as video chips.

- *Facility Testing* — Verify that each stated requirement facility is met.
- *Field Testing* — Verify the system works correctly in the real environment.
- *Middleware Testing* — Verify the middleware software works correctly, for example, the common interfaces and accessibility among clients and servers.
- *Multimedia Testing* — Verify the multimedia system features, which use video, graphics, and sound.
- *Online Help Testing* — Verify the system's online help features work properly.
- *Operability Testing* — Verify system will work correctly in the actual business environment.
- *Package Testing* — Verify installed software package works correctly.
- *Parallel Testing* — Verify system behaves the same in the old and new version.
- *Port Testing* — Verify system works correctly on different operating systems and computers.
- *Procedure Testing* — Verify nonautomated procedures work properly, for example, operation, DBA, and the like.
- *Production Testing* — Verify the system will work correctly during actual ongoing production and not just in the test lab environment.
- *Real-Time Testing* — Verify systems in which time issues are critical and there are response time requirements.
- *Reliability Testing* — Verify the system works correctly within predefined expected failure duration, for example, mean time to failure (MTF).
- *Serviceability Testing* — Verify service facilities of the system work properly, for example, mean time to debug a defect and maintenance procedures.
- *SQL Testing* — Verify the queries, data retrievals, and updates.
- *Storage Testing* — Verify that the system storage requirements are met, for example, sizes of spill files and amount of main or secondary storage used.

Step 3: Review/Approve System Tests

Task 1: Schedule/Conduct the Review

The system test plan review should be scheduled well in advance of the actual review, and the participants should have the latest copy of the test plan.

As with any interview or review, it should contain certain elements. The first is defining what will be discussed; the second is discussing the details; and the third is summarization. The final element is timeliness. The reviewer should state up front the estimated duration of the review and set the ground rule that if time expires before completing all items on the agenda, a follow-on review will be scheduled.

The purpose of this task is for development and the project sponsor to agree and accept the system test plan. If there are any suggested changes to the test plan during the review, they should be incorporated into the test plan.

Task 2: Obtain Approvals

Approval is critical in a testing effort because it helps provide the necessary agreement among testing, development, and the sponsor. The best approach is with a formal sign-off procedure of a system test plan. If this is the case, use the management approval sign-off forms. However, if a formal agreement procedure is not in place, send a memo to each key participant including at least the project manager, development manager, and sponsor. In the document attach the latest test plan and point out that all their feedback comments have been incorporated and that if you do not hear from them, it is assumed that they agree with the plan. Finally, indicate that in a spiral development environment, the system test plan will evolve with each iteration but that you will include them in any modification.

Step 4: Execute the System Tests

Task 1: Regression Test the System Fixes

The purpose of this task is to retest the system tests that discovered defects in the previous system test cycle for this build. The technique used is regression testing. Regression testing is a technique that detects spurious errors caused by software modifications or corrections.

A set of test cases must be maintained and available throughout the entire life of the software. The test cases should be complete enough so that all the software's functional capabilities are thoroughly tested. The question arises as to how to locate those test cases to test defects discovered during the previous test spiral. An excellent mechanism is the retest matrix.

As described earlier, a retest matrix relates test cases to functions (or program units). A check entry in the matrix indicates that the test case is to be retested when the function (or program unit) has been modified due to an enhancement(s) or correction(s). No entry means that the test does not need to be retested. The retest matrix can be built before the first testing spiral but needs to be maintained during subsequent spirals. As functions (or program units) are modified during a development spiral, existing or new test cases need to be created and checked in the retest matrix in preparation for the next test spiral. Over time with subsequent spirals, some functions (or program units) may be stable with no recent modifications.

Consideration to selectively remove their check entries should be undertaken between testing spirals.

Task 2: Execute the New System Tests

The purpose of this task is to execute new system tests that were created at the end of the previous system test cycle. In the previous spiral, the testing team updated the function/GUI, system fragment, and acceptance tests in preparation for the current testing spiral. During this task, those tests are executed.

Task 3: Document the System Defects

During system test execution, the results of the testing must be reported in the defect tracking database. These defects are typically related to individual tests that have been conducted. However, variations to the formal test cases often uncover other defects. The objective of this task is to produce a complete record of the defects. If the execution step has been recorded properly, the defects have already been recorded on the defect tracking database. If the defects are already recorded, the objective of this step becomes to collect and consolidate the defect information.

Tools can be used to consolidate and record defects depending on the test execution methods. If the defects are recorded on paper, the consolidation involves collecting and organizing the papers. If the defects are recorded electronically, search features can easily locate duplicate defects.

Part 19
Conduct Acceptance Testing

Acceptance testing is a user-run test that demonstrates the application's ability to meet the original business objectives and system requirements and usually consists of a subset of system tests (see Exhibit 19.1). It includes discussions on how to prepare for the acceptance test, design and script the acceptance tests, execute the acceptance tests, and report anomalies discovered during the test.

Step 1: Complete Acceptance Test Planning

Task 1: Finalize the Acceptance Test Types

In this task the initial acceptance testing type list is refined and the actual tests to be performed are selected.

Acceptance testing is an optional user-run test that demonstrates the ability of the application to meet the user's requirements. The motivation for this test is to demonstrate rather than be destructive, that is, to show that the system works. Less emphasis is placed on the technical issues and more on the question of whether the system is a good business fit for the end user. Users usually perform the test. However, the users sometimes define "special tests," such as intensive stress or volume tests, to stretch the limits of the system even beyond what was tested during the system test.

Task 2: Finalize the Acceptance Test Schedule

In this task, the acceptance test schedule should be finalized and includes the testing steps (and perhaps tasks), target begin dates and target end dates, and responsibilities. It should also describe how it will be reviewed, tracked, and approved. For acceptance testing, the test team usually consists of user representatives. However, the team test environment and test tool are probably the same as used during system testing. A sample acceptance test schedule is shown in Exhibit 19.2.

Task 3: Organize the Acceptance Test Team

The acceptance test team is responsible for designing and executing the tests, evaluating the test results, and reporting any defects to development,

215

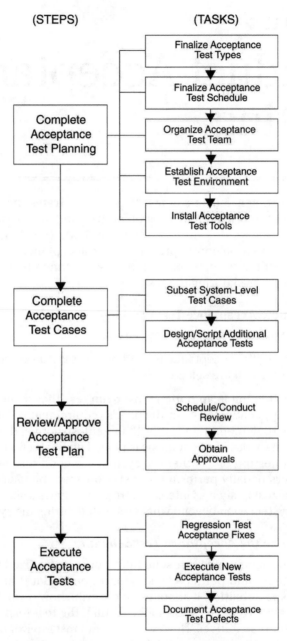

(STEPS)   (TASKS)

Finalize Acceptance Test Types

Finalize Acceptance Test Schedule

Complete Acceptance Test Planning

Organize Acceptance Test Team

Establish Acceptance Test Environment

Install Acceptance Test Tools

Complete Acceptance Test Cases

Subset System-Level Test Cases

Design/Script Additional Acceptance Tests

Review/Approve Acceptance Test Plan

Schedule/Conduct Review

Obtain Approvals

Execute Acceptance Tests

Regression Test Acceptance Fixes

Execute New Acceptance Tests

Document Acceptance Test Defects

Exhibit 19.1. Conduct Acceptance Testing (Steps/Tasks)

using the defect tracking system. When development corrects defects, the test team retests the defects to ensure the correction. The acceptance test team typically has representation from the user community, because this is their final opportunity to accept the system.

Exhibit 19.2. Acceptance Test Schedule

Test Step	Begin Date	End Date	Responsible
General Setup			
Organize the acceptance test team	8/1/04	8/7/04	Smith, Test Manager
Establish the acceptance test environment	8/8/04	8/9/04	Smith, Test Manager
Establish the acceptance test tools	8/10/04	8/10/04	Jones, Tester
Acceptance testing			
Design/script the tests	12/11/04	12/15/04	Jones, Baker (user), Testers
Test review	12/16/04	12/16/04	Smith, Test Manager
Execute the tests	12/17/04	12/22/04	Jones, Baker (user), Tester
Retest acceptance defects	12/23/04	12/25/04	Jones, Baker (user), Tester

The acceptance test team is led by a test manager whose responsibilities include:

- Organizing the test team
- Establishing the test environment
- Organizing the testing policies, procedures, and standards
- Ensuring test readiness
- Working the test plan and controlling the project
- Tracking test costs
- Ensuring test documentation is accurate and timely
- Managing the team members

Task 4: Establish the Acceptance Test Environment

During this task, the acceptance test environment is finalized. Typically, the test environment for acceptance testing is the same as that for system testing. The purpose of the test environment is to provide the physical framework necessary for the testing activity. For this task, the test environment needs are established and reviewed before implementation.

The main components of the test environment include the physical test facility, technologies, and tools. The test facility component includes the physical setup. The technologies component includes the hardware platforms, physical network and all its components, operating system software, and other software, such as utility software. The tools component includes any specialized testing software: automated test tools, testing libraries, and support software.

217

The testing facility and workplace needs to be established. It may range from an individual workplace configuration to a formal testing lab. In any event, it is important that the testers be together and in close proximity to the development team. This facilitates communication and the sense of a common goal. The testing tools that were acquired need to be installed.

The hardware and software technologies need to be set up. This includes the installation of test hardware and software, and coordination with vendors, users, and information technology personnel. It may be necessary to test the hardware and coordinate with hardware vendors. Communication networks need to be installed and tested.

Task 5: Install Acceptance Test Tools

During this task, the acceptance test tools are installed and verified for readiness. A trial run of sample tool test cases and scripts should be performed to verify that the test tools are ready for the actual acceptance test. Some other tool readiness considerations include:

- Test team tool training
- Tool compatibility with operating environment
- Ample disk space for the tools
- Maximizing the tool potentials
- Vendor tool help hotline
- Test procedures modified to accommodate tools
- Installing the latest tool changes
- Assuring the vendor contractual provisions

Step 2: Complete Acceptance Test Cases

During this step, the acceptance test cases are designed and scripted. The conceptual acceptance test cases are transformed into reusable test scripts with test data created. To aid in the development of scripting the test cases, the GUI-based Function Test Matrix template in Appendix E7 can be used to document acceptance-level test cases, with the "function" heading replaced with the acceptance test name.

Task 1: Subset the System-Level Test Cases

Acceptance test cases are typically (but not always) developed by the end user and are not normally considered the responsibility of the development organization, because acceptance testing compares the system to its original requirements and the needs of the users. It is the final test for the end users to accept or reject the system. The end users supply the test resources and perform their own tests. They may or may not use the same test environment that was used during system testing. This depends on whether the test will be performed in the end user's environment. The latter is the recommended approach.

Typically, the acceptance test consists of a subset of system tests that have already been designed during system testing. Therefore, the current task consists of identifying those system-level tests that will be used during acceptance testing.

Task 2: Design/Script Additional Acceptance Tests

In addition to the system-level tests to be rerun during acceptance testing, they may be "tweaked" with special conditions to maximize the acceptability of the system. For example, the acceptance test might require that a certain throughput be sustained for a period of time with acceptable response time tolerance limits; for example, 10,000 transactions per hour are processed with a mean response time of three seconds, with 90 percent less than or equal to two seconds. Another example might be that an independent user "off the street" sits down with the system and the document to verify that he can use the system effectively.

The user might also envision other tests not designed during system testing. These may become more apparent to the user than they would have been to the developer because the user knows the business requirements and is intimately familiar with the business operations. She might uncover defects that only a user would see. This also helps the user to get ready for the real installation and production.

The acceptance test design might even include the use of live data, because the acceptance of test results will probably occur more readily if it looks real to the user. There are also unusual conditions that might not be detected unless live data is used.

Step 3: Review/Approve Acceptance Test Plan

Task 1: Schedule/Conduct the Review

The acceptance test plan review should be scheduled well in advance of the actual review and the participants should have the latest copy of the test plan.

As with any interview or review, it should contain certain elements. The first defines what will be discussed; the second discusses the details; the third summarizes; and the final element is timeliness. The reviewer should state up front the estimated duration of the review and set the ground rule that if time expires before completing all items on the agenda, a follow-on review will be scheduled.

The purpose of this task is for development and the project sponsor to agree and accept the system test plan. If there are any suggested changes to the test plan during the review, they should be incorporated into the test plan.

Task 2: Obtain Approvals

Approval is critical in a testing effort because it helps provide the necessary agreements among testing, development, and the sponsor. The best approach is with a formal sign-off procedure of an acceptance test plan. If this is the case, use the management approval sign-off forms. However, if a formal agreement procedure is not in place, send a memo to each key participant, including at least the project manager, development manager, and sponsor. Attach to the document the latest test plan and point out that all feedback comments have been incorporated and that if you do not hear from them, it is assumed they agree with the plan. Finally, indicate that in a spiral development environment, the system test plan will evolve with each iteration but that you will include them in any modification.

Step 4: Execute the Acceptance Tests

Task 1: Regression Test the Acceptance Fixes

The purpose of this task is to retest the tests that discovered defects in the previous acceptance test cycle for this build. The technique used is regression testing. Regression testing detects spurious errors caused by software modifications or corrections.

A set of test cases must be maintained and available throughout the entire life of the software. The test cases should be complete enough so that all the software's functional capabilities are thoroughly tested. The question arises as to how to locate those test cases to test defects discovered during the previous test spiral. An excellent mechanism is the retest matrix.

As described earlier, a retest matrix relates test cases to functions (or program units). A check entry in the matrix indicates that the test case is to be retested when the function (or program unit) has been modified due to an enhancement(s) or correction(s). No entry means that the test does not need to be retested. The retest matrix can be built before the first testing spiral but needs to be maintained during subsequent spirals. As functions (or program units) are modified during a development spiral, existing or new test cases need to be created and checked in the retest matrix in preparation for the next test spiral. Over time with subsequent spirals, some functions (or program units) may be stable with no recent modifications. Consideration to selectively remove their check entries should be undertaken between testing spirals.

Task 2: Execute the New Acceptance Tests

The purpose of this task is to execute new tests that were created at the end of the previous acceptance test cycle. In the previous spiral, the testing team updated the function/GUI, system fragment, and acceptance tests in preparation for the current testing spiral. During this task, those tests are executed.

Task 3: Document the Acceptance Defects

During acceptance test execution, the results of the testing must be reported in the defect-tracking database. These defects are typically related to individual tests that have been conducted. However, variations to the formal test cases often uncover other defects. The objective of this task is to produce a complete record of the defects. If the execution step has been recorded properly, the defects have already been recorded on the defect-tracking database. If the defects are already recorded, the objective of this step becomes to collect and consolidate the defect information.

Tools can be used to consolidate and record defects depending on the test execution methods. If the defects are recorded on paper, the consolidation involves collecting and organizing the papers. If the defects are recorded electronically, search features can easily locate duplicate defects.

Part 20
Summarize/Report Spiral Test Results

See Appendix F23, Project Completion Checklist, which can be used to confirm that all the key activities have been completed for the project.

Step 1: Perform Data Reduction

Task 1: Ensure All Tests Were Executed/Resolved

During this task, the test plans and logs are examined by the test team to verify that all tests were executed (see Exhibit 20.1). The team can usually do this by ensuring that all the tests are recorded on the activity log and examining the log to confirm that the tests have been completed. When there are defects that are still open and not resolved, they need to be prioritized and deployment workarounds need to be established.

Task 2: Consolidate Test Defects by Test Number

During this task, the team examines the recorded test defects. If the tests have been properly performed, it is logical to assume that, unless a defect test document was reported, the correct or expected result was received. If that defect was not corrected, it would have been posted to the test defect log. The team can assume that all items are working except those recorded on the test log as having no corrective action or unsatisfactory corrective action. The test number should consolidate these defects so that they can be posted to the appropriate matrix.

Task 3: Post Remaining Defects to a Matrix

During this task, the uncorrected or unsatisfactorily corrected defects should be posted to a special function test matrix. The matrix indicates which test-by-test number tested which function. The defect is recorded in the intersection between the test and the functions for which that test occurred. All uncorrected defects should be posted to the function/test matrix intersection.

(STEPS)   (TASKS)

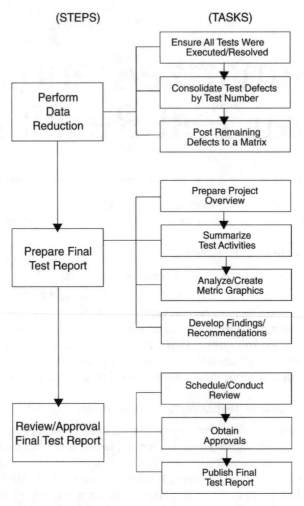

Exhibit 20.1. Summarize/Report Spiral Test Results

Step 2: Prepare Final Test Report

The objective of the final spiral test report is to describe the results of the testing, including not only what works and what does not, from above, but the test team's evaluation regarding performance of the application when it is placed into production.

For some projects, informal reports are the practice, whereas in others very formal reports are required. The following is a compromise between the two extremes to provide essential information not requiring an inordinate amount of preparation (see Appendix E15, Spiral Testing Summary Report; also see Appendix E29, Final Test Summary Report, which can be used as a final report of the test project with key findings).

Task 1: Prepare the Project Overview

An objective of this task is to document an overview of the project in paragraph format. Some pertinent information contained in the introduction includes the project name, project objectives, the type of system, the target audience, the organizational units that participated in the project, why the system was developed, what subsystems are involved, the major and subfunctions of the system, and what functions are out of scope and will not be implemented.

Task 2: Summarize the Test Activities

The objective of this task is to describe the test activities for the project including such information as the following:

- *Test Team* — The composition of the test team, for example, test manager, test leader, and testers, and the contribution of each, such as test planning, test design, test development, and test execution.
- *Test Environment* — Physical test facility, technology, testing tools, software, hardware, networks, testing libraries, and support software.
- *Types of Tests* — Spiral (how many spirals), system testing (types of tests and how many), and acceptance testing (types of tests and how many).
- *Test Schedule (Major Milestones)* — External and internal. External milestones are those events external to the project but which may have a direct impact on it. Internal milestones are the events within the project to which some degree of control can be administered.
- *Test Tools* — Which testing tools were used and for what purpose, for example, path analysis, regression testing, load testing, and so on.

Task 3: Analyze/Create Metric Graphics

During this task, the defect and test management metrics measured during the project are gathered and analyzed. It is hoped that the defect tracking has been automated and will be used to make the work more productive. Reports are run and metric totals and trends are analyzed. This analysis will be instrumental in determining the quality of the system and its acceptability for use and also be useful for future testing endeavors. The final test report should include a series of metric graphics. Following are the suggested graphics.

Defects by Function. The objective of Exhibit 20.2 is to show the number and percentage of defects discovered for each function or group. This analysis will flag the functions that have the most defects. Typically, such functions had poor requirements or design. In the example below, the

Exhibit 20.2. Defects Documented by Function

Function	Number of Defects	Percent of Total
Order Processing		
Create new order	11	6
Fulfill order	5	3
Edit order	15	8
Delete order	9	5
Subtotal	40	22
Customer Processing		
Create new customer	6	3
Edit customer	0	0
Delete customer	10	6
Subtotal	16	9
Financial Processing		
Receive customer payment	0	0
Deposit payment	5	3
Pay vendor	9	5
Write a check	4	2
Display register	6	3
Subtotal	24	13
Inventory Processing		
Acquire vendor products	3	2
Maintain stock	7	4
Handle back orders	9	5
Audit inventory	0	0
Adjust product price	6	3
Subtotal	25	14
Reports		
Create order report	23	13
Create account receivable report	19	11
Create account payable report	35	19
Subtotal	77	43
Grand totals	182	100

Exhibit 20.3. Defects Documented by Tester

Tester	Number of Defects	Percent of Total
Jones	51	28
Baker	19	11
Brown	112	61
Grand Totals	182	100

reports had 43 percent of the total defects, which suggests an area that should be examined for maintainability after it is released for production.

Defects by Tester. The objective of Exhibit 20.3 is to show the number and percentage of defects discovered for each tester during the project. This analysis flags those testers who documented fewer than the expected number of defects. These statistics, however, should be used with care. A tester may have recorded fewer defects because the functional area tested may have relatively fewer defects, for example, tester Baker in Exhibit 20.3. On the other hand, a tester who records a higher percentage of defects could be more productive, for example, tester Brown.

Defect Gap Analysis. The objective of Exhibit 20.4 is to show the gap between the number of defects that has been uncovered and the number that has been corrected during the entire project. At project completion these curves should coincide, indicating that the majority of the defects uncovered have been corrected and the system is ready for production.

Defect Severity Status. The objective of Exhibit 20.5 is to show the distribution of the three severity categories for the entire project, for example, critical, major, and minor. A large percentage of defects in the critical category indicate that there existed a problem with the design or architecture of the application, which should be examined for maintainability after it is released for production.

Test Burnout Tracking. The objective of Exhibit 20.6 is to indicate the rate of uncovering defects for the entire project and is a valuable test completion indicator. The cumulative (e.g., running total) number of defects and defects by time period help predict when fewer and fewer defects are being discovered. This is indicated when the cumulative curve "bends" and the defects by time period approach zero.

Root Cause Analysis. The objective of Exhibit 20.7 is to show the source of the defects, for example, architectural, functional, usability, and so on. If the majority of the defects are architectural, this will pervade the whole system and require a great deal of redesign and rework. High percentage

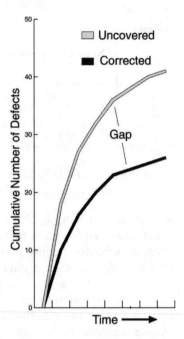

Exhibit 20.4. Defect Gap Analysis

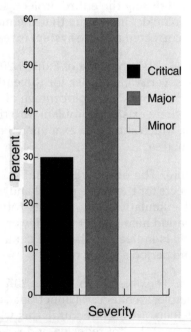

Exhibit 20.5. Defect Severity Status

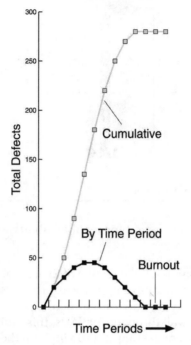

Exhibit 20.6. Test Burnout Tracking

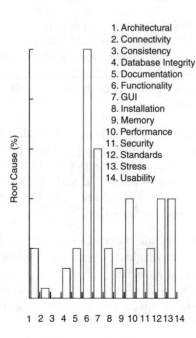

1. Architectural
2. Connectivity
3. Consistency
4. Database Integrity
5. Documentation
6. Functionality
7. GUI
8. Installation
9. Memory
10. Performance
11. Security
12. Standards
13. Stress
14. Usability

Exhibit 20.7. Root Cause Analysis

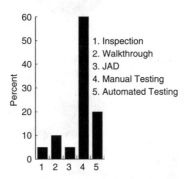

Exhibit 20.8. Defects by How Found

categories should be examined for maintainability after it is released for production.

Defects by How Found. The objective of Exhibit 20.8 is to show how the defects were discovered, for example, by external customers, manual testing, and the like. If a very low percentage of defects was discovered through inspections, walkthroughs, or JADs, this indicates that there may be too much emphasis on testing and too little on the review process. The percentage differences between manual and automated testing also illustrate the contribution of automated testing to the process.

Defects by Who Found. The objective of Exhibit 20.9 is to show who discovered the defects, for example, external customers, development, quality assurance testing, and so on. For most projects, quality assurance testing will discover most of the defects. However, if external or internal customers discovered the majority of the defects, this indicates that quality assurance testing was lacking.

Functions Tested and Not. The objective of Exhibit 20.10 is to show the final status of testing and verify that all or most defects have been corrected and the system is ready for production. At the end of the project all test cases should have been completed and the percentage of test cases run with errors and/or not run should be zero. Exceptions should be evaluated by management and documented.

System Testing Defect Types. Systems testing consists of one or more tests that are based on the original objectives of the system. The objective of Exhibit 20.11 is to show a distribution of defects by system testing type. In the example, performance testing had the most defects, followed by compatibility and usability. An inordinate percentage of performance tests indicates a poorly designed system.

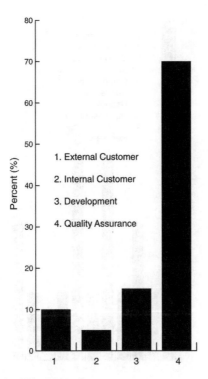

Exhibit 20.9. Defects by Who Found

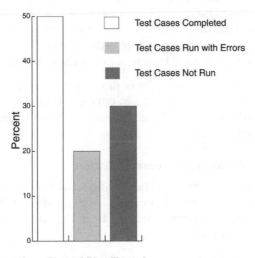

Exhibit 20.10. Functions Tested/Not Tested

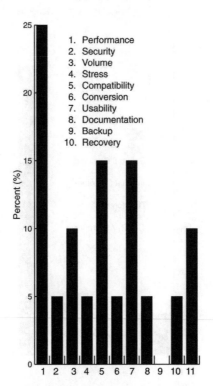

Exhibit 20.11. System Testing by Root Cause

Acceptance Testing Defect Types. Acceptance testing is an optional user-run test that demonstrates the ability of the application to meet the user's requirements. The motivation for this test is to demonstrate rather than destroy, for example, to show that the system works. Less emphasis is placed on the technical issues and more is placed on the question of whether the system is a good business fit for the end user.

There should not be many defects discovered during acceptance testing, as most of them should have been corrected during system testing. In Exhibit 20.12, performance testing still had the most defects, followed by stress and volume testing.

Task 4: Develop Findings/Recommendations

A finding is a variance between what is and what should be. A recommendation is a suggestion on how to correct a defective situation or improve a system. Findings and recommendations from the test team constitute the majority of the test report.

The objective of this task is to develop the findings and recommendations from the testing process and document "lessons learned." Previously,

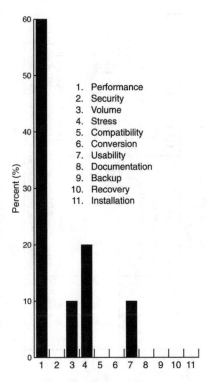

Exhibit 20.12. Acceptance Testing by Root Cause

data reduction has identified the findings, but they must be put in a format suitable for use by the project team and management.

The test team should make the recommendations to correct a situation. The project team should also confirm that the findings are correct and the recommendations reasonable. Each finding and recommendation can be documented in the Finding/Recommendation matrix depicted in Exhibit 20.13.

Step 3: Review/Approve the Final Test Report

Task 1: Schedule/Conduct the Review

The test summary report review should be scheduled well in advance of the actual review and the participants should have the latest copy of the test plan.

As with any interview or review, it should contain certain elements. The first is defining what will be discussed; the second is discussing the details; the third is summarization; and the final element is timeliness. The reviewer should state up front the estimated duration of the review and set

Exhibit 20.13. Finding/Recommendations Matrix

Finding Description[a]	Business Function[b]	Impact[c]	Impact on Other Systems[d]	Costs to Correct[e]	Recommendation[f]
Not enough testers were initially assigned to the project	N/A	Caused the testing process to lag behind the original schedule	N/A	Contracted 5 additional testers from a contract agency	Spend more resource planning in future projects
Defect tracking was not monitored adequately by development	N/A	Number of outstanding defects grew significantly	N/A	Authorized overtime for development	QA needs to stress the importance of defect tracking on a daily basis in future projects
Automated testing tools did contribute significantly to regression testing	N/A	Increased testing productivity	N/A	N/A	Utilize testing tools as much as possible
Excessive number of defects in one functional area	Reports	Caused a lot of developer rework time	N/A	Excessive developer overtime	Perform more technical design reviews early in the project
Functional area not compatible with other systems	Order Processing	Rework costs	Had to redesign the database	Contracted an Oracle database DBA	Perform more database design reviews early in the project
30 percent of defects had critical severity	N/A	Significantly impacted the development and testing effort	N/A	Hired additional development programmers	Perform more technical reviews early in the project and tighten up on the sign-off procedures

Function/GUI had the most defects	N/A	Required a lot of rework	N/A	Testers authorized overtime	Perform more technical reviews early in the project and tighten up on the sign-off procedures
Two test cases could not be completed because performance load test tool did not work properly	Stress testing order entry with 1000 terminals	Cannot guarantee system will perform adequately under extreme load conditions	N/A	Delay system delivery until new testing tool acquired (2 months delay at $85,000 loss in revenue, $10,000 for tool)	Loss of revenue overshadows risk. Ship system but acquire performance test tool and complete stress test

[a] This includes a description of the problem found from the defect information recorded in the defect tracking database. It could also include test team, test procedures, or test environment findings and recommendations.

[b] Describes the business function that was involved and affected.

[c] Describes the effect the finding will have on the operational system. The impact should be described only as major (the defect would cause the application system to produce incorrect results) or minor (the system is incorrect, but the results will be correct).

[d] Describes where the finding will affect application systems other than the one being tested. If the finding affects other development teams, they should be involved in the decision on whether to correct the problem.

[e] Management must know both the costs and the benefits before it can make a decision on whether to install the system without the problem being corrected.

[f] Describes the recommendation from the test team on what action to take.

the ground rule that if time expires before completing all items on the agenda, a follow-on review will be scheduled.

The purpose of this task is for development and the project sponsor to agree and accept the test report. If there are any suggested changes to the report during the review, they should be incorporated.

Task 2: Obtain Approvals

Approval is critical in a testing effort, because it helps provide the necessary agreement among testing, development, and the sponsor. The best approach is with a formal sign-off procedure of a test plan. If this is the case, use the management approval sign-off forms. However, if a formal agreement procedure is not in place, send a memo to each key participant, including at least the project manager, development manager, and sponsor. In the document, attach the latest test plan and point out that all their feedback comments have been incorporated and that if you do not hear from them, it is assumed that they agree with the plan. Finally, indicate that in a spiral development environment, the test plan will evolve with each iteration but that you will include them in any modification.

Task 3: Publish the Final Test Report

The test report is finalized with the suggestions from the review and distributed to the appropriate parties. The purpose has short- and long-term objectives.

The short-term objective is to provide information to the software user to determine if the system is ready for production. It also provides information about outstanding issues, including testing not completed or outstanding problems, and recommendations.

The long-term objectives are to provide information to the project regarding how it was managed and developed from a quality point of view. The project can use the report to trace problems if the system malfunctions in production, for example, defect-prone functions that had the most errors and which ones were not corrected. The project and organization also have the opportunity to learn from the current project. A determination of which development, project management, and testing procedures worked, and which didn't work, or need improvement, can be invaluable to future projects.

Section IV
Test Project
Management

TEST PROJECT MANAGEMENT

Project management, according to the American Society for Quality (ASQ), is the application of knowledge, skills, tools and techniques to meet the requirements of a project. Project management knowledge and practices are best described as a set of processes. A critical project process is software testing. The following section describes the implementation considerations for managing this endeavor.

The objectives of this section are to:

- Describe basic project management principles.
- Contrast general project management and test management.
- Describe how to effectively estimate testing projects.
- Describe the defect management subprocess.
- Discuss the advantages and disadvantages of the offshore and onshore models.
- List the steps for integrating the testing activity into the development methodology.

Part 21
Overview of General Project Management

Although project management is considered as a fast emerging profession that is being consolidated with planning and execution of multiple projects, it remained in its nondefinitional form for centuries. Project management can be traced back to the architectural monuments built in the earlier centuries. Each one of these architectural marvels was itself a project that was initiated, planned, executed, controlled, and closed. One can visualize the amount of planning and execution activities involved in the evolution of the pyramids in Egypt, the hanging gardens of Babylon, or the battles fought by Caesar. Project management had its roots in the construction industry for centuries; however, it gained the current popularity only through software project management activities.

The shortening of software project life cycles (where the start date and end date of the projects are determined in advance) has highlighted the importance of project management activities. Project planning and execution have gained increased popularity because many projects had not reached their logical goals within the stipulated time sequence, due to poor planning There are numerous examples in the software industry where a project that has not been systematically planned and executed has resulted in failure and been cancelled by the project sponsors.

Although the knowledge and experience of the project team contributes to the project's success or failure, it is the project management approach employed by the project manager that is the key factor influencing the success of a project. The following are some project management characteristics that dramatically improve the probability of successful projects.

Define the Objectives

The following is a well-known quote that illustrates the importance of project objectives.

> If you don't know where you are going you are guaranteed to get there.
>
> **Lewis Carroll,** *Alice in Wonderland*

If one studies the history of unsuccessful projects, it is evident that unclear objectives are the primary culprit in failure. Ever-changing requirements, without considering the effect on project objectives, may be the single most critical factor that contributes to a project failure. A useful technique at the project manager's disposal is a requirement change matrix that helps synchronize the completion of the project within the planned date.

As an example of project objectives, a company that wishes to migrate its application to a more robust database and system with multiple platforms and applications could define the project objectives as follows:

- Eliminate cost to support multiple operating systems.
- Eliminate the operational and credit risk by improving data integrity.
- Provide a robust, 24/7, downtime free service to the clients.

Define the Scope of the Project

The project manager needs to clearly define the project scope. If the project scope is not clear, the project manager cannot define a comprehensive planning and execution strategy. It is not possible to follow the waterfall model in a spiral development environment where it is impossible to freeze requirements before one starts planning and designing activities. But as a prudent project manager, one should freeze the higher-level objectives and deliverables of the project before pursuing major design activities. When directions are imposed to initiate the project with unclear objectives, document the risks and assumptions, and convey it to the project sponsors.

Identify the Key Activities

When the project scope is reasonably clear and documented, identify all the possible key activities that need to be accomplished to reach the objectives. This is necessary because each activity that contributes to the project is included within its own schedule and cost implications. If any one of these key activities is not accounted for, the project manager will be viewed as disorganized.

Estimate Correctly

Cost estimation is another critical factor that determines the success or failure of most software projects. Some examples of cost include:

- Software
- People resources
- Infrastructure and other costs
- Training

Various estimation models have emerged to estimate the schedule and cost for projects. From function points, COCOMO to domain-specific, project-specific cost estimation models it is the responsibility of the project manager to choose the best project estimation model. Unless a project manager is able to identify the activity that needs to be performed for completing the project, the estimate tends to explode and eventually affect the cost, schedule, and the project deliverables. Prudence should be exercised to choose the best model. Always apply a margin for error in the estimation.

The basic COCOMO model estimates the effort required to develop software in three modes of development (organic, semidetached, or embedded mode) using only DSI (delivered source instructions) as an input. The basic model is good for quick, early, and rough order-of-magnitude estimates.

Design

As with requirements, design is one more crucial activity that requires focus by the project managers. In the software industry, where new technology emerges every other day, the project manager should foresee the changes while designing the application. The corporate charter and goals should be given due consideration when identifying the advantages of the emerging technologies. For example, when the corporate goal projects five million users growth over the decade, if the designs are based on the existing technology, scaling up the problem may crop up after a few years and the application will not survive the test of time. This will incur additional expenses for the company that could have been avoided had the corporate goals been considered while designing.

But just because new technologies emerge, the project manager should avoid the tendency to choose it unless it is warranted by the business corporate goals. For example, if the corporate growth is projected for 10 million users over the next five years, it would be imprudent to embrace technology that caters to 100 million users.

While designing, the design constraints and alternatives should also be considered. The project manager should identify and manage the explicit and implicit design constraints.

Manage People

Team members' under performance is the source of most software project failures. This is one of the crucial factors that a project manager must consider. Choosing the right people for the right job is a challenging project management task. Motivation and retention is an art that the project manager must master.

Leadership

Leadership is one of the crucial factors in project management. A leader should lead by example. There is considerable difference between a manager and leader. Anybody can manage a well-established system, whereas a leader alone will take the organization to greater heights. The leader should align herself with the company vision and establish the direction for the team.

Motivating and inspiring the team to accomplish its targets is one of the primary leadership qualities. Retention is another crucial factor in the software projects. Attrition at the critical stages of projects will certainly affect the progress of the project. Promotions, pay hikes, and other fringe benefits alone are not sufficient to motivate a leader. Challenging projects are one of the contributing factors for retention of a leader's talents. The leader should have the necessary independence to choose the appropriate resources for the project. Simply dumping an available resource into the project may cause havoc, because projects are time-bound activities, not training grounds.

Although there is speculation among project management experts that project managers need not be technical specialists, the knowledge in functional and technical areas is an added advantage for a project manager to manage the projects effectively.

Leadership traits are best described by sixth-century B.C. Chinese wisdom as follows:

> A leader is best when his [colleagues] scarcely know that he exists.
>
> Bad when they fear him. Worse when they despise him.
>
> But of a good leader, at the end of the day, when his work is done and his goals achieved, they will all say, "We did this ourselves."

Communication

Communication is another key factor in the success of all projects. When the project leader is unable to clearly communicate the project objectives to the project team the communication gap arises, which affects the quality of the project. It is the responsibility of the project leader to communicate in a clear unambiguous manner and to communicate effectively. Similarly, individuals receiving direction should also ensure that the message is understood on the same wavelength as it is passed from the sender.

In the virtual world where global and physical distance do not make any difference, clear communication is an essential contributor for the successful and fruitful completion of the goals. Establishing clear communication channels is the primary responsibility of the project manager, irrespective of whether the communication is written, verbal, listening or speaking, or internal or external to the projects.

Solving Problems

As projects are always constrained by time and scope, cost problems always emerge. Project management does not end after preparing a detailed project plan that includes the risks and assumptions for the project. It is the primary responsibility of the project manager to continue analyzing these risks while the project is in progress. In the event that any of these risks are materializing, action must be taken to solve the issues.

The problem root causes should be identified and the necessary action must be initiated to solve the problems. The project manager should be able to distinguish between the causes and problems and should take appropriate decisions to solve the problems before they explode to a greater level.

Continuous Monitoring

The project manager must always align the project activities with the project goals. The project should be monitored at the macrolevel. Several projects that have been managed by technical gurus have failed simply for the reason that they have been micromanaged. Continuous monitoring helps to identify the symptoms in the earlier stages and will help to resolve them at the proper time before further damage is caused to the project. The following tips will help the project manager perform effective monitoring:

- Daily status and activity report
- Weekly progress report
- Risk and assumptions analysis report
- Review reports
- Downtime reports
- Defect reports

There are several software tools available for project and task scheduling; however, comprehensive project progress monitoring cannot be satisfied by a software tool. Project monitoring requires a great deal of diligence from the experience of the project manager and the decision needs to be taken early rather than waiting until a problem escalates.

Manage Changes

Change management is yet another critical activity for effective project management. There are several software tools available for the project managers to monitor the changes to occur in the requirements, schedule, and environments. Changes in the scope and time have far-reaching implications for the project deliverables. When the project is inundated with scope creep, the project manager should reassess the cost and time implications and should convey them to the project sponsors.

Change management in the development and test environment for code promotion is yet another area that requires much disciplined activity from the project team. There exist very good version control software products such as PVCS. Although general management consists of planning, organizing, staffing, executing, and controlling an ongoing operation, a project manager should possess additional skills of estimation and scheduling as projects are specific activities with definite start and end dates. Functional knowledge, technical knowledge, and management experience will help produce better project managers.

Each project will complete with specific deliverables such as a specification document and functional software. But within the project life cycle, each cycle will consist of an entry and exit criterion. At the end of every exit criterion the project manager should assess the situation and decide whether it is appropriate to move to the next phase of the project.

A program is a group of projects managed in coordinated ways. When the project manager matures and starts managing multiple projects he becomes a program manager.

Program managers with technical and development experience derive the futuristic vision of the product or company, create design, and define strategy for all aspects. They understand the nuances of project management and guide the project managers.

Part 22
Test Project Management

In the previous chapter we have discussed the concepts of project management. Within project management a number of new management hierarchies are emerging due to the continuous expansion occurring in software project management. The responsibilities that have been executed by a single person are now divided into multiple positions and responsibilities due to the size of the projects. Below are some of the familiar titles we hear:

- Program manager
- Technical project manger
- Development project manager
- Quality assurance manager
- Test project manager
- Configuration manager
- Release manager
- System manager
- Resource manager

In past years these responsibilities were shouldered by a single individual.

Test project management has emerged as a specialized management activity in the last couple of years. This section analyzes how the test project manager differs from the other project manager roles and how the test project manager distinguishes himself in his roles and responsibilities.

In previous years, software testing was a subset of the software development life cycle and developers performed the validation in the software programs coded by them and released them to the users for verification of the critical business flows before implementing to production. The volume of business losses due to the inherent bugs in the systems has led the business to consider the concept of independent verification and validation. Verification is ensuring that the test specification is satisfied whereas validation ensures that the original business objectives are satisfied. Validation is commonly related to user acceptance testing. Inasmuch as developers do not like to break their own code, which is their brainchild, the concept of independent testing has gained more attention.

Historically, the development team construes themselves as the creators of the system and the QA community is considered a necessary evil. This is more prevalent when there is an independent testing group. As the test team often works in a hostile atmosphere, they need to equip themselves more strongly in both functional and testing skills. The test team should be involved during the requirement and functional specification stages. In recent years, major losses caused in the financial and insurance sectors have forced the stakeholders to involve the test team even in the requirement stage.

The following are some best practice testing principles to increase the probability of the project's success.

Understand the Requirements

Although the developers concentrate on their programs and modules, the test team needs to understand the overall application. If a programmer understands the functional and design specifications of the functions assigned to her, she can perform well. But the testers should broaden their vision to understand the entire functionality of the application. Testers should be comfortable with the inputs, expected results, data flow between modules, and between interfaces. Unless they have a thorough knowledge of the functionality of the system it is difficult to gain overall insight into the application. Thus, before the tester pursues testing an application, considerable time needs to be spent understanding the complexities of the application functionality.

The knowledge in the business and application system will help the test managers to:

- Create a complete and meaningful test plan and test cases for the application.
- Substantiate the tester's arguments while defending defects discovered in the system.
- Improve leadership capabilities by extending help to other testers.
- Suggest valid improvements to the system.

Unless the test project manager is comfortable in the business domain in which he is operating, it is difficult for him to critically evaluate the test conditions and cases. Because testing often occurs at the end of the development cycle, unless the test project manager understands the application requirements, it is difficult to deliver quality software to the end users.

Test Planning

The 70:30 project management concept considers two different types of project managers. Structural planning is the basis for sound testing. Instead of unstructured planning, a good test project manager spends 70 percent of the time systematically planning and preparing the test strategy, testware, and test execution methodologies. The result is a quality application delivered within scheduled timelines.

The test project manager should be proactive to:

- Decide on the proper strategy depending upon the types of testing required.
- Prepare the test cases and scripts.
- Review all the test documents.
- Implement traceability to ensure good test coverage.
- Plan the data requirements and availability.
- Plan the execution schedule.

Test Execution

The role of a tester is to ensure that no known bugs exist in the system. A tester coming from a development background probably has the natural instincts to test the positive flow and avoid exceptions, or negative conditions.

To overcome this, the tester needs to change his perspective. He needs to crack the system, create implicit test conditions and cases, and see the system from a user perspective. The role of QA/testing is gaining more importance because:

- Many systems in production are still afflicted with bugs.
- Defects lead to unexpected downtime for the business.
- The financial loss caused due to bugs and downtime is too high,
- The corporation's board is becoming responsible for the unexpected business loss due to bugs, and
- Bugs in mission-critical applications can be catastrophic.

The test manager must perform his role by verifying and validating the system from the business user requirement. Even if hundred of defects are discovered by the QA/tester, it is common to not be appreciated when one unknown defect is unearthed in production.

Identify and Improve Processes

Although test managers work within defined boundaries of processes and procedures established within their work environment, there is always room for continuous process improvement. The following useful tips will expedite continuous process improvement:

- *Process Improvement* — Identify the loose ends in the process and bridge the gaps with innovative quality improvement processes. However, there is always is scope when improving any process.

- *Defect Analysis* — Analyze the pattern in the defects identified in the previous releases of the application and tighten the test cases to capture the hidden defects.
- *Requirements Review* — Perform a complete review for ambiguous statements in the requirements documents, which may give rise to different interpretations and ultimately to bugs in the system.
- *Risk Mitigation* — Expect the unexpected and always have a contingency plan upon which to fall back. Continuously review the risk and mitigation plan during the planning and execution phase of testing.

Essential Characteristics of a Test Project Manager

The test project manager is a key element in ensuring a quality application. The following are some key activities that will help maximize the efficiency of the test project manager.

Requirement Analysis

Business users do not have to be superior communicators of their requirements. The business analysts will document the business user requirements. When business users sign off on the requirement documents they implicitly assume certain conditions based on their intuitive knowledge in the business. The test manager should consider these implicit conditions also while writing and reviewing the test conditions. If an implicit condition is not tested, then the testing is not complete and it will not certainly satisfy the end-user requirements.

Gap Analysis

The gaps among the requirement document and functional and design specifications may explode like a grenade when the project goes live and a typical business scenario emerges. The test project manager should spend considerable time analyzing the gap between the requirements and specifications so that the rework costs will be minimal. A gap document will demonstrate the gaps between these two documents and provide confidence to the business regarding their final requirements. Gaps (if any) in the other baseline documents such as use cases or architecture should also be analyzed by the test project manager.

Lateral Thinking in Developing Test Cases

The test project manager should exhibit lateral thinking in designing the test cases. Thinking beyond the perceived client expectations brings out critical business issues that would otherwise crop up at a later stage in production. The test project manager should analyze the assumptions, risks, and design considerations and constitute special test cases to test them.

Avoid Duplication and Repetition

The ability and efficiency of the test project manager is exhibited when the test cases are comprehensive with full coverage and are not repetitive. Executing the same type of test cases for different conditions reduces the efficiency and consumes more effort of the testers. Equivalence clause partitioning is a testing technique (see Appendix G) that should be used so that the business functions that are tested in a set of test cases are not repeated in multiple test cases.

Test Data Generation

It is the responsibility of the test manager to ensure that all the test cases generated are executed with the required test data. Test data generation is a vital part of the test planning activity. The data guidelines should be generated during the test planning stage to ensure that all the data required for executing all the test cases is made available in the test environment.

Validate the Test Environment

The test environment should be defined in the test strategy document. All the interfaces that are required to execute the test cases should be available or the testers will not be able to complete their tests. The test manager should prepare a checklist for testing the environment before executing the test cases.

Test to Destroy

The test manager's attitude should be to break the software with effective test cases. Test cases should be designed in such a way that all possible live situations are visualized and represented as test cases. As mentioned above, the lateral thinking will help the test manager to prepare critical test cases that may at times cause the software to crash. If the test cases are prepared with this killer attitude, they will make hidden bugs in the system surface.

Analyze the Test Results

The testing does not end with the successful execution of test cases and reporting of defects as they arise. The test manager should analyze the results of all the test cases to ensure that they behave as expected. Sometimes the analysis will bring out the hidden test cases that were not visualized while preparing the test cases. For example, the specification document will define the norms for a start date, tenure, and end date for a product. The implicit test condition needs to be designed to check that the start date couldn't be greater than the end date.

For performance testing, analysis is an important step in the testing process. The test manager should be equipped to analyze the performance test results and interpret them. The baseline performance measures should be compared with the results and recommendations should be made for better tuning of the system.

Do Not Hesitate to Accept Help from Others

The more a test manager is flexible, the higher the probability that the software will be stable in a shorter testing life cycle. Instead of assuming and taking things for granted, the test manager and team can approach the business users to verify and validate the test results. For example, in the case of performance tests where more technical knowledge is required to analyze the test results, the developer can be consulted.

Convey Issues as They Arise

When they arise, the various issues during test execution should be conveyed to the stakeholders. This will help to reduce the test cycle time. The status report and progressive reports on test planning and execution should be elaborate enough to provide top management a realistic evaluation of the testing processes.

Improve Communication

Communication between various teams is a vital aspect for the test project management. The communication should convey the required message and should be addressed to the correct person for whom it is intended. It is the responsibility of the communicator to make the recipient understand the view on the same wavelength. Improper communication has caused projects to fail. Unlike development, testing requires effective communication whereby the test managers and testers need to communicate and influence various other groups.

Always Keep Updating Your Business Knowledge

It is because of that business the software industry survives. Software development exists to support the business. If there were no business, most of the software companies would cease to exist. Updating business knowledge is an ongoing process for the test managers and team. Unless the test manager is very strong in business knowledge, she will not be able to convince the developers or business of the importance of the defects that have been discovered in the system.

Learn the New Testing Technologies and Tools

The software industry is one of the most fast-changing industries with new technologies emerging every day. If the test manager does not update himself with the changing technologies he will be outdated. More efficient software testing tools are emerging. From the first generation tools, now fourth generation software-testing tools are arriving. If the test project manager does not update his knowledge of these tools, his effort estimation will suffer which will affect the cost and time of the project.

Deliver Quality

The ultimate purpose of software testing is to deliver quality that is measured by what the user originally wanted. It is the primary responsibility of the test project manager to also deliver quality software. The software should be tested completely for the requirements and the test project manager should ensure full coverage.

Improve the Process

With every project the test project manager learns new concepts that will refresh her test processes. The test process should undergo continuous process improvement.

Create a Knowledge Base

The expertise gathered in various projects should be documented so that the knowledge is reused in other projects. It is the responsibility of the test project manager to document the positive and negative factors that were encountered in each test project execution.

Repeat the Success

This is illustrated in testing when the test team defines implicit conditions from the requirements documents. Everyone thinks in a different way but think logically. Place yourself in the shoes of the business users. The test manager's interaction with other project members may give rise to different perspectives, which will fine-tune your test cases to unearth a hidden bug.

Part 23
Test Estimation

When faced with a critical schedule crunch, a key question is whether one is managing the test project or the project is managing the project manager (PM). Testing activities, cost, and schedule are estimated by project management. Unfortunately, systematic testing efforts are not considered when the overall project schedule is defined. The test project manager is typically not brought into a project until the project has already progressed halfway. The project manager is normally requested to work within the predefined schedule for the testing effort. In this case, the project is going to manage the test project manager. Because of the late involvement, the PM is unable to make a retrospective test estimation effort and/or readjust the schedule. In this section some estimation best practices for the test project management are discussed.

Effort estimation is concerned with the cost of resources needed to complete a project. In software testing projects the following are the major costs having an impact on resources:

- Number of testers required for the project and the cost of hiring them
- Cost of hardware and other administrative requirements for them to work during the project
- The software cost that needs to be installed on the machines, including the cost of automation tools required for testing

Finalizing the testing scope is the primary task of the test project manager to start the effort estimation. The work breakdown structure (WBS) is the widely used technique to estimate the effort. For testing projects the scope is divided into smaller tasks to a granular level of estimating how much one person can accomplish in one day. This is called a person day. The total number of person days is defined and the number of resources required to complete the tasks is estimated.

The sample project plan shown in Exhibits 23.1 and 23.2 defines the typical tasks that are performed in a testing project.

Of the various activities in the project plan, planning and execution are the key activities that determine the cost of resources and schedules required for the testing projects. During these two crucial phases of testing, various key deliverables are estimated. This will ensure the test team

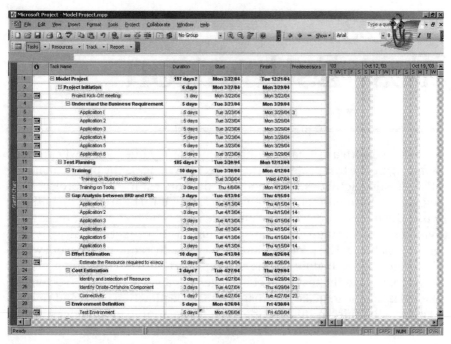

Exhibit 23.1. Sample Project Plan

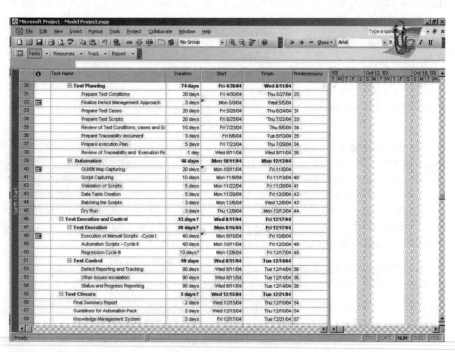

Exhibit 23.2. Sample Project Plan (continued)

will have a focused approach and the delivery of the deliverables will bring each task to a logical end so that the project can proceed with the next task in the plan. However, it is not always necessary that a particular task should be completed to start the next task. The project manager should analyze the task dependencies. A task dependency is the relationship between two tasks in which one task depends on the start or finish of another task in order to begin or end. The task that depends on the other task is the successor, and the task it depends on is the predecessor.

The following describe some typical test dependencies and why they are important to test management.

Finish-to-Start: (FS)

Task (B) cannot start until task (A) finishes. For example, if you have two tasks "Test Script writing" and "Test Execution," "Test Execution" can't start until "Test Script writing" completes. This is the most common type of dependency.

Start-to-Start: (SS)

Task (B) cannot start until task (A) starts. For example, if we have two tasks "Test Script writing" and "Run Plan preparation," "Run Plan preparation" can't begin until "Test Script writing" starts.

Finish-to-Finish: (FF)

Task (B) cannot finish until task (A) finishes. For example, if you have two tasks, "Test Execution complete" and "Test Closure Report," "Test Closure Report" can't finish until "Test Execution complete" finishes.

Start-to-Finish (SF)

Task (B) cannot finish until task (A) starts. This dependency type can be used for "just-in-time scheduling" up to a milestone or the project finish date to minimize the risk of a task finishing late, if its dependent task slips. This dependency type applies when a related task needs to finish before a milestone or project finish date. However, it does not matter exactly when and one does not want a late finish to affect the just-in-time task. You can create an SF dependency between the task you want scheduled just in time (the predecessor) and its related task (the successor). Then if you update the progress on the successor task, it won't affect the scheduled dates of the predecessor task.

Critical Activities for Test Estimation

Test scope document, test strategy, test conditions, test cases, test scripts, traceability, and test execution/run plan are the critical activities for the test planning phase. The number of test iterations and the defect management process are the critical activities during the execution stage.

The following describe each testing activity.

Test Scope Document

The scope of testing is derived from the various baseline documents available for testing the application. They may be the business requirement document, functional specification document, technical design documents, use case documents, documentation manuals available for the application, or even the application under test itself. While arriving at the scope of testing the test manager should consider the various dependent applications that are required to execute the tests such as interfaces between the applications. Unless the scope of testing is complete one cannot proceed with the estimation.

Test Strategy

A test strategy outlines what to plan and how to plan it. An unrealistic test strategy leads to untested software whereas a successful strategy is a foundation for testing success. A well-planned test strategy ensures a well-designed product can be successfully released to achieve the fullest potential in the market. The purpose of the strategy is to clarify the major tasks and approach toward the test project. It should be very clear, unambiguous, and specific to the objective of the project.

Test strategies can cover a wide range of testing and business topics, such as:

- Overview of the client, project, and application
- Scope of testing
- Inclusions, exclusions, and assumptions
- Plans for recruitment, team structure, and training
- Test management, metrics, and improvement
- Test environment, change control, and release strategy
- Test techniques, test data, and test planning
- Roles and responsibilities
- High-level schedule
- Entry and exit criteria
- Defect reporting and monitoring process
- Regression test processes
- Performance test analysis approach
- Test automation and test tool assessment
- Approaches to risk assessment, costs, and quality through the organization
- Sign-off criteria and analysis
- Deliverable of the test project

Test Condition

A test condition is an abstract extraction of the testable requirements from the baseline documents. Test conditions may be explicitly or implicitly in the requirement documents. A test condition has one or more associated test cases.

Test Case

A test case is a set of test inputs, execution conditions, and expected results developed for a particular objective to validate a specific functionality in the application under test.

The intensity of the testing is proportional to the number of test cases. Confidence in the quality of the product and test process is established when the number of test cases increases. This is true because each test case reflects different condition scenarios, or business flow, in the application under test. Test cases form the foundation to design and develop test scripts.

Test Script

A test script is the collection or set of related test cases arranged in the execution flow for testing specific business functionality. A test script contains the conditions tested, number of test cases tested in that script, prerequisites, test data required for the testing, and instructions to verify the test results.

The advantage of test scripts is that someone other than the individual who prepared the test script can execute it. This provides repeatability and helps when additional resources are deployed during the peak period of test execution.

Execution/Run Plan

The execution/run plan addresses the logical sequence and dependent execution of the test scripts. For example, the batch run dates must be matched with the business functionalities scripts before arriving at the execution plan. This logical sequencing of test cases and scripts will help the test project manager effectively monitor the execution progress. The stakeholders can be updated on the status of the project.

Factors Affecting Test Estimation

While estimating the test effort, the test project manager should consider the following factors:

- Stability and availability of the test environment
- The turnaround time for review of testware

- Availability of required test professionals and their expertise levels in functionality and testing concepts
- Timely delivery of the software for testing
- Availability of external and internal interfaces attached to the application under testing
- The change management process planned for promoting code after fixing the bugs
- Risk escalation and mitigation procedure
- The turnaround time for bug fixes
- Choice of automation tools and required expertise
- Timely completion of earlier test execution such as unit testing
- Number of stakeholders and the business issue resolution turnaround time
- Availability of estimated test data

Test Planning Estimation

Of the various test planning activities, the effort required to prepare the test conditions, test cases, test scripts, test data, and execution plan are critical. There are other deliverables that consume the effort of the test team such as traceability and the dependency matrix, resource allocations, and other project management deliverables. Normally 15 percent of total effort is spent by these activities but may vary depending upon the project. The project manager should use prudence when deciding the time required for all other activities and include them in the effort. Normally the test conditions are prepared first and mapped with the business requirement documents to ensure coverage. The test conditions are further extrapolated into test cases by establishing the various data values required to extensively test a condition.

It is recommended that the entire application be decomposed into various modules and subapplications and for each of those applications testware developed (conditions, cases, scripts) that will help to scope out the estimation effort. However, the test conditions and test cases do not always require the same effort. Test conditions/cases are further drilled down to complex, medium, and simple conditions/cases. Deciding the complexity of the conditions/cases requires the collective wisdom, technical, and functional expertise of the entire project team.

The number of test conditions/cases, and the time to prepare each of those complex, medium, and simple scripts constitute the major effort of the test planning activity. Prudence of the project manager and the expertise of the team will help to define the work effort. Sometimes, sample conditions/cases or scripts will be created for a particular application and the logic will be extended to other applications for estimating the effort.

In addition to critical testware such as conditions, cases, and scripts, the time required for other planning activities such as the preparation of the test plan, strategy, review of each of these testware deliverables, and preparation of the run/execution plan should be taken into consideration to arrive at the cumulative test planning effort.

Test Execution and Controlling Effort

The execution test estimation effort is influenced by the following factors:

- The complexity level of the test conditions and cases
- The number of iterations planned
- The defect fix turnaround time agreed upon in the strategy
- Availability of the required data
- Number and type of batch runs planned (for mainframe applications)
- Defect management and resolution process
- Change management process

The test project manager should use judgment in defining the effort required to execute the complex, medium, and simple scripts. The following should also be estimated to determine the total effort required in the execution phase:

- Number of test cycles planned for the test execution phase
- Number of interfaces with the application
- Number of batch runs

Test Result Analysis

This is another critical activity that is very important to ensure that the software is developed according to the requirement specifications. The functional test automation and script capturing activities referred to in the project plan should be taken into consideration in the estimation. The test automation approach, the number of iterations of load and stress testing, and analysis effort of the test results also should be added to the effort. This varies among the projects and the functional area of the project and the experience level of the test managers and team.

Effort Estimation — Model Project

The following describes how to effectively use an estimation template.

The critical activities for effort estimation involving functional testing are defined in the model. The time for each of these activities is arrived at based on the parameters defined and the experiences from the project team. Exhibit 23.3 shows the tasks with which the project manager, test lead, and test engineer are typically associated.

Exhibit 23.3. Activities for Estimating Effort

Test Initiation and Planning		Resources
Understanding the application		PM^aTL^b
Training the rest of the team members/ambiguity review	TE^c	TL
Project plan/test strategy		PM
Test conditions/scenarios	TE	
Review of test conditions		PM
Test cases	TE	
Test scripts	TE	
Internal review of test scripts		PM
Preparation of coverage/trace matrix	TE	TL
Data requirements/guidelines	TE	TL
Preparation of run plan		TL
Internal review of run plan		PM
Sign off by business		
Test Execution		
Day 0 verification - environment check		PM
Validation of test scripts with application	TE	TL
Iteration 1 (100 percent) (execution & defect review)	TE	TL
Iteration 2 (50 percent) (execution & defect review)	TE	TL
Iteration 3 (50 percent) (automation)	TE	PM
Test Closure		
Final report preparation		PM
Business review and sign off		

^a PM Project Manager
^b TL Test Lead
^c TE Test Engineer

Test cases are classified as simple, medium, and complex based upon the time preparation and execution times for these scripts. The baseline times required by project management activities and other project-related activities are estimated and entered into Exhibit 23.4.

Exhibit 23.5 shows the total effort for test planning, test execution, and test closure activities separately for test engineers and test project managers. The total person days are calculated for each of these effort parameters and total person months are calculated. Normally 22 working days are

Exhibit 23.4. Baseline Effort Estimation

Condition to Case	
Simple	1
Medium	3
Complex	5
Buffer	20%
Case to Script	
10	1

No. of Test Cases per Day	
Planning	**Execution**[b]
30	15

No. of Test Scripts per Day	
Planning	**Execution**[a]
2	1

Timelines	
Day-Hr	8
Week-Day	5
Month-Day	22

Project Schedule	
Planning	**Execution**
35	25

Note: Project Baselines — Values can be changed depending on the project requirements.

[a] Including bug/defect regression.

taken for a month to arrive at a person month. The exhibit also shows that the total number of individuals required can be calculated, which is calculated from the person months. If the test execution schedule is already defined in the overall milestone project plan, one can estimate the number of resources required to complete the project within the given time.

Exhibit 23.5. Total Effort and Number of Individuals Required

No.	Resource	Test Planning / Scripting	Test Execution	Test Closure	Total
		(All Effort in Person Days)			
1	Test Engineers				
2	Project Manager/Test Lead				
	Total Person Days				
	Total Person Months	60.0	30.0	10.0	100.0
	Ratio	60.0%	30.0%	10.0%	100.0%
Person Months (Only TE Effort)		0	0	0	0
Team Size		4	3	0	7

The project team should establish the baseline as to how many test conditions, test cases, and test scripts can be prepared and executed by the individual tester per day. This is critical to this estimate and will differ on different projects. Similarly, review activities should be calculated as a percentage of the critical activity for each of those activities.

The project management activity should take into consideration the defect management process, daily defect meeting, conference calls, and other meetings expected during the planning and execution stages of the projects.

Part 24
Defect Monitoring and Management Process

A defect is a product anomaly. Any variation found in the product that does not comply with business requirements or business is considered a defect. No product can be produced with 100 percent perfection and the product becomes completely acceptable to the business with the continuous improvements over a period of time. Each product has its own life cycle.

During the software testing, the test engineers find various types of defects that need to be reported to the owners of the system and the developers to carry out the required modifications. Defect reporting and tracking the defects to closure are important activities of the test project management. During the test execution phase a defect report (see Appendix E12) is produced and circulated to the stakeholders and a defect meeting is arranged periodically to evaluate the "correctness" of the defect so that the developers can modify the code.

The test strategy document (see Appendix E16) specifies the defect management process for the project. It clearly spells out the test engineer's behavior when she finds a defect in the system. Numerous defect management tools are available for logging in and monitoring the defects. Some of the popular defect management tools are described in Section V, Modern Software Testing Tools.

Test engineers will prepare the defect log (see Appendix E9) noting when they encountered errors while testing. This forms the basis for recording the defects into the database. The test log documents a chronological record of the relevant details of each test. This includes the results of the test, including discrepancies between the expected and actual results.

The test report (see Appendix E12) summarizes the discrepancies in the test log. It includes the expected and actual test results, the environment, and so forth. In addition, relevant information to help isolate the problem

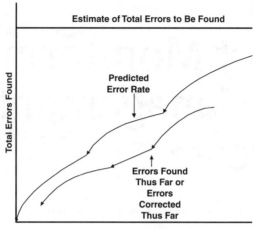

Exhibit 24.1. Defect Tracking

is documented. Every defect must be analyzed and entered into the error tracking system. Trend curves should be published periodically. There are many ways to graphically illustrate the error trends.

Some trend curves are:

- Total errors found over time
- Errors found by cause, for example, operator and program errors
- Errors found by how found, for example, discovered by user
- Errors found by system, for example, order entry or accounts receivable
- Errors found by the responsible organization, for example, support group or operations

Exhibit 24.1 shows a graph of time versus the number of errors detected and the predicted error rate provides an estimate of progress toward completion. This shows whether error correction is a bottleneck in the test process. If so, additional development resources should be assigned. It also demonstrates the difference between the predicted and actual error rates relative to the total number of projected errors.

Defect Reporting

A defect report describes defects in software and documentation. Defect reports have a priority rating that indicates the impact the problem has on the customer. The defects will be reported using a standard format with the following information:

- Defect number
- Defect date

- Module ID
- Test case/script number
- Test case description
- Expected result
- Defect description
- Severity
- Defect category
- Status
- Responsibility
- Defect log
- Developer's comment
- Tester's comment
- Client comment

Defect Meetings

Defect meetings are the best way to disseminate information among the testers, analysts, development, and the business.

- Meetings are conducted at the end of every day between the test team and development team to discuss test execution and defects. This is where the defects are formally categorized in terms of the defect type and severity.
- Before the defect meetings with the development team, the test team should have internal discussions with the test project manager on the defects reported. This process ensures that all defects are accurate and authentic to the best knowledge of the test team.

Defect Classifications

Defects that are detected by the tester are classified into categories based upon the defect. This helps test planning and prioritization. The following are some sample classifications that can vary depending upon the requirement of the project:

- *Showstopper (X):* The impact of the defect is severe and the system cannot be tested without resolving the defect because an interim solution may not be available.
- *Critical (C):* The impact of the defect is severe; however, an interim solution is available. The defect should not hinder the test process in any way.
- *Noncritical (N):* All defects that are not in the X or C category are deemed to be in the N category. These are also the defects that could potentially be resolved via documentation and user training. These can be GUI defects or some minor field-level observations. Exhibit 24.2 depicts the life cycle flow of the defects. A defect has the initial state of "New" and eventually has a "Closed" state.

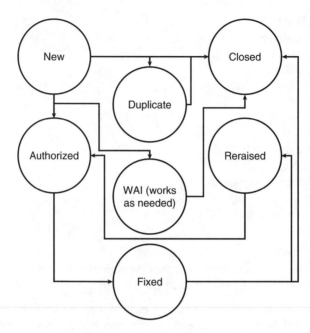

Exhibit 24.2. Defect Life Cycle

Defect Priority

Priority is allotted to the defects either while entering them in the defect reports or on the basis of the discussions in the defect meetings. The scheduled defect fixing is based upon the assigned priority. The following are the most common priority types:

- *High:* Further development and testing cannot occur until the defect has been repaired. The software system cannot be used until the repair is done.
- *Medium:* The defect must be resolved as soon as possible because it is impairing development and testing activities. Software system use will be severely affected until the defect is fixed.
- *Low:* The defect is an irritant that should be repaired but which can be repaired after a more serious defect has been fixed.

Defect Category

Defects are categorized into different categories as per the testing strategy. The following are the major categories of defects normally identified in a testing project.

- *Works as Intended (WAI):* Test cases to be modified. This may arise when the tester's understanding may be incorrect.

- *Discussion Items:* Arises when there is a difference of opinion between the test and the development team. This is marked to the domain consultant for final verdict.
- *Code Change:* Arises when the development team has to fix the bug.
- *Data Related:* Arises when the defect is due to data and not coding.
- *User Training:* Arises when the defect is not severe or technically not feasible to fix; it is decided to train the user on the defect. This should ideally not be critical.
- *New Requirement:* Inclusion of functionality after discussion.
- *User Maintenance:* Masters and parameter maintained by the user causing the defect.
- *Observation:* Any other observation not classified in the above categories such as a user-perspective GUI defect.

Defect Metrics

The analysis of the defects can be done based on the severity, occurrence, and category of the defects. As an example, defect density is a metric, which gives the ratio of defects in specific modules to the total defects in the application. Further analysis and derivation of metrics can be done based on the various components of the defect management.

- *Defect Age:* Defect age is the time duration between the points of identification of the defect to the point of closure of the defect. This would give a fair idea on the defect set to be included for smoke test during regression.
- *Defect Density:* Defect density is usually calculated per thousand source lines of code (KSLOC) as shown below. This can be helpful in that a measure of defect density can be used to (1) predict the remaining defects when compared to the expected defect density, (2) determine if the amount of testing is sufficient, and (3) establish a database of standard defect densities.

$$Dd = D/KLSOC$$

where

D = the number of defects,
$KSLOC$ = the number of noncommented lines of source code (numbered per thousand), and
Dd = the actual defect density.

When one plots defect density versus module size, the curve is typically U-shaped and concaved upwards (see Exhibit 24.3). Very small and very large modules are associated with more bugs than those of intermediate size. A different way of viewing the same data is to plot lines of code per module versus total bugs. The curve looks roughly logarithmic and then flattens (corresponding to the minimum in the defect density curve), after

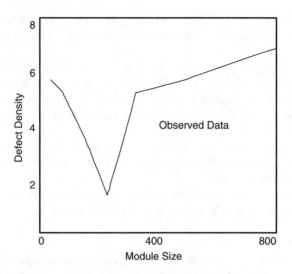

Exhibit 24.3. Defect Count and Density versus Module Size

which it goes up as the square of the number of the lines of code (which is what one might intuitively expect for the whole curve, following Brooks' Law).

Brooks' Law predicts that adding programmers to a late project makes it later. More generally, it predicts that costs and error rates rise as the square of the number of programmers on a project.

The increasing incidence of bugs at small module sizes holds across a wide variety of systems implemented in different languages and has been demonstrated by different studies.

Part 25
Integrating Testing into Development Methodology

The following describes testing as a process rather than a life cycle phase. A quality assurance department that treats testing as a life cycle phase should integrate the concepts in this section into its current systems development methodology. If the development methodology provides for testing throughout the design and maintenance methodology but is not well defined, the testing approach must be expanded and modified to correspond to the process described in this manual.

Testing must be integrated into the systems development methodology. Considered as a separate function, it may not receive the appropriate resources and commitment. Testing as an integrated function, however, prevents development from proceeding without testing.

The integration of testing into a systems development methodology is a two-part process.

1. The testing steps and tasks are integrated into the systems development methodology through addition or modification of tasks for developmental personnel to perform during the creation of an application system.
2. Defects must be recorded and captured. This process is the equivalent of problem reporting in operational application systems. The test manager must be able to capture information about the problems or defects that occur; without this information, it is difficult to improve testing.

Usually, the person responsible for the systems development methodology integrates testing into it. In many organizations, this is the quality assurance function. If no one is directly responsible for the systems development methodology, the test manager should assume responsibility for testing integration. If testing, which can take half of the total development effort, is not already an integral part of the current systems development methodology, the integration process will be especially time consuming.

Step 1. Organize the Test Team

Integrating a new test methodology is difficult and complex. Some organizations habitually acquire new design methodologies without fully implementing them, a problem that can be obviated with proper planning and management direction.

To make a test design methodology work, a team of key people from the testing function must be appointed to manage it. The group should be representative of the overall testing staff and respected by their peers. The test management team should consist of three to seven individuals. With fewer than three members, the interaction and energy necessary to successfully introduce the testing methodology may not occur. With more than seven members, management of the team becomes unwieldy.

Whether a supervisor is appointed chairperson of the test management team or a natural leader assumes the role, this individual ensures that the team performs its mission.

The project sponsor should ensure that the test management team:

- Understands testing concepts and the standard for software testing discussed in this manual
- Customizes and integrates the standard for software testing into the organization's systems design and maintenance methodology
- Encourages adherence to and support of the integrated test methodology and agrees to perform testing in the manner prescribed by the methodology

Management should not attempt to tell the test management team which aspects of the software testing standard should be adopted, how that testing methodology should be integrated into the existing design methodology, or the amount of time and effort needed to perform the task. Management should set the tone by stating that this manual will be the basis for testing in the organization but that the test management team is free to make necessary modifications.

Step 2. Identify Test Steps and Tasks to Integrate

Section III defines the steps and tasks involved in the client/server and Internet testing methodology. These should be evaluated to determine which are applicable to the organization and design methodology. Some of the tasks may already be performed through design methodology, the test management team may consider them unnecessary, or the team may decide to combine tasks.

The test team must consider three areas when performing this step: the test team must agree on the general objectives of testing, it must understand how the design methodology works, and it must understand the test methodology presented in this manual.

Step 3. Customize Test Steps and Tasks

The material covered in this text may not be consistent with the methodology in place and will need customizing for each organization. The test team can either perform this task itself or assign it to others (e.g., to the group in charge of design methodology).

Customization usually includes the following:

- *Standardizing vocabulary* — Vocabulary should be consistent throughout the design methodology. If staff members understand and use the same vocabulary, they can easily move from job to job within the organization. Vocabulary customization may mean changing vocabulary in the testing standard or integrating the testing vocabulary into the systems development methodology.
- *Changing the structure of presentation* — The way the testing steps and tasks have been described may differ from the way other parts of the design methodology are presented. For example, this manual has separate sections for forms and text descriptions of the software testing tools. If the systems development methodology integrates them into single units, they may need to be rearranged or reordered to make them consistent with the development manual.

Customization can work two ways. The process can be customized for individual application systems. During test planning, the test team would determine which tasks, worksheets, and checklists are applicable to the system being developed and then create a smaller version of the process for test purposes. In addition, the processes described in this manual can be customized for a particular development function. The test standards and procedures can be customized to meet specific application and test needs.

Step 4. Select Integration Points

This step involves selecting points in development methodology to integrate test steps and tasks. It requires a thorough understanding of the systems development methodology and the software tasks. The two key criteria for determining where to integrate these tasks are:

1. *What data is needed* — The test task can be inserted into the design methodology only after the point at which the needed information has been produced.
2. *Where the test products are needed* — The testing tasks must be completed before the products produced by that task are needed in the systems development methodology.

If these two rules are followed, both the earliest and latest points at which the tasks can be performed can be determined. The tasks should be inserted into the systems development methodology within this time-frame.

Step 5. Modify the Development Methodology

This step generally involves inserting the material into the systems development methodology documentation and must be performed by someone familiar with the design process. All the information needed to modify the systems development methodology is available at this point.

Step 6. Incorporate Defect Recording

An integral part of the tester's workbench is the quality control function, which can identify problems and defects uncovered through testing as well as problems in the testing process itself. Appropriate recording and analysis of these defects is essential to improving the testing process.

The next part of this section presents a procedure for defect recording and analysis when the testing process is integrated into the systems development methodology. This procedure requires categorizing defects and ensuring that they are appropriately recorded throughout the systems development methodology.

The most difficult part of defect recording is convincing development staff members that this information will not be used against them. This information is gathered strictly for the improvement of the test process and should never be used for performance appraisals or any other individual evaluations.

Step 7. Train in Use of the Test Methodology

This step involves training analysts, users, and programmers in use of the test methodology. Once testing is integrated into the systems development methodology, people must be trained and motivated to use the test methodology, a more difficult job.

Test management team members play a large role in convincing their peers to accept and use the new methodology — first, by their example, and second, by actively encouraging co-workers to adopt the methodology. An important part of this step is creating and conducting testing seminars, which should cover the following.

- *Testing concepts and methods* — This part of the training recaps the material in Appendix F.
- *Test standards* — Individuals responsible for testing must know the standards against which they are measured. The standards should

be taught first, so team members know why they are performing certain tasks (e.g., test procedures), and the procedures second. If they feel that the procedures are just one way of testing, they may decide there are better ways. On the other hand, if they know the objective for performing the test procedures (e.g., meeting test standards), they are more likely to take an interest in learning and following the test procedures.

- *Test methodology* — The methodology incorporated into the systems development methodology should be taught step by step and task by task. An analyst, user, or programmer should initially perform tasks under the direction of an instructor. This helps ensure that these professionals fully understand how the task should be performed and what results should be expected.

Until the individuals responsible for testing have been trained and have demonstrated proficiency in testing processes, management should allow for some testing errors. In addition, until individuals have demonstrated mastery of the test procedures, they should be closely supervised during the execution of those procedures.

Part 26
On-Site/Offshore Model

Outsourcing has emerged as a major concept in the twentieth century when a number of manufacturing products were outsourced to China and Japan. The offshore outsourcing model can provide exceptional value to clients. Increased efficiency and cost advantage are the two basic elements that increased the outsourcing approach. When the IT boom evaporated and companies were forced to maintain their profit line, they often turned toward outsourcing the development, testing, and maintenance to Asian countries such as India, China, and others. This part analyzes the important elements of outsourcing with special reference to testing and the advantages and issues involved.

Step 1: Analysis

The corporate management should evaluate the outsourcing option. It should not be chosen as a matter of routine. A committee should carefully study the following aspects and submit a report to the senior management to make a decision on outsourcing.

Some questions that need to be answered include the following:

- Could the products, development, testing, or maintenance be outsourced?
- What part of the project can be outsourced?
- What experiences have other companies had with outsourcing?
- Are there options available for the line of product in the market?
- What are the short-term versus long-term business processes to outsource?
- Are the requirements defined beforehand?
- Are there frequent changes in the business process outsourcing project?
- Does the client's location have the extra capacity it needs?

Management should analyze the report and only if the product could be successfully outsourced with substantial benefits to the company, should the decision to outsource be taken.

Step 2: Determine the Economic Tradeoffs

Once the management has decided to outsource the product, then the cost benefit should be analyzed. This can be done in two ways:

1. The advantages of outsourcing in terms of cost within the same geographical location
2. The advantages of outsourcing among the various competitive outsourcing clients available

Corporate should not be carried out by the cost-benefit studies projected by the vendors for outsourcing (see the Vendor Evaluation Excel spreadsheet on the CD). These studies are prepared with the primary objective of capturing the new business and have not taken into consideration various recurring and unexpected project costs that normally form part of any project operation. Eighty percent cost saving may land a company in the hands of a vendor who is not going to deliver a quality product within the schedule. Normally studies show that around 40 to 50 percent benefits are accrued to the outsourcing firms in terms of cost. Any projections above this industry average are questionable.

Step 3: Determine the Selection Criteria

Outsourcing projects have become catastrophic to many firms in the United States for the simple reason that the selection process adopted by them is wrong.

- *Geographical Locations:* The location of the outsourcing country is a primary factor in selecting the outsourcing partner. Countries such as India and China get more outsourcing projects due to their geographical locations because the 24/7 work atmosphere can be ensured in these locations. When U.S. companies start their operations in the morning, already two rounds of shifts are completed for the requirement sent to these locations as of the earlier day. The project management group often finds it very difficult to evaluate the output received as the day begins.
- *Optimum Utilization:* Maximum usage of the previous hardware resources can be done if the work is carried out 24/7 in different locations. Because the globe is interconnected by IPLC and VPN the load to the server can be distributed across locations and maximum utilization of the servers can be ensured.
- *Quality Deliverables:* The quality of the deliverables from the vendor should be evaluated with respect to compliance with the company's quality standards and with respect to international quality standards.

Project Management and Monitoring

The success of the on-site/offshore model depends on the effective project management practices adopted by the companies. Several companies that

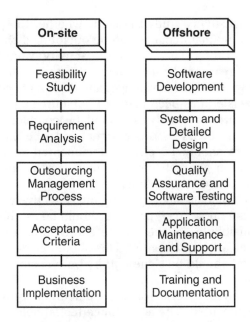

Exhibit 26.1. Onshore versus Offshore Activities

have started experimenting with this model have retracted. Unless clear project management practices defining the clear role and responsibilities for the on-site/offshore team are established, this model is bound to face several obstacles in delivering the expected cost advantages results.

Outsourcing Methodology

Having decided to outsource, the outsourcing methodology should clearly define what to outsource, and what cannot be outsourced. Potential activities that can be outsourced are shown in Exhibit 26.1. Of course, the activities depend heavily on (1) completeness of the requirements, (2) effectiveness of communication, (3) whether the project supports operating effectiveness or strategy, and (4) the existence of well-defined project management, quality assurance, and development.

Operational effectiveness is concerned with working cheaper or faster. Strategy is about the creation of a long-term competitive advantage for the business. An application development that is strategic and has multiple spiral iterations should not outsource the entire development and quality assurance activities. An application development project with well-defined requirements and that will not have a major effect on the operations of the business is a candidate for offshoring.

On-Site Activities

- The initial feasibility study to decide whether the particular development/testing/maintenance can be outsourced should be decided by the corporation. This part of the activity cannot be outsourced for obvious reasons. As indicated, this study will result in a cost-benefit analysis and the advantages and disadvantages of outsourcing.
- When a decision has been made to outsource a part or whole process, a requirement analysis should be conducted to decide the portion of the business process that is to be outsourced. These requirements should be clearly documented so that there is no communication gap between the management and the vendor on the deliveries and expectations.
- The project management process for effectively monitoring and managing the outsourced projects should be established. The roles and responsibilities of the on-site coordinator and offshore team should be clearly documented. This should be decided by the management and should be signed off by both senior management and the vendor.
- The acceptance criteria for the outsourced projects should be clearly documented. The acceptance test should be conducted by the corporation by involving the actual end users or business analysts. Proper guidelines and checklists should be created for the acceptance criteria.
- The business implementation should be done by the corporate office as this cannot be outsourced.

Offshore Activities

The following are potential activities that could be outsourced:

- *Development* — Outsourcing a software development process is the major activity that has been stabilized across the globe. A number of software companies have emerged in regions such as India, China, and Southeast Asia, which lends effective support to businesses in the United Kingdom and the United States in the development of software code. These companies accredit themselves with the international standards such as CMM, ISO, and other international auditing standards, and a clear process is established for verifying the deliverables.
- *High-Level and Detailed Design* — With the English-speaking knowledge gained by these countries and the globe shrinking with networks, in addition to software development, other related activities such as high-level design and system design could be transferred offshore.

- *System Testing* — With the global connectivity made simple and low-cost, many of the testing activities can be outsourced. Because system design and development happens in the offshore development centers, system testing can be performed offshore. This reduces the cost of hiring additional resources at higher cost or dislocating the business resources from their routines that will indirectly affect business growth.
- *Quality Assurance* — Quality assurance and software testing are other important activities that are candidates for outsourcing by U.S. companies. This directly relates to the outsourcing of development and other related activities. Most of these vendors have developed expertise in modern software testing tools and they execute these automated test scripts from anywhere across the globe.
- *Support and Maintenance* — Application maintenance and support (AMS) is another critical activity that is extended to the long-term outsourcing of maintenance and support of the critical applications. Many of the call centers for critical applications such as U.K. Railways and major telecom companies have already been moved to countries such as India.
- *Follow-Up Activities* — Any other related documentation work that relates to software development, design development, or quality assurance related documentation can easily be outsourced by the standards for the deliverables. With the development of Internet tools such as Placeware even training can be outsourced to remote locations.

Implementing the On-Site/Offshore Model

Once it has been decided to outsource after the initial analysis phase, the outsourcing should be managed in a phased manner. Phasing should not affect the existing business activities of the company. The following five phases define the process.

Knowledge Transfer

In this phase the offshore core team can visit the client site to understand the application that is to be outsourced. These technical and business resources communicate with the existing resources and internalize the functional, technical, and operational aspects of the applications. Normally a client coordinator is nominated to plan, act as liaison, monitor, and evaluate knowledge transfer sessions with active participation. The offshore team makes a reverse presentation of its understanding of the system so that the client coordinator is convinced of its knowledge acquisition. This team will prepare training and other documentation to be passed on to the rest of the offshore team.

This team will consist of identified process experts from the outsourced company who will document the process followed up at the client place. These processes will be integrated or aligned with the vendor's process so that the client deliverables will pass any audit requirements.

Detailed Design

Once the initial knowledge acquisition phase is complete, the technical team will prepare a detailed design for the hardware, software, and connectivity requirements, which are to be in place to start the operations from the remote locations. The technical team from the client side will authenticate this design. Once the technical detail area is approved, the infrastructure team at the remote location will start to put the environment in place. The client's server and applications will be connected and a sanity test will be performed for verification.

The business analyst team will prepare a migration plan for migrating the planned activities such as development, testing, design, or maintenance in a phased manner.

Milestone-Based Transfer

The on-site/offshore transition process provides a framework to shift the responsibility of development, testing, design, support, and maintenance from on-site to offshore with a step-by-step methodology without affecting the normal business of the client. Key milestones for smooth transfer are:

- Establish the environment at the offshore location.
- Train the offshore resources.
- Plan the move of the identified activities in a phased manner.
- Obtain offshore stability.

Steady State

Over a period of time the offshore environment will be stabilized and the deliverables will start flowing to the on-site location with the anticipation of improved quality and less cost. This is a critical period where the on-site project management activities should meticulously review the deliverables and have conference calls to clarify issues with the offshore team and other related activities. Once this steady state is achieved, the model is established.

Application Management

Once the design, development, and testing are completed and the product has gone live, the further enhancements (new requirements arising out of business necessity will require change in the code) need ongoing maintenance. Moreover, during the normal business cycle jobs such as data

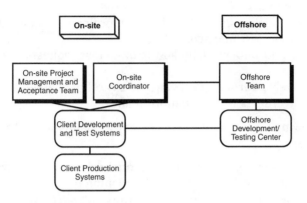

Exhibit 26.2. Relationship Model

backup and purging the data can be outsourced. As the vendor companies have specialized in the business domain they will be in a better position to offer these services on a long-term basis at low cost.

Ideally, 20 to 30 percent of work is done on-site whereas 70 to 80 percent is outsourced offshore depending upon the criticality of the project. Usually, requirement analysis, development of detailed specifications, critical support, and implementation are performed on-site, and development and testing are outsourced offshore.

The following are the important prerequisites for an effective on-site/offshore model to deliver the desired results.

Relationship Model

The relationship model should be established for a successful on-site/offshore model. Exhibit 26.2 shows a higher-level relationship model. The roles and responsibilities for the project manager at the on-site client, on-site vendor coordinator, and the offshore team should be clearly established.

Some of the generic responsibilities of the on-site client team are:

- Initiate and participate in all status conference calls.
- Coordinate and provide information on testing requirements.
- Provide clarifications and other required data to the offshore team.
- Review offshore test deliverables and sign off on the quality of deliverables.
- Single point of contact with offshore project manager in obtaining clarifications raised and in obtaining approvals on the test deliverables from the respective on-site departments and divisions.
- Establish and maintain optimal turnaround time for clarifications and deliverables.

- Approve timesheets.
- Finalize timelines/schedule for test projects in consultation with offshore project manager.
- Prepare and publish daily status of all test requests outstanding to all parties.
- Proactively inform requests and/or any other changes that will affect the deliverables of the offshore team.

The following are some of the generic responsibilities of the on-site client team:

- A single point of contact for the offshore team in interacting with the on-site coordinator should be identified.
- The time and methodology for the daily/weekly/monthly status review calls should be decided and the participants in these various calls should be decided at the various stakeholders' levels.
- Overall project management activities and the review process should be defined.
- A weekly/monthly status report formats and contents should be decided.
- Prepare and publish daily progress through status report.
- Follow up with on-site coordinator in getting clarifications for issues raised by development/test team engineers.
- Support and review process for all project-related test documents and deliverables prepared by development and test team engineers.
- Allocate test projects to offshore test engineers.
- Identify resources for ramp-up and ramp-down depending upon the project requirements at the various phases of the project.
- Prepare a project plan and strategy document.
- Convey project-related issues proactively to on-site coordinator.
- Responsibility for the quality of the deliverables should be explicitly declared.
- Responsibility for project tracking and project control should be decided.
- Conduct daily and weekly team meetings.
- Collect timesheets and submit them to on-site coordinator.
- Finalize timelines/schedule for test projects in consultation with on-site coordinator.

Standards. Several companies that have experimented with on-site/offshore models to minimize their costs ended up in failure primarily due to the incompatibility between the sourced and vendor companies on the technical standards and guidelines. Although the companies are CMM compliant and ISO certified, there are vast differences in the standards adopted between them for the same source code or testing methodology.

The standards of the vendor companies should be evaluated and synchronized with the standards and guidelines of the outsourced company. The development standards, testing methodology, test automation standards, documentation standards, and training scope should be clearly defined in advance. Apart from the above the following should also be taken into consideration:

- Request for proposals (RFP) procedures
- Change request procedures
- Configuration management
- Tools
- Acceptance criteria

The acceptance criterion is another critical factor that should be defined with the help of the end users who are going to ultimately use the system. If the standards and deliverables are not acceptable to them, the project is going to fail in the implementation phase.

Benefits of On-Site/Offshore Methodology

The ultimate advantages of this model are time, money and communication. The case study described in Exhibit 26.3 demonstrates the ideal usage of the offshore model and describes the approximate benefit that companies may reap with the onshore/offshore model. The statistics may vary from 80 to 40 percent.

In the case study the XYZ Company will have the following parameters to evaluate in this analysis (critical success factors are noted in parameters 10 to 13).

1. The number of resources required — five.
2. The schedule for the project is assumed as six months.
3. The cost of on-site existing resources is assumed as $80 per hour.
4. Eight hours per day and 22 days per month are considered.
5. Offshore resources are considered at the cost of $150 per day.
6. Initial knowledge transfer is assumed for two weeks at nominal cost.
7. Project management cost is estimated at 30 percent of the resource cost.
8. Initial environment establishment cost and subsequent maintenance cost are assumed nominally.
9. A percentage of recurring administrative cost included.
10. The requirements have undergone complete reviews and sign-offs by the stakeholders.
11. Communication has been established by the project manager and is excellent.
12. The project is nonstrategic to the business.
13. Complete standards have been established and documented.

Exhibit 26.3. Example Cost-Benefit Case Study:
Cost-Benefit Analysis between On-Site and Offshore Models

#	Description	Rate	No. of Days	No. of Persons	Total
					(Amounts in $)
1	**On-site** for 5 persons for 6 months	640	132	5	422,400
	PM effort 30 percent on the total cost				126,720
	Total				549,120
2	**Offshore** for 5 persons for 6 months	150	132	5	99,000
	PM effort 30 percent on the total cost				29,700
	Knowledge transfer at on-site				25,000
	Initial network connectivity				50,000
	Recurring cost (maintenance)				5,000
	Communication expenses				5,000
	Administrative expenses				5,000
	Total				218,700
	Analysis:				
	Diff. between on-site and offshore				330,420
	Percent gain on offshore model over on-site model				60.17

Although it can be quite difficult to satisfy the expected demand for IT resources in Western countries, it is a completely different scenario in countries such as China and India where there are many available programmers with good academic backgrounds. These vendor companies typically possess an extensive, highly specialized knowledge base.

Another advantage is that we can engage these resources only for required times, not on a continuous basis. This has the potential of substantially saving the cost for the company.

Due to the geographic location advantage of these regions, 24/7 service can be achieved from these vendors. The service requests that are sent at the end of the day in the United States are delivered at the beginning of the next working day.

Most of these outsourcing companies are CMM level 5 with ISO certification with established processes and procedures that enhance the quality of deliverables.

The onshore/offshore model can enable the organizations to concentrate on their core business, carry out business reengineering, and provide information that is valid, timely, and adequate to assist decision making at the top management level and quality and cost control at the middle and lower levels

On-Site/Offshore Model Challenges

Out of Sight. The offshore team being out of sight intensifies the fear of loss of control for the on-site project managers. This can be overcome by visiting the stakeholders and vendors' facilities offshore to provide confidence. Second, the established processes, methodologies, and tools, which are industry standard due to CMM and ISO and IEEE standards, will provide additional confidence.

Establish Transparency. The vendors should provide the clients with complete transparency and allow them to actively participate in recruiting offshore resources and utilizing their own resources on-site, as they deem appropriate.

Security Considerations. The security considerations on the secrecy of the data can be overcome by a dedicated network set up exclusively for the client.

Project Monitoring. The failure of established project management practices can be attended to by tailoring the project management practices to suit to the requirements of the clients.

Management Overhead. When the overall cost benefit is evaluated, the management overhead, which will be additional, expenses using this model can be substantial.

Cultural Differences. Although fluency in the English language is considered an advantage for outsourcing most of the projects from Europe and the United States, the cultural differences can create difficulties. However, individuals tend to adapt to the different cultural environment very quickly.

Software Licensing. This is another problem relating to global licensing or regional restrictions on the use of software licenses that needs to be dealt with on a case-to-case basis.

The Future of Onshore/Offshore

Several companies have attempted and are attempting the onshore/offshore model in order to reduce IT costs. Although the cost savings are clear, the quality of the offshore deliverables depends heavily on the clear onshore project management practices and standards. Even though there is a 24/7 work paradigm because of the overlap in global time differences, communication and cultural adjustments are critical success factors.

However, offshoring is a mistake when technology companies confuse operating effectiveness and strategy. Operational effectiveness is concerned with working cheaper or faster. Strategy is about the creation of a long-term competitive advantage, which for technology companies is usually the ability to create innovative software.

Outsourcing developers and quality assurance testing is feasible when the software developed isn't a key part of the pipeline of innovation for products a company actually sells. For example, when Web site design or back-office software such as accounts payable or inventory control is outsourced, that can be an effective approach because it improves operational effectiveness. But writing and testing innovative software cannot be produced on an assembly line. It requires hard-to-find development, design, and testing skills. Farming out development efforts overseas will not create a competitive advantage. When a technology company outsources a majority of its software development, that company may lose its capacity to be innovative and grow its competitive edge.

Section V
Modern Software Testing Tools

Test automation can add a lot of complexity and cost to a test team's effort. However, it can also provide some valuable assistance if it is done by the right people, with the right training and right environment, and in the right context.

The flourish of automated testing tools is a reaction to advances in Web-based, client/server, and mainframe software development tools that have enabled developers to build applications rapidly and with increased functionality. Testing departments must cope with software that is dramatically improved, but increasingly complex. New testing tools have been developed to aid in the quality assurance process.

The objectives of this section are to:

- Describe a brief history of software testing.
- Describe the evolution of automated software testing tools.
- Describe futuristic testing tools.
- Describe when a testing tool is useful.
- Describe when not to use a testing tool.
- Provide a testing tool selection checklist.
- Discuss types of testing tools.
- Provide descriptions of modern and popular testing tools.
- Describe a methodology to evaluate testing tools.

Part 27
A Brief History of Software Testing

Modern testing tools are becoming more and more advanced and user-friendly. The following discussion describes how the software testing activity has evolved, and is evolving, over time. This sets the perspective on where automated testing tools are going.

Software testing is the activity of running a series of dynamic executions of software programs that occurs after the software source code has been developed. It is performed to uncover and correct as many of the potential errors as possible before delivery to the customer. As pointed out earlier, software testing is still an "art." It can be considered a risk management technique; the quality assurance technique, for example, represents the last defense to correct deviations from errors in the specification, design, or code.

Throughout the history of software development, there have been many definitions and advances in software testing. Exhibit 27.1 graphically illustrates these evolutions. In the 1950s, software testing was defined as "what programmers did to find bugs in their programs." In the early 1960s the definition of testing underwent a revision. Consideration was given to exhaustive testing of the software in terms of the possible paths through the code, or total enumeration of the possible input data variations. It was noted that it was impossible to completely test an application because: (1) the domain of program inputs is too large, (2) there are too many possible input paths, and (3) design and specification issues are difficult to test. Because of the above points, exhaustive testing was discounted and found to be theoretically impossible.

As software development matured through the 1960s and 1970s the activity of software development was referred to as "computer science." Software testing was defined as "what is done to demonstrate correctness of a program" or as "the process of establishing confidence that a program or system does what it is supposed to do" in the early 1970s. A short-lived computer science technique that was proposed during the specification, design, and implementation of a software system was software verification through "correctness proof." Although this concept was theoretically

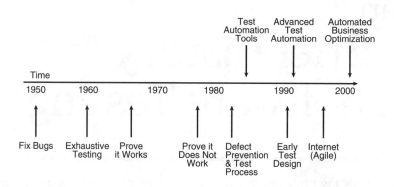

Exhibit 27.1. History of Software Testing

promising, in practice it was too time consuming and insufficient. For simple tests, it was easy to show that the software "works" and prove that it will theoretically work. However, because most of the software was not tested using this approach, a large number of defects remained to be discovered during actual implementation. It was soon concluded that "proof of correctness" was an inefficient method of software testing. However, even today there is still a need for correctness demonstrations, such as acceptance testing, as described in various sections of this book.

In the late 1970s it was stated that testing is a process of executing a program with the intent of finding an error, not proving that it works. He emphasized that a good test case is one that has a high probability of finding an as-yet-undiscovered error. A successful test is one that uncovers an as-yet-undiscovered error. This approach was the exact opposite up to this point.

The above two definitions of testing present (prove that it works versus prove that it does not work) the "testing paradox" with two underlying and contradictory objectives:

1. To give confidence that the product is working well
2. To uncover errors in the software product before its delivery to the customer (or the next state of development)

If the first objective is to prove that a program works. It was determined that "we shall subconsciously be steered toward this goal; that is, we shall tend to select test data that have a low probability of causing the program to fail."

If the second objective is to uncover errors in the software product, how can there be confidence that the product is working well, inasmuch as it was just proved that it is, in fact, not working! Today it has been widely accepted by good testers that the second objective is more productive than the first objective, for if one accepts the first objective, the tester will subconsciously ignore defects trying to prove that a program works.

The following good testing principles were proposed:

- A necessary part of a test case is a definition of the expected output or result.
- Programmers should avoid attempting to test their own programs.
- A programming organization should not test its own programs.
- Thoroughly inspect the results of each test.
- Test cases must be written for invalid and unexpected, as well as valid and expected, input conditions.
- Examining a program to see if it does not do what it is supposed to do is only half the battle. The other half is seeing whether the program does what it is not supposed to do.
- Avoid throwaway test cases unless the program is truly a throwaway program.
- Do not plan a testing effort under the tacit assumption that no errors will be found.
- The probability of the existence of more errors in a section of a program is proportional to the number of errors already found in that section.

The 1980s saw the definition of testing extended to include defect prevention. Designing tests is one of the most effective bug prevention techniques known. It was suggested that a testing methodology was required, specifically that testing must include reviews throughout the entire software development life cycle and that it should be a managed process. He promoted the importance of testing not just a program but the requirements, design, code, tests themselves, and the program.

"Testing" traditionally (up until the early 1980s) referred to what was done to a system once working code was delivered (now often referred to as system testing), however, testing today is "greater testing," where a tester should be involved in almost any aspect of the software development life cycle. Once code is delivered to testing, it can be tested and checked but if anything is wrong the previous development phases have to be investigated. If the error was caused by a design ambiguity, or a programmer oversight, it is simpler to try to find the problems as soon as they occur, not wait until an actual working product is produced. Studies have shown that about 50 percent of bugs are created at the requirements (what do we want the software to do?) or design stages, and these can have a compounding effect and create more bugs during coding. The earlier a bug or issue is found in the life cycle, the cheaper it is to fix (by exponential amounts). Rather than test a program and look for bugs in it, requirements or designs can be rigorously reviewed. Unfortunately, even today, many software development organizations believe that software testing is a back-end activity.

In the mid-1980s automated testing tools emerged to automate the manual testing effort to improve the efficiency and quality of the target application. It was anticipated that the computer could do more tests of a program than a human could do manually and do them more reliably. These tools were initially fairly primitive and did not have advanced scripting language facilities (see the following section, Evolution of Automated Testing Tools, for more details).

In the early 1990s the power of early test design was recognized. Testing was redefined to be "the planning, design, building, maintaining and executing tests and test environments." This was a quality assurance perspective of testing that assumes that good testing is a managed process, a total life cycle concern with testability.

Also in the early 1990s more advanced capture/replay testing tools offered rich scripting languages and reporting facilities. Test management tools helped manage all the artifacts from requirements and test design, to test scripts and test defects. Also, commercially available performance tools arrived to test the performance of the system. These tools tested stress and load-tested the target system to determine their breaking points. This was facilitated by capacity planning.

Although the concept of a test as a process throughout the entire software development life cycle has persisted, in the mid-1990s with the popularity of the Internet, software was often developed without a specific testing standard model, making it much more difficult to test. Just as documents could be reviewed without specifically defining each expected result of each step of the review, so could tests be performed without explicitly defining everything that had to be tested in advance. Testing approaches to this problem are known as "agile testing." The techniques include exploratory testing, rapid testing, and risk-based testing.

In the early 2000s Mercury Interactive introduced an even broader definition of testing when they introduced the concept of business technology optimization (BTO). BTO aligns the IT strategy and execution with business goals. It helps govern the priorities, people, and processes of IT. The basic approach is to measure and maximize value across the IT service delivery life cycle to ensure applications meet quality, performance, and availability goals. Topaz is an interactive digital cockpit that reveals vital business availability information in real-time to help IT and business executives prioritize IT operations and maximize business results. It provides end-to-end visibility into business availability by presenting key business process indicators in real-time, as well as their mapping to the underlying IT infrastructure.

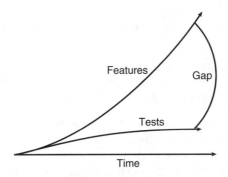

Exhibit 27.2. Motivation for Test Automation (From "Why Automate," Linda Hayes, Worksoft, Inc white paper, 2002, www.worksoft.com. With permission.)

Evolution of Automated Testing Tools

Test automation started in the mid-1980s with the emergence of automated capture/replay tools. A capture/replay tool enables testers to record interaction scenarios. Such tools record every keystroke, mouse movement, and response that was sent to the screen during the scenario. Later, the tester may replay the recorded scenarios. The capture/replay tool automatically notes any discrepancies in the expected results. Such tools improved testing efficiency and productivity by reducing the manual testing efforts.

Linda Hayes, a pioneer in test automation, points out that the cost justification for test automation is simple and can be expressed in a single exhibit (Exhibit 27.2). As this exhibit suggests, over time the number of functional features for a particular application increases due to changes and improvements to the business operations that use the software. Unfortunately, the number of people and the amount of time invested in testing each new release either remain flat or may even decline. As a result, the test coverage steadily decreases, which increases the risk of failure, translating to potential business losses.

For example, if the development organization adds application enhancements equal to 10 percent of the existing code, this means that the test effort is now 110 percent as great as it was before. Because no organization budgets more time and resources for testing than they do for development, it is literally impossible for testers to keep up.

This is why applications that have been in production for years often experience failures. When test resources and time can't keep pace, decisions must be made to omit the testing of some functional features. Typically, the newest features are targeted because the oldest ones are assumed to still work. However, because changes in one area often have an unintended impact on other areas, this assumption may not be true. Ironically, the greatest risk is in the existing features, not the new ones, for the simple reason that they are already being used.

Test automation is the only way to resolve this dilemma. By continually adding new tests for new features to a library of automated tests for existing features, the test library can track the application functionality.

The cost of failure is also on the rise. Whereas in past decades software was primarily found in back-office applications, today software is a competitive weapon that differentiates many companies from their competitors and forms the backbone of critical operations. Examples abound of errors in the tens or hundreds of millions — even billions — of dollars in losses due to undetected software errors. Exacerbating the increasing risk is the decreasing cycle times. Product cycles have compressed from years into months, weeks, or even days. In these tight timeframes, it is virtually impossible to achieve acceptable coverage with manual testing.

Capture/replay automated tools have undergone a series of staged improvements. The evolutionary improvements are described below.

Static Capture/Replay Tools (without Scripting Language)

With these early tools, tests were performed manually and the inputs and outputs were captured in the background. During subsequent automated playback, the script repeated the same sequence of actions to apply the inputs and compare the actual responses to the captured results. Differences were reported as errors. The GUI menus, radio buttons, list boxes, and text were stored in the script. With this approach the flexibility of changes to the GUI was limited. The scripts resulting from this method contained hard-coded values that must change if anything at all changed in the application. The costs associated with maintaining such scripts were astronomical, and unacceptable. These scripts were not reliable, even if the application had not changed, and often failed on replay (pop-up windows, messages, and other things can happen that did not happen when the test was recorded). If the tester made an error entering data, the test had to be rerecorded. If the application changed, the test had to be rerecorded.

Static Capture/Replay Tools (with Scripting Language)

The next generation of automated testing tools introduced scripting languages. Now the test script was a program. Scripting languages were needed to handle conditions, exceptions, and the increased complexity of software. Automated script development, to be effective, had to be subject to the same rules and standards that were applied to software development. Making effective use of any automated test tool required at least one trained, *technical* person — in other words, a *programmer.*

Variable Capture/Replay Tools

The next generation of automated testing tools introduced added variable test data to be used in conjunction with the capture/replay features. The difference between static capture/replay and variable is that in the former case the inputs and outputs are fixed, whereas in the latter the inputs and outputs are variable. This is accomplished by performing the testing manually, and then replacing the captured inputs and expected outputs with variables whose corresponding values are stored in data files external to the script. Variable capture/replay is available from most testing tools that use a script language with variable data capability. Variable capture/replay and extended methodologies reduce the risk of not performing regression testing on existing features and improving the productivity of the testing process.

However, the problem with variable capture/replay tools is that they still require a scripting language that needs to be programmed. However, just as development programming techniques improved, new scripting techniques emerged. The following describes two of these techniques.

Functional Decomposition Approach. The focus of the functional decomposition script development approach (like structured software development) is to reduce all test cases to their most fundamental tasks, and write the following types of scripts: user-defined functions, business function scripts, and "subroutine" or "utility" scripts that perform these tasks independently of each other. Some examples of what these scripts do include:

- Navigation (e.g., "Access Loan Screen from Main Menu")
- Specific (Business) Function (e.g., "Post a Loan")
- Data Verification (e.g., "Verify Loan Payment Updates Current Balance")
- Return Navigation (e.g., "Return to Main Menu")

In order to effectively use these scripts, it is necessary to separate data from function. This allows an automated test script to be written for a business function, using data files to provide both the input and the expected-results verification. A hierarchical architecture is employed, using a structured or modular design.

The highest level is the driver script, which is the engine of the test. The driver script contains a series of calls to one or more "test case" scripts. The test case scripts contain the test case logic, calling the business function scripts necessary to perform the application testing. Utility scripts and functions are called as needed by drivers, main, and business function scripts. These are described in more detail below.

- *Driver Scripts:* Perform initialization (if required); then call the test case scripts in the desired order.

- *Test Case Scripts:* Perform the application test case logic using business function scripts.
- *Business Function Scripts:* Perform specific business functions within the application.
- *Subroutine Scripts:* Perform application-specific tasks required by two or more business scripts.
- *User-Defined Functions:* General, application-specific, and screen-access functions.

Test Plan Driven ("Keyword") Approach. This approach uses the test case document developed by the tester using a spreadsheet containing table-driven "keywords." This approach maintains most of the advantages of the functional decomposition approach, while eliminating most of the disadvantages. Using this approach, the entire process is data-driven, including functionality.

The keywords control the processing. Templates like "Loan Payments" shown in Exhibit 27.3 are created using a spreadsheet program, such as Microsoft Excel, and then copied to create additional test cases. This file is read by a controller script for the application, and processed. When a keyword is encountered, a list is created using data from the remaining columns. This continues until a "null" (blank) in the field/screen name field is encountered. The controller script then calls a utility script associated with the keyword and passes the "list" as an input parameter. The utility script continues processing until "end-of-list," then returns to the "Controller" script, which continues processing the file until "end-of-file" is reached.

Each of the keywords causes a utility script to be called that processes the remaining columns as input parameters in order to perform specific functions. An advantage of this approach is that it can be run as a manual test. The numerical dollar data and "Check" (bold font) in the Input/Verification Data column indicates what would need to be changed if one were to copy this test case to create additional tests.

This approach has all of the advantages of functional decomposition, as well as the following:

- The detail test plan can be written in spreadsheet format containing all input and verification data. Therefore, the tester only needs to write this once, rather than writing it in Word and then creating input and verification files as is required by the functional decomposition method.
- The test plan does not necessarily have to be written using Excel. Any format can be used from which either "tab-delimited" or "comma-delimited" files can be saved, e.g., Access Database.

Exhibit 27.3. Test Plan Template (Loan Payments)

Key Word	Field/ Screen Name	Input/ Verification Data	Pass/Fail	Comments
Start test:	Screen	Main menu	Pass	Verify starting point
Enter:	Selection	3	Pass	Select loan option
Action:	Press_key	F4	Pass	Access loan screen
Verify:	Screen	Loan posting	Pass	Verify screen accessed
			Pass	
Enter:	Loan amount	$125.87	Pass	Enter loan data
	Loan method	Check	Pass	
			Pass	
Action:	Press_key	F9	Pass	Process loan
			Pass	
Verify:	Screen	Loan payment screen	Pass	Verify screen remains
			Pass	
Verify_data:	Loan amount	$125.87	Pass	Verify updated data
	Current balance	$1,309.77	Pass	
	Status message	Loan posted	Pass	
Action:	Press_key	F12	Pass	Return to main menu
Verify:	Screen	Main menu	Pass	Verify return to menu

- If someone proficient in the automated tool's scripting language (prior to the detail test plan being written) can create utility scripts, then the tester can use the automated test tool immediately via the "spreadsheet-input" method, without needing to learn the scripting language.
- The tester need only learn the keywords required, and the specific format to use within the test plan. This allows the tester to be productive with the test tool very quickly, and allows more extensive training in the test tool to be scheduled at a more convenient time.
- After a number of generic utility scripts have already been created for testing an application, most of these can be reused to test another. This allows the organization to get their automated testing "up and running" (for most applications) within a few days, rather than weeks.

Historical Software Testing and Development Parallels

In some ways software testing and automated testing tools are following similar paths to traditional development. The following is a brief evolution of software development and shows how deviations from prior best practices are also being observed in the software testing process.

The first computers were developed in the 1950s and FORTRAN was the first 1GL programming language. In the late 1960s, the concept of "structured programming" stated that any program can be written using three simple constructs: simple sequence, if/then/else, and do while statements. There were other prerequisites such as the program being a "proper program" whereby there must exist only one entry and one exit point. The focus was on the process of creating programs.

In the 1970s the development community focused on design techniques. They realized that structured programming was not enough to ensure quality — a program must be designed before it can be coded. Techniques such as Yourdon's, Myers', and Constantine's structured design and composite design techniques flourished and were accepted as best practice. The focus still had a process orientation.

The philosophy of structured design was *partitioning* and *organizing* the pieces of a system. By partitioning is meant the division of the problem into smaller subproblems, so that each subproblem will eventually correspond to a piece of the system. Highly interrelated parts of the problem should be in the same piece of the system; that is, things that belong together should go together. Unrelated parts of the problem should reside in unrelated pieces of the system; for example, things that have nothing to do with each other don't belong together.

In the 1980s it was determined that structured programming and software design techniques were still not enough: the requirements for the programs must first be established for the right system to be delivered to the customer. The focus was on quality that occurs when the customer receives exactly what she wanted in the first place.

Many requirement techniques emerged such as Data Flow Diagrams (DFDs). An important part of a DFD is a "store," a representation of where the application data will be stored. The concept of a "store" motivated practitioners to develop a logical view representation of the data. Previously the focus was on the physical view of data in terms of the database. The concept of a data model was then created: a simplified description of a real-world system in terms of data, for example, a logical view of data. The components of this approach included entities, relationships, cardinality, referential integrity, and normalization. These also created a controversy as to which came first: the process or data, a chicken-and-egg argument. Until this logical representation of data, the focus was on the processes that interfaced to databases. Proponents of the logical view of data initially insisted that the data was the first analysis focus and then the process. With time, it was agreed that both the process and data must be considered jointly in defining the requirements of a system.

In the mid-1980s the concept of information engineering was introduced. It was a new discipline that led the world into the information age. With this approach there is more interest in understanding how information can be stored and represented, how information can be transmitted through networks in multimedia forms, and how information can be processed for various services and applications. Analytical problem-solving techniques, with the help of mathematics and other related theories, were applied to the engineering design problems. Information engineering stressed the importance of taking an enterprise view to application development rather than a specific application. By modeling the entire enterprise in terms of processes, data, risks, critical success factors, and other dimensions it was proposed that management would be able to manage the enterprise in a more efficient manner.

During this same timeframe, fourth generation computers embraced microprocessor chip technology and advanced secondary storage with fantastic rates with storage devices holding tremendous amounts of data. Software development techniques had vastly improved and 4GLs made the development process much easier and faster. Unfortunately, the emphasis on quick turnaround of applications led to a backwards trend of fundamental development techniques to "get the code out" as quickly as possible.

Extreme Programming

Extreme programming (XP) is an example of such a trend. XP is an unorthodox approach to software development and it has been argued that it has no design aspects. The extreme programming methodology proposes a radical departure from commonly accepted software development processes. There are really two XP rules: Do a Little Design and No Requirements, Just User Stories. Extreme programming disciples insist that "there really are no rules, just suggestions. XP methodology calls for small units of design, from ten minutes to half an hour, done periodically from one day between sessions to a full week between sessions. Effectively, nothing gets designed until it is time to program it."

Although most people in the software development business understandably consider requirements documentation to be vital, XP recommends the creation of as little documentation as possible. No upfront requirement documentation is created in XP and very little is created in the software development process.

With XP, the developer comes up with test scenarios before she does anything else. The basic premise behind test-first design is that the test class is written before the real class; thus the end purpose of the real class is not simply to fulfill a requirement, but simply to pass all the tests that are in the test class. The problem with this approach is that independent testing is needed to find out things about the product the developer did not think about or was not able to discover in his own testing.

Part 28
Software Testing Trends

Today many companies are still struggling with the requirements phase, which is often minimized (or bypassed) to get the application "out the door." Testers constantly ask, "How do you test software without a requirements specification?" The answer is, you can't. This lack of good requirements has resulted in a loss of billions of dollars each year dealing with the rippling effect, which occurs when one phase of the development life cycle has not been sufficiently completed before proceeding to the next. For example, if the requirements are not fully defined, the design and coding will reflect the wrong requirements. The application project will have to constantly go back to redefine the requirements and then design and code. The efficiency of 4GLs in some ways has diminished previously learned lessons in software development.

Unfortunately, the above historical development trends are being followed in software testing, as listed below.

Automated Capture/Replay Testing Tools

The original purpose of automated test tools was to automate regression testing to verify that software changes do not adversely affect any portion of the application already tested. This requires that a tester has developed detailed test cases that are repeatable, and the suite of tests is run every time after there is a change to the application. With the emergence of automated testing tools many have embraced this as the final frontier for the testing effort.

However, on many occasions testing tools are attempted with no testing process or methodology. A test process consists of test planning, test design, test implementation, test execution, and defect management. Automated testing tools must integrate within the context of a testing process. The testing process must be embedded into the development methodology to be successful. Having some testing process is also not enough. Many companies decline and even fail at the same time they are reforming their processes. They are winning Baldrige Awards and creating dramatic new efficiencies, savings, and improvements in product quality and customer

301

service. Companies experiencing this paradox have clearly gotten a process right. But that differs from getting the right process right. The selection and usage of an automated testing tool does not guarantee success.

Test Case Builder Tools

Companies purchase a lot of automated testing tools but soon realize that they need a programmer or tester with programming experience to create and maintain the scripts. The emphasis becomes getting the automated test script (a program) to work. The scripting effort is a development project within a development project and requires a great deal of programming effort. Many testers do not have a programming background and developers do not want to do testing.

Automated testing tools are just a delivery mechanism of the test data to the target application under test. Automated testing tools are typically used for function/GUI testing. Tools are the interface between the test data and the GUI to verify the target application responds as defined by the requirements (if there are any). The creation of the test data/scenarios is a manual process in which a tester (or business analyst) translates the requirements (usually written in a word processor such as Microsoft Word) to test data.

This is a very time-consuming and difficult problem in which humans are not very efficient. There are numerous testing techniques (see Appendix G) that aid in the translation, but this translation is still a human effort from one formalism to another, for example, an English language statement to test data/scenarios. It is ironic that so much attention has been given to developing test scenarios with little or no concern about the quality of the test data.

Advanced Leading-Edge Automated Testing Tools

Because most test efforts require hundreds, if not thousands, of test cases, this leads to an extensive development effort when a capture/replay tool uses a scripting language. This is time consuming, as automating an hour of manual testing can require ten hours of coding and debugging. The net result is another development effort within the test cycle, which is not planned, staffed, or budgeted. For testers who do not have a programming background there is a steep learning curve to learn how to use these tools. As the inevitable changes are made to the application, even minor modifications can have an extensive impact on the automated test library. A single change to a widely used function can affect dozens of test cases or more. Not only do the changes have to be mapped to the affected scripts and any necessary modifications made, but also the results have to be tested. Eventually the maintenance effort takes so much of the test cycle time that testers are forced to revert to manual testing to meet their deadlines. At this point, the tool becomes shelfware.

The focus of future automated testing tools will have a business perspective rather than a programming view. Business analysts will be able to use such tools to test applications from a business perspective without having to write test scripts.

Instead of requiring one to learn a scripting language, or to document their tests so someone else can code them into scripts, the most advanced automated testing tools let one document and automate in one step with no programming effort required. Application experts with business knowledge will be able to learn to develop and execute robust automated tests using simple drop-down menus.

Original Software's "TestBench" Suite is an example of such tools; see Taxonomy of Testing Tools section for more details. Also see www.origsoft. com, which describes the tool in detail.

Original Software's TestBench suite, for example, uses a simple "point-and-click" interface in all of its record and playback modules, to guarantee the type of fast start required by business and the ease of use that makes the tools accessible to even the least technical end-users. It really is as simple as using a VCR and completely bypasses the need for any scripting language or programming knowledge. And yet, these modules still deliver powerful high-level functions such as:

- *Self Healing Script (SHS) technology* with which existing test scripts can be run over new versions of applications without the need for tedious and time-consuming maintenance.
- *Variable data,* which enables multiple business scenarios to be tested with a single script. Integration between TestBench and the TestSmart feature means that optimum quality variable data can be created.
- *Tracked fields* to enable data created during the running of an application (e.g., purchase reference numbers) to be captured and used throughout playback.
- *Script progression logic* with which individual scripts and other test modules can be linked into a sequence that recreates an entire business process. The launch sequence of scripts and modules can change automatically according to the data presented during a test run, so a whole range of possible scenarios can be recreated from just one sequence.

The TestBench record and playback modules all come with the ability to integrate with a range of server-side databases — which means that all scripts, script sequences, test results, documentation, etc. can be stored in one central repository, accessible by all authorized team members. This vastly improves test process efficiency by eliminating the duplication of resources and ensuring that the knowledge of how to test an application or a particular process is not held by just one individual. Features such as these guarantee the highest levels of availability and usability to fulfill the requirements of the business perspective and avoid the shelfware scenario described above, and such tools are at the core of the future of automated software testing.

Advanced Leading-Edge Test Case Builder Tools

These tools can even accomplish advanced tasks such as providing test data from spreadsheets without writing a single line of code.

As pointed out previously, the focus of test automation to date has been on getting the scripts to work. But from where does the data come? How does the tester know the right test data is being used by the script and how does the tester know there is adequate requirement coverage by the data?

This is a fundamental element that is typically missing from capture/replay automated tools up to now. What is not being addressed is the quality of the test data input and test scenarios to the scripts. Typically the automated testing tool scripter is assigned to the testing department. Because this is a very specialized and intensive programming effort, the focus is on getting the script working correctly. It is assumed someone else will provide the test data/test scenarios

Smartware Technology's TestSmart™ is an example of such a tool; see the Taxonomy of Testing Tools section for more details.

Necessary and Sufficient Conditions

Automated testing tools to date do not satisfy the necessary and sufficient conditions to achieve quality. These tools are as good as the quality of the test data input from the automated test scripts.

GIGO stands for Garbage In, Garbage Out. Computers, unlike humans, will unquestioningly process the most nonsensical input data and produce nonsensical output. Of course a properly written program will reject input data that is obviously erroneous but such checking is not always easy to specify and is tedious to write. GIGO is usually said in response to users who complain that a program didn't "do the right thing" when given imperfect input. This term is also commonly used to describe failures in human decision making due to faulty, incomplete, or imprecise data. This is a sardonic comment on the tendency human beings have to put excessive trust in "computerized" data.

The necessary and sufficient conditions for quality are that a robust tool be the deliverer of quality test data/test scenarios to be exercised against the target application based upon what the application should do or not do. For most commercial applications, the data is key to the test result. Not just entering or verifying data values, but knowing what the state of the data is supposed to be so you can predict expected results. Getting control of the test data is fundamental for any test effort, because a basic tenet of software testing is that you must know both the input conditions of the data and the expected output results to perform a valid test. If you don't know either of these, it's not a test; it's an experiment, because you don't know what will happen. This predictability is important for manual testing, but for automated testing it's essential.

But for many systems you can't even get started until you have enough test data to make it meaningful and if you need thousands or millions of data records, you've got a whole new problem. In an extreme case, testing an airline fare pricing application required tens of thousands of setup transactions to create the cities, flights, passengers, and fares needed to exercise all of the requirements. The actual test itself took less time than the data setup. Other necessary conditions are the people and process. The right people need to be trained and there must be a solid testing process in place before test automation can be attempted.

Test Data/Test Case Generation

Historically there are four basic strategies for assembling a test data environment: production sampling, starting from scratch, seeding data, or generating it. Each strategy is considered including the advantages and disadvantages of each. After this discussion, a fifth, or cutting-edge, approach generating not only test data but test scenarios and the expected results (based upon the requirements) is discussed.

Sampling from Production

The most common test data acquisition technique is to take it from production. This approach seems both logical and practical: production represents reality, in that it contains the actual situations the software must deal with and it offers both depth and breadth while ostensibly saving the time required to create new data.

There are at least three major drawbacks, however. The test platform seldom replicates production capacity, and so a subset must be extracted. Acquiring this subset is not as easy as taking every *N*th record or some flat percentage of the data: the complex interrelationships between files means that the subset must be internally cohesive. For example, the selected transactions must reference valid selected master accounts, and the totals must coincide with balances and histories. Simply identifying these relationships and tracing through all of the files to ensure that the subset makes sense can be a major undertaking in and of itself. Furthermore, it is difficult to know how large a sample is necessary to achieve coverage of all critical states and combinations.

The second major drawback of this approach is that the tests themselves and the extracted data must be constantly modified to work together. Going back to our basic tenet, we must know the input conditions for a valid test, in this case, the data contents. Each fresh extraction starts everything over. If a payroll tax test requires an employee whose year-to-date earnings will cross over the FICA limit on the next paycheck, for example, the person performing the test must either find such an employee in the subset, modify one, or add one. If the test is automated, it too must be modified for the new employee number and related information. Searching for an employee that meets all the conditions you are interested in is like searching for a needle in a haystack. Thus, the time savings are illusory because there is limited repeatability: all effort to establish the proper test conditions is lost every time the extract is refreshed.

And finally, this approach obviously cannot be employed for new systems under development, inasmuch as no production data is available.

Starting from Scratch

The other extreme is to start from scratch, in effect reconstructing the test data each time. This approach has the benefit of complete control; the content is always known and can be enhanced or extended over time, preserving prior efforts. Internal cohesion is ensured because the software itself creates and maintains the interrelationships, and changes to file structures or record layouts are automatically incorporated.

But reconstructing test data is not free from hazards. The most obvious is that, without automation, it's highly impractical for large-scale applications. But less obvious is the fact that some files cannot be created through online interaction: they are system generated only through interfaces or processing cycles. Thus, it may not be possible to start from a truly clean slate.

A compelling argument also might be made that data created in a vacuum, so to speak, lacks the expanse of production: unique or unusual situations that often arise in the real world may not be contemplated by test designers. Granted, this technique allows for steady and constant expansion of the test data as necessary circumstances are discovered, but it lacks the randomness that makes production so appealing.

Seeding the Data

Seeding test data is a combination of using production files and creating new data with specific conditions. This approach provides a dose of reality tempered by a measure of control.

This was the strategy adopted by a major mutual fund to enable test automation. Without predictable repeatable data there was no practical means of reusing automated tests across releases. Although much of the data could be created through the online interface, such as funds, customers, and accounts, other data had to be extracted from production. Testing statements and tax reports, for example, required historical transactions that could not be generated except by multiple execution cycles. So, the alternative to acquiring the data from production and performing the necessary maintenance on the tests proved to be less time consuming. Once the data was assembled, it was archived for reuse.

It's still not easy. You must still surmount the cohesion challenge, ensuring that the subset you acquire makes sense, and you must still have an efficient means of creating the additional data needed for test conditions. Furthermore, you must treat the resulting data as the valuable asset that it is, instituting procedures for archiving it safely so that it can be restored and reused.

Although a popular and sensible concept, reuse brings its own issues. For time-sensitive applications, which many if not most are, reusing the same data over and over is not viable unless you can roll the data dates forward or the system date back. For example, an employee who is 64 one month may turn 65 the next, resulting in different tax consequences for pension payouts.

Furthermore, modifications to file structures and record layouts demand data conversions, but this may be seen as an advantage because, it is hoped, the conversions are tested against the testbed before they are performed against production.

Generating Data Based upon the Database

Generated test data can obviously be used to create databases with enough information to approximate real-world conditions for testing capacity and performance. If you need to ensure that your database design can support millions of customers or billions of transactions and still deliver acceptable response times, generation may be the only practical means of creating these volumes.

Test data generators begin with the description of the file or database that is to be created. In most cases, the tools can read the database tables directly to determine the fields and their type, length, and format. The user can then add the rules, relationships, and constraints that govern the generation of valid data.

Standard "profiles" are also offered, which can automatically produce billions of names, addresses, cities, states, zip codes, Social Security numbers, test dates, and other common data values such as random values, ranges, and type mixes. User-customizable data types are also available in most products, which can be used for generating unique SIC (standard industrialization classification) business codes, e-mail addresses, and other data types.

A more critical feature, and more difficult to implement, is support for parent/child and other relationships in complex databases. For example, a parent record, such as a customer account master, must be linked with multiple child records, such as different accounts and transactions. This type of functionality is essential for relational database environments where referential integrity is key.

Some users have found it easier to use a test data generator to create data that is then read by an automated test tool and entered into the application. This is an interesting combination of data generating and seeding. The synergy between test data generation and test automation tools is a natural, and in some cases the test data generation capability is being embedded in test execution products.

Databases can contain more than just data, such as stored procedures or derived foreign keys that link other tables or databases. In these cases, it is not feasible to generate data directly into the tables. Too often maintaining database integrity is a project unto itself.

And, of course, in the end volume is its own challenge. More is not necessarily better. Too much data will take too long to generate, will require too much storage, and may create even more issues than not enough.

Generating Test Data/Test Cases Based upon the Requirements

Functional testing is a different animal, however. If you are testing business rules, such as whether an account whose balance owed is more than 90 days past due will permit additional credit purchases to be posted, then you must know precisely which account number contains the condition and which transactions will be entered against it. Although it may be easy to generate huge volumes of accounts whose balances are all over the map in terms of their amounts and due dates, it is not as simple to know exactly which accounts satisfy which business rules.

In this context, the same issues exist as they do for simply sampling production data. Even if you are comfortable that your data sample is representative of the types of conditions that must be tested, it's another matter altogether to know which accounts meet which requirements. Testing complex business rules may require knowing the exact state of several variables that are spread over multiple databases, tables, and/or files, and finding that precise combination may be like looking for a needle in a haystack.

The latest test case builder tools derive the test data directly from the requirements. The output of such tools is the input to the automated testing scripts that do not require business knowledge. How novel — test scripts and the test data/test case scenarios are based upon the requirements! Such cutting edge test tools bridge the gap between the requirements and testing phases.

Advanced test case generation tools have the following characteristics:

- Input the raw unprocessed test data from a test grid or external source such as Microsoft's Excel. For GUI the data could be the values in a drop-down list, the text field data, the radio button conditions, and so on.
- Capability of reengineering existing parameterized test data to raw unprocessed test data from an external source such as Microsoft Excel.
- Generate optimized "pair-wise" positive and negative test data from the raw unprocessed parameters and values.
- Capability for the analyst/tester to build business rules in English prose statements from the requirements when rigorous requirements exist, achieved by simple point and clicking. The English prose must be able to handle any complex conditional expression.
- Based upon the condition tested against the optimized "pairwise" test data an action or otherwise action is applied to the test data to reflect how the application should or should not behave. This results in a set of rows of optimized test scenarios.
- Capability for the analyst/tester to build interface rules in English prose statements to modify the input set to (1) modify the input set based upon one or more conditions, and (2) generate ranges for test data that is important for performance/load/stress testing. This feature is used when rigorous requirements are not necessarily rigorous or even available.
- Capability of exporting the optimized test data to Excel or other medium which can then be input to an automated testing tool (current or future automated tool).
- Provide a cross-reference matrix to associate the business rules with the resulting test scenario test data. This is bidirectional traceability, which is important for maintenance efforts.
- Capability of creating an expected result in the test data based upon the application of the business rules. This allows the script to compare the actual and expected values.

Smartware Technologies's TestSmart™ is an example of this cutting edge tool approach; TestSmart™ has also been seamlessly integrated with Original Software's TestBench Suite of testing tools as characterized above. With Original's simple "point-and-click" interface, the user can generate intelligent test cases and replay them using the replay portion of the TestBench Suite.

With TestSmart™, one does not have to manually create test cases by entering symmetric row tests in a test grid or an Excel spreadsheet. All that is necessary from the user are the parameters and respective column values, e.g., GUI dropdown caption name and the respective values. A set of optimized test cases will be generated. To be even more sophisticated, the user can easily enter business rules by point and click to constrain the optimized test data to reflect how the application or system should or should not behave. See www.smartwaretechnologies.com, which describes the tool in detail. A free trial version is available from this Smartware Technologies, Inc. Web site.

Part 29
Taxonomy of Testing Tools

Testing Tool Selection Checklist

Finding the appropriate tool can be difficult. Several questions need to be answered before selecting a tool. Appendix F19, Testing Tool Selection Checklist, lists questions to help the QA team evaluate and select an automated testing tool.

The following categorizes currently available tool types based upon their tool objectives and features. In the section called Vendor Tool Descriptions, popular vendors supporting each tool category are discussed.

- *Function/Regression Tools* — These tools help you test software through a native graphical user interface. Some also help with other interface types. Another example is Web test tools that test through a browser, for example, capture/replay tools.
- *Test Design/Data Tools* — These tools help create test cases and generate test data.
- *Load/Performance Tools* — These tools are often also GUI test drivers.
- *Test Process/Management Tools* — These tools help organize and execute suites of test cases at the command line, API, or protocol level. Some tools have graphical user interfaces, but they don't have any special support for testing a product that has a native GUI. Web test tools that work at the protocol level are included here.
- *Unit Testing Tools* — These tools, frameworks, and libraries support unit testing, which is usually performed by the developer, usually using interfaces below the public interfaces of the software under test.
- *Test Implementation Tools* — These tools assist with testing at runtime.
- *Test Evaluation Tools* — Tools that help you evaluate the quality of your tests. Examples include code coverage tools.
- *Static Test Analyzers* — Tools that analyze programs without running them. Metrics tools fall in this category.
- *Defect Management Tools* — Tools that track software product defects and manage product enhancement requests. Manages defect states from defect discovery to closure.

- *Application Performance Monitoring/Tuning Tools* — Tools that measure and maximize value across the IT service delivery life cycle to ensure applications meet quality, performance, and availability goals.
- *Runtime Analysis Testing Tools* — Tools that analyze programs while running them.

Vendor Tool Descriptions

Exhibit 29.1 provides an overview of some testing tools. The descriptions are listed alphabetically and are cross-referenced to the tool description and vendor Web site information. No tool is favored over another.

When You Should Consider Test Automation

A testing tool should be considered based on the test objectives. As a general guideline, one should investigate the appropriateness of a testing tool when the human manual process is inadequate. For example, if a system needs to be stress tested, a group of testers could simultaneously log on to the system and attempt to simulate peak loads using stopwatches. However, this approach has limitations. One cannot systematically measure the performance precisely or repeatably. For this case, a load-testing tool can simulate several virtual users under controlled stress conditions.

A regression testing tool might be needed under the following circumstances:

- Tests need to be run at every build of an application, for example, time-consuming, unreliable, and inconsistent use of human resources.
- Tests are required using multiple data values for the same actions.
- Tests require detailed information from system internals such as SQL and GUI attributes.
- There is a need to stress a system to see how it performs.

Testing tools have the following benefits:

- Much faster than their human counterpart
- Run without human intervention
- Provide code coverage analysis after a test run
- Precisely repeatable
- Reusable, just as programming subroutines
- Detailed test cases (including predictable "expected results"), which have been developed from functional specifications and/or technical design documentation
- Stable testing environment with a test database that can be restorable to a known constant, so that the test cases are able to be repeated each time there are modifications made to the application

Exhibit 29.1. Testing Tool Name versus Tool Category[a]

	Function/Regression Tools	Test Design/Data Tools	Load/Performance Tools	Test Process/Management Tools	Unit Testing Tools	Test Implementation Tools	Test Evaluation Tools	Static Test Analyzer Tools	Defect Management Tools	Application Performance Monitoring/Tuning Tools	Runtime Analysis Testing Tools
Abbott	√										
Access for DB2						√					
Advanced Defect Tracking									√		
ALLPAIRS	√										
AllPairs.java	√										
Android	√										
Application Expert			√								
ApTest Manager				√							
AQtest					√						
ASSENT								√			
Assertion Definition Language (ADL)	√										
Astra Load Test			√								
Astra Quick Test	√										
Aunit					√						
AutoIt	√										
AutomX	√										
AutoPilot	√										
AutoTester Client/Server for use with SAP R/3				√							
AutoTester for OS/2	√										
AutoTester for Windows	√										
Bug Tracker Software									√		
BugAware									√		
Buggit									√		

Exhibit 29.1. Testing Tool Name versus Tool Category[a] (Continued)

	Function/Regression Tools	Test Design/Data Tools	Load/Performance Tools	Test Process/Management Tools	Unit Testing Tools	Test Implementation Tools	Test Evaluation Tools	Static Test Analyzer Tools	Defect Management Tools	Application Performance Monitoring/Tuning Tools	Runtime Analysis Testing Tools
CAPBAK	✓										
Certify	✓										
Check					✓						
CitraTest	✓										
ClearDDTS									✓		
ClearMaker								✓			
ClearQuest									✓		
ClientVantage			✓								
Clover							✓				
CodeSurfer								✓			
CodeTEST								✓			✓
Compare for Servers						✓					
cUnit					✓						
DARTT	✓										
Datagen2000	✓										
DateWise FileCompare						✓					
Defect Agent									✓		
DGL	✓										
Eggplant for Mac OS X	✓										
Elementool									✓		
e-Monitor	✓										
EMOS Framework	✓										
E-SIM				✓							
e-Tester	✓										

Exhibit 29.1. Testing Tool Name versus Tool Category[a] (Continued)

	Function/Regression Tools	Test Design/Data Tools	Load/Performance Tools	Test Process/Management Tools	Unit Testing Tools	Test Implementation Tools	Test Evaluation Tools	Static Test Analyzer Tools	Defect Management Tools	Application Performance Monitoring/Tuning Tools	Runtime Analysis Testing Tools
eValid	√										√
Eventcorder suite	√										
File-AID/CS		√									
HarnessIt					√						
Hindsight/SQA								√			
HtmlUnit					√						
IBM Rational Robot	√										
IBM Rational Test Realtime										√	√
imbus GUI Test Case Library	√										
iSTROBE			√								
Jacareto	√										
Jemmy	√										
Jenny	√										
jfcUnit	√										
LDRA Testbed							√				
LoadRunner			√								
LOGISCOPE toolset							√				
Marathon	√										
McCabe Coverage Server								√			
McCabe Enterprise Quality				√							
McCabe QA								√			
McCabe Reengineer								√			
McCabe Test								√			
McCabe TRUEtrack									√		

315

Exhibit 29.1. Testing Tool Name versus Tool Category[a] (Continued)

	Function/Regression Tools	Test Design/Data Tools	Load/Performance Tools	Test Process/Management Tools	Unit Testing Tools	Test Implementation Tools	Test Evaluation Tools	Static Test Analyzer Tools	Defect Management Tools	Application Performance Monitoring/Tuning Tools	Runtime Analysis Testing Tools
MemCheck for Windows						✓					✓
Merant Tracker									✓		
METRIC								✓			
Metrics Tools								✓			
Move for Legacy	✓										
NetworkVantage			✓								
NUnit					✓						
Orchid	✓										
Ozibug									✓		
Panorama C/C++	✓										
Panorama-2	✓										
Perl X11::GUITest	✓										
Phantom	✓										
Pounder	✓										
Problem Tracker									✓		
ProjecTrak Bug									✓		
Protune										✓	
PVCS Tracker									✓		
QADirector®				✓							
QARunTM	✓										
QC/Replay	✓										
QES/Architect				✓							
QES/DatEZ (date-easy)	✓										
QES/EZ for GUI	✓										

Exhibit 29.1. Testing Tool Name versus Tool Category[a] (Continued)

	Function/Regression Tools	Test Design/Data Tools	Load/Performance Tools	Test Process/Management Tools	Unit Testing Tools	Test Implementation Tools	Test Evaluation Tools	Static Test Analyzer Tools	Defect Management Tools	Application Performance Monitoring/Tuning Tools	Runtime Analysis Testing Tools
qftestJUI	√										
QStudio for Java Pro								√			
QStudio JAVA								√			
QtUnit					√						
Quick Test Professional	√										
QuickBugs									√		
Rational Functional Tester for Java and Web	√										
Rational Performance Tester			√								
Rational PureCoverage							√				
Rational Purify						√					√
Rational Purify Plus											√
Rational Robot	√										
Rational TeamTest	√										
Rational Test RealTime Coverage							√				
Rational Test RealTime System Testing				√							
Reconcile				√							
Remedy Quality Management									√		
SAFS (Software Automation Framework Support)	√										
SDTF - SNA Development Test Facility				√							
ServerVantage			√								
Silk Vision										√	
SilkPerformer			√								

Exhibit 29.1. Testing Tool Name versus Tool Category[a] (Continued)

	Function/Regression Tools	Test Design/Data Tools	Load/Performance Tools	Test Process/Management Tools	Unit Testing Tools	Test Implementation Tools	Test Evaluation Tools	Static Test Analyzer Tools	Defect Management Tools	Application Performance Monitoring/Tuning Tools	Runtime Analysis Testing Tools
Silkperformer lite			√								
SilkPilot				√							
Silkplan pro				√							
SilkRadar									√		
SilkRealizer						√					
SilkTest	√										
Silktest international	√										
Smalltalk Test Mentor	√										
Smart TestTM		√			√						
SQA TeamTest: ERP Extension for SAP	√										
SQA TestFoundation for PeopleSoft	√										
SSW Code Auditor								√			
STATIC								√			
Strobe/APM			√								
TagUnit					√						
Tasker	√										
TCAT C/C++							√				
TCAT for Java							√				
TCAT-PATH							√				
TDGEN	√										
Test Case Manager (TCM)				√							
Test Mentor - Java Edition					√						
Test Now	√										

Exhibit 29.1. Testing Tool Name versus Tool Category[a] (Continued)

	Function/Regression Tools	Test Design/Data Tools	Load/Performance Tools	Test Process/Management Tools	Unit Testing Tools	Test Implementation Tools	Test Evaluation Tools	Static Test Analyzer Tools	Defect Management Tools	Application Performance Monitoring/Tuning Tools	Runtime Analysis Testing Tools
Test Station				√							
TestAgent	√										
TestBase	√										
TestBed								√			
TestBench for iSeries	√										
TestDirector				√					√		
Tester	√										
TestGUI	√										
Test Manager				√							
TestQuest Pro Test Automation System	√										
TestSmith	√										
TestWorks				√							
TestWorks/Advisor								√			
TestWorks/Coverage											√
TET (Test Environment Toolkit)				√							
TMS				√							
T-Plan Professional				√							
TrackRecord									√		
TRecorder	√										
TrueJ								√			
T-SCOPE											√
Turbo Data	√										
Unified TestPro (UTP)	√										

Exhibit 29.1. Testing Tool Name versus Tool Category[a] (Continued)

	Function/Regression Tools	Test Design/Data Tools	Load/Performance Tools	Test Process/Management Tools	Unit Testing Tools	Test Implementation Tools	Test Evaluation Tools	Static Test Analyzer Tools	Defect Management Tools	Application Performance Monitoring/Tuning Tools	Runtime Analysis Testing Tools
Vermont High Test Plus	√										
VersaTest			√								
Visual Test	√										
WebKing	√										
WinRunner	√										
XMLUnit					√						
xrc - X Remote Control	√										
XRunner	√										
XSLTunit					√						
X-Unity					√						
ZeroDefect									√		
ZeroFault							√				

[a] Each tool is described on the CD.

When You Should NOT Consider Test Automation

In spite of the compelling business case for test automation, and despite the significant investments of money, time, and effort invested in test automation tools and projects, the majority of testing is still performed manually. Why? There are three primary reasons why test automation fails: the steep learning curve, the development effort required, and the maintenance overhead.

The learning curve is an issue for the simple reason that traditional test scripting tools are basically specialized programming languages, but the best testers are application experts, not programmers.

This creates a skills disconnect that requires an unreasonable learning curve. Application experts, who make ideal testers because of their business knowledge, are unlikely to have programming skills. Gaining these skills takes months if not years, and without these skills the script libraries are usually not well-designed for maintainability.

Most test tool vendors are aware of this shortcoming and attempt to address it through a capture/replay facility. This is an approach that ostensibly allows a tester to perform the test manually while it is automatically "recorded" into a test script that can later be replayed. Although this approach appears to address the learning curve, in reality it often causes more problems than it solves.

First, a recorded test script is fragile and easily subject to failure. Because it has no error handling or logic, the smallest deviation in the application behavior or data will cause the script to either abort or make errors. Furthermore, it combines both script and data into a single program, which yields no reusability or modularity. The end result is essentially unstructured, poorly designed code.

Also, although it may appear easy to record a script, it is not as easy to modify or maintain it. The reason software is tested is because something has changed, which means the scripts must also be modified. Making extensive script changes and debugging errors is time consuming and complex.

Once companies discover that capture/replay is not a viable long-term solution, they either give up or begin a development effort.

Contrary to popular belief, it is not always wise to purchase a testing tool. Some factors that limit a testing tool include:

- *Unrealistic expectations* — The IT industry is notorious for latching onto any new technology solution thinking that it will be a panacea. It is human nature to be optimistic about any new technology. The vendor salespeople present the rosiest picture of their tool offerings. The result is expectations that are often unrealistic.
- *Lack of a testing process* — A prerequisite for test automation is that a sound manual testing process exists. The lack of good testing practices and standards will be detrimental to test automation. Automated testing tools will not automatically find defects unless well-defined test plans are in place.
- *False sense of security* — Even though a set of automated test scripts runs successfully, this does not guarantee that the automated testing tool has located all the defects. This assumption leads to a false sense of security. Automation is as good as the test cases and test input data.

- *Technical difficulties* — Automated testing tools themselves unfortunately have defects. Technical environmental changes such as the operating system can severely limit automated testing tools.
- *Organizational issues* — Test automation will have an impact on the organization, for it transcends projects and departments. For example, the use of data-driven test scripts requires test input data, typically in the form of rows in an Excel spreadsheet. This data will probably be supplied by another group, such as the business system analysts, not the testing organization.
- *Cost* — A testing tool may not be affordable to the organization, for example, the cost/performance tradeoff.
- *Culture* — The development culture may not be ready for a testing tool, because it requires the proper skills and commitment to long-term quality.
- *Usability testing* — There are no automated testing tools that can test usability.
- *One-time testing* — If the test is going to be performed only once, a testing tool may not be worth the required time and expense.
- *Time crunch* — If there is pressure to complete testing within a fixed timeframe, a testing tool may not be feasible, because it takes time to learn, set up, and integrate a testing tool into the development methodology.
- *Ad hoc testing* — If there is no formal test design and test cases, a regression testing tool will be useless.
- *Predictable results* — If tests do not have predictable results, a regression testing tool will be useless.
- *Instability* — If the system is changing rapidly during each testing spiral, more time will be spent maintaining a regression testing tool than it is worth.

Part 30
Methodology to Evaluate Automated Testing Tools

This part provides an outline of the steps involved in acquiring, implementing, and using testing tools. The management of any significant project requires that the work be divided into tasks for which completion criteria can be defined. The transition from one task to another occurs in steps; to permit the orderly progress of the activities, the scheduling of these steps must be determined in advance. A general outline for such a schedule is provided by the steps described. The actual time schedule depends on many factors that must be determined for each specific tool use.

Step 1: Define Your Test Requirements

The goals to be accomplished should be identified in a format that permits later determination that they have been met (i.e., Step 15). Typical goals include reducing the average processing time of C++ programs by one fifth, achieving complete interchangeability of programs or data sets with another organization, and adhering to an established standard for documentation format. The statement of goals should also identify responsibilities, particularly the role that headquarters staff may have, and specify coordination requirements with other organizations. When a centralized management method is employed, the statement of goals may include a budget and a desired completion date. Once these constraints are specified, funding management may delegate the approval of the acquisition plan to a lower level.

Step 2: Set Tool Objectives

The goals generated in Step 1 should be translated into desired tool features and requirements that arise from the development and operating environment identified. Constraints on tool cost and availability may also be added at this step. For example, a typical tool objective for a program format is to provide header identification, uniform indentation, and the facility to print listings and comments separately for all Pascal programs. In addition, the program must be able to run on the organization's specific computer under its operating system. Only tools that have been in commercial use for at least one year and at no fewer than N sites should be considered. (The value of N is predetermined by the number of sites the organization has.)

Step 3a: Conduct Selection Activities for Informal Procurement

The following tasks should be performed when an informal procurement plan is in effect.

Task 1: Develop the Acquisition Plan

The acquisition plan communicates the actions of software management both up and down the chain of command. The plan may also be combined with the statement of tool objectives (Step 2). The acquisition plan includes the budgets and schedules for subsequent steps in the tool introduction, a justification of resource requirements in light of expected benefits, contributions to the introduction expected from other organizations (e.g., the tool itself, modification patches, or training materials), and the assignment of responsibility for subsequent events within the organization, particularly the identification of the software engineer. Minimum tool documentation requirements are also specified in the plan.

Task 2: Define Selection Criteria

The selection criteria include a ranked listing of attributes that should support effective tool use. Typical selection criteria include:

- The ability to accomplish specified tool objectives
- Ease of use
- Ease of installation
- Minimum processing time
- Compatibility with other tools
- Low purchase or lease cost

Most of these criteria must be considered further to permit objective evaluation, but this step may be left to the individual who does the scoring. Constraints that have been imposed by the preceding events or are generated at this step should be summarized together with the criteria.

Task 3: Identify Candidate Tools

This is the first step for which the software engineer is responsible. The starting point for preparing a list of candidate tools is a comprehensive tool catalogue. Two lists are usually prepared, the first of which does not consider the constraints and contains all tools that meet the functional requirements. For the feasible candidates, literature should be requested from the developer and then examined for conformance with the given constraints. At this point, the second list is generated, which contains tools that meet both the functional requirements and the constraints. If this list is too short, some constraints may be relaxed.

Task 4: Conduct the Candidate Review

The user must review the list of candidate tools prepared by the software engineer. Because few users can be expected to be knowledgeable about software tools, specific questions should be raised by software management, including the following:

- Will this tool handle the present file format?
- Are tool commands consistent with those of the editor?
- How much training is required?

Adequate time should be allowed for this review, and a due date for responses should be indicated. Because users often view this as a low-priority, long-term task, considerable follow-up by line management is required. If possible, tools should be obtained for trial use, or a demonstration at another facility should be arranged.

Task 5: Score the Candidates

For each criterion identified in Task 2, a numeric score should be generated on the basis of the information obtained from the vendor's literature, tool demonstrations, the user's review, observation in a working environment, or the comments of previous users. Once weighting factors for the criteria have been assigned, the score for each criterion is multiplied by the appropriate factor; the sum of the products represents the overall tool score. If the criteria are merely ranked, the scoring will consist of a ranking of each candidate under each criterion heading. Frequently during this process, a single tool will be recognized as clearly superior.

Task 6: Select the Tool

This decision is reserved for software managers; they can provide a review of the scoring and permit additional factors that are not expressed in the criteria to be considered. For example, a report from another agency may state that the selected vendor did not provide adequate service. If the selected tool did not receive the highest score, the software engineer must review the tool characteristics thoroughly to avoid unexpected installation difficulties. (Tool selection concludes the separate procedure for informal procurement. The overall procedure continues with Step 4.)

Step 3b: Conduct Selection Activities for Formal Procurement

The following tasks should be performed when a formal tool procurement plan is in effect.

Task 1: Develop the Acquisition Plan

This plan must include all the elements mentioned for Task 1 of Step 3a, plus the constraints on the procurement process and the detailed responsibilities for all procurement documents (e.g., statement of work and technical and administrative provisions in the request for proposal).

Task 2: Create the Technical Requirements Document

The technical requirements document is an informal description of tool requirements and the constraints under which the tool must operate. It uses much of the material from the acquisition plan but should add enough detail to support a meaningful review by the tool user.

Task 3: Review Requirements

The user must review the technical requirements for the proposed procurement. As in the case of Step 3a, Task 4, the user may need to be prompted with pertinent questions, and there should be close management follow-up for a timely response.

Task 4: Generate the Request for Proposal

The technical portions of the request for proposal should be generated from the technical requirements document and any user comments on it. Technical considerations typically include:

- A specification of the tool as it should be delivered, including applicable documents, a definition of the operating environment, and the quality assurance provisions;
- A statement of work for which the tool is procured. This includes any applicable standards for the process by which the tool is generated (e.g., configuration management of the tool) and documentation or test reports to be furnished with the tool. Training and operational support requirements are also identified in the statement of work; and
- Proposal evaluation criteria and format requirements. These criteria are listed in order of importance. Subfactors for each may be identified. Any restrictions on the proposal format (e.g., major headings, page count, or desired sample outputs) may be included.

Task 5: Solicit Proposals

This activity should be carried out by administrative personnel. Capability lists of potential sources are maintained by most purchasing organizations.

When the software organization knows of potential bidders, those bidders' names should be submitted to the procurement office. Responses should be screened for compliance with major legal provisions of the request for proposal.

Task 6: Perform the Technical Evaluation

Each proposal received in response to the request for proposal should be evaluated in light of the previously established criteria. Failure to meet major technical requirements can lead to outright disqualification of a proposal. Those deemed to be in the competitive range are assigned point scores that are then considered together with cost and schedule factors, which are separately evaluated by administrative personnel.

Task 7: Select a Tool Source

On the basis of the combined cost, schedule, and technical factors, a source for the tool is selected. If this is not the highest-rated technical proposal, managers should require additional reviews by software management and the software engineer to determine whether the tool is acceptable. (Source selection concludes the separate procedure for formal procurement. The overall procedure continues with Step 4.)

Step 4: Procure the Testing Tool

In addition to verifying that the cost of the selected tool is within the approved budget, the procurement process considers the adequacy of licensing and other contractual provisions and compliance with the fine print associated with all government procurements. The vendor must furnish the source program, meet specific test and performance requirements, and maintain the tool. In informal procurement, a trial period use may be considered if this has not already taken place under one of the previous steps.

If the acquisition plan indicates the need for outside training, the ability of the vendor to supply the training and any cost advantages from the combined procurement of the tool and the training should be investigated. If substantial savings can be realized through simultaneously purchasing the tool and training users, procurement may be held up until outside training requirements are defined (Step 7).

Step 5: Create the Evaluation Plan

The evaluation plan is based on the goals identified in Step 1 and the tool objectives derived in Step 2. It describes how the attainment of these objectives should be evaluated for the specific tool selected. Typical items to be covered in the plan are milestones for installation and dates and performance levels for the initial operational capability and for subsequent enhancements. When improvements in throughput, response time, or turn-around time are expected, the reports for obtaining these data should be identified. Responsibility for tests, reports, and other actions must be assigned in the plan, and a topical outline of the evaluation report should be included.

The acceptance test procedure is part of the evaluation plan, although for a major tool procurement it may be a separate document. The procedure lists the detailed steps that are necessary to test the tool in accordance with the procurement provisions when it is received, to evaluate the inter-action of the tool with the computer environment (e.g., adverse effects on throughput), and to generate an acceptance report.

Step 6: Create the Tool Manager's Plan

The tool manager's plan describes how the tool manager is selected, the responsibilities for the adaptation of the tool, and the training that is required. The tool manager should be an experienced systems program-mer who is familiar with the current operating system. Training in the oper-ation and installation of the selected tool in the form of review of documen-tation, visits to the tool's current users, or training by the vendor must be arranged. The software engineer is responsible for the tool manager's plan, and the tool manager should work under the software engineer's direction. The tool manager's plan must be approved by software management.

Step 7: Create the Training Plan

The training plan should first consider the training that is automatically provided with the tool (e.g., documentation, test cases, and online diagnos-tics). These features may be supplemented by standard training aids sup-plied by the vendor for in-house training (e.g., audio- or videocassettes and lecturers). Because of the expense, training sessions at other locations should be considered only when nothing else is available. The personnel to receive formal training should also be specified in the plan, and adequacy of in-house facilities (e.g., number of terminals and computer time) should be addressed. If training by the tool vendor is desired, this should be iden-tified as early as possible to permit training to be procured along with the tool (see Step 4). Users must be involved in the preparation of the training plan; coordination with users is essential. The training plan must be pre-pared by the software engineer and approved by software management. Portions of the plan must be furnished to the procurement staff if outside personnel or facilities are used.

Step 8: Receive the Tool

The tool is turned over by the procuring organization to the software engineer.

Step 9: Perform the Acceptance Test

The software engineer or staff should test the tool in an as-received condition with only those modifications made that are essential for bringing the tool up on the host computer. Once a report on the test has been issued and approved by the software manager, the tool is officially accepted.

Step 10: Conduct Orientation

When it has been determined that the tool has been received in a satisfactory condition, software management should hold an orientation meeting for all personnel involved in the use of the tool and tool products (e.g., reports or listings generated by the tool). The objectives of tool use (e.g., increased throughput or improved legibility of listings) should be directly communicated. Highlights of the evaluation plan should be presented, and any changes in duties associated with tool introduction should be described. Personnel should be reassured that allowances will be made for problems encountered during tool introduction and reminded that the tool's full benefits may not be realized for some time.

Step 11: Implement Modifications

This step is carried out by the tool manager in accordance with the approved tool manager plan. It includes modifications of the tool, the documentation, and the operating system. In rare cases, some modification of the computer (e.g., channel assignments) may also be necessary. Typical tool modifications involve deletion of unused options, changes in prompts or diagnostics, and other adaptations made for efficient use in the current environment. In addition, the modifications must be thoroughly documented.

Vendor literature for the tool should be reviewed in detail and tailored to the current computer environment and to any tool modifications that have been made. Deleting sections that are not applicable is just as useful as adding material that is required for the specific programming environment. Unused options should be clearly marked or removed from the manuals. If the tool should not be used for some resident software (e.g., because of language incompatibility or conflicts in the operating system interface), warning notices should be inserted in the tool manual.

Step 12: Train Tool Users

Training is a joint responsibility of the software engineer and the tool users and should help promote tool use. The software engineer is responsible for the content (in accordance with the approved training plan), and the tool user controls the length and scheduling of sessions. The tool user should be able to terminate training steps that are not helpful and to extend portions that are helpful but need further explication. Retraining or training in the use of additional options may be necessary and can provide an opportunity for users to talk about problems associated with the tool.

Step 13: Use the Tool in the Operating Environment

The first use of the tool in the operating environment should involve the most qualified user personnel and minimal use of options. This first use should not be on a project with tight schedule constraints. Resulting difficulties must be resolved before expanded service is initiated. If the first use is successful, use by additional personnel and use of further options may commence.

User comments on training, first use of the tool, and the use of extended capabilities should be prepared and furnished to the software engineer. Desired improvements in the user interface, in the speed or format of response, and in the use of computer resources are all appropriate topics. Formal comments may be solicited shortly after the initial use, after six months, and again after one year.

Step 14: Write the Evaluation Report

Using the outline generated in Step 5, the software engineer prepares the evaluation report. User comments and toolsmith observations provide important input to this document. Most of all, the document must discuss how the general goals and tool objectives were met. The report may also include observations on the installation and use of the tool, cooperation received from the vendor in installation or training, and any other lessons learned.

Tool and host computer modifications are also described in this report. It may contain a section of comments useful to future tool users. The report should be approved by software management and preferably by funding management as well.

Step 15: Determine Whether Goals Have Been Met

Funding management receives the evaluation report and should determine whether the goals that were established in Step 1 have been met. This written determination should address:

- Attainment of technical objectives
- Adherence to budget and other resource constraints
- Timeliness of the effort
- Cooperation from other agencies
- Recommendations for future tool acquisitions

Appendices

Appendix A
Spiral Testing Methodology

The following is a graphical representation of the spiral testing methodology and consists of an overview relating the methodology to Deming's Plan, Do, Check, Act (PDCA) quality wheel, parts, steps, and tasks.

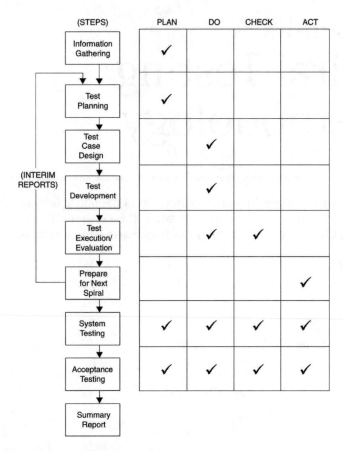

Exhibit A.1. Continuous Improvement

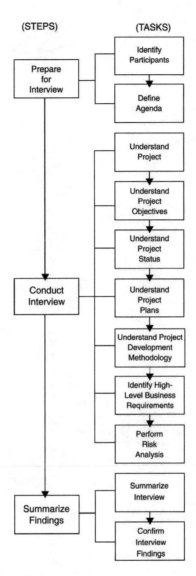

(STEPS) (TASKS)

Exhibit A.2. Information Gathering

(STEPS) (TASKS)

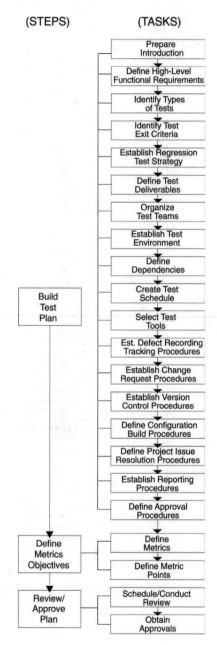

Exhibit A.3. Test Planning

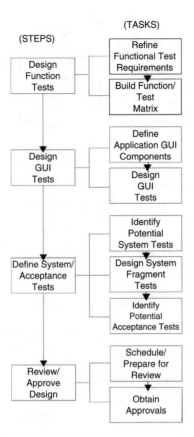

Exhibit A.4. Test Case Design

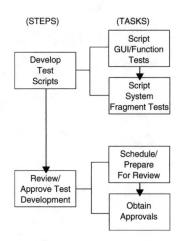

Exhibit A.5. Test Development

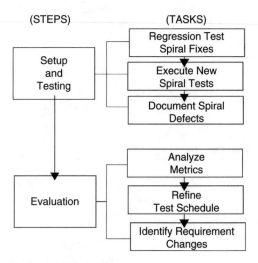

Exhibit A.6. Test Execution/Evaluation

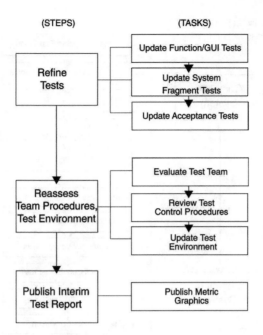

Exhibit A.7. Prepare for the Next Spiral

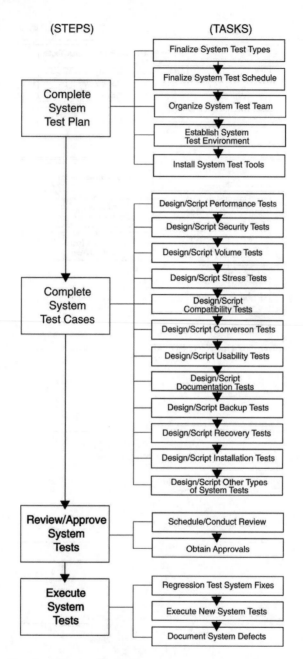

(STEPS)   (TASKS)

Finalize System Test Types

Finalize System Test Schedule

Complete System Test Plan

Organize System Test Team

Establish System Test Environment

Install System Test Tools

Design/Script Performance Tests

Design/Script Security Tests

Design/Script Volume Tests

Design/Script Stress Tests

Complete System Test Cases

Design/Script Compatibility Tests

Design/Script Converson Tests

Design/Script Usability Tests

Design/Script Documentation Tests

Design/Script Backup Tests

Design/Script Recovery Tests

Design/Script Installation Tests

Design/Script Other Types of System Tests

Review/Approve System Tests

Schedule/Conduct Review

Obtain Approvals

Execute System Tests

Regression Test System Fixes

Execute New System Tests

Document System Defects

Exhibit A.8. Conduct System Testing

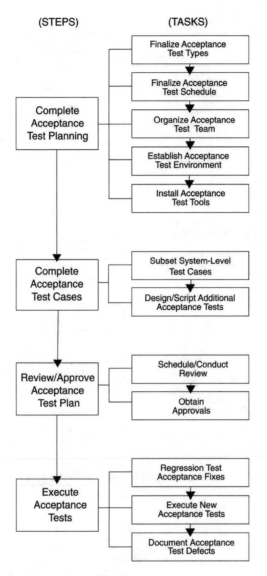

(STEPS) (TASKS)

Complete Acceptance Test Planning
- Finalize Acceptance Test Types
- Finalize Acceptance Test Schedule
- Organize Acceptance Test Team
- Establish Acceptance Test Environment
- Install Acceptance Test Tools

Complete Acceptance Test Cases
- Subset System-Level Test Cases
- Design/Script Additional Acceptance Tests

Review/Approve Acceptance Test Plan
- Schedule/Conduct Review
- Obtain Approvals

Execute Acceptance Tests
- Regression Test Acceptance Fixes
- Execute New Acceptance Tests
- Document Acceptance Test Defects

Exhibit A.9. Conduct Acceptance Testing

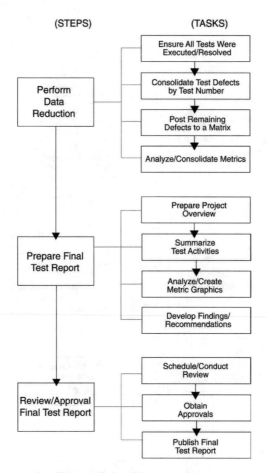

(STEPS) (TASKS)

Exhibit A.10. Summarize/Report Spiral Test Results

Appendix B
Software Quality Assurance Plan

This appendix provides a sample software quality assurance plan for an application project. The details of the project are obscured to emphasize the plan's general philosophy and techniques.

1. Purpose
2. Reference Document
   2.1 The MIS Standard
   2.2 MIS Software Guidelines
   2.3 The Software Requirements Specification
   2.4 The Generic Project Plan
   2.5 The Generic Software Test Plan
   2.6 The Software Configuration Management Plan
3. Management
   3.1 The Organizational Structure
   3.2 Tasks and Responsibilities
       3.2.1 Project Leader (Lead Software Engineer)
       3.2.2 Software Development Groups
       3.2.3 The Testing Subcommittee
4. Documentation
   4.1 The Software Requirements Specification
   4.2 System User Guide
   4.3 The Installation Guide
   4.4 Test Results Summary
   4.5 Software Unit Documentation
       4.5.1 The Preliminary Design Document
       4.5.2 Detailed Design Document
       4.5.3 Other Documents
   4.6 Translator Software Units
5. Standards, Practices, and Conventions
6. Reviews and Inspections
7. Software Configuration Management
8. Problem Reporting and Corrective Action
9. Tools, Techniques, and Methodologies
10. Code Control

APPENDICES

Appendix C
Requirements Specification

The requirements specification is a specification for a software product, program, or application that performs functions in a specific environment organized by feature (source: IEEE Recommended Practice for Software Requirements Specifications).

APPENDICES

Appendix D
Change Request Form

The sample change request form below serves as the document vehicle to record and disseminate the actions of change control.

Change Request Form

Report Number: _____   Change Request No: _____

System Affected: _____

Subsystem Affected: _____

Documentation Affected: _____

Problem Statement:

_____

_____

_____

_____

_____

Action Required:

_____

_____

_____

_____

_____

_____

Appendix E
Test Templates

E1: Unit Test Plan

The unit test plan is based on the program or design specification and is required for a formal test environment. The following is a sample unit test plan table of contents.

1. Introduction Section
   a. Test Strategy and Approach
   b. Test Scope
   c. Test Assumptions
2. Walkthrough (Static Testing)
   a. Defects Discovered and Corrected
   b. Improvement Ideas
   c. Structured Programming Compliance
   d. Language Standards
   e. Development Documentation Standards
3. Test Cases (Dynamic Testing)
   a. Input Test Data
   b. Initial Conditions
   c. Expected Results
   d. Test Log Status
4. Environment Requirements
   a. Test Strategy and Approach
   b. Platform
   c. Libraries
   d. Tools
   e. Test Procedures
   f. Status Reporting

E2: System/Acceptance Test Plan

The system or acceptance test plan is based on the requirement specifications and is required for a formal test environment. System testing evaluates the functionality and performance of the whole application and consists of a variety of tests including performance, usability, stress, documentation, security, volume, recovery, and so on. Acceptance testing is a user-run test that demonstrates the application's ability to meet the original business objectives and system requirements and usually consists of a subset of system tests.

The following is a sample test plan table of contents.

1. Introduction
   a. System Description (i.e., brief description of system)
   b. Objective (i.e., objectives of the test plan)
   c. Assumptions (e.g., computers available all working hours, etc.)
   d. Risks (i.e., risks if unit testing is not completed)
   e. Contingencies (e.g., backup procedures, etc.)
   f. Constraints (e.g., limited resources)
   g. Approval Signatures (e.g., authority to sign off on document)
2. Test Approach and Strategy
   a. Scope of Testing (i.e., tests to be performed)
   b. Test Approach (e.g., test tools, black-box)
   c. Types of Tests (e.g., unit, system, static, dynamic, manual)
   d. Logistics (e.g., location, site needs, etc.)
   e. Regression Policy (e.g., between each build)
   f. Test Facility (i.e., general description of where test will occur)
   g. Test Procedures (e.g., defect fix acceptance, defect priorities, etc.)
   h. Test Organization (e.g., description of QA/test team)
   i. Test Libraries (i.e., location and description)
   j. Test Tools (e.g., capture/playback regression testing tools)
   k. Version Control (i.e., procedures to control different versions)
   l. Configuration Building (i.e., how to build the system)
   m. Change Control (i.e., procedures to manage change requests)
3. Test Execution Setup
   a. System Test Process (e.g., entrance criteria, readiness, etc.)
   b. Facility (e.g., details of test environment, lab)
   c. Resources (e.g., staffing, training, timeline)
   d. Tool Plan (e.g., specific tools, packages, special software)
   e. Test Organization (e.g., details of who, roles, responsibilities)
4. Test Specifications
   a. Functional Decomposition (e.g., what functions to test from functional specification)
   b. Functions Not to Be Tested (e.g., out of scope)
   c. Unit Test Cases (i.e., specific unit test cases)
   d. Integration Test Cases (i.e., specific integration test cases)
   e. System Test Cases (i.e., specific system test cases)
   f. Acceptance Test Cases (i.e., specific acceptance test cases)
5. Test Procedures
   a. Test Case, Script, Data Development (e.g., procedures to develop and maintain)
   b. Test Execution (i.e., procedures to execute the tests)

    c. Correction (i.e., procedures to correct discovered defects)

    d. Version Control (i.e., procedures to control software component versions)

    e. Maintaining Test Libraries

    f. Automated Test Tool Usage (i.e., tool standards)

    g. Project Management (i.e., issue and defect management)

    h. Monitoring and Status Reporting (i.e., interim vs. summary reports)

6. Test Tools

    a. Tools to Use (i.e., specific tools and features)

    b. Installation and Setup (i.e., instructions)

    c. Support and Help (e.g., vendor help line)

7. Personnel Resources

    a. Required Skills (i.e., manual/automated testing skills)

    b. Roles and Responsibilities (i.e., who does what when)

    c. Numbers and Time Required (e.g., resource balancing)

    d. Training Needs (e.g., send staff to tool training)

8. Test Schedule

    a. Development of Test Plan (e.g., start and end dates)

    b. Design of Test Cases (e.g., start and end dates by test type)

    c. Development of Test Cases (e.g., start and end dates by test type)

    d. Execution of Test Cases (e.g., start and end date by test type)

    e. Reporting of Problems (e.g., start and end dates)

    f. Developing Test Summary Report (e.g., start and end dates)

    g. Documenting Test Summary Report (e.g., start and end dates)

E3: Requirements Traceability Matrix

The requirements traceability matrix below is a document that traces user requirements from analysis through implementation. It can be used as a completeness check to verify that all requirements are present or that there are no unnecessary/extra features, and as a maintenance guide for new personnel. At each step in the development cycle, the requirements, code, and associated test cases are recorded to ensure that the user requirement is addressed in the final system. Both the user and developer have the ability to easily cross-reference the requirements to the design specifications, programming, and test cases.

User Requirement Reference	System Requirements Reference	Design Specification	Coding Component Reference	Unit Test Case Reference	Integration Test Case Reference	System Test Case Reference	Acceptance Test Case Reference
1.1 Customer must be valid	1.1.2 Online customer screen	Customer screen specification	CUS105, CUS217	CUS105.1.1, CUS2171.1	Int1.25, Int1.26	Sys4.75, Sys4.76	Acc2.25, Acc2.26
•	•	•	•	•	•	•	•
•	•	•	•	•	•	•	•
•	•	•	•	•	•	•	•

E4: Test Plan (Client/Server and Internet Spiral Testing)

The client/server test plan is based on the information gathered during the initial interview(s) with development and any other information that becomes available during the course of the project. Because requirement specifications are probably not available in the spiral development environment, this test plan is a "living document." Through every spiral, new information is added, and old information is updated as circumstances change. The major testing activities are the function, GUI, system, acceptance, and regression testing. These tests, however, are not necessarily performed in a specific order and may be concurrent.

The cover page of the test plan includes the title of the testing project, author, current revision number, and date last changed. The next page includes an optional section for sign-offs by the executive sponsor, development manager, testing manager, quality assurance manager, and others as appropriate.

The following is a sample test plan table of contents.

1. Introduction
    1.1   Purpose
    1.2   Executive Summary
    1.3   Project Documentation
    1.4   Risks
2. Scope
    2.1   In Scope
    2.2   Test Requirements
        2.2.1   High-Level Functional Requirements
        2.2.2   User Business/Interface Rules
    2.3   GUI Testing
    2.4   Critical System/Acceptance Testing
        2.4.1   Performance Testing
        2.4.2   Security Testing
        2.4.3   Volume Testing
        2.4.4   Stress Testing
        2.4.5   Compatibility Testing
        2.4.6   Conversion Testing
        2.4.7   Usability Testing
        2.4.8   Documentation Testing
        2.4.9   Backup Testing
        2.4.10 Recovery Testing
        2.4.11 Installation Testing
    2.5   Regression Testing
    2.6   Out of Scope
3. Test Approach
    3.1   General Test Structure

APPENDICES

E5: Function/Test Matrix

The function/test matrix below cross-references the tests to the functions. This matrix provides proof of the completeness of the test strategies and illustrates in graphic format which tests exercise which functions.

	Test Case				
	1	**2**	**3**	**4**	**5**
Business Function					

E6: GUI Component Test Matrix
(Client/Server and Internet Spiral Testing)

With the GUI component test matrix below, each GUI component is defined and documented by name and GUI type. During GUI testing, each component is tested against a predefined set of GUI tests.

| **Name** | **Window** | GUI Type | | | | **P/F** | **Date** | **Tester** |
		Menu	**Form**	**ICON**	**Control**			
Main Window	√							
Customer-Order Window	√							
Edit-Order Window	√							
Menu Bar		√						
Tool Bar					√			
.								
.								
.								

E7: GUI-Based Functional Test Matrix
(Client/Server and Internet Spiral Testing)

Below is a GUI-based Function Test matrix template that can be used to document GUI-based test cases. It includes functions and associated GUI objects or foundation components (windows, menus, forms, icons, and controls). Each test includes a requirements number, test objective, test procedure (step or script), expected results, whether the test passed or failed, the tester, and the date of the test. It thus also serves as a test case log.

Function (Enter the Name)

Case No.	REQ No.	Test Objective	Case Steps	Expected Results	(P/F)	Tester	Date
			1. 2. 3.				
GUI object (menu, icon, List Box, etc.)							
			1. 2. 3.				
GUI object (menu, icon, List Box, etc.)							
			1. 2. 3.				
GUI object (menu, icon, List Box, etc.)							
			1. 2. 3.				
GUI object (menu, icon, List Box, etc.)							
			1. 2. 3.				

E8: Test Case

The test case below defines the step-by-step process whereby a test is executed. It includes the objectives and conditions of the test, the steps needed to set up the test, the data inputs, and the expected and actual results. Other information, such as the software, environment, version, test ID, screen, and test type, are also provided.

Date: _____ Tested by: _____
System: _____ Environment: _____
Objective: _____ Test ID _____ Req. ID _____
Function: _____ Screen: _____
Version: _____ Test Type: _____
(Unit, Integ., System, Accept.)

Condition to Test:

_____
_____
_____
_____

Data/Steps to Perform:

_____
_____
_____
_____

Expected Results:

_____
_____
_____

Actual Results: Passed ☐ Failed ☐

_____
_____
_____
_____

E9: Test Case Log

The test case log below documents the test cases for a test type to be executed during testing. It also records the results of the tests, which provides the detailed evidence for the test log summary report and enables one to reconstruct the test, if necessary.

Test Name: Enter Name of Test
Test Case Author: Enter Test Case Author Name
Tester Name: Enter Tester Name
Project ID/Name: Enter Name of Project
Test Cycle ID: Enter Test Cycle ID
Date Tested: Enter Date Test Case Was Completed

Test Case ID	Test Objective ID	Category	Condition	Expected Results	Actual Results	Requirement ID
Enter ID	Enter ID from Test Plan	Enter the Test Category (edit, numeric, presentation, etc.)	Enter Specific Test Condition	Describe the Specific Results Expected Upon Executing the Condition	Record "Pass" or "Fail"	Enter the ID that Traces Back to the Specific Requirement

E10: Test Log Summary Report

The test log summary report below documents the test cases from the tester's test logs, eight in progress or completed, for the status reporting and metric collection.

Completed By:	Enter the Tester Name of the Report	**Report Date:**	Enter Date of the Report
Project ID/Name	Enter Project Identifier/Name	**Testing Name/Event:**	Enter the Name of the Type of Test (Unit, Integration, System, Acceptance)
Total Number of Test Cases	Enter Total Number of Test Cases	**Testing Sub-Type:**	Enter Name of Testing Subtype (Interface, Volume, Stress, User, Parallel Testing)

Week/ Month	Current Period	Project to Date	% Started	Current Period	% Open	Current Period	Project to Date	% Completed
Enter Test Period	Enter Number of Test Cases Started for the Period	Enter Total Test Cases Started to Date	Total Number Test Cases Started/ Total Number of Test Cases	Enter Number of Test Cases Started for this Period	Total Number of Test Cases Started/Total Number of Test Cases	Enter Number of Test Cases Started for this Period	Enter Total Test Cases Started to Date	Total Number Test Cases Started/Total Number of Test Cases
Total:								

E11: System Summary Report

A system summary report should be prepared for every major testing event. Sometimes it summarizes all the tests. The following is an outline of the information that should be provided.

1. General Information
1.1 Test Objectives. The objectives of the test, including the general functions of the software tested and the test analysis performed, should be summarized. Objectives include functionality, performance, etc.

1.2 Environment. The software sponsor, development manager, the user organization, and the computer center at which the software is to be installed should be identified. The manner in which the test environment may be different from the operation environment should be noted, and the effects of this difference assessed.

1.3 References. Applicable references should be listed, including:
   a. Project authorization
   b. Previously published documents on the project
   c. Documentation concerning related projects
   d. Standards and other reference documents

2. Test Results and Findings
The results and findings of each test should be presented separately.

2.1 Test (Identify)
   2.1.1 Validation Tests. Data input and output results of this test, including the output of internally generated data, should be compared with the data input and output requirements. Findings should be included.

   2.1.2 Verification Tests. Variances with expected results should be listed.

2.2 Test (Identify). The results and findings of the second and succeeding tests should be presented in a manner similar to the previous paragraphs.

3. Software Function and Findings
3.1 Function (Identify)
   3.1.1 Performance. The function should be briefly described. The software capabilities that were designed to satisfy this function should be described. The findings on the demonstrated capabilities from one or more tests should be included.

   3.1.2 Limits. The range of data values tested should be identified. The deficiencies, limitations, and constraints detected in the software during the testing with respect to this function should be noted.

3.2 Function (Identify). The findings on the second and succeeding functions should be presented in a manner similar to Paragraph 3.1.

4. Analysis Summary

4.1 Capabilities. The capabilities of the software as demonstrated by the tests should be described. When tests were to demonstrate fulfillment of one or more specific performance requirements, findings showing the comparison of the results with these requirements should be prepared. The effects of any differences in the test environment compared with the operational environment should be assessed.

4.2 Deficiencies. Software deficiencies as demonstrated by the tests should be listed, and their impact on the performance of the software should be assessed. The cumulative or overall impact on performance of all detected deficiencies should be summarized.

4.3 Graphical Analysis. Graphs can be used to demonstrate the history of the development project including defect trend analysis, root cause analysis, and so on. (Project wrap-up graphs are recommended as illustrations.)

4.4 Risks. The business risks faced if the software is placed in production should be listed.

4.5 Recommendations and Estimates. For each deficiency, estimates of time and effort required for its correction should be provided along with recommendations on:
a. Urgency of each correction
b. Parties responsible for corrections
c. How the corrections should be made

4.6 Opinion. The readiness of the software for production should be assessed.

E12: Defect Report

The defect report below documents an anomaly discovered during testing. It includes all the information needed to reproduce the problem, including the author, release/build number, open/close dates, problem area, problem description, test environment, defect type, how it was detected, who detected it, priority, severity, status, and so on.

Software Problem Report

Defect ID: (Required)
   Computer generated

Author: (Required)
   Computer generated

Release/Build#: (Required)
   Build where issue was discovered

Open Date: (Required)
    Computer generated

Close Date: (Required)
    Computer generated when QA closes

Problem Area: (Required)
    e.g., add order, etc.

Defect or Enhancement: (Required)
    Defect (default)
    Enhancement

Problem Title: (Required)
    Brief, one-line description

Problem Description:
    A precise problem description with screen captures, if possible

Current Environment: (Required)
    e.g., Win95T/Oracle 4.0 NT

Other Environment(s):
    e.g., WinNT/Oracle 4.0 NT

Defect Type: (Required)
    Architectural
    Connectivity
    Consistency
    Database Integrity
    Documentation
    Functionality (default)
    GUI
    Installation
    Memory
    Performance
    Security and Controls
    Standards and Conventions
    Stress
    Usability
    Who Detected: (Required)
    External Customer
    Internal Customer
    Development
    Quality Assurance (default)

How Detected: (Required)
    Review
    Walkthrough
    JAD
    Testing (default)

Assigned To: (Required)
    Individual assigned to investigate problem

Priority: (Required)
    Critical
    High (default)
    Medium
    Low

Severity: (Required)
    Critical
    High (default)
    Medium
    Low

Status: (Required)
    Open (default)
    Being Reviewed by Development
    Returned by Development
    Ready for Testing in the Next Build
    Closed (QA)
    Returned by (QA)
    Deferred to the Next Release

Status Description:
    (Required when Status = "Returned by Development," "Ready for
        Testing in the Next Build")

Fixed by:
    (Required when Status = "Ready for Testing in the Next Build")

Planned Fix Build#:
    (Required when Status = "Ready for Testing in the Next Build")

E13: Test Schedule

The test schedule below includes the testing steps (and perhaps tasks), the target begin and end dates, and responsibilities. It should also describe how the test will be reviewed, tracked, and approved.

Test Step	Begin Date	End Date	Responsible
First Spiral			
Information gathering			
Prepare for Interview	xx/xx/xx	xx/xx/xx	
Conduct Interview	xx/xx/xx	xx/xx/xx	
Summarize Findings	xx/xx/xx	xx/xx/xx	
Test Planning			
Build Test Plan	xx/xx/xx	xx/xx/xx	
Define the Metric Objectives	xx/xx/xx	xx/xx/xx	
Review/Approve Plan	xx/xx/xx	xx/xx/xx	
Test Case Design			
Design Function Tests	xx/xx/xx	xx/xx/xx	
Design GUI Tests	xx/xx/xx	xx/xx/xx	
Define the System/Acceptance Tests	xx/xx/xx	xx/xx/xx	
Review/Approve Design	xx/xx/xx	xx/xx/xx	
Test Development			
Develop Test Scripts	xx/xx/xx	xx/xx/xx	
Review/Approve Test Development	xx/xx/xx	xx/xx/xx	
Test Execution/Evaluation			
Setup and Testing	xx/xx/xx	xx/xx/xx	
Evaluation	xx/xx/xx	xx/xx/xx	
Prepare for the Next Spiral			
Refine the tests	xx/xx/xx	xx/xx/xx	
Reassess Team, Procedures, and Test Environment	xx/xx/xx	xx/xx/xx	
Publish Interim Report	xx/xx/xx	xx/xx/xx	
•			
•			
•			

Test Step	Begin Date	End Date	Responsible
Last Spiral…			
Test Execution/Evaluation			
Setup and Testing	xx/xx/xx	xx/xx/xx	
Evaluation	xx/xx/xx	xx/xx/xx	
•			
•			
•			
Conduct System Testing			
Complete System Test Plan	xx/xx/xx	xx/xx/xx	
Complete System Test Cases	xx/xx/xx	xx/xx/xx	
Review/Approve System Tests	xx/xx/xx	xx/xx/xx	
Execute the System Tests	xx/xx/xx	xx/xx/xx	
Conduct Acceptance Testing			
Complete Acceptance Test Plan	xx/xx/xx	xx/xx/xx	
Complete Acceptance Test Cases	xx/xx/xx	xx/xx/xx	
Review/Approve Acceptance Test Plan	xx/xx/xx	xx/xx/xx	
Execute the Acceptance Tests	xx/xx/xx	xx/xx/xx	
Summarize/Report Spiral Test Results			
Perform Data Reduction	xx/xx/xx	xx/xx/xx	
Prepare Final Test Report	xx/xx/xx	xx/xx/xx	
Review/Approve the Final Test Report	xx/xx/xx	xx/xx/xx	

E14: Retest Matrix

A retest matrix is a tool that relates test cases to functions (or program units) as shown below. A check entry in the matrix indicates that the test case is to be retested when the function (or program unit) has been modified due to an enhancement(s) or correction(s). No entry means that the test does not need to be retested. The retest matrix can be built before the first testing spiral but needs to be maintained during subsequent spirals. As functions (or program units) are modified during a development spiral, existing or new test cases need to be created and checked in the retest matrix in preparation for the next test spiral. Over time with subsequent spirals, some functions (or program units) may be stable with no recent modifications. Consideration to selectively remove their check entries should be undertaken between testing spirals.

Business Function	Test Case				
	1	2	3	4	5
Order Processing					
Create New Order					
Fulfill Order					
Edit Order					
Delete Order					
Customer Processing					
Create New Customer					
Edit Customer					
Delete Customer					
Financial Processing					
Receive Customer Payment					
Deposit Payment					
Pay Vendor					
Write a Check					
Display Register					
Inventory Processing					
Acquire Vendor Products					
Maintain Stock					
Handle Back Orders					
Audit Inventory					
Adjust Product Price					
Reports					
Create Order Report					
Create Account Receivables Report					
Create Account Payables					
Create Inventory Report					

E15: Spiral Testing Summary Report (Client/Server and Internet Spiral Testing)

The objective of the Final Spiral Test Report is to describe the results of the testing, including not only what works and what does not, but the test team's evaluation regarding performance of the application when it is placed into production.

For some projects, informal reports are the practice, whereas in others very formal reports are required. The following is a compromise between the two extremes to provide essential information not requiring an inordinate amount of preparation.

I. Project Overview
II. Test Activities
   A. Test Team
   B. Test Environment
   C. Types of Tests
   D. Test Schedule
   E. Test Tools
III. Metric Graphics
IV. Findings/Recommendations

E16: Minutes of the Meeting

The Minutes of the Meeting below is used to document the results and follow-up actions for the project information-gathering session. The following is a sample that is also included in the CD in the back of the book.

Meeting Purpose		Meeting Date	
Start Time		End Time	
Attended By			
Distribution List			

Important Discussions:

Discussion Item #1	Details	Comments

Discussion Item #2	Details	Comments

Discussion Item #3	Details	Comments

Discussion Item #4	Details	Comments

Action Items:

a.

b.

c.

d.

e.

f.

g.

h.

i.

j.

k.

E17: Test Approvals

The Test Approvals matrix is to formally document management approvals for test deliverables. The following is a sample that is also included in the CD in the back of the book.

Deliverable Approvals

Test Deliverable Name	Approval Status	Approver	Approved Date

E18: Test Execution Plan

The Test Execution Plan below is used to plan the activities for the execution phase. The following is a sample that is also included in the CD in the back of the book.

Project Name:_____

Project Code: _____

Activity No.	Activities/ Sub-Tasks	Planned Date		Re- source	Total Test Cases/ Scripts	Test Cases/ Scripts Completed	Comments
		Start Date	**End Date**				

Date: _____

E19: Test Project Milestones

The Test Project Milestones matrix below is used to identify and track the key test milestones. The following is a sample that is also included in the CD in the back of the book.

Milestone	Date Due	Actual Due

E20: PDCA Test Schedule

The PDCA Test Schedule matrix below is used to plan and track the Plan, Do, Check, Act test phases. The following is a sample that is also included in the CD in the back of the book.

Test Step	Start Date	End Date	Responsible
Information Gathering			
Test Planning			
Test Case Design			
Test Development			
Test Execution/Evaluation			
Prepare for the Next Test Iteration			
Conduct System Testing			
Conduct Acceptance Testing			
Summarize Tests/Project Closure			

E21: Test Strategy

The Test Strategy below is used to document the overall testing approach for the project. The following is a sample table of contents that is also included in the CD in the back of the book.

1. Introduction
    1.1 Project Overview
        <An introduction to the project including an outline of the project scope>

    1.2 About the Client
        <Client's business in association with the project>

    1.3 Application/System Overview
        <A concise and high-level explanation of our understanding of the functionality of the application and the break-up of business functions>

2. Testing Scope
    <General application scope should be provided in this section>

    2.1 Testing Objectives
        <Test objectives as they relate to specific requirements>

    2.2 Types of Tests
        <Types of testing such as functionality testing, nonfunctionality testing, operational acceptance testing, regression testing, performance testing, etc. should be mentioned here>

    2.3 Within Scope
        <Transactions, reports, interfaces, business functions, etc.>

    2.4 Out of Scope
        <Define what is NOT specifically covered in testing>

    2.5 Assumptions
        <Test assumptions in conjunction with the test scope>

    2.6 Baseline Documents
        <The list of baseline documents, prototype with version numbers>

3. Testing Approach
    3.1 Testing Methodology
        3.3.1 Entry Criteria
            <List of criteria that need to be fulfilled before test planning should begin>

        3.3.2 Test Planning Approach
            <The approach to be adopted in preparing necessary test wares, e.g., manual test cases or automated test scripts, approach for creating test data, etc.>

3.3.3 Test Documents
<List of test documents, their definition and purpose>

3.3.4 Test Execution Methodology
<A description of how the tests will be executed>

3.3.5 Test Execution Checklist
<List of items that need to be available to the test team prior to the start of test execution>

3.3.6 Test Iterations
<Number of iterations of testing planned for execution, the entry and exit criteria, and the scope of each test iteration>

3.3.7 Defect Management
<Entire defect management process. It includes defect meeting, defect resolution, etc.>

3.3.8 Defect Logging and Defect Reporting
<A note on defect logging process and a sample defect log template that will be used during test execution should be mentioned here>

3.3.9 Defect Classification and Defect Life Cycle
<A detailed note on the life cycle of a defect, the different defect severity levels, defect categories>

3.3.10 Defect Meetings
<A detailed defect meeting procedure indicating the parties to the defect meeting, their responsibilities, and the frequency of defect meeting>

3.3.11 Exit Criteria
<Exit criteria for test execution>

4. Resources
   4.1 Skills Required for the Project
   <An analysis of the skills required for executing the project>

   4.2 Training Schedule
   <Project specific training needs with a timetable>

   4.3 Offshore
      4.3.1 Test Personnel
      <List of test team personnel and their role in the project along with date of inclusion in the project>

      4.3.2 Roles and Responsibilities

4.4 On-Site

    4.4.1 Test Personnel

        <List of test team personnel and their role in the project along with date of inclusion in the project>

    4.4.2 Roles and Responsibilities

4.5 Client

    <Roles and responsibilities of client or client's representative>

4.6 Test Infrastructure

    4.6.1 Hardware

        <List of hardware requirements for test execution>

    4.6.2 Software

        <List of software requirements for test execution>

5. Project Organization and Communication

<Project organization chart, the turnaround time for the review, and sign-off for the documents submitted to the clients>

5.1 Escalation Model

    <In case of issues and concerns, the escalation procedure and timelines to escalate>

5.2 Suspension and Resumption Criteria

    <List of circumstances under which test activities will be suspended or resumed should be mentioned here>

5.3 Risk, Contingency, and Mitigation Plan

    <Risks of the project, contingency, and mitigation plan for the risks identified>

5.4 Schedule

    5.4.1 Milestones

        <A high-level schedule for the different stages of the project with clear indication of milestones planned with a list of activities>

    5.4.2 Detailed Plan

        <A detailed project plan using MS-Project with all identified tasks and subtasks, resources to be used with dates fitting into the milestones as mentioned in the high-level schedule>

    5.4.3 Deliverables

        <A list of deliverables associated with the project as mentioned in the test documents, the mechanism for obtaining client acceptance for the deliverables>

6. Appendix

<Appendix, as mentioned in any of the sections above, should be mentioned here>

E22: Clarification Request

The Clarification Request matrix below is used to document questions that may arise while the tester analyzes the requirements. The following is a sample that is also included in the CD in the back of the book.

Project Name:_____

Project Code: _____

Issue No.	Document Reference	Application/ Function	Date Raised	Clarification Requested	Raised By	Status	Response

E23: Screen Data Mapping

The Screen Data Mapping matrix below is used to document the properties of the screen data. The following is a sample that is also included in the CD in the back of the book.

Item No.	Test Case ID	Screen Reference (Optional)	Field Name	Data Required	Data Type	Data Format	Comments
1	TS-01		Account Number	aabbcc	alphabets		
2	TS-01		Account Number	10099	numeric	######	
3	TS-05		As-of Date	31101999	date	dd-mm-yyyy	

E24: Test Condition versus Test Case

The Test Condition versus Test Case matrix below is used to associate a requirement with each condition that is mapped to one or more test cases. The following is a sample that is also included in the CD in the back of the book.

Item No.	Requirement Details/Source (Fun. Spec./Bus. Req./Other)	Condition No.	Test Condition	Test Case No.

E25: Project Status Report

The Project Status Report below is used to report the status of the testing project for all key process areas. The following is a sample that is also included in the CD in the back of the book.

Purpose: This template consolidates the QA Project-related activities in all key process areas. It is published to all project stakeholders weekly.

Project Name	_____	**Project Code**	_____
Project Start Date	_____	**Project Manager**	_____
Project Phase	_____	**Week No. & Date**	_____
Distribution	_____		

Key Activities

	Details	Remarks
Deliverables		
Decisions		

Weekly Progress for This Week

Item	Key Processes	Activities/ Milestone, Deliverable	Planned		Actual		Status/ Remarks	Owner
			Start Date	End Date	Start Date	End Date		

Unplanned Activities

Item	Activities	Start Date	End Date	Effort (Person Hours)	Comments

Activities Planned for Next Week

Item	Activities	Start Date	End Date	Effort (Person Hours)	Comments

Planned but Not Completed
Change Requests (New)
Change Requests (Outstanding)
Issues (New)
Issues (Outstanding)

E26: Test Defect Details Report

The Test Defect Details Report below is used to report the detailed defect status of the testing project for all key process areas. The following is a sample that is also included in the CD in the back of the book.

Item No.	Defect ID	Script ID	Test Case Description	Expected Result	Actual Results	Detected By	Defect Status	Severity	Priority	Reported Date	Closed Date
1			Log-in page not getting displayed	Log-in page should be displayed	Log-in page is not displaying	Bill	Open	3	1		
2			Text box is not enabled	Text box should be enabled		Joe	Closed	2	2		
3			User is not allowed to enter values	User should be allowed to enter values		Sam	Fixed	3	3		
4			Area 3 is not getting displayed on the list	Module 3 should get displayed on the list		Sally	Closed	2	4		
5			Error message is displayed	Error message should not be displayed		June	Open	2	5		

E27: Defect Report

The Defect Report below is used to report the details of a specific defect. The following is a sample that is also included in the CD in the back of the book.

Defect ID	Date	Test Script ID	Test Case Description	Expected Result	Actual Result	Status	Severity	Defect Type	Tester Comment	Developer Comment	Client Comment

E28: Test Execution Tracking Manager

The Test Execution Tracking Manager is an Excel spreadsheet that provides a comprehensive and test cycle view of the number of test cases that passed/failed, the number of defects discovered by application area, the status of the defects, percentage completed, and the defect severities by defect type. The template is located in the CD in the back of the book.

E29: Final Test Summary Report

The Final Test Summary Report below is used as a final report of the test project with key findings.

The following is a sample table of contents that is also included in the CD in the back of the book.

1. Introduction
   1.1 Executive Summary
       <Highlights of the project in terms of schedule, size, and defect counts, as well as important events that happened during the life of the project, which would be of interest to the management>

   1.2 Project Overview
       <This section covers the business of the client and overview of the project>

   1.3 Scope of Testing
       <A note on the scope of testing and details regarding the scope of testing>

2. Test Methodology
   2.1 Test Documents
       <A brief note on the test documents>

   2.2 Test Iterations
       <The details of test iterations carried out>

   2.3 Defect Management
       <A brief note explaining the Defect Management process followed during execution>

3. Measurements
   3.1 Traceability Matrix
       <The details of the trace from the requirements through to the scripts>

   3.2 Planned versus Actual
       <Details of Planned versus Actual schedule with reasons for variation>

   3.3 Test Scripts Summary
       <The Final Test Scripts summary at the end of Test Execution>

   3.4 Features Untested/Invalid
       <Details pertaining to the scripts that were untested, invalid, or not delivered and the reasons>

4. Findings
   4.1 Final Defect Summary
   <Summary of Defects at the end of test execution>
   4.2 Deferred Defects
   <Details of test cases that failed and are in deferred status with reasons for deferring the defect>

5. Analysis
   5.1 Categorywise Defects
   <A chart should be generated to display the count of defects categorywise>

   5.2 Statuswise Defects
   <A chart should be generated to display the count of defects statuswise>

   5.3 Severitywise Defects
   <A chart should be generated to display the count of defects severitywise>

   5.4 Issues
   <Details of issues experienced during the course of the project that were documented and highlighted to management>

   5.5 Risks
   <Defects reported should be analyzed and any risks that could affect the business that we foresee>

   5.6 Observations
   <Any other critical events that cannot be classified under issues and risks>

6. Test Team
   <Names and roles of personnel from all parties involved during the project>

7. Appendices
   <Appendices, as referred to in any of the sections above, should be mentioned here>

Appendix F
Checklists

A very powerful quality control testing tool is a checklist. It is powerful because it statistically differentiates between two extremes. It can be used for fact gathering during problem identification, cause analysis, or it can check progress during implementation of a solution.

Observed results or conditions are recorded by entering or not entering check marks opposite items on a list. Information gathered in this way is limited to simple yes/no answers. It also quantifies or counts the data entered for subsequent tallying and analysis.

F1: Requirements Phase Defect Checklist

The requirements phase defect checklist below is used to verify the functional needs and specifications for the system. A check in the Missing column means that the item was not included. A check in the Wrong column means the item was incorrectly used. A check in the Extra column means that the item has been discovered but not originally identified. The Total column totals the number of missing and extra items.

Defect Category	Missing	Wrong	Extra	Total
1. Business rules (or information) are inadequate or partially missing.				
2. Performance criteria (or information) are inadequate or partially missing.				
3. Environment information is inadequate or partially missing.				
4. System mission information is inadequate or partially missing.				
5. Requirements are incompatible.				
6. Requirements are incomplete.				
7. Requirements are missing.				
8. Requirements are incorrect.				
9. The accuracy specified does not conform to the actual need.				
10. The data environment is inadequately described.				
11. The external interface definitions are erroneous.				
12. User training has not been considered adequately.				
13. Initialization of the system state has not been considered.				
14. The functions have not be adequately defined.				
15. The user needs are inadequately stated.				
16. Quality metrics have not been specified adequately, e.g., maintainability, transportability, etc.				

F2: Logical Design Phase Defect Checklist

The logical design phase defect checklist below is used to verify the logical design of the system. A check in the Missing column means that the item was not included. A check in the Wrong column means the item was incorrectly used. A check in the Extra column means that the item has been discovered but not originally identified. The Total column totals the number of missing and extra items.

Defect Category	Missing	Wrong	Extra	Total
1. The data has not been adequately defined.				
2. Entity definition is incomplete.				
3. Entity cardinality is incorrect.				
4. Entity attribute is incomplete.				
5. Normalization is violated.				
6. Incorrect primary key.				
7. Incorrect foreign key.				
8. Incorrect compound key.				
9. Incorrect entity subtype.				
10. The process has not been adequately defined.				
11. Parent process is incomplete.				
12. Child process is incomplete.				
13. Process inputs/outputs are incorrect.				
14. Elementary processes are not defined correctly.				
15. Mutually exclusive process problem.				
16. Parallel links problem.				
17. Event-triggered processes not defined properly.				
18. Incorrect entity/process create association.				
19. Incorrect entity/process read association.				
20. Incorrect entity/process update association.				
21. Incorrect entity/process delete association.				

F3: Physical Design Phase Defect Checklist

The physical design phase defect checklist below is used to verify the physical design of the system. A check in the Missing column means that the item was not included. A check in the Wrong column means the item was incorrectly used. A check in the Extra column means that the item has been discovered but not originally identified. The Total column totals the number of missing and extra items.

Defect Category	Missing	Wrong	Extra	Total
1. Logic or sequencing is erroneous.				
2. Processing is inaccurate.				
3. Routine does not input or output required parameters.				
4. Routine does not accept all data within the allowable range.				
5. Limit and validity checks are made on input data.				
6. Recovery procedures are not implemented or are inadequate.				
7. Required processing is missing or inadequate.				
8. Values are erroneous or ambiguous.				
9. Data storage is erroneous or inadequate.				
10. Variables are missing.				
11. Design requirements are inaccurately or incorrectly understood.				
12. Database is not compatible with the data environment.				
13. Modular decomposition reflects a high intermodular dependence.				
14. Major algorithms are not evaluated for accuracy or speed.				
15. Control structure is not expandable.				
16. Control structure ignores the processing priorities.				
17. Interface protocols are incorrect.				
18. Logic to implementing algorithms is incorrect.				

Defect Category	Missing	Wrong	Extra	Total
19. Data is not converted according to correct format.				
20. No consideration is given to the effects of round-off or truncation.				
21. Indices are not checked for validity.				
22. Infinite loops are permitted.				
23. Module specifications are incorrectly understood.				
24. Database rules are violated.				
25. Logic is incomplete for all cases.				
26. Special cases are neglected.				
27. Error handling is deficient.				
28. Timing considerations are neglected.				
29. Requirement specifications are misallocated among the various software modules.				
30. Interface specifications are misunderstood or misimplemented.				
31. System is functionally correct but does not meet performance requirements.				
32. Software is not sufficiently complex to match the problem being solved.				
33. Arithmetic overflow and underflow are not properly addressed.				
34. Actions in response to given inputs are inappropriate or missing.				
35. Algorithmic approximations provide insufficient accuracy or erroneous results for certain values of the input.				
36. There are errors in the detailed logic developed to solve a particular problem.				
37. Singular or critical input values may yield unexpected results that are not appropriately accounted for in the code.				
38. An algorithm is inefficient or does not compute the result as rapidly as a more efficient algorithm.				
39. An algorithm does not cover all the necessary cases.				

Defect Category	Missing	Wrong	Extra	Total
40. An algorithm is incorrect or converges to the wrong solution.				
41. Logic errors exist.				
42. A design oversight occurs.				

F4: Program Unit Design Phase Defect Checklist

The program unit design phase defect checklist below is used to verify the unit design of the system. A check in the Missing column means that the item was not included. A check in the Wrong column means the item was incorrectly used. A check in the Extra column means that the item has been discovered but not originally identified. The Total column totals the number of missing and extra items.

Defect Category	Missing	Wrong	Extra	Total
1. Is the if-then-else construct used incorrectly?				
2. Is the dowhile construct used incorrectly?				
3. Is the dountil construct used incorrectly?				
4. Is the case construct used incorrectly?				
5. Are there infinite loops?				
6. Is it a proper program?				
7. Are there goto statements?				
8. Is the program readable?				
9. Is the program efficient?				
10. Does the case construct contain all the conditions?				
11. Is there dead code?				
12. Does the program have self-modifying code?				
13. Is the algorithm expression too simple?				
14. Is the algorithm expression too complicated?				
15. Is the nesting too deep?				
16. Is there negative Boolean logic?				
17. Are there compounded Boolean expressions?				
18. Is there jumping in and out of loops?				

APPENDICES

F5: Coding Phase Defect Checklist

The coding phase defect checklist below is used to verify the conversion of the design specifications into executable code. A check in the Missing column means that the item was not included. A check in the Wrong column means the item was incorrectly used. A check in the Extra column means that the item has been discovered but not originally identified. The Total column totals the number of missing and extra items.

Defect Category	Missing	Wrong	Extra	Total
1. Decision logic or sequencing is erroneous or inadequate.				
2. Arithmetic computations are erroneous or inadequate.				
3. Branching is erroneous.				
4. Branching or other testing is performed incorrectly.				
5. There are undefined loop terminations.				
6. Programming language rules are violated.				
7. Programming standards are violated.				
8. The programmer misinterprets language constructs.				
9. Typographical errors exist.				
10. Main storage allocation errors exist.				
11. Iteration schemes are unsuccessful.				
12. I/O format errors exist.				
13. Parameters or subscripts are violated.				
14. Subprogram invocations are violated.				
15. Data errors exist.				
16. A subprogram is nonterminating.				
17. There are errors in preparing or processing input data.				
18. Tape handling errors exist.				
19. Disk handling errors exist.				
20. Output processing errors exist.				
21. Error message processing errors exist.				
22. Software interface errors exist.				
23. Database interface errors exist.				

Defect Category	Missing	Wrong	Extra	Total
24. User interface errors exist.				
25. Indexing and subscripting errors exist.				
26. Iterative procedural errors exist.				
27. Bit manipulation errors exist.				
28. Syntax errors exist.				
29. Initialization errors exist.				
30. There is confusion in the use of parameters.				
31. There are errors in loop counters.				
32. Decision results are incorrectly handled.				
33. Variables are given multiple names or are not defined.				
34. Errors are made in writing out variable names.				
35. Variable type and dimensions are incorrectly declared.				
36. There is confusion about library program names.				
37. External symbols are incorrectly resolved.				
38. Compiler errors exist.				
39. Singularities and external points exist.				
40. Floating point underflow errors exist.				
41. Floating point overflow errors exist.				
42. Floating point and integer division by zero is allowed.				
43. A sequencing error exists.				
44. There is a failure to save and restore appropriate registers in real-time systems.				
45. The software interface to connected hardware systems is incorrect.				

F6: Field Testing Checklist

The field test below is limited to a specific field or data element and is intended to validate that all of the processing related to that specific field is performed correctly.

Item	Yes	No	N/A	Comments
1. Were all codes validated?				
2. Can fields be updated properly?				
3. Is the field large enough for collecting the totals?				
4. Is the field adequately described in the program?				
5. Can the field be initialized properly?				
6. Do all references to the field use the proper field name?				
7. If the field's contents are restricted, are those restrictions validated?				
8. Were rules established for identifying and processing invalid field data? (If not, this data must be developed for the error-handling transaction type. If so, test conditions must be prepared to validate the specification processing for invalid field data.)				
9. Is a wide range of typical valid processing values included in the test conditions?				
10. For numerical fields, have the upper and lower values been tested?				
11. For numerical fields, has a zero value been tested?				
12. For numerical fields, has a negative test condition been prepared?				
13. For alphabetical fields, has a blank condition been prepared?				
14. For an alphabetic or alphanumeric field, has a test condition longer than the field length been prepared to check truncation processing?				
15. Were all valid conditions tested on the basis of the data dictionary printout?				

Item	Yes	No	N/A	Comments
16. Were systems specifications reviewed to determine whether all valid conditions are tested?				
17. Do owners of data elements know whether all valid conditions are tested?				
18. Have owners of data elements reported their results?				

F7: Record Testing Checklist

The record test below validates that records can be created, entered, processed, stored, and output correctly.

Item	Yes	No	N/A	Comments
1. Were conditions prepared for testing the processing of the first record?				
2. Were conditions determined for validating the processing of the last record?				
3. Were all multiple records per transaction processed correctly?				
4. Were all multiple records on a storage medium (i.e., permanent or temporary file) processed correctly?				
5. Were all variations in record size tested (e.g., a header with variable length trailers)?				
6. Can the job control language be checked for each record type?				
7. Can processing be done for two records with the same identifier (e.g., two payments for the same accounts receivable file)?				
8. Can the first record stored on a storage file be retrieved?				
9. Can the last record stored on a storage file be retrieved?				
10. Can all of the records entered be stored properly?				
11. Can all of the stored records be retrieved?				
12. Do interconnecting modules have the same identifier for each record type?				
13. Can the data entry function prepare the proper records from the data entry documentation?				
14. Is the user documentation useful to users?				
15. Do individual module record descriptions conform to the system record descriptions?				

Item	Yes	No	N/A	Comments
16. Does the storage definition of records conform to the system definition of records?				
17. Are record descriptions common throughout the entire software system?				
18. Do current record formats coincide with the formats used on files created by other systems?				

F8: File Test Checklist

The file test below verifies that all needed files are included in the system being tested, that they are properly documented in the operating infrastructure, and that the files connect properly with the software components that need data from those files.

Item	Yes	No	N/A	Comments
1. Is a condition available for testing each file?				
2. Is a condition available for testing each file's interface with each module?				
3. Are test conditions available for validating each job control condition (or the equivalent in environments in which there is no JCL)?				
4. Is a condition available for validating that the correct version of each file will be used?				
5. Is a condition available for testing that records placed on a file will be returned intact?				
6. Are conditions available for validating that each file is properly closed after the last record is processed for that file?				
7. Are conditions available for validating that each record type can be processed from beginning to end of the system intact?				
8. Are conditions available for validating that all records entered are processed through the system?				
9. Are conditions available for validating that files that are mounted but not used are properly closed at the end of processing?				
10. Are test conditions available for creating a file for which no prior records exist?				
11. Is a condition available for validating the correct closing of a file when all records on the file have been deleted?				
12. Are conditions available for validating the correctness of all the job control statements?				

F9: Error Testing Checklist

The error test below identifies errors in data elements, data element relationships, record and file relationships, as well as logical processing conditions.

Item	Yes	No	N/A	Comments
1. Were functional errors identified by the brainstorming session with end users/customers?				
2. Were structural error conditions identified by the brainstorming session with project personnel?				
3. Were functional error conditions identified for the following cases:				
Rejection of invalid codes?				
Rejection of out-of-range values?				
Rejection of improper data relationships?				
Rejection of invalid dates?				
Rejection of unauthorized transactions of the following types:				
• Invalid value?				
• Invalid customer?				
• Invalid product?				
• Invalid transaction type?				
• Invalid price?				
Alphabetic data in numeric fields?				
Blanks in a numeric field?				
An all-blank condition in a numeric field?				
Negative values in a positive field?				
Positive values in a negative field?				
Negative balances in a financial account?				
Numeric in an alphabetic field?				
Blanks in an alphabetic field?				
Values longer than the field permits?				
Totals that exceed maximum size of total fields?				
Proper accumulation of totals (at all levels for multiple-level totals)?				

Item	Yes	No	N/A	Comments
Incomplete transactions (i.e., one or more fields missing)?				
Obsolete data in the field (i.e., a formerly valid code no longer valid)?				
A new value that will become acceptable but is not acceptable now (e.g., a new district code for which the district has not yet been established)?				
A postdated transaction?				
Change of a value that affects a relationship (e.g., if the unit digit is used to control year, switching from 9 in 89 to 0 in 90 can still be processed)?				
4. Does the data dictionary list of field specifications generate invalid specifications?				
5. Are tests performed for the following architectural error conditions:				
Page overflow?				
Report format conformance to design layout?				
Posting of data to correct portion of reports?				
Printed error messages representative of the actual error condition?				
All instructions executed?				
All paths executed?				
All internal tables?				
All loops?				
All PERFORM type routines?				
All compiler warning messages?				
The correct version of the program?				
Unchanged portions of the system revalidated after any part of the system is changed?				

F10: Use Test Checklist

The use test below tests the end user's ability to use the system and involves an understanding of both system output and that output's ability to lead to a correct action.

Item	Yes	No	N/A	Comments
1. Are all end-user actions identified?				
2. Are they identified in enough detail so that contribution of information system output items can be related to those actions?				
3. Is all the information used in taking an action identified and related to the action?				
4. Is the output from the system under test related to specific actions?				
5. Does the end user correctly understand the output reports and screens?				
6. Does the end user understand the type of logic and computation performed to produce the output?				
7. Can the end user identify the contribution the output makes to the actions taken?				
8. Can the end user identify whether the actions taken are correct?				
9. If not, can another party determine the correctness of the actions taken?				
10. Is the relationship between system output and business actions defined?				
11. Does interpretation of the matrix indicate that the end user does not have adequate information to take an action?				
12. Does analysis of the matrix indicate that the end user is making an abnormal number of incorrect actions?				
13. If so, is the end user willing to let the system be modified to provide better information for taking actions?				

F11: Search Test Checklist

The search test below verifies locating records, fields, and other variables, and helps validate that the search logic is correct.

Item	Yes	No	N/A	Comments
1. Were all internal tables identified?				
2. Were all internal lists of error messages identified?				
3. Were all internal logic paths (when there are multiple choices) identified?				
4. Was the search logic identified? (In some cases, algorithms are used to identify the needed entity.)				
5. Were all authorization routines identified?				
6. Were all password routines identified?				
7. Was all business processing logic requiring a search identified (e.g., logic requiring the lookup of a customer record)?				
8. Were database search routines identified?				
9. Were subsystem searches identified (e.g., finding a tax rate in a sales tax subsystem)?				
10. Were complex search logics identified (e.g., those requiring two or more conditions or two or more records-searching for accounts more than both 90 days old and $100)?				
11. Were search routines for processing modules identified?				
12. Were test conditions graded for all of the preceding search conditions?				
13. Was the end user interviewed to determine the type of one-time searches that might be encountered in the future?				
14. If so, can these searches be done with reasonable effort (confirmed by the project group)?				
15. If no, was the end user informed of the cost of conducting the searches or reconstructing the system to meet those needs?				

F12: Match/Merge Checklist

The match/merge test below ensures that all the combinations of merging and matching are adequately addressed. The test typically involves two or more files: an input transaction and one or more files or an input transaction and an internal table.

Item	Yes	No	N/A	Comments
1. Were all files associated with the application identified? (In this transaction, files include specialized files, databases, and internal groupings of records used for matching and merging.)				
2. Were the following match/merge conditions addressed:				
Match/merge of records of two different identifiers (e.g., inserting a new employee on the payroll file)?				
A match/merge on which there are no records on the matched/merged file?				
A match/merge in which the matched/merged record is the lowest value on the file?				
A match/merge in which the matched/merged record is the highest value on the file?				
A match/merge in which the matched/merged record is the same value as an item on a file (e.g., adding a new employee when the employee's payroll number is the same as an existing payroll number on the file)?				
A match/merge for which there is no input file or transactions being matched/merged? (The objective is to see that the matched/merged file is adequately closed.)				
A match/merge in which the first item on the file is deleted?				
A match/merge in which the last item on the attached/merged file is deleted?				
A match/merge in which two incoming records have the same value?				

Item	Yes	No	N/A	Comments
A match/merge in which two incoming records indicate a value on the matched/merged file is to be deleted?				
A match/merge condition when the last remaining record on the matched/merged file is deleted?				
A match/merge condition in which the incoming matched/merged file is out of sequence or has a single record out of sequence?				
Were these test conditions applied to the totality of match/merge conditions that can occur in the software being tested?				

F13: Stress Test Checklist

The stress test below validates the performance of software that is subjected to a large volume of transactions.

Item	Yes	No	N/A	Comments
1. Were all desired performance capabilities identified?				
2. Were all system features contributing to the test identified?				
3. Were the following system performance capabilities identified:				
Data entry operator performance?				
Communications line performance?				
Turnaround performance?				
Availability and uptime performance?				
Response time performance?				
Error-handling performance?				
Report-generation performance?				
Internal computational performance?				
Performance in developing actions?				
4. Are the following system features (that can impair performance) identified:				
Internal computer processing speed?				
Communications line transmission speed?				
Efficiency of programming language?				
Efficiency of database management system?				
Number of input terminals and entry stations?				
Skill level of data entry staff?				
Backup for computer terminals?				
Backup for data entry staff?				
Expected downtime with central processing site?				
Expected frequency and duration of abnormal software terminations?				

Item	Yes	No	N/A	Comments
Queueing capabilities?				
File-storage capabilities?				
5. Are the stress conditions realistic for validating software performance (as confirmed by project personnel)?				

F14: Attributes Testing Checklist

The attributes test below involves verifying the attributes that are quality and productivity characteristics of a system being tested. An example includes the ease of introducing changes into the software.

Item	Yes	No	N/A	Comments
1. Have software attributes been identified?				
2. Have software attributes been ranked?				
3. Do end users or customers agree with the attribute ranking?				
4. Have test conditions been developed for the very important attributes?				
5. For correctness attributes, are the functions accurate and complete?				
6. For the file integrity attribute, is the integrity of each file or subschema validated?				
7. For the authorization attribute, are there authorization procedures for each transaction?				
8. For the audit trail attribute, do test conditions verify that each business transaction can be reconstructed?				
9. For the continuity-of-processing attribute, can the system be recovered within a reasonable time span and transactions captured or processed during the recovery period?				
10. For the service attribute, do turnaround and response times meet user needs?				
11. For the access control attribute, is the system limited to authorized users?				
12. Does the compliance attribute conform to MIS standards, the systems development methodology, and appropriate policies, procedures, and regulations?				
13. For the reliability attribute, is incorrect, incomplete, or obsolete data processed properly?				
14. For the ease-of-use attribute, can users use the system effectively, efficiently, and economically?				

Item	Yes	No	N/A	Comments
15. For the maintainability attribute, can the system be changed or enhanced with reasonable effort and on a timely basis?				
16. For the portability attribute, can the software be moved efficiently to other platforms?				
17. For the coupling attribute, can the software integrate properly with other systems?				
18. For the performance attribute, do end users consider the software's performance acceptable?				
19. For the ease-of-operation attribute, are operations personnel able to effectively, economically, and efficiently operate the software?				

F15: States Testing Checklist

The states test below verifies special conditions relating to both the operating and functional environments that may occur.

Item	Yes	No	N/A	Comments
1. Has the state of empty master files been validated?				
2. Has the state of empty transaction files been validated?				
3. Has the state of missing master records been validated?				
4. Has the state of duplicate master records been validated?				
5. Has the state of empty tables been validated?				
6. Has the state of insufficient quantity been validated?				
7. Has the state of negative balances been validated?				
8. Has the state of duplicate input been validated?				
9. Has the state of entering the same transaction twice (particularly from a terminal) been validated?				
10. Has the state of concurrent updates (i.e., two terminals calling on the same master record at the same time) been validated?				
11. Has the state in which there are more requests for service or products than there are services and products to support them been validated?				

F16: Procedures Testing Checklist

The procedures test below verifies the software to verify the operating, terminal, and communications procedures.

Item	Yes	No	N/A	Comments
1. Have start-up procedures been validated?				
2. Have query procedures been validated?				
3. Have file mounting procedures been validated?				
4. Have updating procedures been validated?				
5. Have backup procedures been validated?				
6. Have off-site storage procedures been validated?				
7. Have recovery procedures been validated?				
8. Have terminal operating procedures been validated?				
9. Have procedures needed to operate the terminal when the main computer is down been validated?				
10. Have procedures needed to capture data when the terminals are down been validated?				

F17: Control Testing Checklist

The control test below validates the ability of internal controls to support accurate, complete, timely, and authorized processing. These controls are usually validated by auditors assessing the adequacy of control, which is typically dictated by law.

Item	Yes	No	N/A	Comments
1. Have the business transactions processed by the software been identified?				
2. Has a transaction flow analysis been prepared for each transaction?				
3. Have controls for the transaction flow been documented?				
4. Do data input controls address:				
Accuracy of data input?				
Completeness of data input?				
Timeliness of data input?				
Conversion of data input into a machine-readable format?				
The keying of input?				
Data input processing schedules?				
Assignment of data input duties (e.g., originating, entering, and processing data and distributing output)?				
End users' input (with the help of the control group)?				
Input of all source documents?				
Batching techniques?				
Record counts?				
Predetermined control totals?				
Control logs?				
Key verification?				
Preprogrammed keying formats?				
Editing for input?				
Input data elements?				
Data validation editing techniques?				

413

Item	Yes	No	N/A	Comments
Monitoring for overrides and bypasses?				
Restriction of overrides and bypasses to supervisory personnel?				
Automatic recording and submission of overrides and bypasses to supervisors for analysis?				
Automatic development of control counts during data entry?				
Recording of transaction errors?				
Monitoring of rejected transactions for correcting and reentering them on a timely basis?				
Written procedures for data input processes?				
Appropriate error messages for all data error conditions?				
Security for data entry terminals?				
Passwords for entering business transactions through terminals?				
Shutting down of terminals after predefined periods of inactivity?				
Reports of unauthorized terminal use?				
Built-in identification codes for terminals?				
Logs of transactions entered through terminals? Interactive displays that tell terminal operators which data is entered?				
5. Do data entry controls include the following controls:				
Accuracy of new data?				
Completeness of new data?				
Timely recording of new data?				
Procedures and methods for creating new data?				
Security for blank source documents?				
Checking of cross-referenced fields?				
Pre-numbered documents?				
Transaction authorization?				
Systems overrides?				

Item	Yes	No	N/A	Comments
Manual adjustments?				
Batching of source documents?				
Control totals for source documents?				
A correction procedure for errors made on source documents?				
A retention repository for source documents?				
Transmission of source documents for data entry?				
Confirmation by the data entry function to the source document function that the documents are entered? (For online systems, data origination and data entry are performed concurrently.)				
Prompt messages for data entry operators?				
6. Do processing controls address:				
Input throughout processing?				
Instructions for operations personnel on how to control processing?				
Abnormal termination or conditions?				
Operation logs for review by supervisors?				
Procedures for reconciling record counts and control totals?				
Reconciliation of processing control totals and manually developed control totals?				
Procedures ensuring that the right versions of programs are run?				
Procedures ensuring that the right versions of files are used?				
Maintenance of run-to-run totals?				
Reconciliation of processing from last to current run (or between different time periods)?				
Validation of new data?				
Manual validation of override and bypass procedures after processing?				
Maintenance of transaction history files?				

Item	Yes	No	N/A	Comments
Procedures for controlling errors?				
Correct and timely reentry of rejected transactions?				
Recording of correct accounting classifications?				
Concurrent update protection procedures?				
Error messages printed out for each error condition?				
Identical procedures for processing corrected and original transactions?				
7. Do data output controls address:				
Accountable documents (e.g., bank checks)?				
Accountable documents damaged in output preparation?				
Completeness of output?				
Review of output documents for acceptability and completeness?				
Reconciliation of output documents for record counts and control totals?				
Identification of output products?				
Delivery of output products to the right locations?				
Delivery of output products on a timely basis?				
Appropriate security for output products?				
The end user's assigned responsibility for the accuracy of all output?				
Logs for output production and delivery?				
Clear output error messages?				
A history of output errors?				
Users informed of output product errors?				
Users informed of abnormal terminations?				
A phone number users can call for help in understanding output?				

Item	Yes	No	N/A	Comments
A phone number users can call for information about the output production schedule?				
The number of copies of output?				
Procedures that determine who gets online output?				
Control totals for online output?				
Written procedures for online output?				
Procedures for user responses made on the basis of output information?				
8. Has the level of risk for each control area been identified?				
9. Has this level of risk been confirmed by the audit function?				
10. Have end users or customers been notified of the level of control risk?				

F18: Control Flow Testing Checklist

The control flow test below validates the control flow of transactions through the system under test. It determines whether records can be lost or misprocessed during processing.

Item	Yes	No	N/A	Comments
1. Have all branches been tested in both directions?				
2. Have all statements been executed?				
3. Have all loops been tested?				
4. Have all iterations of each loop been tested?				
5. Have all execution paths been tested?				
6. Have all subroutines and libraries been called in and executed during testing?				

F19: Testing Tool Selection Checklist

Finding the tool that is appropriate for a project can be difficult. Several questions need to be answered before selecting a tool. The testing tool selection checklist below lists the questions to help the QA team evaluate and select an automated testing tool.

Item	Yes	No	N/A	Comments
1. How easy is the tool for your testers to use? Is it something that can be picked up quickly, or is training going to be required?				
2. Do any of the team members already have experience using the tool?				
3. If training is necessary, are classes, books, or other forms of instruction available?				
4. Will the tool work effectively on the computer system currently in place?				
5. Or is more memory, faster processors, etc. going to be needed?				
6. Is the tool itself easy to use?				
7. Does it have a user-friendly interface?				
8. Is it prone to user error?				
9. Is the tool physically capable of testing your application? Many testing tools can only test in a GUI environment, whereas others test in non-GUI environments.				
10. Can the tool handle full project testing? That is, is it able to run hundreds if not thousands of test cases for extended periods of time?				
11. Can it run for long periods of time without crashing, or is the tool itself full of bugs?				
12. Talk to customers who currently or previously have used the tool. Did it meet their needs?				
13. How similar were their testing needs to yours and how well did the tool perform?				
14. Try to select a tool that is advanced enough so the costs of updating tests don't overwhelm any benefits of testing.				

Item	Yes	No	N/A	Comments
15. If a demo version is available, try it out before you make any decisions.				
16. Does the price of the tool fit in the QA department or company budget?				
17. Does the tool meet the requirements of the company testing methodology?				

F20: Project Information Gathering Checklist

This checklist is used to verify the information available and required at the beginning of the project. For all negative responses the QA testing manager should assess the impact and document it as an issue. This can be accomplished through weekly status reports and/or e-mail. The following is a sample that is also included in the CD in the back of the book.

Context	Activity	Yes	No	Comments
Proposal Phase				
	Is the QA team prepared to make QA estimates?	☐	☐	
	Has the Proposal been reviewed and approved?	☐	☐	
	Has Estimation and Risk Assessment been completed?	☐	☐	
	Have Initial Work Products been sent to the Project server?	☐	☐	
	Vendor Contract (if applicable)	☐	☐	
	Has the Contract been reviewed and approved?	☐	☐	Need process defined in QA Project Plan
	Does the Master Contract and Proposal exist?	☐	☐	
	Has the Proposal and communications been defined?	☐	☐	
	Has the Project Acceptance Notes/Communication been defined?	☐	☐	
Project Initiation				
	Has a Project Folder has been created?	☐	☐	
	Has the Project Manager been trained on his role?	☐	☐	
	Has the Project kick-off meeting been completed?	☐	☐	
	Was the Manager who made the proposal present in the Project kick-off meeting?	☐	☐	
Project Plan & Scheduling				
	Have Audits and Reviews been planned?	☐	☐	
	Have the Project goals been identified?	☐	☐	

Context	Activity	Yes	No	Comments
	Has Configuration Management been discussed?	☐	☐	
	Has the Staffing Plan been discussed?	☐	☐	
	Has the Training Plan been discussed?	☐	☐	
	Has the Status reporting method and frequency been discussed?	☐	☐	
	Has the Project scheduling been discussed?	☐	☐	
	Does the Project schedule include all the activities in the project?	☐	☐	
	Has the QA Project Management plan been reviewed by the Project Manager and others?	☐	☐	
	Has the QA Project schedule been reviewed by the team?	☐	☐	
Testing Process Overview				
	Has the Testing process been reviewed and approved by Project Manager?	☐	☐	
Project Folder				
	Has the Estimation and Risk been discussed?	☐	☐	
	Have the Roles and responsibilities been discussed?	☐	☐	
	Have the Critical resources been planned?	☐	☐	
	Have the Project dependencies been identified?	☐	☐	
	Has the Project Folder been reviewed by the Quality Test for completeness?	☐	☐	

F21: Impact Analysis Checklist

The impact analysis checklist is used to help analyze the impacts of changes to the system. For all negative responses the test manager will assess the impact and document it as an issue to the concerned parties. This can be accomplished through weekly status reports or e-mail. The following is a sample that is also included in the CD in the back of the book.

Context	Activity	Yes	No	Comments
	Is the Enhanced Business Requirement available?	☐	☐	
	Is the New Functional Specification Document for new requirements available?	☐	☐	
	Have you understood the additional/new requirements?	☐	☐	
	Is the Prototype document for new release available?	☐	☐	
	Are you able to identify the proposed changes?	☐	☐	
	Are you able to identify the applications affected by the enhancements?	☐	☐	
	Has the test scope been adequately defined for the enhancements?	☐	☐	
	Have the test conditions/cases been prepared for the enhancements and impacted application areas?	☐	☐	
	Have you prepared a Test Plan/Strategy?	☐	☐	
	Have you prepared the test data requirements for all the conditions/cases?	☐	☐	
	Has the automation scope for the new/additional requirements been completed?	☐	☐	
	Has the impact on the existing scripts been analyzed?	☐	☐	
	Has the Test Execution Plan been documented for the new release?	☐	☐	
	Has the Traceability matrix document been prepared?	☐	☐	

Context	Activity	Yes	No	Comments
	Are there any architectural changes due to new requirements?	☐	☐	
	Are there any changes to the database(s) due to new requirements?	☐	☐	
	Have the GUI changes due to new requirements been analyzed?	☐	☐	

F22: Environment Readiness Checklist

The environment readiness checklist is to verify the readiness of the environment for testing before starting test execution. For all negative responses the test manager will assess the impact and document it as an issue to the concerned parties. This can be accomplished through weekly status reports or e-mail. The following is a sample that is also included in the CD in the back of the book.

Context	Items to Be Checked	Yes	No	Comments
	Has the Client signed off on the Test Strategy?	☐	☐	
	Is the Test Environment Ready?	☐	☐	
	Hardware	☐	☐	
	<Input Each Component>	☐	☐	
	Software	☐	☐	
	<Input Each Component>	☐	☐	
	Is the Testbed created?	☐	☐	
	Is Data available as per expected format (Test Data Guidelines — Planning)?	☐	☐	
	Is the Data actually populated?	☐	☐	
	Is the populated data sufficient?	☐	☐	
	Has the Software transfer been completed and the initial version been loaded (Load Management)?	☐	☐	
	Have the User IDs and Passwords been set up to access the environment from Client/Developers?	☐	☐	
	Logistics	☐	☐	
	Is the Testing Team available and ready to start testing?	☐	☐	
	Is the Test Lab setup complete?	☐	☐	
	Is the Interaction model (Project Planning) defined and established as documented in the Test Strategy?	☐	☐	
	Is the Client aware of the Defect Management process as defined in the Strategy?	☐	☐	

Context	Items to Be Checked	Yes	No	Comments
	Is the Entry Criteria defined and established per the Project Strategy plan?	☐	☐	
	\<Enter each Criteria here\>	☐	☐	
Any Other Potential Issues:				

F23: Project Completion Checklist

The project completion checklist is used to confirm that all the key activities have been completed for the project. The following is a sample that is also included in the CD in the back of the book.

Context	Activity	Status			Comments
		Yes	**No**	**Required/ Optional**	
	Are all the test cases executed?	☐	☐	R	
	Are all the defects either closed or deferred?	☐	☐	R	
	Are all Change Requests closed?	☐	☐	R	
	Is the soft base delivered certified?	☐	☐	O	
	Has user training been completed?	☐	☐	O	
	Are the deliverables handed over to the customer?	☐	☐	R	
	Is project sign-off obtained from the customer?	☐	☐	O	
	Does the Project Directory contain the latest version of the documents?	☐	☐	R	
	Are all the documents archived and put in data warehouse?	☐	☐	R	
	Have Customer Feedback Forms been sent to Customer?	☐	☐	O	
	Has the Customer Supplied material been returned or released to other projects and the same communicated to the Customer?	☐	☐	R	
	Has the Formal Project Closure communicated? (Customer, Senior Manager, Onsite Team, Quality Team, Inter Groups and Project Team)	☐	☐	R	
	Have the project directories been backed up?	☐	☐	R	

Context	Activity	Status			Comments
		Yes	No	Required/ Optional	
	Have the media been stored in a fireproof cabinet?	☐	☐	R	
	Has the Project Directory been withdrawn from the server?	☐	☐	R	
	Has the project been marked as Closed in project database?	☐	☐	R	
	Have all Metric data collection been completed?	☐	☐	R	
	Has the Skill database been updated?	☐	☐	O	

F24: Unit Testing Checklist

The unit testing checklist is used to verify that unit testing has been thorough and comprehensive. The following is a sample that is also included in the CD in the back of the book.

Expected Testing Actions	Completed			Comments/Explanation
	Yes	No	N/A	
Was every field verified to allow only data of the correct format to be entered [e.g., numeric (signed/unsigned), alphabetic, alphanumeric (special characters), date, valid and invalid]? Check error messages for invalid data?				
Was every field verified to allow only data of allowable values to be entered (e.g., tables, ranges, minimum, maximum)? Check error messages for invalid data?				
Was every field verified that business rules for the field were enforced (e.g., mandatory/not mandatory when another field is present, relational edits)?				
Was every error message tested?				
Was every field verified to handle all invalid values?				
Were all upper and lower case field conditions verified?				
Were all internal tables verified or addressed to have sufficient capacity to provide for maximum volumes (e.g., dataset population, number of transactions to accept)? Check error messages?				
For numerical fields, have all zero values have been tested?				
Were all valid data conditions tested based on data dictionary definitions?				

Expected Testing Actions	Completed			Comments/Explanation
	Yes	No	N/A	
Were the specifications reviewed to ensure conditions have been tested?				
Were all alpha fields validated for "blank" conditions?				
Was it verified that all data is being retrieved from and written to the correct physical database?				
Were all fields initialized properly?				
Were all fields that are protected validated?				
Was all data being retrieved from and written to appropriate files and fields verified?				
Was every calculation verified to provide correct results over the entire ranges of involved data items based on the business rules?				
Was every output value and its format verified? (e.g., Rounding/Truncation).				
Was data passed to all other systems verified to be in the correct format by the receiving system?				
Was data passed from other systems verified to be in the correct format?				
Were all required security requirements, as specified in the design specification, verified?				
Were all outputs verified to identify the security level classification appropriate to the information being present?				
Were all error conditions trapped and handled according to the standards for the environment(s) in which the software item will execute (e.g., error codes, error messages)?				

Expected Testing Actions	Completed			Comments/Explanation
	Yes	No	N/A	
Was it verified that the software items do not leave corrupted data when unexpected error conditions occur (e.g., General Protection Fault, Syntax Error, abnormal exit)?				
Were all messages verified to be clear and understandable by typical end users of the software item?				
Did typical users of the instructions verify all the instructions to be concise and understandable?				
Did the typical audience of the documentation verify the documentation to be clear and understandable?				
Were all tabs, buttons, hyperlinks, and field tabbing operated in a logical manner according to the REL IT standards in which the software item will execute?				
Were all commands verified to be available using either a mouse or keyboard?				
Were tests performed to indicate that response times meet requirements as specified and will be acceptable in the environment(s) where the software item will execute (run-time for large volumes)?				
Was the code reviewed?				
Were all undefined loop iterations verified?				
Were all the programming standards satisfied?				
Were invalid codes verified?				
Were invalid data relationships verified?				
Were invalid date formats verified?				

Expected Testing Actions	Completed			Comments/Explanation
	Yes	No	N/A	
Were page overflows verified?				
Was it verified that the software items meet all standards applicable to the environment(s) in which the software item is expected to execute?				
Was it verified that the software items meet all requirements imposed by corporate standards regarding financial controls and privacy.				
Was it verified that the software could be adapted to execute in the specific environment(s) in which it is required to execute?				
Comments:				

Completed by: _____   Accepted by: _____

Date _____   Date _____

Developer   Development Manager

F25: Ambiguity Review Checklist

The ambiguity review checklist is used to assist in the review of a functional specification of structural ambiguity (not to be confused with content reviews). For all negative responses the QA project manager will assess and document it as an issue to the concerned parties for resolution. This can be accomplished through weekly status reports or e-mail. The following is a sample that is also included in the CD in the back of the book.

Context	Task	Yes	No	Comments
Complexity	Are the requirements overly complex?	☐	☐	
Dangling Else	Are there cases where the else part of a condition is missing?	☐	☐	
Ambiguity of References	Are there cases where there are references that are not clearly defined?	☐	☐	
Scope of Action	Are there cases where the scope of the action for a condition is not clearly defined?	☐	☐	
Omissions	Are there causes without effects?	☐	☐	
	Are there missing effects?	☐	☐	
	Are there effects without causes?	☐	☐	
	Are there missing causes?	☐	☐	
Ambiguous Logical Operators	Is there compound usage of "and/or" that are not clear?	☐	☐	
	Are there implicit connectors?	☐	☐	
	Is the use of "or" correctly used?	☐	☐	
Negation	Are there cases of scope negation?	☐	☐	
	Are there cases of unnecessary negation?	☐	☐	
	Are there cases of double negation?	☐	☐	
Ambiguous Statements	Are there cases of ambiguous verbs?	☐	☐	
	Are there cases of ambiguous adverbs?	☐	☐	
	Are there cases of ambiguous adjectives?	☐	☐	
	Are there cases of ambiguous variables?	☐	☐	
	Are there cases of aliases?	☐	☐	

Context	Task	Yes	No	Comments
Random Organization	Are there cases of mixed causes and effects?	☐	☐	
	Are there cases of random case sequences?	☐	☐	
Built-in Assumptions	Are there cases of functional/environmental knowledge?	☐	☐	
Ambiguous Precedence Relationships	Are there cases where the sequences of events are not clear?	☐	☐	
Implicit Cases	Are there implicit cases?	☐	☐	
Etc.	Are there examples of "etc.?"	☐	☐	
I.e. versus e.g.	Are "i.e." and "e.g." used correctly?	☐	☐	
Temporal Ambiguity	Are there cases of timing ambiguities?	☐	☐	
Boundary Ambiguity	Are there boundary ambiguities?	☐	☐	

F26: Architecture Review Checklist

The architecture review checklist is used to review the architecture for completeness and clarity. For all negative responses the test manager will assess the impact and document it as an issue to the concerned parties for resolution. This can be accomplished through weekly status reports or e-mail. The following is a sample that is also included in the CD in the back of the book.

Area	Task	Yes	No	Comments
	Has an overview description of the system been documented?			
	Has the 2 or 3 tier architecture been defined?			
	Have the database and access been defined?			
	Have servers been defined?			
	Have the protocols been defined, e.g., HTTP, JSP, PeopleSoft, Tuxedo?			
	Is the vendor in-house or outsourced?			
	Has the point of contact to resolve technical architecture problems been defined?			
	Has the platform been defined?			
	Is there a network diagram?			
	Has the test equipment been defined?			
	Has load balancing been defined?			
	Have the business processes been defined?			
	Are there common tasks that may be performed more often than others?			
	Have peak volumes been defined?			
	Have the Web servers been identified?			

F27: Data Design Review Checklist

The data design review checklist is used to review the logical and physical design for clarity and completeness. For all negative responses the QA project manager will assess the impact and document it as an issue to the concerned parties for resolution. This can be accomplished through weekly status reports or e-mail, depending upon the severity. The following is a sample that is also included in the CD in the back of the book.

Context	Task	Status		
		Yes	No	Remarks
Logical Design				
	Has the data been inadequately defined?	☐	☐	
	Are the data entity definitions incomplete?	☐	☐	
	Are the cardinalities defined incorrectly?	☐	☐	
	Are the attributes defined adequately?	☐	☐	
	Are there normalization violations?	☐	☐	
	Are the primary keys defined incorrectly?	☐	☐	
	Are the foreign keys defined incorrectly?	☐	☐	
	Are the compound keys defined incorrectly?	☐	☐	
	Are the entity subtypes defined incorrectly?	☐	☐	
	Are the parent processes incomplete?	☐	☐	
	Are the child processes incomplete?	☐	☐	
	Are the process inputs and outputs interactions with the entities incomplete?	☐	☐	
	Are the elementary entities defined correctly?	☐	☐	
	Are there parallel linkage problems?	☐	☐	
	Are event-trigger processes designed incorrectly?	☐	☐	
	Are there entity/process associations incorrectly defined?	☐	☐	
	Are there entity/process read associations incorrectly defined?	☐	☐	
	Are there entity/process update associations incorrectly defined?	☐	☐	
	Are there entity/process delete associations incorrectly defined?	☐	☐	

F28: Functional Specification Review Checklist

The functional specification review checklist is used to review a functional specification for content completeness and clarity (not to be confused with ambiguity reviews). For all negative responses the QA project manager will assess the impact and document it as an issue to the concerned parties for resolution. This can be accomplished through weekly status reports or e-mail. The following is a sample that is also included in the CD in the back of the book.

Context	Task	Yes	No	Comments
Introduction				
	Are the purpose, scope, and organization of the functional specification documented?	☐	☐	
Software Overview				
Product Description	Is there a description of why the product is being developed and a list of the important features and capabilities?	☐	☐	
Product Functional Capabilities	Is there a list of the functions that the software will be required to perform?	☐	☐	
	For several functional capabilities, is there a table (or some other format) to illustrate the relationships between the functional capabilities? Note: This may be an update to the Requirements documentation	☐	☐	
User Characteristics	Are the intended users of the software in terms of job function, specialized knowledge, or skill levels described?	☐	☐	
User Operations and Practices	Is there a description of how the users will normally use the software, and the tasks they will frequently perform?	☐	☐	
General Constraints	Are algorithm limitations, user interface limitations, and data limitations described?	☐	☐	
Assumptions	Are all the assumptions described?	☐	☐	
Other Software	Is there a description of how the system interfaces with other software?	☐	☐	

Context	Task	Yes	No	Comments
Specific Functional Descriptions				
Description	Is the role of each function described?	☐	☐	
Inputs	Are all input sources specified?	☐	☐	
	Are all input accuracy requirements specified?	☐	☐	
	Are all input range values specified?	☐	☐	
	Are all input frequencies specified?	☐	☐	
	Are all input formats specified?	☐	☐	
Processing	If calculations using methods or specific standards are used, are they referenced?	☐	☐	
	Are database definitions included?	☐	☐	
Outputs	Are the outputs of the function described?	☐	☐	
	Where there is a user interface, is it included?	☐	☐	
	Are all output destinations specified?	☐	☐	
	Are all output accuracy requirements specified?	☐	☐	
	Are all output range values specified?	☐	☐	
	Are all output frequencies specified?	☐	☐	
	Are all output formats specified?	☐	☐	
Reports				
	Are all report formats specified?	☐	☐	
	Are all calculations/formulas used in reports specified?	☐	☐	
	Are all report data filter requirements specified?	☐	☐	
	Are all report sorting requirements specified?	☐	☐	
	Is a report totaling requirements specified?	☐	☐	
	Are all report formatting requirements specified?	☐	☐	

Context	Task	Yes	No	Comments
Nonfunctional				
	Are all performance requirements specified for each function?	☐	☐	
	Are all design constrains specified for each function?	☐	☐	
	Are all attributes specified for each function?	☐	☐	
	All security requirements specified for each function?	☐	☐	
	Are all maintainability requirements specified for each function?	☐	☐	
	Are all database requirements specified for each function?	☐	☐	
	Are all operational requirements specified for each function?	☐	☐	
	Are all installation requirements specified for each function?	☐	☐	
Interfaces				
	Are all user interfaces specified?	☐	☐	
	Are all batch interfaces specified?	☐	☐	
	Are all hardware interfaces specified?	☐	☐	
	Are all software interfaces specified?	☐	☐	
	Are all communications interfaces specified?	☐	☐	
	Are all interface design constraints specified?	☐	☐	
	Are all interface security requirements specified?	☐	☐	
	Are all interface maintainability requirements specified?	☐	☐	
	Are all human–computer interactions specified for user interfaces?	☐	☐	
	Have all internal interfaces been identified?	☐	☐	
	Have all internal interface characteristics been specified?	☐	☐	

Context	Task	Yes	No	Comments
	Are error message requirements described?	☐	☐	
	Are input range checking requirements described?	☐	☐	
	Is the order of choices and screens corresponding to user preferences defined?	☐	☐	
Additional Requirements				
Database	Are any specific requirements relating to the database, such as data base type, capability to handle large text fields, real-time capability, multi-user capability and special requirements relating to queries and forms, defined?	☐	☐	
Administration	Are there any periodic updating or data management requirements defined?	☐	☐	
User Documentation	Are there user-documentation requirements to be delivered with the software defined?	☐	☐	
Other Requirements	Are there requirements not already covered above that need to be considered during the design of the software?	☐	☐	
Timing				
	Are all expected processing times specified?	☐	☐	
	Are all data transfer rates specified?	☐	☐	
	Are all system throughput rates specified?	☐	☐	
Hardware	Is the minimum memory specified?	☐	☐	
	Is the minimum storage specified?	☐	☐	
	Is the maximum memory specified?	☐	☐	
	Is the maximum storage specified?	☐	☐	

Context	Task	Yes	No	Comments
Software	Are the required software environments/OSs specified?	☐	☐	
	Are all of the required software utilities specified?	☐	☐	
	Are all purchased software products that are to be used with the system specified?	☐	☐	
Network	Is the target network specified?	☐	☐	
	Are the required network protocols specified?	☐	☐	
	Is the required network capacity specified?	☐	☐	
	Is the required/estimated network throughput rate specified?	☐	☐	
	Is the estimated number of network connections specified?	☐	☐	
	Are minimum network performance requirements specified?	☐	☐	
	Are the maximum network performance requirements specified?	☐	☐	

F29: Prototype Review Checklist

The prototype review checklist is used to review a prototype for content completeness and clarity. For all negative responses the test manager will assess the impact and document it as an issue to the concerned parties for resolution. This can be accomplished through weekly status reports or e-mail. The following is a sample that is also included in the CD in the back of the book.

Context	Item	Yes	No	Comments
	Does the prototype reflect the initial client requirements?			
	Does the prototype design reflect the initial requirements?			
	Has a detailed interactive/visual user interface been created?			
	Is there an easy connection of the user interface components to the underlying functional behavior?			
	Does the prototyping tool provide an easy to learn language?			
	Is modification to the resulting prototyping tool language easy to perform?			
	Simplicity: Does the user interface provide an appropriate means of allowing a client to assess the underlying functional behavior as described by the initial requirements?			
	Is the prototype simple to use?			
	Conciseness: Does the prototype contain full-scale user interfaces without extraneous details?			
	Does the prototype contain a data model defining the data structures for the application itself?			
	Is the volatility/persistence of the data represented?			
	Does the prototype accommodate new requirements?			
	Does the prototype address poorly defined requirements?			

F30: Requirements Review Checklist

The requirements review checklist is used to verify that the testing project requirements are comprehensive and complete. For all negative responses the test manager will assess the impact and document it as an issue to the concerned parties for resolution. This can be accomplished through weekly status reports or e-mail. The following is a sample that is also included in the CD in the back of the book.

Context	Task	Status Yes	No	Comments
Clarity				
	Are the requirements written in nontechnical understandable language?	☐	☐	
	Is each characteristic of the final product described with a unique terminology?	☐	☐	
	Is there a glossary in which the specific meaning(s) of each term is (are) defined?	☐	☐	
	Could the requirements be understood and implemented by an independent group?	☐	☐	
Completeness				
	Is there an indexed table of contents?	☐	☐	
	Are all figures, tables, and diagrams labeled?	☐	☐	
	Are all figures, tables, and diagrams cross-referenced?	☐	☐	
	Are all of the requirements defined?	☐	☐	
	Are all of the requirements related to functionality included?	☐	☐	
	Are all of the requirements related to performance included?	☐	☐	
	Are all of the requirements related to design constraints included?	☐	☐	
	Are all of the requirements related to attributes included?	☐	☐	
	Are all of the requirements related to external interfaces included?	☐	☐	
	Are all of the requirements related to databases included?	☐	☐	
	Are all of the requirements related to software included?	☐	☐	

Context	Task	Status		
		Yes	**No**	**Comments**
	Are all of the requirements related to hardware included	☐	☐	
	Are all of the requirements related to inputs included?	☐	☐	
	Are all of the requirements related to outputs included?	☐	☐	
	Are all of the requirements related to reporting included?	☐	☐	
	Are all of the requirements related to security included?	☐	☐	
	Are all of the requirements related to maintainability included?	☐	☐	
	Are all of the requirements related to criticality included?	☐	☐	
	Are possible changes to the requirements specified?	☐	☐	
Consistency				
	Are there any requirements describing the same object that conflict with other requirements with respect to terminology?	☐	☐	
	Are there any requirements describing the same object that conflict with respect to attributes?	☐	☐	
	Are there any requirements that describe two or more actions that conflict logically?	☐	☐	
	Are there any requirements that describe two or more actions that conflict temporally?	☐	☐	
Traceability				
	Are all requirements traceable back to a specific user need?	☐	☐	
	Are all requirements traceable back to a specific source document or person?	☐	☐	
	Are all requirements traceable forward to a specific design document?	☐	☐	
	Are all requirements traceable forward to a specific software module?	☐	☐	

Context	Task	Status		
		Yes	**No**	**Comments**
Verifiability				
	Are any requirements included that are impossible to implement?	☐	☐	
	For each requirement is there a process that can be executed by either a human or a machine to verify the requirement?	☐	☐	
	Are there any requirements that will be expressed in verifiable terms at a later time?	☐	☐	
Modifiability				
	Is the requirements document clearly and logically organized?	☐	☐	
	Does the organization adhere to an accepted standard?	☐	☐	
Content				
General				
	Is each requirement relevant to the problem and its solution?	☐	☐	
	Are any of the defined requirements really designing details?	☐	☐	
	Are any of the defined requirements really verification details?	☐	☐	
	Are any of the defined requirements really project management details?	☐	☐	
	Is there an introduction section?	☐	☐	
	Is there a general description section?	☐	☐	
	Is there a scope section?	☐	☐	
	Is there a definitions, acronyms, and abbreviations section?	☐	☐	
	Is there a product perspective section?	☐	☐	
	Is there a product functions section?	☐	☐	
	Is there a user characteristics section?	☐	☐	
	Is there a general constraints section?	☐	☐	
	Is there an assumptions and dependencies section?	☐	☐	
	Is there a specific requirements section?	☐	☐	
	Are all of the necessary appendices present?	☐	☐	

Context	Task	Status		
		Yes	No	Comments
	Are all of the necessary figures present?	☐	☐	
	Are all of the necessary tables present?	☐	☐	
	Are all of the necessary diagrams present?	☐	☐	
Reliability				
	Are the consequences of software failure specified for each requirement?	☐	☐	
	Is the information to protect from failure specified?	☐	☐	
	Is a strategy for error detection specified?	☐	☐	
	Is a strategy for correction specified?	☐	☐	
Hardware				
	Are the hardware details specified?	☐	☐	
Software				
	Are the required software details specified?	☐	☐	
Communications				
	Are the required communication/network details specified	☐	☐	

F31: Technical Design Review Checklist

The technical design review checklist is used to review the technical design for clarity and completeness. For all negative responses the QA project manager will assess the impact and document it as an issue to the concerned parties for resolution. This can be accomplished through weekly status reports or e-mail, depending upon the severity. The following is a sample that is also included in the CD in the back of the book.

Context	Task	Yes	No	Comments
Technical Design				
	Is the logic sequencing erroneous?	☐	☐	
	Is the processing inaccurate?	☐	☐	
	Do procedures handle input or output parameters incorrectly?	☐	☐	
	Do procedures not accept all data within allowable ranges?	☐	☐	
	Are limit and validity checks made on input data?	☐	☐	
	Are there recovery procedures not implemented or that are inadequate?	☐	☐	
	Is required logic missing or inadequate?	☐	☐	
	Are values erroneous or ambiguous?	☐	☐	
	Is data storage erroneous or inadequate?	☐	☐	
	Is variable missing or not declared properly?	☐	☐	
	Is the database not compatible with the data environment?	☐	☐	
	Does the modular structure reflect a high inter-modular dependence?	☐	☐	
	Are there algorithms not evaluated for accuracy or speed?	☐	☐	
	Is the control structure not expandable?	☐	☐	
	Do control structures ignore the processing priorities?	☐	☐	
	Are the interface protocols incorrectly used?	☐	☐	
	Is data not converted according to the correct format?	☐	☐	
	Is there no consideration to round-off or truncation?	☐	☐	

Context	Task	Yes	No	Comments
	Are the indices used incorrectly?	☐	☐	
	Are there infinite loops?	☐	☐	
	Are database rules violated?	☐	☐	
	Are there special cases not covered?	☐	☐	
	Is error handling deficient?	☐	☐	
	Are timing considerations neglected?	☐	☐	
	Are interface specifications misunderstood or implemented wrongly?	☐	☐	
	Are the functional specifications misallocated among the various software modules?	☐	☐	
	Is the system functionality correct but does not meet performance requirements?	☐	☐	
	Is the system not sufficiently complex to match the problem being solved?	☐	☐	
	Are there actions in response to given inputs that are inappropriate or missing?	☐	☐	
	Do algorithmic approximations provide insufficient accuracy or erroneous results for certain values of the input?	☐	☐	
	Are there errors in the detailed logic developed to solve a particular problem?	☐	☐	
	Do singular or critical input values yield unexpected results that are not appropriately accounted for in the code?	☐	☐	
	Are there algorithms that do not cover all the necessary cases?	☐	☐	
	Are there algorithms that are incorrect or produce the wrong solution?	☐	☐	

F32: Test Case Preparation Review Checklist

This is used to ensure that test cases have been prepared as per specifications. For all negative responses the test case preparation review checklist test manager will assess the impact and document it as an issue to the concerned parties for resolution. This can be accomplished through weekly status reports or e-mail. The following is a sample that is also included in the CD in the back of the book.

Context	Activity	Status		
		Yes	No	Comments
	Is the Approved Test Plan available?	☐	☐	
	Are the resources identified to implement the test plan?	☐	☐	
	Are the baseline documents available?	☐	☐	
	Is the domain knowledge imparted to team members to work with the application?	☐	☐	
	Has the test condition document been completed?	☐	☐	
	Have test cases have been developed for all the requirements?	☐	☐	
	Has the traceability been verified?	☐	☐	
	Have all the basic flows in use cases been covered?	☐	☐	
	Have all the alternate flows in use cases been covered?	☐	☐	
	Have any changed requirements been covered fully?	☐	☐	
	Have nontestable requirements been escalated?	☐	☐	
	Have the test cases been written for data flow across interfaces?	☐	☐	
	Have the test cases been written for all types of tests defined in the project plan?	☐	☐	
	Have all the positive and negative cases been identified?	☐	☐	
	Are all boundary cases identified?	☐	☐	
	Have test cases been written for nonfunctional requirements?	☐	☐	
	Have test cases been written for GUI/hyperlink testing in Web applications?	☐	☐	
	Have test cases been written to test date integrity?	☐	☐	

Appendix G
Software Testing Techniques

G1: Basis Path Testing

Basis path testing is a white-box technique that identifies test cases based on the flows or logical paths that can be taken through a program. A basis path is a unique path through the program where no iterations are allowed. Basis paths are atomic level paths, and all possible paths through the system are linear combinations of them. Basis path testing also produces a cyclomatic metric, which measures the complexity of a source code module by examining the control structures.

Consider the following small program, which reads records from a file and tallies the numerical ranges of a field on each record to illustrate the technique.

PROGRAM: FIELD-COUNT

```
Node Statement
1.   Dowhile not EOF
        read record
2.      if FIELD_COUNTER > 7 then
3.         increment COUNTER_7 by 1
        else
4.         if FIELD_COUNTER > 3 then
5.            increment COUNTER_3 by 1
           else
6.            increment COUNTER_1 by 1
7.         endif
8.      endif
9.   End_While
10. End
```

In theory, if the loop were to be iterated 100 times, 1.5×10 test cases would be required to perform exhaustive testing, which is not achievable. On the other hand, with basis testing there are four basis test cases required to test the program, as shown below.

$1 \rightarrow 10$

$1 \rightarrow 2 \rightarrow 3 \rightarrow 8 \rightarrow 9 \rightarrow 1 \rightarrow 10$

$1 \rightarrow 2 \rightarrow 4 \rightarrow 5 \rightarrow 7 \rightarrow 8 \rightarrow 9 \rightarrow 1 \rightarrow 10$

$1 \rightarrow 2 \rightarrow 4 \rightarrow 6 \rightarrow 7 \rightarrow 8 \rightarrow 9 \rightarrow 1 \rightarrow 10$

Mathematically, all possible paths in the program can be generated by linear combinations of the four basis paths. Experience shows that most of the potential defects will be discovered by executing the four basis path test cases, which demonstrates the power of the technique. The number of basis paths is also the cyclomatic complexity metric. It is recommended that the cyclomatic for a program module should not exceed 10. As the calculations are very labor intensive, there are testing tools to automate the process. See Section V, Modern Software Testing Tools, for more details.

Basis path testing can also be applied to integration testing when program modules are integrated. The use of the technique quantifies the integration effort involved as well as the design-level complexity.

G2: Black-Box Testing

Black-box or functional testing is one in which test conditions are developed based on the program or system's functionality; that is, the tester requires information about the input data and observed output, but does not know how the program or system works. Just as one does not have to know how a car works internally to drive it, it is not necessary to know the internal structure of a program to execute it. The technique focuses on testing the program's functionality against the specification. With black-box testing, the tester views the program as a black-box and is completely unconcerned with the internal structure of the program or system. Some examples in this category include: decision tables, equivalence partitioning, range testing, boundary value testing, database integrity testing, cause-effect graphing, orthogonal array testing, array and table testing, exception testing, limit testing, and random testing.

A major advantage of black-box testing is that the tests are geared to what the program or system is supposed to do, and it is natural and understood by everyone. This should be verified with techniques such as structured walkthroughs, inspections, and JADs. A limitation is that exhaustive input testing is not achievable, because this requires that every possible input condition or combination be tested. In addition, because there is no knowledge of the internal structure or logic, there could be errors or deliberate mischief on the part of a programmer, which may not be detectable with black-box testing. For example, suppose a disgruntled payroll programmer wanted to insert some job security into a payroll application he is developing. By inserting the following extra code into the application, if the employee were to be terminated, that is, if his employee ID no longer exists in the system, justice would sooner or later prevail.

Extra Program Logic

```
if my employee ID exists
   deposit regular pay check into my bank account
else
   deposit an enormous amount of money into my bank account
   erase any possible financial audit trails
   erase this code
```

G3: Bottom-Up Testing

The bottom-up testing technique is an incremental testing approach where the lowest-level modules or system components are integrated and tested first. Testing then proceeds hierarchically to the top level. A driver, or temporary test program that invokes the test module or system component, is often required. Bottom-up testing starts with the lowest-level modules or system components with the drivers to invoke them. After these components have been tested, the next logical level in the program or system component hierarchy is added and tested driving upward.

Bottom-up testing is common for large complex systems, and it takes a relatively long time to make the system visible. The menus and external user interfaces are tested last, so users cannot have an early review of these interfaces and functions. A potential drawback is that it requires a lot of effort to create drivers, which can add additional errors.

G4: Boundary Value Testing

The boundary value testing technique is a black-box technique that focuses on the boundaries of the input and output equivalence classes (see Equivalence Class Partitioning Testing). Errors tend to congregate at the boundaries. Focusing testing in these areas increases the probability of detecting errors.

Boundary value testing is a variation of the equivalence class partitioning technique, which focuses on the bounds of each equivalence class, for example, on, above, and below each class. Rather than select an arbitrary test point within an equivalence class, boundary value analysis selects one or more test cases to challenge each edge. Focus is on the input space (input equivalence classes) and output space (output equivalence classes). It is more difficult to define output equivalence classes and, therefore, boundary value tests.

Boundary value testing can require a large number of test cases to be created because of the large number of input and output variations. It is recommended that at least nine test cases be created for each input variable. The inputs need to be thoroughly understood, and the behavior must be consistent for the equivalence class. One limitation is that it may be very difficult to define the range of the equivalence class if it involves complex calculations. It is, therefore, imperative that the requirements be as detailed as possible. The following are some examples of how to apply the technique.

Numeric Input Data

Field Ranges. Ex. "Input can range from integers 0 to 100," test cases include –1, 0, 100, 101.

Ex. "Input can range from real numbers 0 to 100.0," test cases include –.00001, 0.0, 100.0, 100.00001.

Numeric Output Data

Output Range of Values. Ex. "Numerical range outputs of actuarial tables can be from $0.0 to $100,000.00"; for example, attempt to create conditions that produce a negative amount, $0.0, $100,000.00, $100,000.01.

Nonnumeric Input Data

Tables or Arrays. Ex. Focus on the first and last rows, for example, read, update, write, delete.

Ex. Try to access a nonexistent table or array.

Number of Items. Ex. "Number of products associated with a model is up to 10"; for example, enter 0, 10, 11 items.

Nonnumeric Output Data

Tables or Arrays. Ex. Focus on the first and last rows, for example, update, delete, insert operations.

Number of Outputs. Ex. "Up to 10 stocks can be displayed"; for example, attempt to display 0, 10, and 11 stocks.

GUI

1. Vertically and horizontally scroll to the end of scroll bars
2. Upper and lower limits of color selection
3. Upper and lower limits of sound selection
4. Boundary gizmos, for example, bounds available sets of available input values
5. Spinners, for example, small edit field with two half-height buttons

6. Flip-flop menu items
7. List box bounds

G5: Branch Coverage Testing

Branch coverage or decision coverage is a white-box testing technique in which test cases are written to ensure that every decision has a true and false outcome at least once; for example, each branch is traversed at least once. Branch coverage generally satisfies statement coverage (see Statement Coverage testing technique), because every statement is on the same subpath from either branch statement.

Consider the following small program, which reads records from a file and tallies the numerical ranges of a field on each record to illustrate the technique.

PROGRAM: FIELD-COUNT

```
Dowhile not EOF
  read record
  if FIELD_COUNTER > 7 then
    increment COUNTER_7 by 1
  else
    if FIELD_COUNTER > 3 then
      increment COUNTER_3 by 1
    else
      increment COUNTER_1 by 1
    endif
  endif
End_While
End
```

The test cases to satisfy branch coverage are as follows:

Test Case	Value (FIELD_COUNTER)
1	>7, ex. 8
2	<= 7, ex. 7
3	>3, ex. 4
4	<= 3, ex. 3

For this particular example, Test Case 2 is redundant and can be eliminated.

G6: Branch/Condition Coverage Testing

Branch/condition coverage is a white-box testing technique in which test cases are written to ensure that each decision and the conditions within a decision take on all possible values at least once. It is a stronger logic-coverage technique than decision or condition coverage because it covers all the conditions that may not be tested with decision coverage alone. It also satisfies statement coverage.

One method of creating testing cases using this technique is to build a truth table and write down all conditions and their complements. Then, if they exist, duplicate test cases are eliminated. Consider the following small program, which reads records from a file and tallies the numerical ranges of a field on each record to illustrate the technique.

PROGRAM: FIELD-COUNT

```
Dowhile not EOF
  read record
  if FIELD_COUNTER > 7 then
    increment COUNTER_7 by 1
  else
    if FIELD_COUNTER > 3 then
      increment COUNTER_3 by 1
    else
      increment COUNTER_1 by 1
    endif
  endif
End_While
End
```

The test cases to satisfy branch/condition coverage are as follows:

Test Case	Value (FIELD_COUNTER)
1	>7, ex. 8
2	<= 7, ex. 7
3	>3, ex. 4
4	<= 3, ex. 3

For this particular example there is only one condition for each decision. If there were more, each condition and its complement would be tested. Again, Test Case 2 is redundant and can be eliminated.

G7: Cause-Effect Graphing

Cause-effect diagrams (also known as Ishikawa or Fishbone diagrams) are useful tools to analyze the causes of an unsatisfactory condition. They have several advantages. One is that they provide a visual display of the relationship of one cause to another. This has proven to be an effective way to stimulate ideas during the initial search. Another benefit is that they provide a way to keep searching for root causes by asking why, what, where, who, and how. Another is that they are graphical representations in which the cause-relationships are easily discernible.

One application of cause-effect graphs was undertaken to understand the inspection process. It discovered that (1) excessive size of materials to be inspected leads to a preparation rate that is too high, (2) a preparation rate that is too high contributes to an excessive rate of inspection, and (3) an excessive rate of inspection causes fewer defects to be found. This analysis using cause-effect graphics provided insights to optimize the inspection process by limiting the size of materials to be inspected and the preparation rate.

Proper preparation for construction of cause-effect diagrams is essential. Visibility is a key requirement. It is advisable to leave a good deal of space between the causes as they are listed, so there can be room for additional notation as the work continues.

Several stages of construction should be expected before a "finished" product is developed. This often consists of enlarging a smaller section of the cause-effect diagram by taking one significant cause and making it the "effect" to be analyzed on another cause-effect diagram.

Cause-effect graphics can also be applied to test case design, particularly function testing. They are used to systematically select a set of test cases that have high probability of detecting program errors. This technique explores the input and combinations of input conditions of a program to develop test cases but does not examine the internal behavior of the program. For each test case derived, the technique also identifies the expected output. The input and output are determined through the analysis of the requirement specifications (see Section V, Modern Software Testing Tools, which automates the process).

The following is a brief overview of the methodology to convert requirements to test cases using cause-effect diagrams. It is followed by an example of how to apply the methodology.

Cause-Effect Methodology

1. Identify all the requirements.
2. Analyze the requirements and identify all the causes and effects.
3. Assign each cause and effect a unique number.
4. Analyze the requirements and translate them into a Boolean graph linking the causes and effects.
5. Convert the graph into a decision table.
6. Convert the columns in the decision table into test cases.

Example. A database management system requires that each file in the database have its name listed in a master index identifying the location of each file. The index is divided into ten sections. A small system is being developed that allows the user to interactively enter a command to display any section of the index at the terminal. Cause-effect graphing is used to develop a set of test cases for the system. The specification for this system is explained in the following paragraphs.

Specification

To display one of the ten possible index sections, a command must be entered consisting of a letter and a digit. The first character entered must be a D (for display) or an L (for list), and it must be in column 1. The second character entered must be a digit (0 through 9) in column 2. If this command occurs, the index section identified by the digit is displayed on the terminal. If the first character is incorrect, error message "Invalid Command" is printed. If the second character is incorrect, error message "Invalid Index Number" is printed.

The causes and effects are identified as follows.

Causes

1. Character in column 1 is D.
2. Character in column 1 is L.
3. Character in column 2 is a digit.

Effects

1. Index section is displayed.
2. Error message "Invalid Command" is displayed.
3. Error message "Invalid Index Number" is displayed.

A Boolean graph (see Exhibit G.1) is constructed through analysis of the specification. This is accomplished by (1) representing each cause and effect by a node by its unique number; (2) listing all the cause nodes vertically on the left side of a sheet of paper and listing the effect nodes on the right side; (3) interconnecting the cause and effect nodes by analyzing the specification. Each cause and effect can be in one of two states: true or false. Using Boolean logic, set the possible states of the causes and determine under what conditions each effect is present; and (4) annotating the graph with constraints describing combinations of causes and effects that are impossible because of syntactic or environmental constraints.

Node 20 is an intermediate node representing the Boolean state of node 1 or node 2. The state of node 50 is true if the states of nodes 20 and 3 are both true. The state of node 20 is true if the state of node 1 or node 2 is true. The state of node 51 is true if the state of node 20 is not true. The state of node 52 is true if the state of node 3 is not true. Nodes 1 and 2 are also annotated with a constraint that states that causes 1 and 2 cannot be true simultaneously.

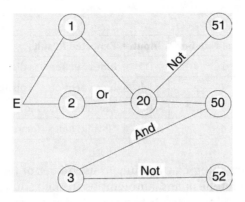

Exhibit G.1. Cause-Effect Graph

Exhibit G.2. Decision Table

	Test Cases			
Causes	1	2	3	4
1	1	0	0	
2	0	1	0	
3	1	1		1
Effects				
50	1	1	0	0
51	0	0	1	0
52	0	0	0	1

Exhibit G.2 shows Exhibit G.1 converted into a decision table. This is accomplished by (1) tracing back through the graph to find all combinations of causes that make the effect true for each effect, (2) representing each combination as a column in the decision table, and (3) determining the state of all other effects for each such combination. After completing this, each column in Exhibit G.2 represents a test case.

For each test case, the bottom of Exhibit G.2 indicates which effect is present (indicated by a 1). For each effect, all combinations of causes that result in the effect are represented by the entries in the columns of the table. Blanks in the table mean that the state of the cause is irrelevant.

Each column in the decision table is converted into the four test cases shown below.

Test Case Number	Input	Expected Results
1	D5	Index Section 5 is displayed
2	L4	Index Section 4 is displayed
3	B2	"Invalid Command"
4	DA	"Invalid Index Number"

Cause-effect graphing can produce a useful set of test cases and can point out incompleteness and ambiguities in the requirement specification. It can be applied to generate test cases in any type of computing application when the specification is clearly stated and combinations of input conditions can be identified. Although manual application of this technique is tedious, long, and moderately complex, there are automated testing tools that will automatically help convert the requirements to a graph, decision table, and test cases. See Section V, Modern Software Testing Tools, for more details.

G8: Condition Coverage

Condition coverage is a white-box testing technique in which test cases are written to ensure that each condition in a decision takes on all possible outcomes at least once. It is not necessary to consider the decision branches with condition coverage using this technique. Condition coverage guarantees that every condition within a decision is covered. However, it does not necessarily traverse the true and false outcomes of each decision.

One method of creating testing cases using this technique is to build a truth table and write down all conditions and their complements. If they exist, duplicate test cases are eliminated.

Consider the following small program, which reads records from a file and tallies the numerical ranges of a field on each record to illustrate the technique.

PROGRAM: FIELD-COUNT

```
Dowhile not EOF
  read record
  if FIELD_COUNTER > 7 then
    increment COUNTER_7 by 1
  else
    if FIELD_COUNTER > 3 then
      increment COUNTER_3 by 1
```

```
      else
         increment COUNTER_1 by 1
      endif
   endif
End_While
End
```

The initial test cases to satisfy condition coverage are as follows:

Test Case	Values (FIELD_COUNTER)
1	>7, e.g., 8
2	<= 7, e.g., 7
3	>3, e.g., 6
4	<= 3, e.g., 3

Notice that Test Cases 2 and 3 are redundant and one of them can be eliminated, resulting in three test cases.

G9: CRUD Testing

A CRUD matrix, or process/data matrix, is optionally developed during the analysis phase of application development, which links data and process models. It helps ensure that the data and processes are discovered and assessed. It identifies and resolves matrix omissions and conflicts and helps refine the data and process models, as necessary. It maps processes against entities, showing which processes create, read, update, or delete the instances in an entity.

The CRUD matrix in Exhibit G.3 is developed at the analysis level of development before the physical system or GUI (physical screens, menus, etc.) has been designed and developed. As the GUI evolves, a CRUD test matrix can be built, as shown in Exhibit G.3. It is a testing technique that verifies the life cycle of all business objects. In Exhibit G.3, each CRUD cell object is tested. When an object does not have full life cycle operations a "–" can be placed in a cell.

A variation of this is to also make unit performance measurements for each operation during system fragment testing.

G10: Database Testing

The following provides a description of how to test databases. It also includes an overview of relational database concepts, which will serve as a reference to the tester.

Integrity Testing

Database integrity testing verifies the structure and format, compliance with integrity constraints, business rules and relationships, edit controls

Exhibit G.3. CRUD Testing

Object	C (Pass/ Fail)	R (Pass/ Fail)	U (Pass/ Fail)	D (Pass/ Fail)	Delete Confirm (Yes/No)	Tester	Date (M/D/Y)
Customer	x	x	x	x			
Order	-	x	x	-			
Payment	-	x	x	-			
Vendor	x	x	x	x			
Check	x	x	-	x			
Register	x	x	x	x			
Product	-	x	x	-			
Stock	x	x	x	x			
Back Order	-	x	x	-			
Inventory	x	-	x	-			
Report	x	x	-	-			
.							
.							
.							
.							

on updates that refresh databases, and database normalization, or denormalization per performance constraints. There are at least six types of integrity tests that need to be performed to verify the integrity of the database.

Entity Integrity. Entity integrity states that each row must always have a primary key value. For example, if team ID is the primary key of the team table, no team can lack a team ID. This can be tested and verified with database integrity reports or queries.

Primary Key Integrity. The value of each primary key must be unique and valid. For example, two teams cannot have the same team ID, and a team ID of "ABC" is invalid when numeric values are required. Another rule is that the primary key must not contain a null value (be empty). This can be tested and verified with database integrity reports or queries.

Column Key Integrity. The values in a column have column-specific rules. For example, the values in a column for the number of members on a team must always be a positive and numeric number and not exceed 7.

This can be tested and verified with database integrity reports or queries. It can also be verified with the following testing techniques: range testing, boundary value testing, field integrity testing, and positive and negative testing.

Domain Integrity. A domain is an object that is a set of data and characteristics that describe those values. For example, "date" could be defined as a basic data type that has a field length, format, and validation rules. Columns can be defined based on domains; in this case a column might be defined as an order date. This can be tested and verified with database queries. It can also be verified with the following testing techniques: range testing, boundary value testing, field integrity testing, and positive and negative testing.

User-Defined Integrity. User-defined integrity checks are specialized validation rules that go beyond the standard row and column checks. User-defined rules for particular data items often must be written manually, using a procedural language.

Another option instead of writing procedures is the use of assertions, if available. Assertions are standalone validation checks that are not linked to a particular row or column, but that are automatically applied.

Referential Integrity. The primary key is a candidate key to uniquely identify a particular entity. With a table of teams, the primary key could be the team number. A foreign key is a key that refers to a primary key in another entity, as a cross reference. For example, part of the key to a member name (from a member entity) may be a team ID, which is the primary key to the team entity.

A table has business rules that govern the relationships among entities. For example, a member must be related to a team, and only one team. A team, on the other hand, may at any given time have no members, only one member, or many members. This is referred to as the cardinality of the entity relationship. Any member "floating around" in the system, without being associated with a team, is an invalid order. A record such as this is referred to as an orphan.

As an example, assume that a team can have one, no, or more members, but a member cannot exist without a team. The test cases shown in Exhibit G.4 should be created to verify referential integrity.

Other database testing approaches include the following.

- *Control Testing* — includes a variety of control issues, which need to be tested.
  - *Security Testing* — protects the database from unauthorized access.
  - *Backup Testing* — verifies the ability to back up the system.

Exhibit G.4. Referential Integrity Test Cases

Test Case	Expected Results
1. Insert a team	No association with the member entity for this record
2. Insert a member	There exists a foreign key relationship to the team entity
3. Attempt to delete a team which has a relationship (foreign key) in the member	Should not do automatically but provide a confirmation prompt
4. Update a member	Team foreign key relation exists to the team entity

- *Recovery Testing* — verifies the restoration of a database to a state known to be correct after some failure has rendered it unreliable.
- *Concurrency Testing* — ensures that parallel processes such as queries and updates do not interfere with each other.
- *Deadlock Control* — ensures that two concurrent processes do not form a "gridlock" and mutually exclude each other from adequate completion.
- *Data Content Verification* — provides periodic audits and comparisons with known reference sources.
- *Refresh Verification* — verifies external systems that refresh the database and data conversions.
- *Data Usage* — includes verifying database editing and updating. Many times, the developer does not create enough or may include too many characters for the columns of an entity. The tester should compare the number of characters on each GUI field to the respective entity field lengths to verify they are the same. Tip: One way to make sure the database column lengths are large enough is to copy a very large document using the Window copy edit feature and then paste it into each GUI field. Some of the testing techniques that can be employed to generate data include range testing, boundary value testing, field integrity testing, and positive and negative testing. Most databases have query facilities that enable the tester to verify that the data is updated and edited correctly in the database.
- *Stored Procedures* — are stored and invoked when specific triggers from the application occur.

Data Modeling Essentials

The purpose of this section is to familiarize the reader with data modeling concepts and terminology in order to perform database and GUI field testing against a relational design (see below: Database Integrity Testing,

Range Testing, Positive and Negative Testing, and Table and Array Testing). It will also serve as a useful reference to relational database design in the context of testing.

What Is a Model? A model is a simplified description of a real-world system that assists its user in making calculations and predictions. Only those aspects of the system that are of interest to the user are included in the model; all others are omitted.

Three different materials are used in creating models:

1. Metal
2. Wood
3. Clay

The most appropriate material is used for the model, even though it may differ from the material used for the system being modeled. The written specifications of a system may be used by themselves as a model of the real world.

A model may be considered as having two features:

1. Shape or structure
2. Content

The structure of the model reflects the invariant aspects of the system, and the content reflects the dynamic aspects. For example, the structure of a predictive meteorological model consists of formulae, whereas the content consists of data (temperature, humidity, wind speed, and atmospheric pressure) gathered from many points over a period of time.

Why Do We Create Models? We must be able to measure real-world systems to be able to understand them, use them effectively, monitor their performance, and predict their future performance. Often, it is impossible to measure the actual system. It may be too expensive or too dangerous. Before an aircraft manufacturer sends a pilot up in a new plane, there must be some assurance that the plane will fly. An automobile manufacturer wants to know what a car will look like before tooling up an assembly line to make it.

We have a requirement to understand, measure, and control a real-world system: the user's business. The easiest way to make timely, cost-effective measurements and predictions about the business system is to create a model of the business. Data is the most appropriate material for our model; hence the name "data model." The structure of our data model should represent the aspects of the user's business that change very little over time. The content of the model (the values stored in the model) represents the information that changes with time. The result is a data model whose structure is stable and, therefore, easily maintained.

Applications that we create will be responsible for adding, changing, and deleting the content of the model and for reporting on the content.

The use of this technique results in the following benefits:

- The relatively stable nature of the data model will allow us to be more responsive to changing business needs. Business changes usually result in changes in how the content is maintained and reported. Changes to the structure of the model occur less frequently and are usually minor.
- The technique we will use will create a data model that is independent of both current business processes (but not business policy) and current data processing technology.
- An additional benefit of this technique is that it can be used in situations where current process-oriented techniques do not work. For example, there are no clearly identifiable processes involved in a management information application. The users cannot specify exactly how data will be used. By creating a data model whose structure reflects the structure of the business, we can support any reasonable inquiry against the data.
- Data analysis starts from the development of the data model.

Tables — A Definition

A table is a list of facts, numbers, and the like, systematically arranged in columns.

Tables are used whenever we need to order information for storage or presentation. They are relatively easy to create and maintain and present information in a clear, unambiguous, simple format. Examples of tables that we may encounter are:

- Table of Contents
- Metric Conversion Table
- Table of Weights and Measures
- Tax Table

Exhibit G.5 illustrates the features of a table.

Exhibit G.5. Sample Table

Name	Address	Telephone Number
Bill Smith	3290 Oak Lane, Dallas, Texas	(972) 329-6723
Joe Jones	129 Cliff Avenue, Austin, Texas	(812) 456-2198
Sue Maddox	1421 Millington Drive, Boca Raton, Florida	(305) 402-5954
Jerry Jones	112 Cowboys Drive, Portland, Oregon	(265) 693-2319

Table Names. A table is identified by its name. Therefore, its name must be unique within the scope of the business.

Columns. A table is divided vertically into columns. All entries in a given column are of the same type and have the same format. A column contains a single piece of data about all rows in the table. Each column must have a name unique within the table. The combination of table name and column name is unique within the business. Examples might be CUSTOMER.NAME, CUSTOMER.NUMBER, EMPLOYEE.NAME, and EMPLOYEE.NUMBER.

Rows. A table is divided horizontally into rows. Each row must be uniquely identifiable. Each row has the same number of cells and contains a piece of data of a different type and format.

Order. The order of rows and columns in a table is arbitrary. That is, the order in which rows and columns are presented does not affect the meaning of the data. In fact, each user of a table may have unique requirements for ordering rows and columns. For this reason, there must be no special significance to the order.

Based on the above definition, tables are useful for documenting data requirements. They can be easily understood by both development and user personnel.

We define a table to represent each object in our model. The table columns provide descriptive information about the object, and the rows provide examples of occurrences of the object.

Entities — A Definition

An entity is a uniquely identifiable person, place, thing, or event of interest to the user, about which the application is to maintain and report data.

When we create a data model, we must first decide which real-world objects are to be included. We include only those objects that are of interest to the users. Furthermore, we include only those objects required by computer applications.

We organize the objects (entities) to be included into groups called entity types. For example, a clothing store might identify customers, products sold, and suppliers of those products as objects to be included in a data model. This grouping, however, is not adequate for a useful model of the real world. Depending on the type of clothing sold by the store, the user may wish to group products by style, type, size, color, and so on. The identification of objects is made difficult by the fuzzy definitions used in the real world. In our model, we must be specific; therefore, we will define as entity types only groups of objects in which each occurrence can be uniquely identified.

Each entity type is given a unique name. Examples are CUSTOMER, SUP-PLIER, and EMPLOYEE.

Identification — Primary Key

Every entity must have a primary key.

To allow us to uniquely identify each occurrence of an entity type, we must define a key called the primary key. Its value may be assigned by the user or by the application. There may be more than one choice for the primary key. For the entity type EMPLOYEE we might choose SOCIAL INSUR-ANCE NUMBER or invent an EMPLOYEE NUMBER. The major requirement is that each value be unique. It is also important that the primary key be one by which the user would naturally identify an occurrence of the entity. You should also choose a key that is not likely to change. It should be as short as possible. This is why serial numbers are popular keys; they are assigned once, they do not change, and they are unique. (Be careful. In the real world, duplicate serial numbers may be inadvertently assigned.)

NOTE: A key is not an access path. It is only a unique identifier.

Compound Primary Keys. A primary key may be composed of more than one column. For example, an automobile can be uniquely identified only by the combination MAKE + MODEL+VEHICLE IDENTIFICATION NUM-BER. A key composed of more than one column is a compound key.

Null Values. In any descriptive information about an entity, it is possible to have a situation where a piece of data for a particular occurrence is not known. For example, when an employee description is added to a person-nel application for the first time, the employee's department number or phone number might not be known. The correct value is not zero or blank; it is unknown. We refer to an unknown value as a null value. We might use blanks or zero or some special indicator to reflect this in a computer appli-cation. However, because null means unknown, you cannot compare null values (e.g., for equal). You also cannot use them in numeric computations, because the result would also be unknown. In our data model, we indicate which columns may contain null values.

We bring this point up here because of the following rule:

A primary key may not be null.

It is important to remember this. A null value means we do not know what the correct value is, but primary key values must be known to uniquely identify each occurrence of the entity type to which they refer. In a compound key, it is possible for the key to contain null values in some, but NOT all, columns.

Identifying Entities. Consider the following list:

- Which is an entity type?
- Which is an entity occurrence?
- Which is neither?
- What would be a suitable key?
    - Automobile
    - Ford
    - Superman
    - Nietzsche
    - Telephone
    - Telephone number
    - House
    - Postal code
    - Aquamarine
    - Seven
    - Marriage

One thing you will discover when trying to identify the entity types and occurrences in the above list is that the user context is important. Consider Automobile. If the user is an automobile dealer, then automobile could be an entity type. However, if the user is attempting to keep track of types of transportation, automobile could be an entity occurrence. Ford might be a make of automobile, a U.S. president, or a way to cross a river.

Telephone number is often treated as if it were an entity type. You might instead think of it as the key that identifies a telephone. It cannot identify a specific physical phone, however, because you can replace the phone with a new one without changing the telephone number. It doesn't identify a specific telephone line, because you can often take the phone number with you when you move to a new location. In fact, the telephone number really identifies a telephone company account.

Aquamarine might be an entity occurrence. What would be the entity type? If your user is a jeweler, the entity type might be Precious Stone; if a paint manufacturer, Color.

Entity Classes. Entities may be grouped for convenience into various classes. Consider the following:

- *Major Entity:* An entity that can exist without reference to other entities (e.g., CUSTOMER, ORDER). These entity types are typically identified early in the data analysis process. In most cases, the primary key of a major entity will consist of a single column.
- *Dependent Entity:* An entity that depends upon and further defines another entity (e.g., ORDER LINE ITEM). These entity types will often be identified during the process of defining relationships or

normalizing and refining the model. The primary key of a dependent entity is always a compound key. These topics are covered later.

- *Minor Entity:* An entity that is used primarily to define valid values within the model (e.g., EMPLOYEE TYPE, CREDIT CODE). These may be ignored in some cases (e.g., if the only valid values are Y and N). The primary key of a minor entity is almost always a single column.

Relationships — A Definition

Each entity in a data model does not exist in solitary splendor. Entities are linked by relationships. A relationship is an association between two or more entities, of interest to the user, about which the application is to maintain and report data.

This is similar to the definition of an entity, and we show that a relationship can be considered as a special type of entity.

Relationship Types. There are three types of relationships:

1. One-to-One
2. One-to-Many
3. Many-to-Many

We now examine each type and see how we document them.

One-to-One. One-to-one relationships are the simplest and, unfortunately, the least common.

A one-to-one relationship links a single occurrence of an entity to zero or one occurrence of an entity. The related entity occurrences are usually of different types, but there is no rule prohibiting them from being of the same type. When the related entities are of the same type, the relationship is called a recursive relationship.

Let's consider a hypothetical example. An enlightened company, which shall remain nameless, has determined that employees work best when they are not forced to share desks or workstations. As a result, each desk is assigned to only one employee and each employee is assigned to one desk.

We document this happy relationship by placing the primary key of either entity into the description of the other entity as a foreign key.

Either Exhibit G.6 or Exhibit G.7 can be used to illustrate the relationship. Look first at Exhibit G.6, the EMPLOYEE table.

The PK in the column headed EMPLOYEE NUMBER indicates that this is the primary key. The FK in the column headed DESK NUMBER indicates that this is a foreign key (i.e., it is a primary key in some other table). The ND in this column enforces the one-to-one relationship by indicating that

Exhibit G.6. Employee Table

Employee	
EMPLOYEE NUMBER	**DESK NUMBER**
PK	FK
	ND
12345	004
23456	003
98751	001

Exhibit G.7. Employee Table

Desk	
DESK NUMBER	**EMPLOYEE NUMBER**
PK	FK
	ND, NL
003	23456
001	98751
002	-NULL-
004	12345

there can be no duplicate values (the same desk cannot be assigned to two different employees).

Exhibit G.7 illustrates the same relationship. The ND indicates that an employee may not be assigned to two different desks. Note, however, that there is an NL indication in the EMPLOYEE NUMBER column in this table. This indicates that a desk may be unassigned.

Although the relationship may be documented either way, there are some guidelines:

- Do NOT document the relationship both ways. Choose one.
- Choose the way that reduces or eliminates the need to record nulls. Note that this typically means placing the foreign key in the entity with the fewest occurrences.

Based on the above guidelines, the relationship in our example is best represented, as in Exhibit G.6, by recording the desk number as a foreign key of the employee (although Exhibit G.7 is not wrong).

471

Exhibit G.8. Employee Table

Employee	
EMPLOYEE NUMBER	**TELPHONE NUMBER**
PK	FK
12345	1111
23456	1954
98751	2654

Exhibit G.9. Telephone Line Table

Telephone Line
TELEPHONE NUMBER
PK
1954
2222
1111
2654

One-to-Many. One-to-many relationships are the most common, and the documentation technique is straightforward. A one-to-many relationship links one occurrence of an entity type to zero or more occurrences of an entity type.

As an example, let's look again at the company described above. When it comes to the assignment of telephones to employees, the company is not so enlightened. Each employee must share a single telephone number and line with other employees. Exhibits G.8 and G.9 illustrate the relationship between telephone numbers and employees.

The documentation of this relationship appears to be the same as for a one-to-one relationship. However, there is only one way to represent a one-to-many relationship. We record the one in the many. In Exhibits G.8 and G.9, we record the telephone number as a foreign key of the EMPLOYEE. To record the relationship the other way would require an array of employee numbers of indeterminate size for each telephone number. There is another important difference. We did not place ND (no duplicates) in the foreign key column. This is because duplicates are allowed; the same telephone number can be assigned to more than one employee.

Exhibit G.10. Employee Table

Employee
EMPLOYEE NUMBER
PK

Exhibit G.11. Project Table

Project
PROJECT NUMBER
PK

Exhibit G.12. Employee/Project Table

Employee/Project	
EMPLOYEE NUMBER	**PROJECT NUMBER**
PK	
FK	FK

So the rule here is easy to remember. There is only one correct way:

Record the one in the many.

Many-to-Many. Many-to-many relationships are the most difficult with which to deal. They also occur frequently enough to make data analysis interesting. A many-to-many relationship links many occurrences of an entity type to many occurrences of an entity type. For an example of this type of relationship, let us again examine the nameless company.

Management believes that the more people assigned to a given project, the sooner it will be completed. Also, because they become nervous at the sight of idle employees, they give each employee several assignments to work on simultaneously.

We cannot document a many-to-many relationship directly, so we create a new entity (see Exhibits G.10, G.11, and G.12) and link it to each of the

Exhibit G.13. Employee Table

Employee
EMPLOYEE NUMBER
11111
22222

Exhibit G.14. Project Table

Project
PROJECT NUMBER
ABCD
WXYZ

entities involved, by a one-to-many relationship (we already know how to do that).

The EMPLOYEE/PROJECT entity has been created to support the relationship between EMPLOYEE and PROJECT. It has a primary key consisting of the primary keys of the entity types it is relating. They are identified as foreign keys. This is an example of a compound key. Any entity may have a compound key that may be completely or partly made up of foreign keys from other entities. This commonly occurs with dependent entities. The EMPLOYEE/PROJECT entity we have created is dependent on EMPLOYEE and PROJECT; it wouldn't exist except for the relationship between them.

Note that the foreign keys that make up the primary key in this entity support one-to-many relationships between EMPLOYEE and EMPLOYEE/PROJECT and between PROJECT and EMPLOYEE/PROJECT. We must now demonstrate that this is equivalent to a many-to-many relationship between EMPLOYEE and PROJECT. An example will best illustrate the approach.

Given two employees and two projects, as in Exhibits G.13 and G.14, we can show that both employees work on both projects by creating occurrences of the EMPLOYEE/PROJECT entity, as in Exhibit G.15.

We can see that EMPLOYEE 11111 is related to two EMPLOYEE/PROJECT occurrences (11111ABCD and 11111WXYZ). Each of these EMPLOYEE/PROJECT entities is in turn related to one PROJECT entity. The result is that each EMPLOYEE occurrence may be related to many PROJECT occurrences through the EMPLOYEE/PROJECT entity. By the same technique, each PROJECT occurrence may be related to many EMPLOYEE occurrences.

Exhibit G.15. Employee/Project Table

Employee/Project	
EMPLOYEE NUMBER	**PROJECT NUMBER**
11111	ABCD
11111	WXYZ
22222	ABCD
22222	WXYZ

Multiple Relationships. There will sometimes be more than one type of relationship between occurrences of the same entity types. When you encounter this situation, identify and document each relationship independently of any others. For instance, in the last example, there might have been a requirement to record the project leader of each project independently of any other employees assigned to the project. This relationship might have been a one-to-many relationship with PROJECT LEADER EMPLOYEE NUMBER a foreign key in the PROJECT table.

Entities versus Relationships. The distinction between entities and relationships is not always clear. Consider the following example.

A customer buys an automobile from a dealer. The sale is negotiated by a salesperson employed by the dealer. The customer may have purchased automobiles from this dealer before, but may have dealt with a different salesperson.

Is the purchase a relationship between customer and salesperson? Is it an entity that is related to customer, salesperson, and automobile? How to treat such a real-world situation is often an arbitrary decision. There is no formal rule to guide you. Fortunately, the technique we use to document entities and relationships can reduce or eliminate the problem.

If we consider a purchase agreement to be an entity, we select a primary key, such as AGREEMENT NUMBER, and define relationships to other entities. There is a one-to-many relationship between SALESPERSON and PURCHASE AGREEMENT and, if we have satisfied customers, between CUSTOMER and PURCHASE AGREEMENT. We document these relationships in Exhibit G.16 by placing CUSTOMER NUMBER and EMPLOYEE NUMBER as foreign keys in PURCHASE AGREEMENT.

If we do not consider the purchase agreement to be an entity, we must then document the relationship between CUSTOMER and SALESPERSON (see Exhibit G.17). Because, in the general case, there is a many-to-many relationship between customers and salespeople, we must create a new entity, CUSTOMER/SALESPERSON, with a compound key of CUSTOMER

Exhibit G.16. Purchase Agreement Table

Purchase Agreement		
AGREEMENT NUMBER	**CUSTOMER NUMBER**	**EMPLOYEE NUMBER**
PK	FK	FK

Exhibit G.17. Customer/Salesperson Table

Customer/Salesperson			
CUSTOMER NUMBER	**EMPLOYEE NUMBER**	**VEHICLE MAKE**	**VIN**
PK			
FK	FK		

NUMBER + EMPLOYEE NUMBER. We will probably have to add VEHICLE MAKE and IDENTIFICATION NUMBER to the primary key to ensure uniqueness.

To change this relationship to an entity, we need only rename it and change the primary key. The columns already in the table will probably still be required.

Attributes — A Definition

An attribute is a characteristic quality of an entity or relationship, of interest to the user, about which the application is to maintain and report data.

Attributes are the data elements or fields that describe entities and relationships. An attribute is represented by a column in a table.

- Primary keys are attributes or sets of attributes that uniquely identify entities.
- Foreign keys are attributes that define relationships between entities.
- Non-key attributes provide additional information about entities (e.g., EMPLOYEE NAME) and relationships (e.g., QUANTITY ORDERED on an order line).

The information in this section applies to all types of attributes. All attributes base their values on domains.

Domain

A domain is a set of possible values of an attribute.

To determine which values are valid for a given attribute, we need to know the rules for assigning values. The set of values that may be assigned to a given attribute is the domain of that attribute.

All attributes of the same type must come from the same domain. For example, the following attributes could describe different entities or relationship:

- Department Number
- Sales Branch Number
- Service Branch Number

They are all based on the domain of possible department numbers. The domain is not a list of the assigned department numbers but a set of the possible department numbers from which values may be selected.

The definition of domains is somewhat arbitrary, and there may be a temptation to create general domains that allow too much freedom. Consider CUSTOMER NUMBER and DEPARTMENT NUMBER. If these attributes are both defined to be based on a domain of any numbers, we could end up with the following:

$$\text{Customer} \quad -12345$$

$$\text{Department} \quad 12.34$$

By restricting the domain to positive integers, we can avoid negative numbers and decimal fractions. However, with a definition this general, we can still combine customers and departments. For example, someone might decide that, whenever an internal order is processed, the CUSTOMER NUMBER field on the order will be sent to the ordering DEPARTMENT NUMBER. To satisfy processing requirements, we would have to place department numbers in the CUSTOMER table, because all valid customers appear there. Now, whenever we reorganize the business, we must update the customer data.

The safest approach in our example is to define the domain of CUSTOMER NUMBERS and the domain of DEPARTMENT NUMBERS separately.

Note: Be careful when defining the domain of fields such as customer number, employee number, or part number. It is natural to think of such fields as numeric. It may even be true that, currently, all assigned values are numeric. Alphabetic characters, however, have a nasty habit of showing up in these identifiers sooner or later.

Domain Names

Each domain should have a name that is unique within the organization. The name and the rules for defining values within the domain should be documented. A single column primary key based on a domain will usually have the same name as the domain (e.g., customer number). If a key (primary or foreign) is compound, each column will usually have the same name as the domain. Where the same domain is referenced more than once by attributes of an entity (e.g., date born, date hired for an employee), the domain name should be part of the attribute column name.

Domains, and the attributes based on them, must be nondecomposable.

The statement above does not mean that attributes should not decay or fall apart from old age. As an example of a decomposable domain and attribute, consider the following.

Whenever an order is recorded, it is assigned an order number. The order number is created according to the following rules:

1. The customer number makes up the first (high order) part of the order number.
2. The order entry date, in the form YYMMDD, is the next part of the order number.
3. The last two positions of the order number hold a sequence number to ensure uniqueness if a customer submits several orders in one day.

Because we use the term order number, there is a temptation to treat this as a single column. Resist the temptation. The primary key in this example is a compound key made up of customer number, order entry date, and a sequence number. Each attribute making up the compound key is based on a different domain. It is now possible to document the fact that there is an attribute in the order that is based on the domain of customer numbers. Any changes in the rules for that domain can be checked for their impact on the order entity.

Having said that all domains must be nondecomposable, we now state two exceptions:

1. Date
2. Time

Date is usually in the form month/day/year. There is usually no need to record this as three separate attributes. Similarly, time may be left as hours/minutes.

Attributes versus Relationships. Just as there is a somewhat arbitrary choice between entities and relationships, there is a similar choice between attributes and relationships. You could consider an attribute as a foreign key from a table of valid values for the attribute. If, for example, you were required to record color of eyes as an attribute of EMPLOYEE, you might set up an entity called COLOR with a primary key of COLOR NAME. You could then create EYE COLOR as a foreign key in EMPLOYEE. This would probably not provide much advantage over a simple attribute. You might even get into trouble. If you chose to add HAIR COLOR as a foreign key related to the same primary key, you could end up with an employee with blue hair and red eyes.

Although the above example may seem trivial, real-world choices are often more subtle. You might choose a foreign key over a simple attribute if you wished to have a table for edit checking or if you needed a long description on reports. The description could be an attribute in the table in which the foreign key was a primary key.

Normalization — What Is It? Normalization is the process of refining an initial set of entities into an optimum model. The purpose is to eliminate data redundancy and to ensure that the data structures are as flexible, understandable, and maintainable as possible.

Normalization is achieved by ensuring that an entity contains only those attributes that depend on the key of the entity. By depend on we mean that each value of the key determines only one value for each attribute of the entity. If the concept is unclear at this point, don't be discouraged; it is explained later in this section. Said another way, normalization means ensuring that:

Each attribute depends on

The Key, The Whole Key, and Nothing But the Key.

Problems of Unnormalized Entities. Exhibit G.18 illustrates the problems that will occur in attempting to maintain an unnormalized entity. The example in Exhibit G.18 is unnormalized because the department name is dependent on the department number, not on the employee number, which is the key of the entity. Consider the effects of the design on the application:

- *Modification Anomaly:* Suppose a corporate reorganization makes it necessary to change the name of department 354 to Advertising and Promotion. A special-purpose program will be required to modify this information accurately and completely everywhere that it appears in the database.
- *Insertion Anomaly:* A new employee is hired for department 220. The clerk maintaining the data may not have all the relevant information. Either he will have to scan the data looking for existing names for

479

Exhibit G.18. Employee Table

Employee				
EMPNO	**NAME**	**SALARY**	**DEPT**	**DEPTNAME**
PK				
00100	CODD, E.F.	65736	220	DEEP THOUGHT
00135	KENT, W.	58200	220	DEEP THOUGHT
00171	LEWIS, W.	49900	220	DEEP THOUGHT
00190	SMITH, S.	64000	220	DEEP THOUGHT
00215	DATE, C.J.	51500	114	PUBLISHING
00529	FLAVIN, M.	35700	354	ADVERTISING
00558	CLARK, G.	33600	354	ADVERTISING

department 220 or, probably, he will guess and assign our new employee to department 220, with DEPTNAME SHALLOW THOUGHT. What is the correct name of the department now?

- *Deletion Anomaly:* Employee number 00215 has retired. Her replacement starts next week. However, by deleting the entry for employee 00215, we have lost the information that tells us that the publishing department exists.
- *Redundancy:* It is possible to reduce the impact of these anomalies by designing programs that take their existence into account. Typically, this results in code that is more complex than it needs to be, and in additional code to resolve inconsistencies. These increase the cost of development and maintenance without eliminating the problems. In addition, the duplication of data will increase file or database sizes and will result in increased operating costs for the application.

All of the above problems are collectively known as the update anomaly.

Steps in Normalization

We explain normalization by discussing a series of examples that illustrate the three basic steps to be followed in reducing unnormalized data to third normal form.

First Normal Form (1NF). Each attribute depends on THE KEY.

Each attribute can only have a single value for each value of a key. The first step in normalization is to remove attributes that can have multiple values for a given value of the key and form them into a new entity.

Exhibit G.19. Customer Table

Customer						
CUSTNO	BRAN	CR CD	CST TYP	ADDR_LINE_1	ADDR_LINE_2	ADDR_LINE_3
PK						
003531	0059	A	C	JOHN BLOGGS	25 MAIN ST.	DALLAS, TEXAS
094425	0047	B	C	SAM HOSER	19 REDUNDANT	HOUSTON, TEXAS
976531	0099	I	I	IBM DEPT 344	3500 STORY	BOCA RATON, FLORIDA

Exhibit G.20. Customer Table

Customer			
CUSTNO	BRAN	CR CD	CST TYP
PK			
003531	0059	A	C
094425	0047	B	C
976531	0099	I	I

For example, consider the following entity (CUSTOMER) whose key attribute is CUSTNO (Customer Number) shown in Exhibit G.19.

In this case, the multivalued attribute consists of the three "attributes" ADDR_LINE_1, ADDR_LINE_2, ADDR_LINE_3. In fact, these are really three elements of an array. The first normal form of this entity is shown in Exhibits G.20 and G.21.

We have created a new entity (CUSTOMER ADDRESS), with a compound key of customer number and line number (to identify each line of a customer's address). This new entity is dependent on the CUSTOMER entity and allows an address to have a variable number of lines (0 to 99).

Multivalued attributes can usually be identified because they are recorded as arrays (ADDR(1), ADDR(2)), including arrays of structures, where each element of the array is, in fact, a different value of the attribute. In some cases, as in the example above, the fact that an attribute is multivalued has been disguised by the use of unique column names. The giveaway is in the similarity of names. Additional examples of giveaways are names like:

- CURRENT_SALESMAN, PREVIOUS_SALESMAN and
- FIRST_BRANCH_OFFICE, SECOND_BRANCH_OFFICE,...

Exhibit G.21. Customer Address Table

Customer Address		
CUSTNO	**LINE NO.**	**ADDR_LINE**
PK		
003531	01	JOHN BLOGGS
003531	02	25 MAIN ST.
003531	03	DALLAS, TEXAS
094425	01	SAM HOSER
094425	02	19 REDUNDANT
094425	03	HOUSTON, TEXAS
976531	01	SALES DEPT 355
976531	02	3500 STORY
976531	03	BOCA RATON, FLORIDA

Exhibit G.22. Product Model Table

Product Model					
PRODNO	**MODNO**	**PROD DESCRIPT**	**MODDESCRIPT**	**QTY ON HAND**	**SOURCE SUPPLY**
PK					
3084	032	4_PLEX CPU	SMALL MEMORY	3	FUJISAWA
3084	064	4_PLEX CPU	MORE MEMORY	2	FUJISAWA
3084	0C8	4_PLEX CPU	OODLES OF MEMORY	0	FUJISAWA
3180	001	TERMINAL	TWINAX CONNECTION	55	DALLAS
3180	002	TERMINAL	COAX CONNECTION	83	DALLAS
3274	A41	CONTROL UNIT	BIG MODEL (LOCAL)	15	SAO PAULO
3274	C41	CONTROL UNIT	BIG MODEL (REMOTE)	29	SAO PAULO
SAO PAULO	C61	CONTROL UNIT	DESK TOP MODEL	11	

Second Normal Form (2NF). Each attribute depends on THE WHOLE KEY.

The second step in normalization is to remove attributes that depend on only a part of the key and form them into a new entity.

Let us examine Exhibit G.22, in which the entity (PRODUCT MODEL) is an entity consisting of all the products and their models. The key is

Exhibit G.23. Product Table

Product		
PRODNO	**PRODDESCRIPT**	**SOURCE**
PK		SUPPLY
3084	4_PLEX CPU	FUJISAWA
3180	TERMINAL	DALLAS
3274	CONTROL UNIT	SAO PAULO

Exhibit G.24. Product Model Table

Product Model			
PRODNO	**MODNO**	**MODDESCRIPT**	**QTY ON HAND**
PK			
FK			
3084	032	SMALL MEMORY	3
3084	064	MORE MEMORY	2
3084	0c8	OODLES OF MEMORY	0
3180	001	TWINAX CONNECTION	55
3180	002	COAX CONNECTION	83
3274	A41	BIG MODEL (LOCAL)	15
3274	C41	BIG MODEL (REMOTE)	29
3274	C61	DESK TOP MODEL	11

PRODNO + MODNO. Let us assume that each product has a single SOURCE OF SUPPLY and that it is necessary to know the QTY ON HAND of each model.

PRODDESCRIPT and SOURCE_OF_SUPPLY in Exhibit G.23 are PRODNO and are removed to form a new PRODUCT entity in Exhibit G.24.

The old PRODUCT MODEL entity is now dependent on the new PRODUCT entity. New models can be added without maintaining product descriptions and source of supply information. Models can be deleted while still retaining information about the product itself.

Dependence of attributes on part of a key is particularly evident in cases where a compound key identifies occurrences of an entity type.

What would be the effect on the above entities if a product could have multiple sources of supply?

Exhibit G.25. Order Table

Order							
ORDNO	**PRODNO**	**MODNO**	**CUSTNO**	**CONTRACT TYPE**	**UNIT PRICE**	**QTY**	**EXTENDED PRICE**
PK	FK	FK					
XN223	4068	067	112339	EMPLOYEE	$1,098	1	$1,098
XQ440	4068	067	990613	INTERNAL	$875	5	$4,375
4068	4068	067	574026	DEALER	$1,170	20	$23,400
XB229	5160	020	390651	RETAIL	$2,960	2	$5,920
ZC875	5360	020	740332	BUSINESS	$33,600	1	$33,600
YS8/13	5360	B40	468916	GOVERN'T	$28,400	4	$113,600

Third Normal Form (3NF). Each attribute depends on NO OTHER BUT THE KEY.

The third step in normalization is to remove attributes that depend on other non-key attributes of the entity.

At this point it should be noted that a non-key attribute is an attribute that is neither the primary key nor a candidate key. A candidate key is an attribute, other than the primary key, that also uniquely identifies each occurrence of an entity. (For example, a personnel file is keyed on employee serial number and also contains a social insurance number, either of which uniquely identifies the employee. The employee serial number might function as the primary key and the social security number would be a candidate key.)

Consider the entity ORDER in Exhibit G.25, each occurrence of which represents an order for a product. As a given, assume that the UNIT PRICE varies from machine to machine and contract to contract.

Here we see a number of attributes that are not dependent on key. UNIT PRICE is dependent on CONTRACT TYPE and PRODNO and TENDED PRICE is dependent on both QTY and UNIT PRICE.

Reduction to third normal form requires us to create a new entity, PRODUCT/MODEL/CONTRACT, whose key is PRODNO + MODNO + CONTRACT TYPE, with UNIT PRICE an attribute of the entity. EXTENDED PRICE is calculated from the values of the other attributes and can be dropped from the table and computed as required. This is known as a derived attribute.

The third normal form should look like those displayed in Exhibits G.26 and G.27.

Exhibit G.26. Order Table

Order					
ORDNO	**PRODNO**	**MODNO**	**CUSTNO**	**CONTRACT TYPE**	**QTY**
PK	FK	FK		FK	
XN223	4068	067	112339	EMPLOYEE	1
XQ440	4068	067	990613	INTERNAL	5
XL715	4068	067	574026	DEALER	20
XB229	5160	020	390651	RETAIL	2
ZC875	5360	B40	740332	BUSINESS	1
YS8/13	5360	B40	468916	GOVERN'T	4

Exhibit G.27. Product/Model/Contract Table

Product/Model/Contract			
PRODNO	**MODNO**	**CONTRACT TYPES**	**UNIT PRICE**
PK			
4068	067	EMPLOYEE	$1,098
4068	067	INTERNAL	$875
4068	067	DEALER	$1,170
5160	020	RETAIL	$2,960
5360	B40	BUSINESS	$33,600
5360	B40	GOVERN'T	$28,400

In this form, prices and quantities may be changed. Data from both entities is joined together to calculate an EXTENDED PRICE. What changes to the model might be required to protect the customer against price changes? What would be the effect on the application if it were decided to maintain the EXTENDED PRICE as an attribute of the ORDER entity?

Model Refinement. This section discusses additional refinements that can be (and, in a real situation, usually must be) incorporated into a data model.

What is important about these refinements is that they introduce constraints in the model, which must be documented in the design and incorporated into the application.

Entity Subtypes. Frequently it is necessary to decompose (break down) a defined entity into subtypes.

A Definition. Entity subtypes:

- Have attributes peculiar to the subtype
- Participate in relationships peculiar to the subtype
- Are identified by a subset of the key of the entity

An entity subtype is not the same as a dependent entity. A dependent entity is identified by a compound key, consisting of the key of the major entity plus additional qualifying attributes.

This need not be so in the case of an entity subtype, which has the same key as the major entity and is, in fact, merely a subclassification of that entity.

For example, all of us are employees and hence are occurrences of the EMPLOYEE entity. Some employees, however, are also marketing reps with attributes (marketing unit, team, territory, quota, etc.) that are unique to their occupation. The MARKETING REP entity is a subtype of the EMPLOYEE entity.

Additional subtypes of the EMPLOYEE entity might be:

- Employee as manager
- Employee as stockholder
- Employee as beneficiary

The existence of entity subtypes raises issues of referential integrity, which we discuss in the next section.

Referential Integrity. Integrity Rule:

> *For any foreign key value in a table, there must be a corresponding primary key value in the same or another table.*

As stated, the rule is very simple. To enforce this rule may require a great deal of complicated application code, preceded (of course) by a significant design effort. Fortunately, some database management systems have built-in features that make the provision of referential integrity much simpler (e.g., the logical insert, replace and delete rules in IMS/VS).

Exhibits G.28, G.29, and G.30 illustrate the problem by means of three entities (customer, product, and order).

In practical terms, adherence to the referential integrity rule means the following:

- A customer can be inserted without integrity checks.
- A product can be inserted without integrity checks.

Exhibit G.28. Customer Table

Customer
CUSTOMER NUMBER
PK
221356
840723
737174

Exhibit G.29. Product Table

Product
PRODUCT CODE
PK
3084XC8
4260067
5360A23

Exhibit G.30. Order Table

Order		
ORDER NUMBER	**CUSTOMER NUMBER**	**PRODUCT CODE**
PK	FK	FK
ZA8845	221356	4260067
YB4320	737174	3084XC8
XN7691	840723	4260067
ZL3940	221356	5360A23

- An order can be inserted, but the customer number foreign key must exist in the CUSTOMER entity, and the product code foreign key must exist in the PRODUCT entity.
- A customer may not be deleted if its primary key exists in the order entity as a foreign key.
- A product may not be deleted if its primary key exists in the order entity as a foreign key.
- An order can be updated, but the customer number foreign key must exist in the CUSTOMER entity and the product code foreign key must

exist in the PRODUCT entity if the values of those attributes are being altered.

Sometimes, adherence to the integrity rules can be more complicated. For example, we might want to permit the creation of a CUSTOMER at the time the order is entered, in which case the application must be coded to enforce a modified rule:

> *An order can be inserted, but the customer number foreign key must exist in the CUSTOMER entity or must be inserted along with its attributes during order insertion. The product code foreign key must exist in the PRODUCT entity.*

If these restrictions seem unduly harsh, ask yourself if you would want a salesman to enter orders for customers and products that do not exist.

Integrity constraints apply to entity subtypes as well. In a sense, a subtype simply has a special (1:1) relationship with another entity in which the primary key of the subtype is also a foreign key into the other entity type. In other words, we cannot appoint Joe Bloggs as a marketing rep unless he is already an employee.

> *Referential integrity rules must be documented as part of the data model.*

The rules, based on the dependency constraints, in this case would be as follows:

- An order can be inserted without dependency checks (although to do so without inserting at least one order line might be meaningless).
- An order line item can be inserted, but the order number foreign key must exist in the ORDER entity or must be inserted along with its attributes during order line insertion.
- An order line can be deleted without dependency checks.
- An order cannot be deleted unless all its dependent order lines have been previously deleted.
- Deletion of the order must trigger the guaranteed deletion of all dependent order lines.

> *The dependency constraints must be documented as part of the data model.*

Dependency Constraints

Constraint Rule. A dependent entity cannot exist unless the entity on which it depends also exists.

The dependency constraint rule is a special form of referential integrity constraint applicable to dependent entities. Some database management

Exhibit G.31. Order Table

Order
ORDER NUMBER
PK
ZA8845
XN7691

Exhibit G.32. Line-Item Table

Line-Item			
ORDER NUMBER	**LINE NUMBER**	**QTY**	**PRODUCT CODE**
PK			FK
FK			
ZA8845	1	10	4260067
ZA8845	2	1	3084XC8
ZA8845	3	5	5160002
XN7691	1	2	5360A23
XN7691	2	18	3180001
XN7691	3	2	3520002

systems automatically enforce most dependency constraints. Others do not.

Exhibits G.31 and G.32 are illustrations of dependency as an ORDER with multiple LINE-ITEMS.

Recursion. A recursive relationship is a relationship between two entities of the same type.

Recursive relationships are found more frequently than one might think. Two of the most common recursive relationships are:

1. Bill-of Materials Explosion/Implosion
2. Organizational Hierarchies

Recursive relationships are a special case among the common relationships (i.e., 1:1, 1:M, M:M) and are modeled in exactly the same way. We can start out by making an EMPLOYEE entity represent the organizational structure of a company, as in Exhibit G.33.

489

Exhibit G.33. Employee Table

Employee		
EMPLOYEE NUMBER	**EMPLOYEE NAME**	**DEPT NUMBER**
PK		
00100	CODD	220
00135	KENT	220
00171	NIJSSEN	220
00190	DATE	220
00326	BOYCE	220
00529	KAGOOL	354
00558	MONGO	354
00721	STEIGLITZ	354
00843	STROHEIM	955

Exhibit G.34. Employee Table

Employee			
EMPLOYEE NUMBER	**EMPLOYEE NAME**	**DEPT NUMBER**	**MGR_EMP NUMBER**
PK			FK
00100	CODD	220	00326
00135	KENT	220	00326
00171	NIJSSEN	220	00326
00190	DATE	220	00326
00326	BOYCE	220	00843
00529	KAGOOL	354	00721
00558	MONGO	354	00721
00721	STEIGLITZ	354	00843
00843	STROHEIM	955	NULL -

The relationship between a manager and his employee (the organizational structure) is a one-to-many relationship. The manager's employee number as a foreign key is shown in Exhibit G.34.

Recursive relationships impose additional integrity constraints. In this case:

- A manager cannot work for himself. This implies that the topmost level of the hierarchy must contain a null value in the MGR_EMP_NUMBER column.
- A manager cannot work for one of his employees; nor can he work for anyone who works for one of his employees ... and so on ad infinitum.

A bill of materials processing model is an example of a many-to-many recursive relationship in which each component is used in many subassemblies and finished products and in which each product contains many components.

As an exercise:

- What would such a model look like?
- What constraints should be placed on the model? Would they differ from the constraints placed on the previous model?

Using the Model in Database Design. All the work of modeling is of no use unless it directly contributes to the database design. In converting the model to a physical database design, some compromises with normalization may be necessary in order to obtain satisfactory performance. The compromises will be:

- Least in implementing a relational design
- Moderate in implementing a hierarchical design
- Greatest in implementing a flat file design

It is not the intent of this section to give complete guidance for implementing the model using a specific database management system (DBMS). This material is covered in IMS database design and relational database design courses.

Relational Design. The first cut at implementing the model using a relational DBMS is to implement the model as it stands.

- Each entity and relationship becomes a table.
- Group logically related entities into databases.
- Each attribute becomes a column in the table.
- A unique index is defined for each primary key (to ensure ROW uniqueness).
- Additional indices are created to support known access paths.
- For each table, an index is chosen by which the data will be clustered, to support the most frequently used access sequence.
- Space calculations are performed.

Subsequent modifications may be required to achieve acceptable performance.

Exhibit G.35. Decision Table

DECISIONS					
	EOF	Y	N	N	N
	FIELD_ COUNTER > 7	-	Y	N	N
	FIELD_ COUNTER > 3	-	-	Y	N
ACTIONS					
	End Program	X			
	Increment FIELD_COUNTER_7 by 1		X		
	Increment FIELD_COUNTER_3 by 1			X	
	Increment FIELD_COUNTER_1 by 1				X

G11: Decision Tables

Decision tables are a technique for representing combinations of actions for the respective set of decisions and are an alternative to flow chart analysis. Each column, therefore, comprises a test case, or path through a flow chart.

Consider the following small program, which reads records from a file and tallies the numerical ranges of a field on each record to illustrate the technique.

PROGRAM: FIELD-COUNT

```
Dowhile not EOF
  read record
  if FIELD_COUNTER > 7 then
    increment COUNTER_7 by 1
  else
    if FIELD_COUNTER > 3 then
      increment COUNTER_3 by 1
    else
      increment COUNTER_1 by 1
    endif
  endif
End_While
End
```

The respective decision table is displayed in Exhibit G.35, and there are four test cases to test the program using decision tables.

Exhibit G.36. Income versus Tax Percent

Income Range	Tax % Due
$1 to $30,500	25
$30,501 to $62,500	27
$62,501 or more	38

Exhibit G.37. Income/Tax Test Cases

Test Case Number	Test Value	Expected Value	Equivalence Partition
1	$25,000	$6,250	$1 to $30,500
2	$40,500	$10,935	$30,501 to $62,500
3	$85,200	$32,376	$62,501 or more

G12: Desk Checking

Desk checking is a human error-detection process in the form of a one-person walkthrough. The typical application is where an individual reads a program, checks it with a checklist, and manually talks test data through it. It can also be applied to requirements and design as a check on the work. This technique provides an evaluation of the quality of the program after it has been written or after the design has been completed.

G13: Equivalence Partitioning

The equivalence partitioning testing technique is a black-box testing technique that partitions the input domain into a set of input classes that can cause multiple behaviors.

From the requirements, each input is divided into partitions. Using this technique, one representative value from each partition is selected and tested. It is assumed that the results predict the results for other values in the partition, which demonstrates the power and economy of this technique.

It is more complicated than a simple range test because a range is divided into a series or one or more ranges because of the different behaviors that can occur. Consider the following application. The income needs to be broken up into three equivalence classes, as the behavior (or tax) varies according to the income value.

An IRS program computes the amount of state income tax based on the income, as is displayed in Exhibits G.36 and G.37.

The following are some other examples of how to apply the technique.

Numeric Input Data

Field Ranges. Ex. "Input can range from integers 0 to 100"; for example, a test case could be 45 (any arbitrary number between 1 and 100).

Ex. "Input can range from real numbers 0.0 to 100.0"; for example, a test case could be 75.0 (any arbitrary number between 0.0 and 100.0).

Numeric Output Data

Output Range of Values. Ex. "Numerical range outputs of actuarial tables can be from $0.0 to $100,000.00"; for example, a test case could be $15,000.00 (any arbitrary number between $0.0 and $100,000.00).

Nonnumeric Input Data

Tables or Arrays. Ex. A test case could be to input from any table row with alphabetic contents.

Number of Items. Ex. "Number of products associated with a model is up to 10"; for example, a test case could be 5 products (any arbitrary number of products between 0 and 10).

Nonnumeric Output Data

Tables or Arrays. Ex. Update, write, delete any table row.

Number of Outputs. Ex. "Up to 10 customers can be displayed"; for example, a test case could be 7 customers displayed (any arbitrary number of customers between 0 and 10).

G14: Exception Testing

With exception testing, all the error messages and exception handling processes are identified, including the conditions that trigger them. A test case is written for each error condition. A test case/error exception test matrix (Exhibit G.38) can be helpful for documenting the error conditions and exceptions.

G15: Free Form Testing

Free form testing, often called error guessing, ad hoc testing, or brainstorming, is a "blue-sky" intuition of where and how errors are likely to occur and is an add-on technique to other testing techniques.

Some testers are naturally adept at this form of testing, which does not use any particular testing technique. It involves intuition and experience to

Exhibit G.38. Test Case/Error Exception Test Matrix

Test Case Name	Error Message/Exception	Passes/Failed	Date	Tester
1				
2				
3				
4				
5				
6				
7				
8				
9				

"smell out" defects. There is no particular methodology for applying this technique, but the basic approach is to enumerate a list of potential errors or errorprone situations and write test cases based on the list.

G16: Gray-Box Testing

Black-box testing focuses on the program's functionality against the specification. White-box testing focuses on the paths of logic. Gray-box testing is a combination of black- and white-box testing. The tester studies the requirements specifications and communicates with the developer to understand the internal structure of the system. The motivation is to clear up ambiguous specifications and "read between the lines" to design implied tests. One example of the use of gray-box testing is when it appears to the tester that a certain functionality seems to be reused throughout an application. If the tester communicates with the developers and understands the internal design and architecture, a lot of tests will be eliminated, because it might be possible to test the functionality only once. Another example is when the syntax of a command consists of 7 possible parameters that can be entered in any order as follows:

```
Command parm1, parm2, parm3, parm4, parm5, parm6, parm7
(enter)
```

In theory, a tester would have to create 7! or 5040 tests. The problem is compounded even more if some of the parameters are optional. If the tester uses gray-box testing, by talking with the developer and understanding the parser algorithm, if each parameter is independent, only 7 tests may be required to test each parameter.

Exhibit G.39. Response Time of 100 Samples (seconds)

2	4	1	6	5	12	4	3	4	10
5	2	7	2	4	1	12	4	2	1
1	2	4	3	5	1	3	5	7	12
5	7	1	2	4	3	1	4	1	2
1	3	5	2	1	2	4	5	1	2
3	1	3	2	6	1	5	4	1	2
7	1	8	4	3	1	1	2	6	1
1	2	1	4	2	6	2	2	4	9
2	3	2	1	8	2	4	7	2	2
4	1	2	5	3	4	5	2	1	2

Exhibit G.40. Response Time Histogram

Average = 3.47 seconds									
0	23	25	10	16	10	4	5	2	5
0 to.9	1 to 1.9	2 to 2.9	3 to 3.9	4 to 4.9	5 to 5.9	6 to 6.9	7 to 7.9	8 to 8.9	9 to ∞

G17: Histograms

A histogram is a graphical description of measured values organized according to the frequency or relative frequency of occurrence. In Exhibit G.39, the table consists of a sample of 100 client/server terminal response times (enter key until a server response) for an application. This was measured with a performance testing tool.

The histogram in Exhibit G.40 illustrates how the raw performance data from the above table is displayed in a histogram. It should be noted that the design specification is for response times to be less than 3 seconds. It is obvious from the data that the performance requirement is not being satisfied and there is a performance problem.

G18: Inspections

Inspections are the most formal, commonly used form of peer review. The key feature of an inspection is the use of checklists to facilitate error detection. These checklists are updated as statistics indicate that certain types of errors are occurring more or less frequently than in the past. The most common types of inspections are conducted on the product design and code, although inspections may be used during any life cycle phase.

Inspections should be short because they are often intensive; therefore, the product component to be reviewed must be small. Specifications or designs that result in 50 to 100 lines of code are usually manageable. This translates into an inspection of 15 minutes to one hour, although complex components may require as much as two hours. In any event, inspections of more than two hours are generally less effective and should be avoided.

Two or three days before the inspection, the producer assembles the input to the inspection and gives it to the coordinator for distribution. Participants are expected to study and make comments on the materials before the review.

The review is led by a participant other than the producer. Generally, the individual who has the greatest involvement in the next phase of the life cycle is designated as reader. For example, a requirements inspection would likely be led by a designer, a design review by an implementer, and so forth. The exception to this is the code inspection, which is led by the designer. The inspection is organized and coordinated by an individual designated as the group leader or coordinator.

The reader goes through the product component, using the checklist as a means to identify common types of errors as well as standards violations. A primary goal of an inspection is to identify items that can be modified to make the component more understandable, maintainable, or usable. Participants discuss any issues that they identified in the preinspection study.

At the end of the inspection, an accept or reject decision is made by the group, and the coordinator summarizes all the errors and problems detected and gives this list to all participants. The individual whose work was under review (e.g., designer, implementer, tester) uses the list to make revisions to the component. When revisions are implemented, the coordinator and producer go through a minireview, using the problem list as a checklist. The coordinator then completes management and summary reports. The summary report is used to update checklists for subsequent inspections.

G19: JADs

A JAD is a technique that brings users and development together to design systems in facilitated group sessions. Studies show that JADs increase productivity over traditional design techniques. JADs go beyond one-on-one interviews to collect information. They promote communication, cooperation, and teamwork among the participants by placing the users in the driver's seat.

JADs are logically divided into phases: customization, session, and wrap-up. Regardless of what activity one is pursuing in development, these components will always exist. Each phase has its own objectives.

1. *Customization* — This phase is key to a JAD and largely consists of preparation for the next phase. Participants include the session leader and JAD analysts. The tasks include organizing the team, defining the JAD tasks and deliverables, and preparing the materials for the next JAD session.
2. *Session* — This phase consists of facilitated sessions where the analysts and users jointly define the requirements and the system design. The session leader facilitates the session and the analyst documents the results.
3. *Wrap-Up* — In this final phase, formal JAD outputs are produced. The facilitated session leader summarizes the visual and other documentation into a JAD document. The design results are fed back to the executive sponsor.

A given development effort may consist of a series of the three phases until the final requirements and design have been completed. When a project has multiple design activity (e.g., different portions of the overall design), a final wrap-up occurs at the completion of the design where the design is reviewed as a whole.

G20: Orthogonal Array Testing

Orthogonal array testing is a statistical technique pioneered by Dr. Genichi Taguchi in manufacturing that helps in the selection of test cases to get a handle on the potentially enormous number of combination factors. It calculates the ideal number of tests required and identifies variations of input values and conditions; for example, it helps in the test selection process to provide maximum coverage with a minimum number of test cases.

Taguchi methods refer to techniques of quality engineering that embody both statistical process control (SPC) and new quality-related management techniques. Most of the attention and discussion of Taguchi methods have been focused on the statistical aspects of the procedure; it is the conceptual framework of a methodology for quality improvement and process robustness that needs to be emphasized.

An example is when the syntax of a command consists of three possible parameters in which there can be three possible values as follows.

```
Command PARM1, PARM2, PARM3 (enter)
PARMx = 1,2,3
```

In theory, a tester would have to create 33 or 27 test combinations, as shown in Exhibit G.41.

Applying orthogonal array testing (OATS), the technique selects test cases so as to test the interactions between independent measures called

Exhibit G.41.   Parameter Combinations (with Total Enumeration)

Test Case	PARM1	PARM2	PARM3	Test Case	PARM1	PARM2	PARM3
1	1	1	1	14	2	2	2
2	1	1	2	15	2	2	3
3	1	1	3	16	3	2	1
4	2	1	1	17	3	2	2
5	2	1	2	18	3	2	3
6	2	1	3	19	1	3	1
7	3	1	1	20	1	3	2
8	3	1	2	21	1	3	3
9	3	1	3	22	2	3	1
10	1	2	1	23	2	3	2
11	1	2	2	24	2	3	3
12	1	2	3	25	3	3	1
13	2	2	1	26	3	3	2
-	-	-		27	3	3	3

factors. Each factor also has a finite set of possible values called levels. In Exhibit G.41, there are three factors (PARM1, PARM2, and PARM3). Each has three levels (1, 2, and 3). The technique calls for the tester to locate the best fit of the number of factors and levels to the possible orthogonal arrays (found in most statistical texts). In Exhibit G.42, the orthogonal array with three factors and three levels is chosen. Each column in the array corresponds to a factor and each row corresponds to a test case. The rows represent all possible pairwise combinations of possible levels for the factors. Thus, only nine test cases are required, which demonstrates the power of the technique.

G21: Pareto Analysis

Pareto diagrams are a special form of a graph that points to where efforts should be concentrated. By depicting events or facts in order of decreasing frequency (or cost or failure rate, etc.), it allows for a quick separation of the "vital few" from the trivial many. The Pareto chart is more commonly known to information systems personnel as the 80–20 rule: that is, 20 percent of the causes make up 80 percent of the frequencies. A Pareto chart is a histogram showing values in descending order, which helps identify the high-frequency causes of problems so that appropriate corrective action can be taken. It is an organized ranking of causes of a problem by type of

Exhibit G.42. Parameter Combinations (OATS)

$L_9(3)^3$ (Orthogonal Array, 3 Factors, 3 Levels)			
Test Case	PARM1	PARM2	PARM3
1	1	1	3
2	1	2	2
3	1	3	1
4	2	1	2
5	2	2	1
6	2	3	3
7	3	1	1
8	3	2	3
9	3	3	2

cause. The objective is to select the most frequent cause or causes of a problem in order to direct action to eliminate those causes.

The four steps in using a Pareto chart include the following:

1. *Identify a problem area.* One problem example is an excessive number of defects discovered during software testing.
2. *Identify and name the causes of the problem.* This is the most time-consuming step because it requires the collection of information from various causes. Causes of defects include: architectural, database integrity, documentation, functionality, GUI, installation, performance, and usability. For most problems, there is little need to identify more than 12 causes. When more than 12 causes can be identified, one approach is to select 11 causes and the 12th cause can be classified as "Other." If the "Other" category becomes significant, then it may need to be broken down into specific causes.
3. *Document the occurrence of the causes of the problem.* The occurrences of the causes need to be documented. Samples from the defect tracking database can be used to obtain these frequencies.
4. *Rank the causes by frequency, using the Pareto chart.* This involves two tasks: to count the problem occurrences by type, and to build a bar chart (or Pareto chart), with the major causes listed on the left-hand side and the other causes listed in descending order of occurrence.

In Exhibit G.43 there are eight defect causes. Approximately 1050 defects have been recorded. Of those, 750 are caused by functionality and database integrity. Thus, 20 percent of the causes account for 71 (or approximately 80 percent) of the frequency. In our example, functionality is the

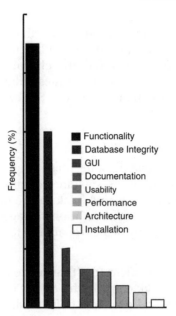

Frequency (%)

■ Functionality
■ Database Integrity
■ GUI
■ Documentation
■ Usability
■ Performance
■ Architecture
□ Installation

Exhibit G.43. Pareto Chart

major cause, and database integrity is the second cause. Emphasis should be placed on eliminating the number of functional and database problems. One approach might be increased unit testing and reviews.

G22: Positive and Negative Testing

Positive and negative testing is an input-based testing technique that requires that a proper balance of positive and negative tests be performed. A positive test is one with a valid input, and a negative test is one with an invalid input. Because there typically are many more negative than positive tests, a suggested balance is 80 percent negative and 20 percent positive tests.

For example, suppose an application accepts stock market or mutual fund five-character symbols and then displays the respective stock or mutual fund name. An example of a positive test is "PHSTX," which is the mutual fund symbol associated with a health science fund. If this symbol displayed some other fund, this would entail a positive test that failed.

Values that are not valid stock or mutual fund symbols are negative tests. Typically, a negative test produces an invalid error message. For example, if "ABCDE" is entered and an invalid error message is displayed, this is a negative test that passed.

Some considerations of negative testing are how much negative testing is enough and how do we anticipate unexpected conditions. Testing the editing of a single alphabetic character field can be complex. One negative test would be "("and should be detected by the system. Should")" be tested? How many other nonalphabetic characters should be tested? Unanticipated conditions are also sometimes difficult to detect. For example, "&" and """ have special meaning with SQL. Should both of these be tested in every field?

G23: Prior Defect History Testing

With prior defect history testing, a test case is created or rerun for every defect found in prior tests of the system. The motivation for this is that defects tend to cluster and regress back to the original problem. Some causes include poor software configuration management procedures, poor coding and unit testing during defect repair, the tendency for bugs to cluster, and so on.

A defect matrix is an excellent tool that relates test cases to functions (or program units). A check entry in the defect matrix indicates that the test case is to be retested because a defect was previously discovered while running this test case. No entry means that the test does not need to be retested.

If this approach is not economical because a large number of defects have been discovered, a test case should be retested on or above a certain defined severity level.

G24: Prototyping

Prototyping is an iterative approach often used to build systems that users are initially unable to describe precisely. The concept is made possible largely through the power of fourth-generation languages and application generators. Prototyping is, however, as prone to defects as any other development effort, maybe more so if not performed in a systematic manner. Prototypes need to be tested as thoroughly as any other system. Testing can be difficult unless a systematic process has been established for developing prototypes.

The following sections describe several prototyping methodologies. They are presented to show the diversity of concepts used in defining software life cycles and to illustrate the effects of prototyping on the life cycle in general.

Cyclic Models

This concept of software development with prototyping consists of two separate but interrelated cyclic models: one consisting of a classical software development cycle and the other of a prototyping cycle that interacts with the classical model during the phases of analysis and design. The major operations are:

- Classical cycle:
  - User request
  - Feasibility
  - Investigation
  - Consideration of prototyping
  - Analysis
  - Design
  - Final proposed design
  - Programming
  - Testing
  - Implementation
  - Operation
  - Evaluation
  - Maintenance
  - (The cycle is repeated.)
- Prototyping cycle:
  - Prototype is designed.
  - Prototype is used.
  - Investigation is conducted using the prototype.
  - Analysis is performed on the investigation.
  - Refinements are made, or a new prototype is built.
  - (This cycle is also repeated.)

The interaction of the two cycles occurs when investigation in the classical cycle uncovers the need to prototype, at which time the prototyping cycle is entered. Prototyping is terminated when analysis, design, or the final proposed design of the classical cycle can be completed based on information discovered or verified in the prototyping cycle.

Fourth-Generation Languages and Prototyping

This method proposes the following life cycle steps:

1. A prototyping team of one analyst/programmer and one end user is formed.
2. User needs are identified by interviewing several end users to define the problem and elicit sample user expectations.
3. A prototype is developed quickly to address most of the issues of the problem and user expectations.
4. The prototype is demonstrated to the end user. The user experiments with it and performs work within a specified time period. If the prototype is not acceptable, it is scrapped.
5. The prototype is refined by including changes identified through use. This step and the previous one are iterated until the system fully achieves the requirements.
6. An end-user test group is formed to provide more feedback on the prototype within a specified period of time.

7. A determination is made as to whether the prototype will be implemented or the system will be rewritten in a conventional language. This decision is based on maintenance considerations, hardware and software efficiency, flexibility, and other system requirements.

Iterative Development Accounting

This model is based on the view that a system is a sequence of specification levels with an increasing amount of detail at each level. These levels are:

- Informal requirements
- Formal requirements
- Design
- Implementation
- Configuration
- Operation

Each level contains more detail than the one preceding it. In addition, each level must be balanced with upper-level specifications. Iterative development imposes development accounting on each level (i.e., a change in one specification level can be made only if the next higher level has been modified to accommodate the change).

A complete history of development is maintained by this accounting technique to ensure that consistency remains throughout all levels. A prototype is developed at each level to show that the specifications are consistent. Each prototype concentrates on the functions to be evaluated at that level. The final prototype becomes the implemented system once testing, installation, and training have been completed.

Evolutionary and Throwaway

Two models are presented here. In the first, the prototype is built and gradually enhanced to form the implemented system. The other is known as the throwaway model.

End users are integral parts of the prototype development in both models and should be trained in the use of a prototyping tool (e.g., a simulation language or 4GL). The two models are described briefly as follows.

- Method 1:
  - The user experiments with and uses a prototype built to respond to the end user's earliest and most tentative needs to perform work.
  - The analyst watches the user to see where prototype refining needs to take place. A series of prototypes, or modifications to the initial prototype, evolve into the final product.

- Method 2:
  - A prototype is implemented. The initial design is developed from this and the end user's feedback. Another prototype is produced to implement the initial design. The final system is implemented in a conventional language.

Application Prototyping

This method proposes the following steps:

1. *Identification of basic needs* — Concentrate on identifying fundamental goals, objectives, and major business problems to be solved and defining data elements, data relations, and functions.
2. *Development of a working model* — Build a working prototype quickly to address the key needs.
3. *Demonstration of prototype* — Present the prototype to all interested users and obtain additional requirements through user feedback.
4. *Completion of prototype* — Iterate between demonstration and enhancement of the prototype until users are satisfied that the organization could provide the service needed from the prototype. Once users agree that the prototype fits the concept of the service needed, it can be enhanced into the final system or rewritten in a more efficient language.

Prototype Systems Development

The stages for this approach are as follows:

1. *Management states the organization's objectives.* These are described in terms of information requirements and the scope of the system boundaries and capabilities. Prototype screens and reports are developed.
2. *End users and management review and approve the prototype.* Full system design, equipment selection, programming, and documentation are completed.
3. *Management reviews and commits to implementing the system.* System tests of the prototype are run in parallel with the old system. Work begins on the next release, which causes an iteration of all three stages.

Data-Driven Prototyping

This methodology consists of the following steps:

1. *Operational review* — Define the project scope and evaluate the environment, current organization, and information structures.
2. *Conceptual design* — Define proposed metadata (i.e., the structure of data and relationships between individual structures), the scenarios

needed to describe service functions that change data states, and types of retrievals.

3. *Data design* — Normalize the metadata.
4. *Heuristic analysis* — Check consistency of requirements against metadata through the use of real data values; this step is iterated with the data design step.
5. *Environment test* — Build programs to support data entry and retrieval (prototype).
6. *Performance monitoring and application tuning.*

Replacement of the Traditional Life Cycle

In this model, the steps include the following:

1. *Rapid analysis* — Results in an incomplete paper model that shows the system context, critical functions, an entity–relationship model of the database, and conceptual tables, screens, attributes, reports, and menus.
2. *Database development* — Uses a relational architecture to create a working database for the use of the prototype.
3. *Menu development* — Expands on the initial concepts defined in rapid analysis and fixes the hierarchical structure of the application.
4. *Function development* — Groups functions by type into modules.
5. *Prototype demonstration* — Iterates by redoing parts as necessary and tuning if possible.
6. *Design, coding, and testing* — Completes the detailed design specifications.
7. *Implementation* — Is based on the evolution of the prototype and completion of all programs, tests, and documentation.

Early-Stage Prototyping

This model can assist in specifying user requirements, verifying the feasibility of system design, and translating the prototype into the final system. The procedure includes the following:

1. A preliminary analysis and requirements specification establish a baseline for future reference.
2. A prototype is defined and implemented, emphasizing the user interface. The prototype is developed by a small development team using prototype development language and tools to assist in rapid development.
3. The prototype is tested in the user's workplace.
4. The prototype is refined by incorporating user comments as quickly as possible.
5. Baseline requirements are refined by incorporating lessons learned from the prototype.

6. The production system is developed through the use of a traditional life cycle with requirements derived from the prototype.

User Software Engineering

This is based on a model of software development that is part formal and part informal and includes the following steps:

1. *Requirements analysis* — Activity and data modeling and identification of user characteristics.
2. *External design* — Develop transactions and user–program interfaces.
3. *Facade development* — Used as a prototype of the user–program interface and revised as needed.
4. *Narrative text* — Used to informally specify the system operations.
5. *Preliminary relational database* — Designed as the basis for a functional prototype of the system.
6. *Functional prototype* — Developed to provide at least some, and perhaps all, of the functions of the proposed system.
7. *Formal specification of the system operations* — May be optionally developed at this point.
8. *System architecture and modules.*
9. *System implementation* — In a procedural language.
10. *Testing and verification* — Performed on the system before the system is released into the production environment.

G25: Random Testing

Random testing is a technique in which a program or system is tested by selecting at random some subset of all possible input values. It is not an optimal testing technique, because it has a low probability of detecting many defects. It does, however, sometimes uncover defects that standardized testing techniques might not. It should, therefore, be considered an add-on testing technique.

G26: Range Testing

Range testing is a technique that assumes that the behavior of any input variable within a predefined range will be the same. The range over which the system behavior should be the same is first selected. Then an arbitrary representative from the range is selected and tested. If it passes, it is assumed that the rest of the values do not have to be tested.

For example, consider the following piece of coding, which calculates the results Z from two input values X and Y:

$$Z = \sqrt{X^2 - Y^2}$$

507

Exhibit G.44. Range Testing Test Cases

Test Case	X Value	Y Value	Z (Expected Result)
1	0	0	0
2	1	0	1
3	1	1	0
4	2	0	2
5	2	1	$\sqrt{3}$
6	2	2	0
7	3	0	3
8	3	1	$\sqrt{8}$
9	3	2	$\sqrt{5}$
10	3	3	0
11	4	0	4
12	4	1	$\sqrt{15}$
13	4	2	$\sqrt{12}$
14	4	3	$\sqrt{7}$
15	4	4	0
16	5	0	5
17	5	1	$\sqrt{24}$
18	5	2	$\sqrt{21}$
19	5	3	4
20	5	4	3
21	5	5	0

If X and Y are positive integers ranging from 0 to 5 and X is greater than or equal to Y, there are 21 possible test cases, as depicted in Exhibit G.44.

Applying this technique has the potential of saving a lot of test generation time. However, it does have the limitation of the assumption that selecting an arbitrary input sample will produce the same system behavior for the rest of the inputs. Additional tests such as the conditions X and Y positive integers and Y greater than X need to be tested as well as the verification of square roots results; for example, we need to determine if the Z variable will accept fractional values as the result of the calculation or truncation (also see Boundary Value Testing).

G27: Regression Testing

Regression testing tests the application in light of changes made during a development spiral, debugging, maintenance, or the development of a new release. This test must be performed after functional improvements or repairs have been made to a system to confirm that the changes have no unintended side effects. Correction of errors relating to logic and control flow, computational errors, and interface errors are examples of conditions that necessitate regression testing. Cosmetic errors generally do not affect other capabilities and do not require that regression testing be performed.

It would be ideal if all the tests in the test suite were rerun for each new spiral, but due to time constraints, this is probably not realistic. A good regression strategy during spiral development is for some regression testing to be performed during each spiral to ensure that previously demonstrated capabilities are not adversely affected by later development spirals or error corrections. During system testing after the system is stable and the functionality has been verified, regression testing should consist of a subset of the system tests. Policies need to be created to decide which tests to include.

In theory, the reliability of a system that has been modified cannot be guaranteed without a full regression test of all tests. However, there are many practical considerations:

- When defects are uncovered, additional regression tests should be created.
- A regression test library should be available and maintained as it evolves.
- There should be a methodology of isolating regression tests that focus on certain areas (see retest and defect matrices).
- If the overall architecture of a system is changed, full regression testing should be performed.
- Automated testing with capture/playback features should be strongly considered (see Section V, Modern Software Testing Tools).

G28: Risk-Based Testing

The purpose of risk management testing is to measure the degree of business risk in an application system to improve testing. This is accomplished in two ways: high-risk applications can be identified and subjected to more extensive testing, and risk analysis can help identify the errorprone components of an individual application so that testing can be directed at those components.

Risk analysis is a formal method for identifying vulnerabilities (i.e., areas of potential loss). Any area that could be misused, intentionally or accidentally,

Exhibit G.45. Sample Run Chart

x (week)	y
1	10
2	50
3	30
4	60
5	25
6	50
7	75
8	45

and result in a loss to the organization is a vulnerability. Identification of risks allows the testing process to measure the potential effect of those vulnerabilities (e.g., the maximum loss that could occur if the risk or vulnerability were exploited).

Risk-based testing is a technique in which test cases are created for every major risk factor that has been previously identified. Each condition is tested to verify that the risk has been averted.

G29: Run Charts

A run chart is a graphical representation of how a quality characteristic varies with time. It is usually a line graph that shows the variability in a measurement or in a count of items. For example, in Exhibit G.45, a run chart can show the variability in the number of defects detected over time. It can show results from a sample of a population or from 100 percent.

A control chart, a special form of run chart, places lines on the chart to represent the limits of permissible variability. These limits could be determined by a design specification or an agreed-upon standard. The control limits are frequently set to show the statistical limit of variabilities that could be due to a chance occurrence. This is calculated by using the averages and range of measurement from each sample of data. Control charts are not only used as an alarm when going outside the limits, but also to examine trends occurring within the limits. For example, if the sequence of ten measurements in Exhibit G.45 is shown to fall above the expected average, it can be assumed that this is not due to mere chance and, therefore, an investigation is in order.

G30: Sandwich Testing

Sandwich testing uses top-down and bottom-up techniques simultaneously and is a compromise between the two. The approach integrates from the top and bottom at the same time, meeting somewhere in the middle of the hierarchical control structure. The meeting point in the middle is defined by the program structure.

It is typically used on large programs but is difficult to justify on small programs. The top level of the hierarchy usually includes the user interfaces to the system, which requires stubs to mimic business functions. The bottom level includes primitive-level modules, which requires drivers to simulate lower-level modules.

G31: Statement Coverage Testing

Statement coverage is a white-box technique that ensures that every statement or line of code (LOC) is executed at least once. It does guarantee that every statement is executed, but it is a very weak code coverage approach and not as comprehensive as other techniques, such as branch coverage, where each branch from a decision statement is executed.

Consider the following small program, which reads records from a file and tallies the numerical ranges of a field on each record to illustrate the technique.

PROGRAM: FIELD-COUNT

```
Dowhile not EOF
   read record
   if FIELD_COUNTER > 7 then
   increment COUNTER_7 by 1
   else
      if FIELD_COUNTER > 3 then
         increment COUNTER_3 by 1
      else
         increment COUNTER_1 by 1
      endif
   endif
End_While
End
```

The test cases to satisfy statement coverage are as follows.

Test Case	Values (FIELD_COUNTER)
1	>7, ex. 8
2	>3, ex. 4
3	<= 3, ex. 3

G32: State Transition Testing

State transition testing is a testing technique in which the states of a system are first identified. Then a test case is written to test the triggers or stimuli that cause a transition from one condition to another state. The tests can be designed using a finite-state diagram or an equivalent table.

Consider the following small program, which reads records from a file and tallies the numerical ranges of a field on each record to illustrate the technique.

PROGRAM: FIELD-COUNT

```
Dowhile not EOF
  read record
  if FIELD_COUNTER > 7 then
    increment COUNTER_7 by 1
  else
    if FIELD_COUNTER > 3 then
      increment COUNTER_3 by 1
    else
      increment COUNTER_1 by 1
    endif
  endif
End_While
End
```

Exhibit G.46 illustrates the use of the testing technique to derive test cases. The states are defined as the current value of COUNTER_7, COUNTER_3, and COUNTER_1. Then the possible transitions are considered. They consist of the end-of-file condition or the value FIELD_COUNTER for each successive record input. For each of these transitions, a definition of how each respective state is transformed is performed. Each transition becomes a test case and the final state is the expected result.

G33: Statistical Profile Testing

With statistical profile testing, statistical techniques are used to develop a usage profile of the system. Based on the expected frequency of use, the tester determines the transaction paths, conditions, functional areas, and data tables that merit focus in testing. The tests are, therefore, geared to the most frequently used part of the system.

G34: Structured Walkthroughs

Structured walkthroughs are more formal than the code-reading reviews. Distinct roles and responsibilities are assigned before the review. Preview preparation is greater, and a more formal approach to problem documentation is stressed. Another key feature of this review is that it is presented by the producer. The most common walkthroughs are those held during

Exhibit G.46. State Transition Table

Initial State	Test Case (Transition)	Final State
COUNTER_7 = X1	1. EOF	COUNTER_7 = X1
COUNTER_3 = X2		COUNTER_3 = X2
COUNTER_1 = X3		COUNTER_1 = X3
		Exit Program
COUNTER_7 = X1	2. Next Record with FIELD_COUNTER > 7	COUNTER_7 = (X1+1)
COUNTER_3 = X2		COUNTER_3 = X2
COUNTER_1 = X3		COUNTER_1 = X3
		Successful
COUNTER_7 = X1	3. Next Record with FIELD_COUNTER < = 7 and FIELD_COUNTER >3	COUNTER_7 = X1
COUNTER_3 = X2		COUNTER_3 = (X2+1)
COUNTER_1 = X3		COUNTER_1 = X3
		Successful
COUNTER_7 = X1	4. Next Record with FIELD_COUNTER < = 3	COUNTER_7 = X1
COUNTER_3 = X2		COUNTER_3 = X2
COUNTER_1 = X3		COUNTER_1 = (X3+1)
		Successful

design and coding; however, recently they have been applied to specifications documentation and test results.

The producer schedules the review and assembles and distributes input. In most cases, the producer selects the walkthrough participants (although this is sometimes done by management) and notifies them of their roles and responsibilities. The walkthrough is usually conducted with less than seven participants and lasts no more than two hours. If more time is needed, there should be a break or the product should be reduced in size. Roles usually included in a walkthrough are producer, coordinator, recorder, and representatives of user, maintenance, and standards organizations.

Although the review is opened by the coordinator, the producer is responsible for leading the group through the product. In the case of design and code walkthroughs, the producer simulates the operation of the component, allowing each participant to comment based on that individual's area of specialization. A list of problems is kept, and at the end of the review, each participant signs the list, or other walkthrough form, indicating whether the product is accepted as is, accepted with recommended changes, or rejected. Suggested changes are made at the discretion of the producer. There are no formal means of follow-up on the review comments. If the walkthrough review is used for products throughout the life cycle, however, comments from past reviews can be discussed at the start of the next review.

G35: Syntax Testing

Syntax testing is a technique in which a syntax command generator generates test cases based on the syntax rules of the system. Both valid and invalid values are created. It is a data-driven black-box testing technique for testing input data to language processors, such as string processors and compilers. Test cases are developed based on rigid data definitions. The valid inputs are described in Backus Naur Form (BNF) notation.

The main advantage of syntax testing is that it ensures that no misunderstandings about valid and invalid data and specification problems will become apparent when employing this technique.

G36: Table Testing

Table testing is a technique that tests the table, which is usually associated with a relational database (the same approaches can be applied to arrays, queues, and heaps). Tables usually come in two forms: sequential and indexed. The following are general tests that need to be performed against tables:

1. Indexed Tables:
    a. Delete the first record in the table.
    b. Delete a middle record in the table.
    c. Delete the last record in the table.
    d. Add a new first record in the table.
    e. Add a new middle record in the table.
    f. Add a new last record in the table.
    g. Attempt to add a duplicate record.
    h. Add a record with an invalid key, for example, garbage in the key field.
    i. Change the key field(s) on a existing record; for example, change an order number.
    j. Delete a nonexisting record; for example, enter a delete key that does not match table entries.
    k. Update and rewrite an existing record.

2. Sequential Tables:
   a. Attempt to delete a record from an empty table.
   b. Read a record from an empty table.
   c. Add a record to a full table.
   d. Delete one record from a one-record table.
   e. Read the last record.
   f. Read the next record after the last record.
   g. Scroll sequentially through the table.
   h. Insert an out-of-sequence record.
   i. Attempt to insert a duplicate record.

G37: Thread Testing

Thread testing is a software testing technique that demonstrates key functional capabilities by testing a string of program units that accomplishes a specific business function in the application.

A thread is basically a business transaction consisting of a set of functions. It is a single discrete process that threads through the whole system. Each function is tested separately, then added one at a time to the thread. The business transaction thread is then tested. Threads are in turn integrated and incrementally tested as subsystems, and then the whole system is tested. This approach facilitates early systems and acceptance testing.

G38: Top-Down Testing

The top-down testing technique is an incremental approach in which the high-level modules or system components are integrated and tested first. Testing then proceeds hierarchically to the bottom level. This technique requires the creation of stubs. When a module or system component is tested, the modules or components it invokes are represented by stubs, which return control back to the calling module or system component with a simulated result. As testing progresses down the program structure, each stub is replaced by the actual code it represents. There is no correct rule of which module to test next; the only rule is that at least one of the modules or system component calling modules must have been tested previously.

Top-down testing allows early discovery of major design flaws occurring at the top of the program, because high-level functions and decisions are tested early, and they are generally located at the top of the control structure. This verifies the program design early. An early prototype or initial design facilitates early demonstrations. Because the menus are often at the top of the control structure, the external interfaces can be displayed early to the user. Stubs need to be created but are generally easier to create than drivers. On the other hand, critical low-level modules or system components are not tested until late in the process. In rare cases, problems with these critical modules or system components may force a redesign.

G39: White-Box Testing

White-box testing, or structural testing, is one in which test conditions are designed by examining paths of logic. The tester examines the internal structure of the program or system. Test data are driven by examining the logic of the program or system, without concern for the program or system requirements. The tester has knowledge of the internal program structure and logic, just as a mechanic knows the inner workings of an automobile. Specific examples in this category include basis path analysis, statement coverage, branch coverage, condition coverage, and branch/condition coverage.

An advantage of white-box testing is that it is thorough and focuses on the produced code. Because there is knowledge of the internal structure or logic, errors or deliberate mischief on the part of a programmer have a higher probability of being detected.

One disadvantage of white-box testing is that it does not verify that the specifications are correct; that is, it focuses only on the internal logic and does not verify the logic to the specification. Another disadvantage is that there is no way to detect missing paths and data-sensitive errors. For example, if the statement in a program should be coded "if $|a-b| < 10$" but is coded "if $(a-b) < 1$," this would not be detectable without specification details. A final disadvantage is that white-box testing cannot execute all possible logic paths through a program, because this would entail an astronomically large number of tests.

Bibliography

1. Arthur, Lowell Jay. 1993. *Improving Software Quality: An Insider's Guide to TQM*. New York: Wiley.
2. Beizeir, Boris. 1984. *Software System Testing and Quality Assurance*. New York: Van Nostrand Reinhold.
3. Beizeir, Boris. 1991. *Software Testing Techniques*, Second Edition. New York: Van Nostrand Reinhold.
4. Beizeir, Boris. 1995. *Black-Box Testing: Techniques for Functional Testing for Testing of Software and Systems*. New York: Wiley.
5. Boehm, Barry W. 1981. *Software Engineering Economics*. Englewood Cliffs, NJ: Prentice Hall.
6. Brooks, Frederick P., Jr. 1995. *The Mythical Man-Month*, Anniversary Edition. Reading, MA: Addison-Wesley.
7. Bruce, Phillip and Sam M. Pederson. 1982. *The Software Development Project: Plan and Management*. New York: Wiley.
8. Buckley, Fletcher J. 1989. *Implementing Software Engineering Practices*. New York: Wiley Series in Software Engineering Practice.
9. Caplan, Frank. 1980. *The Quality System*, Second Edition. Philadelphia: Chilton.
10. Card, David N. with Robert L. Glass. 1990. *Measuring Software Design Quality*. Englewood Cliffs, NJ: Prentice Hall.
11. Charette, Robert N. 1990. *Applications Strategies for Risk Analysis*. New York: McGraw-Hill.
12. Chen, Peter. 1977. *The Entity-Relationship Approach to Logical Database Design*. New York: QED Information Sciences.
13. Cho, C. K. 1980. *An Introduction to Software Quality Control*. New York: Wiley Interscience.
14. Cho, C. K. 1987. *Quality Programming: Developing and Testing Software with Statistical Quality Control*. New York: Wiley.
15. Crandall, Vern J. 1995. The Software Product Development Life Cycle. *Proceedings of the 1995 International Information Technology Quality Conference*, Orlando, FL, April 6.
16. Creech, Bill. 1994. *The Five Pillars of TQM*. New York: Truman Valley /Dutton.
17. Davis, Alan M. 1990. *Software Requirements: Analysis and Specification*. Englewood Cliffs, NJ: Prentice Hall.
18. Davis, Brendan. 1994. *The Economics of Automatic Testing*. Second Edition, New York: McGraw-Hill.
19. DeCarlo, Neil J. and W. Kent Sterett. 1990. History of the Malcolm Baldridge National Quality Award. *Quality Progress* (March): 21–27.
20. DeMarco, Tom. 1979. *Structured Analysis and System Specification*. Englewood Cliffs, NJ: Prentice Hall.
21. DeMarco, Tom. 1982. *Controlling Software Projects: Management, Measurement, and Estimation*. Englewood Cliffs, NJ: Yourdon.
22. Deming, W. E. 1986. *Out of the Crisis*. Cambridge MA: Massachusetts Institute of Technology, Center for Advanced Engineering Study.
23. Deming, W. E. *The Deming Management Method*. New York: Perigee.
24. Dickensen, Brian. 1980. *Developing Structured Systems*. Englewood Cliffs, NJ: Yourdon.
25. Dijkstra, Edsgar. 1968. Go to statement considered harmful. *Communications of the ACM*, 11, 3: 147–178.

26. Fagan, Michael E. 1976. Design and code inspections to reduce errors in program development. *IBM Systems Journal*, 15, 3: 182–211.
27. Fagan, Michael E. 1986. Advances in software inspections. *IEEE Transactions on Software Engineering* (July): 744–751.
28. Flavin, Matt. 1981. *Fundamental Concepts of Information Modeling*. Englewood Cliffs, NJ: Yourdon.
29. Freedman, Daniel and Gerald Weinberg. 1977. *Technical Inspections and Reviews*. Boston, MA: Little, Brown.
30. Freedman, Daniel P. and Weinberg, Gerald M. 1990. *Handbook of Walkthroughs, Inspections, and Technical Reviews*, Third Edition. New York: Dorset House.
31. Gane, Chris and Trish Sarson. 1979. *Structured Systems Analysis: Tools and Techniques*. Englewood Cliffs, NJ: Prentice Hall.
32. Gilb, Tom. 1977. *Software Metrics*. New York: Winthrop.
33. Gilb, Tom. 1988. *Principles of Software Engineering Management*. Reading, MA: Addison-Wesley.
34. Gilb, Tom. 1991. Software metrics: Practical approaches to controlling software projects. *Paper presented at YSG Conference*, Cardiff, Wales. April.
35. Giles, A. C., 1992. *Software Quality: Theory and Management*. New York: Chapman & Hall.
36. Glass, Robert L. 1991. *Software Conflict-Essays on Art & Science of Software Engineering*. Englewood Cliffs, NJ: Yourdon (Prentice Hall).
37. Glass, Robert L. 1991. *Building Quality Software*. Englewood Cliffs, NJ: Prentice Hall.
38. Grady, Robert B. 1989. Dissecting software failures. *HP Journal* (April): 57–63.
39. Grady, Robert B. 1992. *Practical Software Metrics for Project Management and Process Improvement*. Englewood Cliffs, NJ: Prentice Hall.
40. Grady, Robert B. and Deborah L. Caswell. 1987. *Software Metrics: Establishing a Company-Wide Program*. Englewood Cliffs, NJ: Prentice Hall.
41. Gub, Tom et al. 1993. *Software Inspection*. Reading, MA: Addison-Wesley.
42. Hahn, Gerald J. 1995. Deming's impact on industrial statistics: some reflections. *The American Statistician*, 49, 4 (November): 336–341.
43. Halstead, M. 1977. *Elements of Software Science*. New York: Elsevier.
44. Hansen, Kirk. 1983. *Data Structured Program Design*. Topeka, KS: Orr.
45. Hatton, Les. 1997. Re-examining the defect density versus component size distribution. *IEEE Software* (March/April).
46. Hetzel, Bill. 1988. *The Complete Guide to Software Testing*, Second Edition. Wellesley, MA: QED.
47. Hetzel, Bill. 1993. *Making Software Measurement Work: Building an Effective Measurement Program*. Wellesley, MA: QED.
48. Higgins, David. 1979. *Program Design and Construction*. Englewood Cliffs, NJ: Prentice Hall.
49. Higgins, David. 1983. *Designing Structured Programs*. Englewood Cliffs, NJ: Prentice Hall.
50. Hollocker, Charles P. 1990. *Software Reviews and Audits Hand Book*. New York: Wiley.
51. Humphrey, Watts S. 1989. *Managing the Software Process*. Reading, MA: Addison-Wesley.
52. Humphrey, Watts S. 1995. *A Discipline for Software Engineering*. Reading, MA: Addison-Wesley.
53. *IEEE Standard for Measures to Produce Reliable Software*. 1988. Washington, DC: IEEE, Std. 982.
54. *IEEE Standard for Software Verification and Validation Plans*. 1986. Washington, DC: IEEE, Std. 1012–1986 (R1992).
55. *IEEE Standard Glossary of Software Engineering Terminology*. 1990. Washington, DC: IEEE Std. 610.12–1990.

56. Jackson, M. A. 1975. *Principles of Program Design*. New York: Academic.
57. Jackson, M. A. 1983. *System Development*. Englewood Cliffs, NJ: Prentice Hall.
58. Jarvis, Alka S. 1988. How to establish a successful test plan. *EDP Quality Assurance Conference*, Washington, DC, November 14–17.
59. Jarvis, Alka S. 1994. Applying Software Quality. *The Seventh International Software Quality Week*, San Francisco, May 17–20.
60. Jarvis, Alka S. 1995a. Applying Metrics. *First World Congress for Software Quality Conference*, San Francisco, June 20–22.
61. Jarvis, Alka S. 1995b. Exploring the Needs of a Developer and Tester, *Quality Conference 95*, Santa Clara, CA, April 4–7.
62. Jones, Capers. 1986. *Programming Productivity*. New York: McGraw-Hill
63. Jones, Capers. 1993. *Assessment and Control of Software Risks*. Englewood Cliffs, NJ: Yourdon Press Computing Services.
64. Jones, Capers, 1993. *Critical Problems in Software Measurement*. Carlsbad, CA: Infosystems Management.
65. Jones, Capers. 1991. *Applied Software Management: Assuring Productivity and Quality*. New York: McGraw-Hill.
66. Kaner, Cem, Jack Falk, and Hung Quoc Nguyen. 1993. *Testing Computer Software*, Second Edition. New York: Van Nostrand Reinhold.
67. Lewis, William E. 1998. Spiral Testing. *Quality Assurance Institute Annual International Information Technology Quality Conference*, April 13–17, Orlando, FL.
68. Lewis, Robert O. 1992. *Independent Verification & Validation: A Life Cycle Engineering Process for Quality Software*. New York: Wiley.
69. Linger, R. C., H. D. Mills, and B. I. Witt. 1979. *Structured Programming: Theory and Practice*. Reading, MA: Addison-Wesley.
70. Maples, Mike. 1995. Interview. *Information Week*.
71. Marca, David A. and Clement L. Mcgowan. 1988. *SADT: Structured Analysis and Design Technique*. New York: McGraw-Hill.
72. Marciniak, J. 1994. *Encyclopedia of Software Engineering*. New York: Wiley.
73. Marks, David M. 1992. *Testing Very Big Systems*. New York: McGraw-Hill.
74. Martin, James. 1989. *Information Engineering Book I Introduction*. Englewood Cliffs, NJ: Prentice Hall.
75. Martin, James. 1990a. *Information Engineering Book II Planning & Analysis*. Englewood Cliffs, NJ: Prentice Hall.
76. Martin, James. 1990b. *Information Engineering Book III Design & Construction*. Englewood Cliffs, NJ: Prentice Hall.
77. Martin, James, Kathleen Kavanagh Chapman, and Joe Leben. 1991. *Systems Application Architecture: Common User Access*. Englewood Cliffs, NJ: Prentice Hall.
78. McCabe, J. J. and C. W. Butler. 1989. Design complexity measurement and testing. *Communications of the ACM*, 32, 12 (December): 1415–1424.
79. McCabe, Thomas J. 1982. *Structured Testing: A Software Testing Methodology Using Cyclomatic Complexity Metric*. National Bureau of Standards Special Publication, December: 500–599.
80. McConnell, Steve. 1993. *Code Complete: A Practical Handbook of Software Construction*. Redmond, WA: Microsoft.
81. McMenamin, Stephen M. and John F. Palmer. 1984. *Essential Systems Analysis*. Englewood Cliffs, NJ: Yourdon.
82. Metzger, Phillip W. 1981. *Managing a Programming Project*, Second Edition. Englewood Cliffs, NJ: Prentice Hall.
83. Mills, Harlan D. 1983. *Software Productivity*. Boston: Little, Brown.
84. Mills, H. D., R. C. Linger, and A. R. Hevner. 1986. *Principles of Information Systems Analysis and Design*. New York: Academic.
85. Murine, Gerald E. 1988. Integrating software quality metrics with software QA. *Quality Progress* (November): 38–43.

86. Musa, J. D., A. Iannino, and K. Okumoto. 1987. *Software Reliability: Measurement, Prediction, Application.* New York: McGraw-Hill.
87. Myers, Glenford J. 1976. *Software Reliability Principles & Practices.* New York: Wiley.
88. Myers, Glenford J. 1978. *Composite/Structured Design.* New York: Van Nostrand Reinhold.
89. Myers, Glenford J. 1979a. *Reliable Software through Composite Design.* New York: Van Nostrand Reinhold.
90. Myers, Glenford J. 1979b. *The Art of Software Testing.* New York: Wiley.
91. Norwell, MA: Kluwer Academic, 1993.
92. Orr, Ken. 1981. *Structured Requirements Definition.* Topeka, KS: Orr.
93. Page-Jones, Meilir. 1988. *Practical Guide to Structured Systems Design*, Second Edition. Englewood Cliffs, NJ: Yourdon.
94. Page-Jones, Meilir. 1985. *Practical Project Management: Restoring Quality to DP Projects and Systems.* New York: Dorset House.
95. Parnas, D. L. 1972. On the criteria to be used in decomposing systems into modules. *Communications of the ACM* (December): 1053–1058.
96. Perry, William E. 1986. *How to Test Software Packages: A Step-by-Step Guide to Assuring They Do What You Want.* New York: Wiley.
97. Perry, William E. 1991. *Quality Assurance for Information Systems: Methods, Tools, and Techniques.* Wellesley, MA: QED.
98. Peters, Lawrence. 1987. *Advanced Structured Analysis and Design.* Englewood Cliffs, NJ: Prentice Hall.
99. Pressman, Roger S. 1988. *Making Software Engineering Happen: A Guide to Instituting the Technology.* Englewood Cliffs, NJ: Prentice Hall.
100. Pressman, Roger S. 1992. *Software Engineering: A Practitioner's Approach*, Third Edition. New York: McGraw-Hill.
101. Radice, R. A., J. T. Harding, P E. Munnis, and R. W Phillips. 1985. A programming process study. *IBM Systems Journal*, 24, 2: 91–101.
102. Radice, Ronald A. and Richard W. Phillips. 1988. *Software Engineering: An Industrial Approach, Volume I.* Englewood Cliffs, NJ: Prentice Hall.
103. Roper, Marc. 1993. *Software Testing.* New York: McGraw-Hill.
104. Ross, D. T. and K. E. Schoman. 1977. Structured analysis for requirements definition. *IEEE Transactions on Software Engineering*, SE-3, 1 (January): 6–15.
105. Royer, Thomas C., 1992. *Software Testing Management: Life on the Critical Path.* Englewood Cliffs, NJ: Prentice Hall.
106. Rubin, Howard. 1993. *Practical Guide to the Design and Implementation of IS Measurement Programs.* Englewood Cliffs, NJ: Prentice Hall.
107. Sanders, Joe. 1994. *Software Quality: A Framework for Success in Software Development.* Reading, MA: Addison-Wesley.
108. Schulmeyer, G. Gordon. 1990. *Zero Defect Software.* New York: McGraw-Hill.
109. Schulmeyer, W. Gordon and McManus, James. 1992. *Total Quality Management for Software.* New York: Van Nostrand Reinhold.
110. Sharp, Alex. 1993. *Software Quality and Productivity.* New York: Van Nostrand Reinhold.
111. Sommerville, L. 1985. *Software Engineering*, Second Edition, Reading, MA: Addison-Wesley.
112. Stevens, Roger T. 1979. *Operational Test & Evaluation: A Systems Engineering Process.* New York: Wiley-Interscience.
113. Stevens, Wayne P. 1981. *Using Structured Design: How to Make Programs Simple, Changeable, Flexible, and Reusable.* New York: Wiley-Interscience.
114. Stevens, Wayne, Larry Constantine, and Glenford Myers. 1974. Structured design. *IBM Systems Journal*, 13: 115–139.
115. Ward, Paul T. and Stephen J. Mellor. 1985a. *Structured Development for Real Time Systems. Volume 1: Introduction and Tools.* Englewood Cliffs, NJ: Yourdon.

116. Ward, Paul T. and Stephen J. Mellor. 1985b. *Structured Development for Real Time Systems. Volume 2: Essential Modeling Techniques.* Englewood Cliffs, NJ: Yourdon.
117. Ward, Paul T. and Stephen J. Mellor. 1986. *Structured Development for Real Time Systems. Volume 3: Implementation Modeling Techniques.* Englewood Cliffs, NJ: Yourdon.
118. Walton, Mary. 1986. *The Deming Management Method,* New York: A Perigee Book.
119. Warnier, Jean-Dominique. 1974. *Logical Construction of Programs*, Third Edition. New York: Van Nostrand Reinhold.
120. Warnier, Jean-Dominique. 1981. *Logical Construction of Systems.* New York: Van Nostrand Reinhold.
121. Weinberg, Gerald M. 1992. *Software Quality Management: Vol.1: Systems Thinking.* New York: Dorset House.
122. Weinberg, Gerald M. 1993. *Software Quality Management: Vol.2: First-Order Measurement.* New York: Dorset House.
123. Weinberg, Gerald M. 1992. *Quality Software Management: Systems Thinking*, Vol. 1, New York: Dorset House.
124. Weinberg, Gerald M. 1993. *Quality Software Management: First-Order Measurement*, Vol. 2, New York: Dorset House.
125. Weinberg, Gerald M. and Daniela Weinberg. 1979. *On the Design of Stable Systems.* New York: Wiley-Interscience.
126. Weinberg, Victor. 1978. *Structured Analysis.* Englewood Cliffs, NJ: Yourdon.
127. Whitten, Neal. 1990. *Managing Software Development Projects: Formula for Success.* New York: Wiley.
128. Yourdon, Edward. 1975. *Techniques of Program Structure and Design.* Englewood Cliffs, NJ: Prentice Hall.
129. Yourdon, Edward. 1985. *Structured Walkthroughs*, Third Edition. Englewood Cliffs, NJ: Yourdon.
130. Yourdon, Edward. 1989. *Modern Structured Analysis.* Englewood Cliffs, NJ: Yourdon.
131. Youll, David P. 1990. *Making Software Development Visible: Effective Project Control.* New York: Wiley.
132. Yourdon, Edward and Larry L. Constantine. 1979. *Structured Design: Fundamentals of a Discipline of Computer Program and Systems Design.* Englewood Cliffs, NJ: Prentice Hall.
133. Zachman, John. 1987. A framework for information systems architecture. *IBM Systems Journal*, 26, 3.

Glossary

Adaptive Maintenance. Modifications made to a system to accommodate changes in the processing environment.

Algorithm. A set of rules that are supposed to give the correct answer for solving a particular problem.

ANSI. Acronym for the American National Standard Institute, an institute that creates standards for a wide variety of industries, including computer programming languages.

Architecture. Similar to the architecture of a building, the architecture of a computer refers to the design structure of the computer and all its details.

Archive. To store information, to back it up, with the idea of preserving it for a long time.

ASCII. Stands for the American Standard Code for Information Interchange, which is a standardized coding system used by almost all computers and printers.

Assumption. Proposition that must be allowed to reduce the relevant variables of a problem to be manageable.

Attribute. The descriptive characteristic of something.

Backup. The process of making copies of files to enable recovery.

Baseline. (1) A defined set of executables or documents of a specific product, put into a state in which all development and change activity are closely managed in order to support a defined activity at a set time. Examples: Integration Test, Pilots, System Test, Reviews. (2) A product, document, or deliverable that has been formally reviewed, approved, and agreed upon; thereafter serving as a basis for further development, and to which a change can only be implemented through formal change control procedures. Examples: initial deployment of a product; evolution of existing products.

Baseline Measurement. A measurement taken for the specific purpose of determining the initial value of a state.

Benchmark. A test used to measure the relative performance of hardware or software products.

Button. On a computer screen, it is the visual equivalent of a button on a machine.

Cascade. A command in applications that automatically organizes all the windows on the screen in a tidy stack.

Cause-Effect Diagram. A tool used to identify possible causes of a problem by representing the relationship between some effect and its potential cause.

Client/Server. A system architecture in which a client computer cooperates with a server over a network.

Control Chart. A statistical method for differentiating between common and special cause variations as demonstrated by a process.

Corrective Action. The practice and procedure for reporting, tracking, and resolving identified problems both in the software product and the development process. The resolution provides a final solution to the identified problem.

Corrective Maintenance. The identification and removal of code defects.

CPU. The central processing unit, the brains of the computer.

Customer. The individual or organization that receives a product.

Database. A collection of information stored in computerized form.

Defect. Producer's view — product requirement has not been met. Customer's view — anything that causes customer dissatisfaction.

Download. To receive information, typically a file, from another computer.

Drag-and-Drop. Perform tasks by using the mouse to drag an icon onto some other icon.

Emergency Repair. Software repair required immediately.

Entrance Criteria. Quantitative and qualitative measures used to evaluate a products' readiness to enter the next phase or stage of development.

Error. A discrepancy between actual values or conditions and those expected.

Exit Criteria. Quantitative and qualitative measures used to evaluate a product's acceptance for that specific stage or phase of development.

Flowchart. A diagram that shows the sequence of steps of a process.

Formal Review. A type of review typically scheduled at the end of each activity or stage of development to review a component of a deliverable or in some cases, a complete deliverable or the software product and its supporting documentation.

GUI. Graphical user interface — a user interface in which graphics and characters are used on screens to communicate with the user.

Histogram. A graphical description of measured values organized according to the frequency of occurrence.

Icon. A miniature picture used to represent a function.

Impact Analysis. The process of determining which system components are affected by a change to software or hardware.

Incident Report. A report to document an issue or error arising from the execution of a test.

Inputs. Products, services, or information needed to make a process work.

Integration Testing. (1) The testing of combinations of individual, unit-tested pieces of code as they are combined into a complete unit. (2) A testing event driven by temporal cycles determined before the start of the testing phase. This test phase is conducted to identify functional problems with the software product. This is a verification activity.

Intermediate Repair. Software repair before the next formal release, but not immediately (e.g., in a week or so).

ISO9000. A quality series that comprises a set of five documents, which was developed in 1987 by the International Standards Organization (ISO).

Legacy System. Previous application system in production.

Maintenance. Tasks associated with the modification or enhancement of production software.

Management. A team or individual who manage(s) resources.

Management Review and Approval. A management review is the final review of a deliverable. It is conducted by the project manager with the project sponsor to ensure the quality of the business aspects of a work product.

Mean. A value derived by adding several items and dividing the sum by the number of items.

Network. A system that connects computers together and shares resources.

Perfective Maintenance. Enhancement to software performance, maintainability, or understandability.

Policy. Managerial intents and goals regarding a process or products.

Problem. Any deviation from predefined standards.

Problem Reporting. The method of identifying, tracking, and assigning attributes to problems detected within the software product, deliverables, or within the development processes.

Procedure. Step-by-step method that is followed to ensure some standard.

Process. Specific activities that must be performed to accomplish a function.

Process Improvement. To change a process to make it produce a product faster, more economically, or of higher quality.

Productivity. Ratio of output to the input of a process using the same unit of measure.

Quality. The totality of features and characteristics of a product or service that bear on its ability to meet stated or implied needs.

Quality Assurance. An overview process that entails planning and systematic actions to ensure that a product or service conforms to established requirements.

Quality Assurance Evaluation. A type of review performed by the QA organization to ensure that a project is following good quality management practices.

Quality Assurance Organization. A permanently established organization or unit whose primary goal is to review the project and products at various points to ensure that good quality management practices are being followed. Also to provide the testing efforts and all associated deliverables for testing on supported projects. The QA organization must be independent of the project team.

Quality Control. Process by which product quality is compared with standards.

Quality Improvement. Changing a process so that the rate of defects is reduced.

Quality Management. The execution of processes and procedures that ensures quality as an output from the development process.

Regression Testing. Tests used to verify a previously tested system whenever it is modified.

Release Management. A formal release process for nonemergency corrective, perfective, and adaptive projects.

Requirement. A performance standard for an attribute or a function, or the process used to verify that a standard has been met.

Reviews. A process or meeting during which a work product, or a set of work products, is presented to project personnel, project and program managers, users, customers, sponsors, or other interested parties for comment or approval.

Root Cause Analysis. A methodical process based on quantitative data to identify the primary cause in which a defect has been introduced into the product. This is typically more than just repairing the product affected, but establishing how the process or method allows the defect to be introduced into the product to begin with.

Run Chart. A graph of data points in chronological order used to detect trends of a characteristic being measured.

Scatter Plot. A graph that shows whether there is a relationship between two factors.

Software Maintenance. All changes, corrections, and enhancements that occur after an application has been placed into production.

Standard. A measure used to evaluate products or processes and identify nonconformance.

Statistical Process Control. The use of statistics and tools to measure a process.

System Testing. The functional testing of a system to verify that it performs within the limits of the system requirements and is fit for use.

Test Coverage. A measure of the portion of a system under test that is actually tested.

Test Cycle. A set of ordered test conditions that will test a logical and complete portion of a system.

Test Event. A generic term used to describe one of many levels of test. Examples: Unit Test, Integration Test, System Test.

Testing Tool. A manual or automated procedure or software used to test a system.

Test Readiness Review. A formal review conducted primarily to evaluate that all preliminary and entrance criteria have been satisfied and are verifiable before proceeding into a formal test event.

Unit Testing. Testing performed on individual programs to verify that they perform according to their requirements.

User. The customer who uses a product or process.

Validation. A type of evaluation conducted at the end of the development process to assess the software product's ability to meet the specified requirements.

Values. The ideals and customs toward which individuals have a positive regard.

Verification. A type of evaluation to determine if the software products at a given development phase satisfy the imposed conditions, which were determined at the start of that phase.

Vision. A statement that describes the desired future state of something.

Walkthrough. A testing technique to analyze a technical work product.

Window. A rectangle on a screen that represents information.

Index

Index

RENEWALS 458-4574

DATE DUE

MAY 21			
NOV 28			
GAYLORD			PRINTED IN U.S.A.